lonely planet

Dominican Republic

North Coast
(p127)

Península de Samaná
(p108)

Central Highlands
(p161)

Punta Cana & the Southeast
(p78)

Santo Domingo
(p46)

The Southwest & Península de Pedernales
(p183)

THIS EDITION WRITTEN AND RESEARCHED BY

Michael Grosberg,
Kevin Raub

PLAN YOUR TRIP

ON THE ROAD

BEACH, PUNTA CANA P96

HAITIAN MARKET, PEDERNALES P197

Contents

KITESURFING, CABARETE P143

Welcome to the Dominican Republic

The DR is one of the Caribbean's most geographically diverse countries, with stunning mountain scenery, desert scrublands, evocative colonial architecture and beaches galore.

Coastal Country

Hundreds of miles of coastline define the Dominican Republic (DR) – some of it white-sand beaches shaded by rows of palm trees, other parts lined dramatically with rocky cliffs, wind-swept dunes or serene mangrove lagoons. Whether it's fishing villages where the shoreline is used for mooring boats or indulgent tourist playgrounds with aquamarine waters, the sea is the common denominator. Some of the bays and coves where pirates once roamed are the temporary home of thousands of migrating humpback whales, and part of an extensive network of parks and preserves safeguarding the country's natural patrimony.

Peaks & Valleys

Beyond the capital, much of the DR is rural: driving through the vast fertile interior you'll see cows and horses grazing alongside the roads and trucks and burros loaded down with produce. Further inland you'll encounter vistas reminiscent of the European Alps, rivers carving their way through lush jungle and stunning waterfalls. Four of the five highest peaks in the Caribbean rise above the fertile lowlands surrounding Santiago and remote deserts extend through the southwest, giving the DR a physical and cultural complexity not found on other islands.

Past & Present

The country's roller-coaster past is writ large in the physical design of its towns and cities. Santo Domingo's Zona Colonial exudes romance with its beautifully restored monasteries and cobblestone streets where conquistadors once roamed. The crumbling gingerbread homes of Puerto Plata and Santiago remain from more prosperous eras, and scars from decades of misrule are marked by monuments where today people gather to celebrate. New communities have arisen only a few kilometers from the ruins where Christopher Columbus strode and where the indigenous Taíno people left physical traces of their presence carved onto rock walls.

People & Culture

The social glue of the DR is the all-night merengue that blasts from modest corner stores – this is true everywhere from cities such as Santo Domingo, to crumbling San Pedro de Macoris or Puerto Plata where waves crash over the Malecón. Dominicans appreciate their down time and really know how to party, as can be seen at Carnival celebrations held throughout the country and each town's own distinctive fiesta. These events are great windows into the culture, so take the chance to join the fun and elaborate feasts.

Why I Love the Dominican Republic

By Michael Grosberg, Author

Driving along the DR's rural byways, past coconut sellers and men playing dominoes, thick jungly brush often gives way to the idyllic ocean vistas the country is known for. But for me, the country's distinctive appeal lies in everyday village scenes, when Dominicans' informal hospitality can be appreciated. What keeps me going back are the afternoons at beachfront seafood shacks or mountainside-hugging *colmados* (combined corner stores and bars), when the pace slows down and the natural beauty of the surroundings become almost secondary to the warm welcome of locals.

For more about our authors, see p256.

Above: A beach in Punta Cana (p96)

Dominican Republic

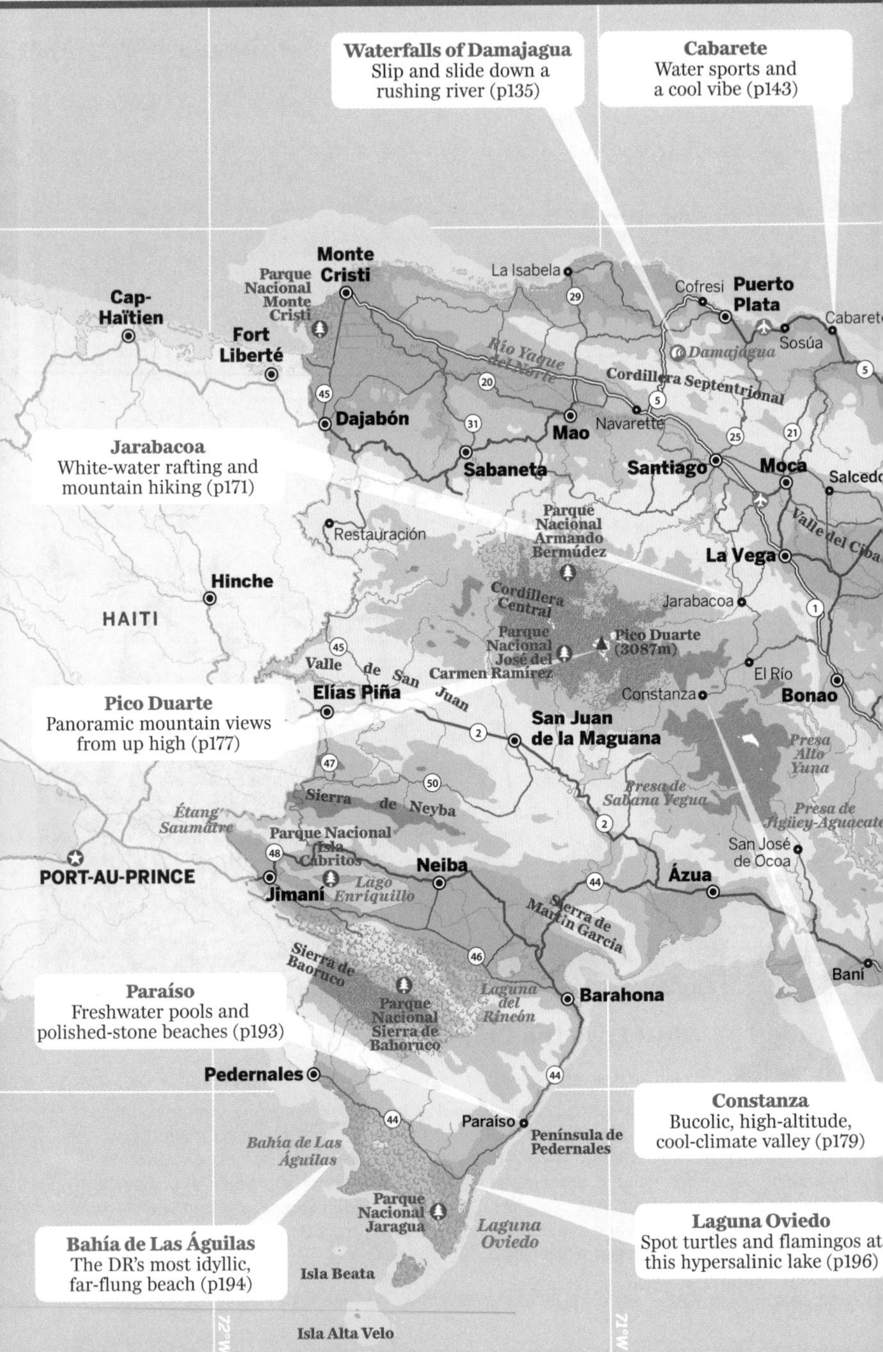

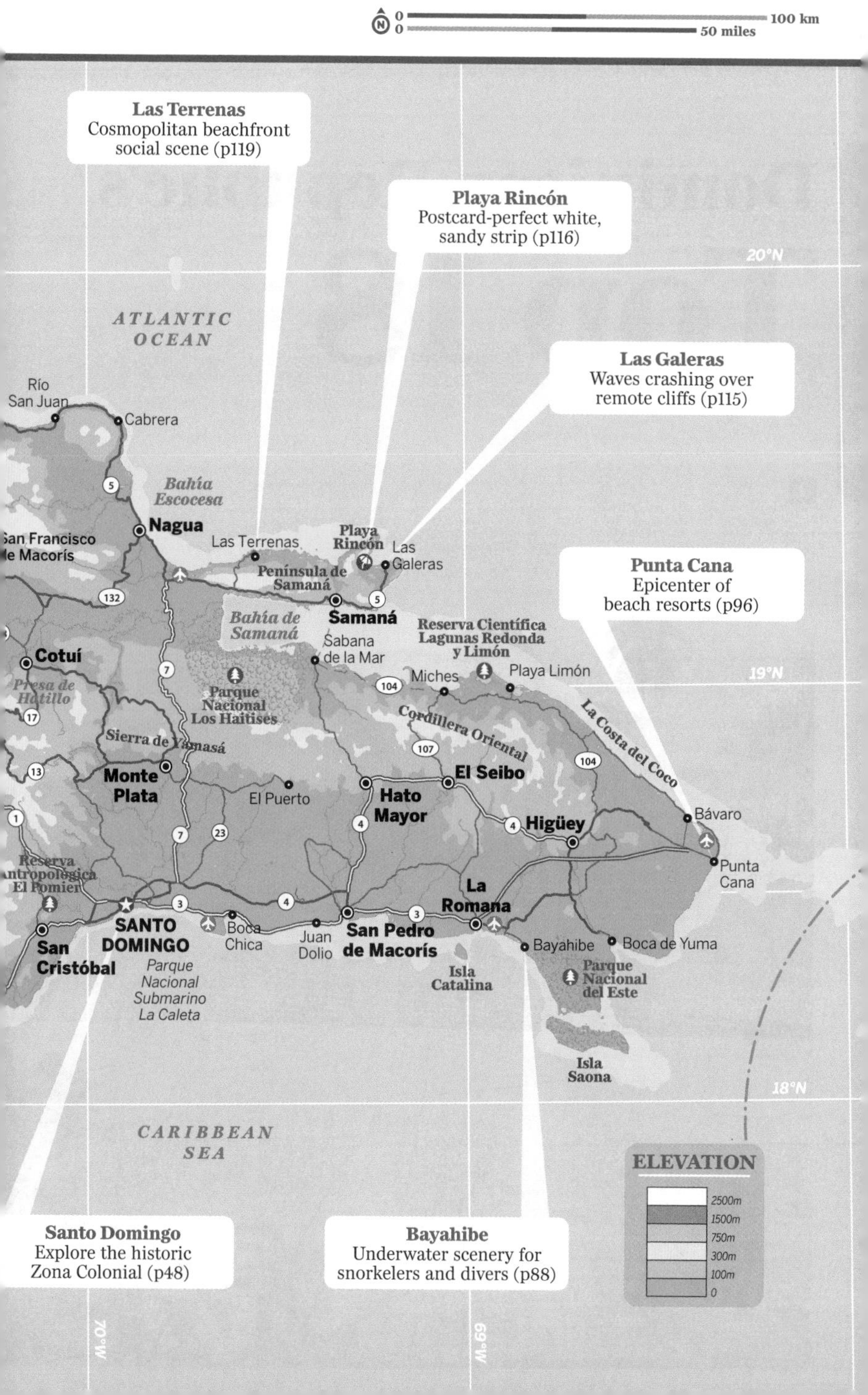

0 100 km
0 50 miles
Las Terrenas
Cosmopolitan beachfront social scene (p119)
Playa Rincón
Postcard-perfect white, sandy strip (p116)
Las Galeras
Waves crashing over remote cliffs (p115)
Punta Cana
Epicenter of beach resorts (p96)
Santo Domingo
Explore the historic Zona Colonial (p48)
Bayahibe
Underwater scenery for snorkelers and divers (p88)
ATLANTIC OCEAN
CARIBBEAN SEA
20°N
19°N
18°N
70°W
69°W
Río San Juan
Cabrera
Bahía Escocesa
Nagua
San Francisco de Macorís
Las Terrenas
Playa Rincón
Las Galeras
Península de Samaná
Samaná
Bahía de Samaná
Sabana de la Mar
Reserva Científica Lagunas Redonda y Limón
Miches
Playa Limón
Cotuí
Presa de Hatillo
Parque Nacional Los Haitises
Sierra de Yamasá
Cordillera Oriental
La Costa del Coco
Monte Plata
El Puerto
Hato Mayor
El Seibo
Higüey
Bávaro
Punta Cana
Reserva Antropológica El Pomier
SANTO DOMINGO
San Cristóbal
Boca Chica
Juan Dolio
San Pedro de Macorís
La Romana
Bayahibe
Boca de Yuma
Parque Nacional Submarino La Caleta
Isla Catalina
Parque Nacional del Este
Isla Saona
ELEVATION
2500m
1500m
750m
300m
100m
0

Dominican Republic's Top 18

1

Santo Domingo's Zona Colonial

1 Take a walk through history in the oldest city in the New World. With its cobblestone streets and beautifully restored mansions, churches and forts, many converted into evocative museums, it's easy to imagine Santo Domingo's landmark quarter (p48) as the seat of Spain's 16th-century empire. But the past and present coexist rather gracefully here; follow in the footsteps of pirates and conquistadors one moment, the next pop into a shop selling CDs from the latest Dominican merengue star. Below left: Museo Alcázar de Colón (p49)

Sun, Sea & Sand at Playa Rincón

2 Consistently rated one of the top beaches in the Caribbean by those in the know – people who courageously brave heatstroke and sunburn in a quest for the ideal – Rincón's (p116) 3km of pitch-perfect sands is second only to Bahía de Las Águilas in the DR. It's large enough for every day-tripper to claim their own piece of real estate without nosy neighbors peeking over the seaweed and driftwood. A thick palm forest provides the backdrop and fresh seafood can be served upon request.

DANIELA DIRSCHERL / GETTY IMAGES ©

2

DOMINICAN REPUBLIC MINISTRY OF TOURISM, WWW.GODOMINICANREPUBLIC.COM ©

Leisurely Las Galeras

3 This sleepy fishing village at the far eastern end of the Península de Samaná is an escape from your getaway. Fewer tourists and therefore less development means that the area around Las Galeras (p115) includes some of the more scenic locales in all the DR. Swaying palm trees back beaches ready-made for a movie set, and waves crash over hard-to-get-to cliffs.

Bahía de Las Águilas

4 The remoteness and loneliness of the country's most far-flung and beautiful beach adds savor and spice to the adventure of getting to Bahía de Las Águilas (p194), a stunning 10km-long stretch of postcard-perfect sand nearly hugging Haiti in an extreme corner of the Península de Pedernales. The fact that you have to take a boat that weaves in and out through craggy cliffs and sea-diving pelicans to get here – and that there won't be hardly any tourists here except for you – only adds to its allure.

Whale Watching

5 North Americans and Europeans aren't the only ones who migrate south to the Caribbean in the winter. Every year, thousands of humpback whales congregate off the Península de Samaná (p108) to mate and give birth, watched (from a respectful distance) by boatloads of their human fans. Get a front row seat to this spectacle from mid-January to mid-March. For an even more intimate experience, week-long live-aboard excursions to the Silver Bank (p132) north of Puerto Plata offer the extremely rare opportunity to snorkel alongside these massive mammals.

Santo Domingo Nightlife & Dancing

6 Get dressed to the nines, do some limbering up and get your dance moves on. Nightclubs (p69) in the seaside resort hotels host some of the best merengue and salsa bands this side of Havana. Downtown has trendy, sceney clubs for the fashionable set, the Zona Colonial is chockablock with spots, from sweaty corner stores and bohemian hangouts to upscale restaurants, wine bars and doormen-guarded hideaways with magnificent colonial-era courtyards.

Above: Plaza España (p53)

8

Resort Relaxing in Punta Cana

7 The heart of Dominican tourism, scores of all-inclusive resorts claim the choicest beachfront property in the southeast of the country. Synonymous with all-you-can-eat buffets and Club Med–like group activities, resorts in Punta Cana (p96) are justly famous for delivering stress-reducing, carefree, indulgent holidays. There are as many families on holiday as there are people getting stuck into the deliciously potent rum cocktails the country is known for.

Las Terrenas Cafe Culture

8 Mellow out in this cosmopolitan beachfront town where French and Italian accents are as common as Dominican. International camaraderie is contagious when every day begins and ends with espresso among baguette-toting foreigners at beachfront open-air cafes and restaurants overlooking the ocean. But Las Terrenas' (p119) relaxed vibe is a marriage between water-sports adventurers swapping tales after an exhausting day, and the more sedentary set content to admire their exploits from afar while relishing the European flare of this former fishing village.

Kitesurfing in Cabarete

9 Do your part for the environment: use wind-powered transportation. Year-round strong offshore breezes make Cabarete (p143) on the DR's north coast one of the undisputed capitals for the burgeoning sport of kitesurfing. Harnessing the wind's power to propel you over the choppy surface of the Atlantic isn't like another day at the beach. It takes training and muscles, not to mention faith, before you can attempt the moves of the pros from around the world who ply their trade here.

10

NICK HANNA / ALAMY ©

11

Mountain Biking the Dominican Alps

10 Hardcore cyclists rave about the rough trails of the DR's central highlands (p161), where they feel like pioneers. Free styling their way on rocky descents, through alpine meadows and through coursing streams, is an adventurer's dream. Less strenuous rides abound, too: pedal along dirt roads through farming communities and sugar-cane fields, and smiles and friendly invitations to stop and grab a Presidente or two will greet you along the way.

Hiking Pico Duarte

11 Hispaniola has some surprisingly rugged terrain in the Central Cordillera, including Pico Duarte (p177), the Caribbean's highest mountain (3087m). You'll need sturdy shoes, warm-weather gear, good stamina and several days, but if you summit when the clouds have dispersed, the views out to both the Atlantic and the Caribbean are more than worth the blisters. Along with the memories of a night huddling around the fire out under the stars, you'll take home a feeling of accomplishment. Above right: Parque Nacional Armando Bermúdez (p177)

Descending the 27 Waterfalls of Damajagua

12 A short drive from Puerto Plata, a hard-won slosh to the far side of the river and a trek through the lush forest lead to these falls (p135). Experiencing this spectacular series of cascades involves wading through clear pools, swimming through narrow, smooth-walled canyons, hiking through forest, and climbing rocks, ropes and ladders through the roaring falls themselves. It's adrenalin-pumping fun when you leap and slide down the falls, with some jumps as high as 10m.

White-Water Rafting

13 The Caribbean's only raftable river, the Río Yaque del Norte (p172) in the central highlands of the DR, is tailor-made for those looking to recharge their batteries after too much sun and sand. Short but intense series of rapids will get the adrenaline going, as will a spill in the cold roiling river. Fortunately, however, there are stretches of flat water where you can loosen your grip on the paddle and gaze at the mountain scenery in the distance.

Mountain Vistas in Constanza

14 The scenery found in the central highlands of the DR is a surprise to most. Cloud-covered peaks whose slopes are a patchwork of well-tended agricultural plots, and galloping forest growth rising from the valley floor, are vistas not often associated with Caribbean islands. A stay on the outskirts of Constanza (p179), truly a world away from the developing coastline, provides tableaus of often spectacular sunsets – it's also this time of day when the temperature begins to dip and the chilly air calls for sweaters and blankets.

Lago Enriquillo

15 Toward the border with Haiti you'll find Lago Enriquillo (p199), a lake 40m below sea level and a remnant of the strait that once bisected the island from Barahona to Port-au-Prince. Several hundred crocodiles call the lake home, and everywhere you'll see rocks of fossilized coral. In the middle of the lake is Isla Cabritos, a national park where seemingly menacing Ricord and rhinoceros iguanas beefier than Buicks roam freely and cacti thrive. Swarms of butterflies color the landscape every June. Bottom: Rhinoceros iguana

14

15

REINHARD DIRSCHERL / GETTY IMAGES ©

ROBERTO GUZMAN / XINHUA PRESS / CORBIS ©

La Vega Carnival

16 Carnival is a huge blowout everywhere in the DR, but especially so in La Vega (p169); the entire city turns out for the parade and every corner and park is transformed into a combination impromptu concert and dance party. Look out for the whips when dancing with costumed devils. Garish, colorful, baroque and elaborately and painstakingly made outfits – capes, demonic masks with bulging eyes and pointed teeth – are worn by marauding groups of revelers.

Aquatic Bayahibe

17 Underwater visibility and consistent ocean conditions make this coastal village (p88), near La Romana in the southeast, the country's best scuba-diving destination bar none. You'll find boat services to the islands of Saona and Catalina, and the island's best wreck dive, the St George, is out here, too. Snorkelers will find themselves equally well catered to, and there's the unique opportunity to spend a few hours cruising the shoreline in a traditional fishing vessel.

Winter Baseball

18 Dominicans don't just worship at Sunday Mass: baseball (p218) makes a solid claim for the country's other religion. Hometown fanatics cheer their team on with a passion equal to bleacher creatures in Yankee Stadium or Fenway Park, but with better dancers and possibly a wider selection of stadium fare. The Dominican league's six teams go *cabeza a cabeza* (head to head) several nights a week – Estadio Quisqueya in Santo Domingo is home field for two longtime rivals – culminating in a championship series at the end of January. Above: Baseball game at Estadio Quisqueya (p70)

Need to Know

For more information, see Survival Guide (p227)

Currency
Dominican peso (RD$)

Language
Spanish

Visas
Generally not required for stays of up to 30 days. Can pay extra fee upon departure for stays of up to 90 days.

Money
ATMs widely available. Credit cards accepted in some hotels and restaurants.

Cell Phones
Local SIM cards can be used or phones can be set for roaming.

Time
Atlantic Standard Time (GMT/UTC minus four hours).

When to Go

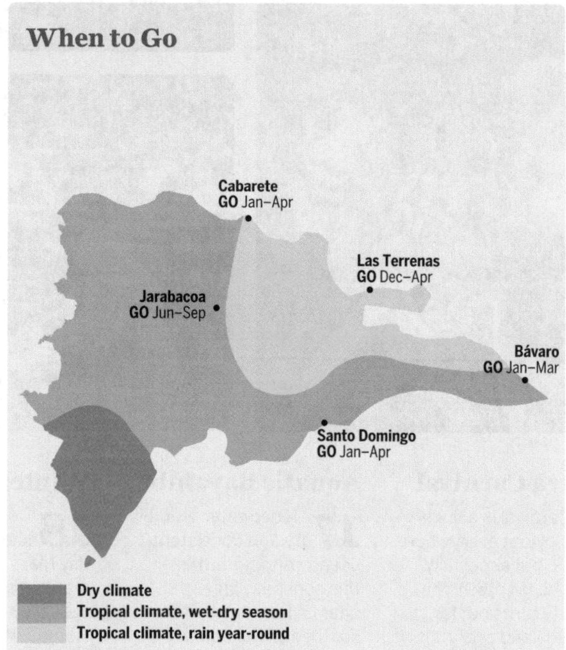

High Season
(mid-Dec–Feb)

➡ July to August and the week before Easter are also high season.

➡ Expect significantly higher hotel prices and crowded beaches.

➡ Most water sports are prohibited throughout the DR during the week before Easter.

Shoulder
(Mar–Jul)

➡ You may see short but strong daily rains in Santo Domingo (through October).

➡ April weather can be idyllic throughout the country.

➡ Standard May to June forecast is pretty much always partly cloudy or partly sunny with chance of afternoon showers.

Low Season
(Aug–early Dec)

➡ Hurricane season, really June to December, but if no storms it's an excellent time to travel.

➡ Temperatures don't vary much (mountains an exception).

➡ Deeply discounted room rates and some properties in resort areas like Cabarete close up in October.

Useful Websites

DR1 (www.dr1.com) Busy online forum with engaged members posting travel and DR-living related news and opinions.

Go Dominican Republic (www.godominicanrepublic.com) Official tourism site.

Debbie's Dominican Travel (www.debbiesdominicantravel.com) Reviews of sites and accommodations.

Dominican Treasures (www.dominicantreasures.com) USAID-supported site promoting sustainable tourism in the DR.

Lonely Planet (www.lonelyplanet.com/dominican-republic) For up-to-date travelers' reports.

Important Numbers

Remember that you must dial ☎1 + 809 or 829 for all calls within the DR, even local ones. There are no regional codes.

Country code	☎1 + 809
Emergency	☎1 + 911
Information	☎1 + 1411

Exchange Rates

Australia	A$1	RD$37.8
Canada	C$1	RD$40
Europe	€1	RD$58.4
Haiti	HTG1	RD$1
Japan	¥100	RD$41
New Zealand	NZ$1	RD$30
UK	UK£1	RD$70
US	US$1	RD$42.7

For current exchange rates see www.xe.com.

Daily Costs

Budget: Less than US$60

- Budget room: RD$1500 (US$35)
- Meal at local *comedor* (eatery): RD$200 (US$4.75)
- Buy all drinks from grocery stores – small bottled water RD$10 and six-pack of 12oz Presidentes RD$62
- Take *motoconchos* (motorcycle taxis) and *guaguas* (small buses) to get around

Midrange: US$60-200

- Internet deal on all-inclusive accommodations: RD$2800 (US$65)
- First-class bus tickets between major destinations: RD$420 (US$10)
- Join group tours for activities such as snorkeling, hiking etc

Top End: Over US$200

- Beachfront resort: RD$8500 (US$200)
- Meal at top restaurant in urban or resort areas: RD$900 (US$21)
- Rent a car for the entire trip or at least for special excursions; gas prices will eat into expenses

Opening Hours

Opening hours vary across the year and are shorter in the shoulder and low seasons. We've provided high-season hours:

Banks 9am-4:30pm Mon-Fri, to 1pm Sat

Bars 8pm-late, to 2am in Santo Domingo

Government Offices 7:30am-4pm Mon-Fri, officially; in practice more like 9am-2:30pm

Restaurants 8am-10pm Mon-Sat (some closed between lunch and dinner); to 11pm or later in large cities and tourist areas

Supermarkets 8am-10pm Mon-Sat

Arriving in the DR

Aeropuerto Internacional Las Américas (Santo Domingo; p236) Taxi fares to the city are US$40. *Motoconchos* can take you to the nearby highway *guagua* stop for the slow, crowded ride 26km west to the center.

Aeropuerto Internacional Punta Cana (Punta Cana; p103) Resort minivans transport the majority of tourists to nearby resorts, but taxis (US$30 to US$80) are plentiful.

Aeropuerto Internacional Gregorío Luperón (Puerto Plata; p134) Many resorts and hotels in the area can arrange minivan pick-up. Taxis cost US$25 to US$40, depending on destination, for the 18km ride.

Getting Around

The DR's relatively small size means even the most distant destination is usually no farther than a half-day's drive away.

Car Most convenient option if seeking freedom of movement, especially if interested in exploring rural and mountain regions.

Bus Two major companies, Caribe Tours and Metro, provide comfortable, frequent service between major cities and towns.

Guaguas Small buses or minivans, least expensive and least comfortable, however often the only available public transport.

Air Most expensive option and sometimes unreliable depending on time of year.

For much more on **getting around**, see p237

First Time

For more information, see Survival Guide (p227)

Checklist

➡ Make sure your passport is valid for at least six months past your arrival date

➡ Inform your debit-/credit-card company

➡ Arrange for appropriate travel insurance

➡ Decide on whether to get any recommended vaccinations

What to Pack

➡ High SPF sunscreen, hat and sunglasses

➡ Bug spray for biting mosquitoes

➡ Minimum one warm weather dressy outfit (if in Santo Domingo, one for every day and night)

➡ Sweater or sweatshirt for cool evenings and even colder buses; full-on cold weather gear if hiking at high altitudes

➡ Bathing suits and flip flops; boots and river shoes for hiking and water-based adventures

➡ Earplugs to get a good night's sleep in the city

➡ Binoculars if you intend to do any birdwatching

Top Tips for Your Trip

➡ Get out into the countryside to see how the majority of Dominicans live. If driving, grab a map and allow time to wander the back roads. Or hop in a *guagua* (local bus) to rub elbows with locals and see how most get around.

➡ If staying at an all-inclusive, experience the local dining scene, whether it's reservations at a nice restaurant or the *plato del día* at a *comedor* (eatery). Best case scenario, chow down late night on *sancocho*, basically, a soupy stew and a Dominican specialty.

➡ Few experiences are more quintessentially Dominican than milking a couple of Presidente *grandes* at a plastic table on a beach or sidewalk patio of a no-name restaurant or *colmodo*.

What to Wear

Dominicans, especially in Santo Domingo, Santiago and other large towns dress well (never shorts or tank tops) and take pride in their appearance, even in the warmest weather when you'd probably rather wear as little as possible. High heels and starched shirts are the norm for nights out. Unless you want to stand out like a sore *turista* and unless you're on the beach or poolside, consider long pants and comfortable, semi-formal tops.

Sleeping

Online room rates are usually cheapest. If you're visiting during the high season, especially in tourist-heavy areas, book early. For more information, see p228.

➡ **Hotels** From boutique European-owned places with style and intimacy, to business-class behemoths in the capital.

➡ **B&Bs** Only a few rooms with owners often living on the premises; breakfast included.

➡ **All-Inclusive Resorts** What most people associate with the DR, quality ranges from top-flight luxury to neglected properties with low standards.

➡ **Apart-hotels & Condos** For longer stays, especially in resort areas with expatriate communities, fully furnished units can be your best bet.

Money

ATMs can be found throughout the DR. Most charge fees (around RD$115) and have relatively low withdrawal limits. Credit and debit cards are widely accepted in cities and tourism-related businesses – Visa and MasterCard are more common than Amex. Many tourist-related businesses, including most midrange and top-end hotels, list prices in US dollars, but accept pesos.

For more information, see p232.

Bargaining

When shopping for souvenirs, whether jewelry, handicrafts or artwork, bargaining is fairly common. Even when the price is marked on the item it's worth a shot, however it's always a casual, low-pressure affair.

Tipping

A shock to many first-timers, most restaurants add a whopping 28% (ITBIS of 18% and an automatic 10% service charge) to every bill. Menus don't always indicate whether prices include the tax and tip.

- **Restaurants** Tips generally not expected since 10% automatically added to total. If especially impressed, you can add whatever else you feel is deserved.
- **Taxis** Typically, you can round up or give a little extra change.
- **Hotels** A 10% service charge is often automatically included; however, a US$1 to US$2 per night gratuity left for cleaning staff is worth considering.

Language

Some amount of English is widely spoken by Dominicans working in the tourism industry. Otherwise, especially in small towns and rural areas, there is little to none. Italian, French and German might come in handy in expat hideaways. Keep in mind, Dominican Spanish is spoken very fast with lots of slang and Dominicans tends to swallow the ends of words, especially those ending in 's' – *tres* sounds like 'tre' and *buenos días* like 'bueno dia.'

Etiquette

Dominicans are generally very polite, but observe relatively few strict rules for dining and etiquette. Generally, it's a laid-back, leisurely culture so be patient if things are moving slower than you'd like.

- Lively background music in restaurants is the norm so loud conversations aren't unusual.
- Rather than calling out, hissing is the preferred method for getting someone's attention.

Eating

Only the most exclusive restaurants require reservations, and those 'specialty' places in all-inclusive resorts. See p34 for more information.

- **Restaurants** Dominican cuisine, *comida criolla*, predominates but international fare, especially Italian, is readily available. Local places usually offer a '*plato del día*' (set menu) option for lunch; restaurants that cater to foreign tourists tend to have inflated prices and mediocre food.
- **Cafes** Coffee drinks and pastries, plus usually a limited menu of simple sandwiches. Stay however long you'd like.
- **Resorts** Buffets, usually with dizzying selection, run the gamut, though least expensive places can be stomach-worrying. Stand-alone restaurants range from bland, generic versions of ethnic cuisine to quality fare.
- **Cafeterías** Selection of fish, chicken and beef with rice and beans, usually displayed under glass.
- **Comedores** Generally they are informal eateries, often hole-in-the-walls.
- **Pica Pollo** Chain-style places specializing in fried chicken.
- **Colmados** Combination corner stores, groceries and bars, you can usually put together a meal here.
- **Car Washes** Combining automobiles and beer, the wisdom of which has to be questioned – these facilities serve drinks and simple food.

If You Like...

White-Sand Beaches

Full of breathtaking beaches, from oases of calm to party hotspots, the country's coastline can satisfy every taste. It is blessed with year-round warm temperatures and waters, so bring a boatload of lotion to avoid sunburned skin.

Playa Rincón Three kilometers of prototypical tropical paradise with a nearby freshwater stream to wash off the salt water. (p116)

Bahía de Las Águilas This far-flung, hard-to-get-to beach with cacti hugging the cliffs is definitely worth the trip. (p194)

Playa del Macao Not far north of Bávaro, a palm-lined beauty, mostly undeveloped but for a surf camp and informal beach shacks. (p97)

Playa Bávaro Long strand of sand and the epicenter of all inclusive resorts. (p97)

Playa Grande Half-moon cove with turquoise water, good surf waves and readily available seafood lunch. (p154)

Playa Limón A 3km-long strip lined with coconut trees, plus wetlands nearby. (p104)

Playa Blanca Tens of kilometers of white sand on the northern coast of Isla Beata, part of Parque Nacional Jaragua. (p197)

Outdoor Adventures

Blessed with a varied geography, both inland and coastal, the DR is an extreme-sport mecca. Ditch the car and try one of these alternative methods of transportation.

Canyoning Involving rappelling, jumping, climbing and swimming down a river, basically emulating a Navy Seal on a recon mission. (p40)

White-water rafting The Rio Yaque outside of Jarabacoa is the only river in the Caribbean for this adrenaline-pumping experience. (p39)

Kitesurfing Skim across the waves at high speeds powered by strong year-round winds in Cabarete. (p37)

Hiking Overnight it to Pico Duarte, the highest peak in the Caribbean for potentially panoramic views. (p41)

Mountain biking Explore the network of little-used trails through striking landscapes and past little-visited villages. (p41)

Relaxing at a Resort

Many of the DR's best beaches are colonized by all-inclusive resorts, the quintessential Caribbean beach break. Certainly, they come in all shapes and sizes, though sprawling 'city-states' seem to be the norm.

Punta Cana The country's largest concentration of developments and widest range of accommodations, with more on the way. (p96)

Playa Dorada Good deals in the geographic center of the North Coast, with easy access to other regional destinations. (p135)

Las Terrenas Of course there's beaches, but also water sports and waterfall adventures in this charming town with a European feel. (p119)

Juan Dolio Convenient because of its close proximity to Santo Domingo, with shallow, calm water. (p79)

Playa Dominicus A small enclave of resorts on a crowded but pretty stretch near the town of Bayahibe. (p91)

Wildlife

A large national park system and an increasing number of scientific preserves ranging from semi-deserts to lush valleys protect the country's biological diversity and a surprising number of endemic species.

Top: Kitesurfers, Cabarete (p143)
Bottom: Beach huts, Bávaro (p96)

Whale-watching These massive mammals take their winter break in Bahía de Samaná. (p111)

Parque Nacional Los Haitises Birdwatching (plus manatees, boas and marine turtles) from a boat cruising through mangrove forest. (p106)

Lago Enriquillo & Isla Cabritos Crocodiles and iguanas (and flamingos and egrets December to April) in a remote saltwater lake and desert island. (p199)

Laguna Oviedo Flamingos, ibis, storks, spoonbills, not to mention egg-laying turtles and iguanas. (p196)

Estero Hondo Climb a watch-tower or hop in a boat to spot a manatee in the mangroves around Punta Rusia. (p157)

Nightlife & Dancing

Whether it's an impromptu neighborhood block party gathering around the local *colmado* (corner store and bar), swanky hotel nightclub or local fiesta, Dominicans love to drink, socialize and get down.

Santo Domingo *Capitaleños* know how to let loose and the city has more bars and night-clubs than anywhere else in the country. (p69)

Santiago Rub elbows and booties at one of the dozen-plus bars and clubs around *el Monumento* in the city's center. (p162)

Cabarete More than just an action-sports destination, the beach here is lined with restau-rants and bars. (p143)

Sosúa Granted, there's a decid-edly raunchy and illicit vibe to nightlife here, but it is lively and diverse. (p137)

Parque Central Wherever you are in the Dominican Republic, every town's central square is usually the nighttime gathering place.

Romantic Getaways

Couples, both those on silver wedding anniversaries and those whose relationships are only a few hours old, will find plenty of places in the DR to make their hearts pound. From secluded hideaways to candle-lit restaurants, there is no shortage of options.

Casa Bonita Out-of-the-way hillside retreat to the south of Barahona. (p195)

Peninsula House The stuff of fairy tales and honeymoons, this exclusive French chateau mansion is perched on a bluff above Playa Cosón. (p126)

Plaza España Come to Santo Domingo for an intimate dinner on the balcony of one of this plaza's many atmospheric restaurants. (p65)

Camp David Balcony views – either the restaurant's or your room's – will make your heart go pitter-patter perched halfway up a mountain outside Santiago. (p165)

Aroma de la Montana Good wine, food, twinkling lights from the valley floor and the DR's only rotating dining room at this restaurant near Jarabacoa. (p176)

Sunset horseback ride It may sound like a cliché but ocean waves lapping at your horse's feet and holding your partner's hand... (p42)

Architecture

In addition to an enduring economic and social legacy, the Spanish colonizers left a physical one in the form of early-16th-century churches and buildings. Homes built by beneficiaries of several industrial boom-bust cycles have also had a lasting impact on urban design.

Zona Colonial Santo Domingo's compact neighborhood of cobblestone streets steeped in history and colonial-era buildings. (p48)

Puerto Plata Elegant, pastel gingerbread Victorian homes around Parque Central. (p129)

San Pedro de Macoris Fine homes, survivors from the late 19th- and early 20th-century sugar-boom days. (p85)

Churches From colonial-era gothic to contemporary post-industrial, Catholic cathedrals are often a town's most striking building. (p222)

Diving & Snorkeling

With hundreds of miles of coastline it's no surprise that the DR's subaquatic adventures are the priority for many visitors. Warm waters and consistently good year-round conditions mean every region has something to offer.

Bayahibe Experienced divers consider this the best destination in the country. (p90)

Playa Frontón Boat out to the reefs here, some of the best on the Península de Samaná. (p115)

Sosúa The base for North Coast underwater adventures as far afield as Luperón and Monte Cristi. (p139)

Boca Chica Two small wrecks and shallow reefs a short drive from Santo Domingo. (p84)

Laguna Dudu A sinkhole with natural spring water leads to several underwater caverns near the town of Cabrera. (p156)

Ruins

Evidence of Hispaniola's rich and tumultuous history, where Carib and Taíno cultures once prospered and Columbus, Cortes, Ponce de Leon and Sir Francis Drake once strode, have been written onto the island's landscape.

La Vega Vieja Remains of a fort built on Columbus's orders and destroyed by an earthquake in 1562. (p171)

Parque Nacional la Isabela Trace the foundation of the second oldest New World settlement on a picturesque ocean bluff. (p157)

Cueva de las Maravillas Easily accessible, massive cave with hundreds of pictographs and petroglyphs. (p88)

Casa Ponce de Leon Spanish explorer's residence when he governed Higüey for the Spanish crown. (p96)

Cueva del Puente Cave of pictographs near the remains of a large Taíno city in the Parque Nacional del Este. (p90)

Reserva Antropólogica Cuevas del Pomier Site of the most extensive pre-historic cave art in the Caribbean. (p188)

Month by Month

TOP EVENTS

Whale-watching Mid-January–mid-March

Carnaval February

Santo Domingo Merengue Festival End of July

Festival of the Bulls August

Winter baseball End of October–end of January

January

The North American winter coincides with whale-watching season in the Bahía de Samaná, making this a popular time of year to visit. Winds on the north coast around Cabarete are generally strongest this time of year.

Whale-Watching

This seasonal display of thousands of humpback whales doing their best impersonation of gymnasts takes place in the Bahía de Samaná and Silver Bank area.

Día de Altagracia

One of the most important religious days of the year falls on January 21, when thousands of pilgrims flock to the basilica in Higüey to pray to the country's patron saint. (p95)

Day of Duarte

On January 26, public fiestas are held in all the major towns, as well as gun salutes in Santo Domingo, celebrating the birthday of the Father of the Country.

February

This is a month of intense partying throughout the DR, hotel prices rise and popular tours can be booked solid. February to March are generally the driest months in Samaná.

Carnaval

Celebrated with great fervor throughout the DR every Sunday in February, culminating in huge blowouts on the last weekend of the month or the first weekend of March. The largest and most traditional Carnivals outside of Santo Domingo are in Santiago, La Vega, Cabral and Monte Cristi.

Master of the Ocean

Called a 'triathlon of the waves', this thrilling competition (www.masterofthe-ocean) in the last week in February sees the world's best windsurfers, kitesurfers and surfers go board to board on Playa Encuentro outside Cabarete.

Independence Day

February 27, 1844, is the day that the DR regained independence from Haiti; the holiday is marked by street celebrations and military parades.

March

Semana Santa (Holy Week), the week before Easter, is when the DR takes a vacation; businesses closed, Dominicans flock to beaches, and reservations are vital. Water sports are mostly prohibited. North American college students arrive for Spring Break.

Sailing Regatta

On the Saturday of Semana Santa, the seaside village of Bayahibe turns out to watch a race of traditionally handcrafted fishing boats.

April

Dominicans travel domestically during the end of April around Good Friday.

This is also a good time to visit Laguna Oviedo and the southwest; from March to June cactus flowers bloom in the desert.

Nighttime Turtle-Watching

Make your way to the out-of-the-way beaches of Parque Nacional Jaragua in the southwest where hawksbill and leatherback turtles lay and hatch their eggs. (p196)

May

Espiritu Santo

Santo Domingo's barrio Villa Mella comes alive to the sounds of drum rhythms on May 3rd when this community celebrates its African heritage in honoring the (formerly) Congo region's paramount diety Kalunga.

June

From May to November Santo Domingo can experience strong daily rains, though usually only for short periods, while from June to September the north coast experiences generally sunny skies.

Puerto Plata Cultural Festival

This week-long festival brings merengue, blues, jazz and folk concerts to the Puerto Plata's Fuerte San Felipe, at the end of the Malecón. (p132)

LUCAS LENA / GETTY IMAGES ©

JANE SWEENEY / GETTY IMAGES ©

Top: Carnaval performer, Santiago (p162)
Bottom: Presidential guards on Independence Day, Santo Domingo (p46)

San Pedro Apóstal

A raucous festival on June 29 in San Pedro celebrating *cocolo* (non-hispanic African) culture. Roving bands of *guloyas* (dancers) perform this traditional dance routine on the streets.

Isla Cabritos Flora & Fauna

Bloooming cactus flowers, butterflies, iguanas and crocodiles all converge in June on this desert island in the middle of Lago Enriquillo.

July

The beginning of the holiday season for Dominicans and Europeans. Scorching temperatures are recorded in the southwest around Lago Enriquillo.

Santo Domingo Merengue Festival

Santo Domingo hosts the country's largest and most raucous merengue festival. For two weeks at the end of July and the beginning of August, the world's top merengue bands play for the world's best merengue dancers all over the city. (p62)

August

The beginning of hurricane season, which can last all the way to December, means you should keep an eye out for developing strong storms. Sunny days generally prevail and you can find good deals on accommodations.

Festival of the Bulls

Higüey's *fiesta patronal* (patronage festival dedicated to the town's saint) sees horseback-borne cowboys and herds of cattle mosey down the city's streets.

Restoration Day

August 16, the day the DR declared its independence from Spain, is marked by general partying and traditional folk dancing and street parades throughout the country but it's especially festive in Santo Domingo and Santiago.

October

Rain showers a few days a week are common throughout the country, especially inland around Santiago. Tropical storms are a threat, however, expect mild temperatures, fewer visitors, some hotel closings and reduced accommodations costs.

Puerto Plata Merengue Festival

During the first week in October the entire length of Puerto Plata's Malecón is closed to vehicular traffic, food stalls are set up and famous merengue singers perform on a stage erected for the event. Also includes a harvest festival and an arts-and-crafts fair. (p132)

Latin Music Festival

This huge, annual three-day event – held at the Olympic Stadium in Santo Domingo – attracts the top names in Latin music, including jazz, salsa, merengue and *bachata* (popular guitar music based on bolero rhythms) players.

November

Winter Baseball

The boys of winter get into full swing in November. Six teams in five cities (Santo Domingo has two) play several games a week.

DR Jazz Festival

Top Dominican and international musicians play on alternating days in Sosúa, Puerto Plata and on the beach in Cabarete from October 31st to November 2nd. (p148)

December

Hotel and flight prices rise as Americans and Canadians begin their yearly migration to the beaches of the Caribbean, including the DR. Surfers head to the north coast where the waves are best from December through March.

Christmas

Decorations are ubiquitous, as early as October, and extended families gather to celebrate the holiday. Specialties like *puerco en puya* (pork roasted on a stick) are part of traditional family meals and holiday songs are played nonstop on the radio.

Itineraries

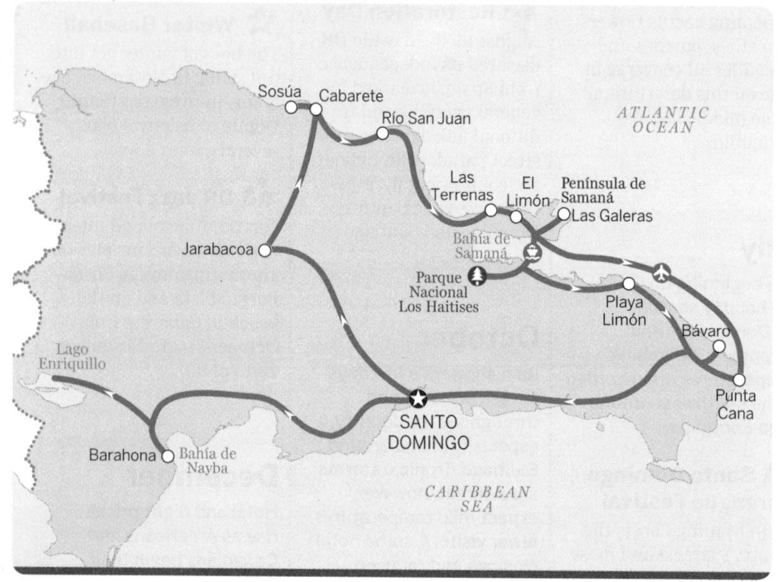

2 WEEKS Dominican Circuit

Start with a couple of days exploring **Santo Domingo**, hitting the Zona Colonial and enjoying the essential Dominican experiences of baseball and dancing to merengue. On day three head to **Jarabacoa**. Visit the waterfalls in the afternoon, with white-water rafting or canyoning the next day. Head north to **Cabarete**, which has world-class water sports and mountain biking. There's great diving and beaches in nearby **Sosúa** and **Río San Juan** – enough to keep you happy for several days. Next you're off to **Península de Samaná**. If it's mid-January to mid-March, go whale-watching. Otherwise take a boat trip to **Parque Nacional Los Haitises** to see the mangroves and cave paintings, or visit the waterfall near **El Limón**. Spend another two days hiking or boating to the beaches around **Las Galeras**. For more nightlife, base yourself in **Las Terrenas**. Allow for some relaxing beach time. The southeast is perfect – go for either deserted **Playa Limón** or perennially popular **Bávaro** and **Punta Cana**. Return to Santo Domingo. To the southwest is a spectacular drive to **Barahona**, and crocodiles in **Lago Enriquillo**. Spend a night or two before returning to Santo Domingo.

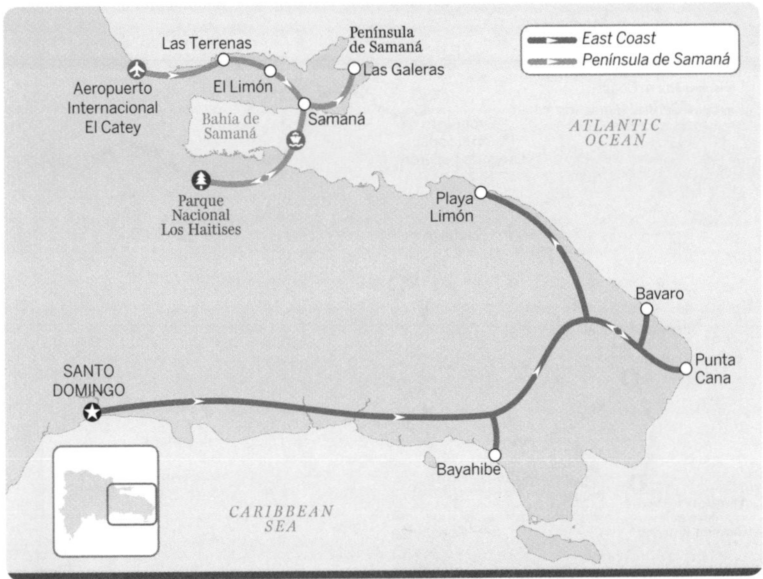

East Coast

Whether you fly into Santo Domingo or directly to the airport outside Punta Cana, allow a full day to explore the old colonial center of **Santo Domingo**.

Base yourself in the southeast at the deservedly popular beaches of **Bávaro** and **Punta Cana**, the hub of Dominican tourism. All-inclusive resorts are tailor-made for families; if all you want to do is splash about in the water, you could do worse than book at the resorts here. Many are particularly child-friendly, and activities include go-karts, bowling, sailing trips and parasailing. Resorts also offer tours to local sights; for more independence, rent a car and head out on your own.

Singles, couples and those seeking nightlife can certainly find their own Shangri-La here as well.

Not far south is **Bayahibe**, a tiny town on the edge of a national park, with the best scuba diving in the DR and a number of excursions, including catamaran tours to an island beach and snorkeling trips. For more privacy head to deserted **Playa Limón** further up the coast.

Península de Samaná

If you can, fly directly into Aeropuerto Internacional El Catey, the closest airport to the peninsula. Otherwise, get in a puddle jumper from another DR airport or consider taking a bus or driving from Santo Domingo – the new highway makes it a painless transfer.

If possible, plan your trip for mid-January to mid-March, when humpback whales migrate to the Bahía de Samaná and boat-based **whale-watching** tours are in full steam.

Otherwise, base yourself either in Las Terrenas or Las Galeras. **Las Terrenas** has a cosmopolitan mix and a relatively sophisticated European vibe. Kitesurfing and other water sports are deservedly popular here and you can choose from day-trips like horseback riding to the waterfall near **El Limón** or a boat trip to **Parque Nacional Los Haitises** to see the mangroves and cave paintings.

Las Galeras is a small laid-back town at the far eastern tip of the peninsula. The beaches around here rival any in the DR and there are chances to really get to the proverbial end of the road.

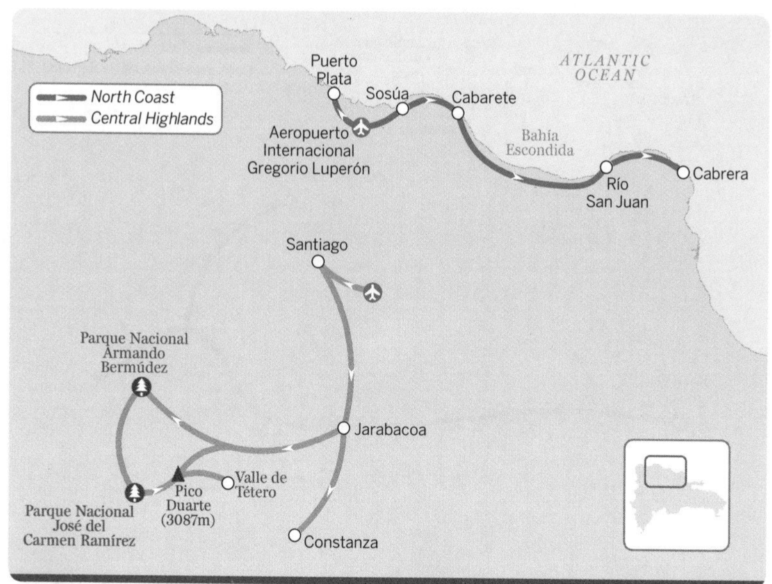

North Coast

Fly into the Aeropuerto Internacional Gregorio Luperón, basically the geographic center of the north coast. From here, choose your base for the week, but allow yourself at least an afternoon in **Puerto Plata**, either at the beginning or end of your trip. Wander the city's downtown streets lined with dilapidated 19th-century homes, educate yourself at one of the city's museums and settle in for a drink at a seafront restaurant.

Active types will want to stay in or around the water-sports mecca of **Cabarete**, east of Puerto Plata; it also has a happening bar and restaurant scene. Carve out several hours or days learning the ropes from the best of kitesurfing, windsurfing or just plain surfing. Of course, the beaches are equally alluring for doing absolutely nothing but sipping cocktails and making headway in a good book.

Scuba divers and those looking for a more raucous nightlife should look into staying in **Sosúa**. Further east near the quiet town of **Río San Juan** are several terrific beaches and snorkeling and diving opportunities nearby. If you have a big group, renting a villa around **Cabrera** is a good choice.

Central Highlands

Fly into the airport outside **Santiago** and spend a day exploring downtown and taking in Dominican painting at the Centro Leon. Don't miss a bar crawl around the Monument, the center of the city's nightlife, and a baseball game at the stadium just north of downtown if you're here during the winter season.

On the following day, head to **Jarabacoa**, gateway to **Parques Nacionales Armando Bermúdez** and **José del Carmen Ramírez**. The two parks cover much of the DR's central mountain range, including **Pico Duarte**, the highest peak (3087m) in the Caribbean. Visit the waterfalls in the afternoon, with white-water rafting, or canyoning and mountain biking for the next day or two. Or arrange your trip around climbing Pico Duarte. The standard trip is three days, but consider arranging a side trip to beautiful **Valle del Tétero**, which adds two days.

Unwind in the mountain town of **Constanza**, only a short drive from Jarabacoa, where you'll find cooler temperatures and stunning views. Rent a 4WD and off-road it through mountain passes to remote valleys and waterfalls.

Top: Cascada El Limón (p122)

Right: Playa Sosúa (p138)

Off the Beaten Track: Dominican Republic

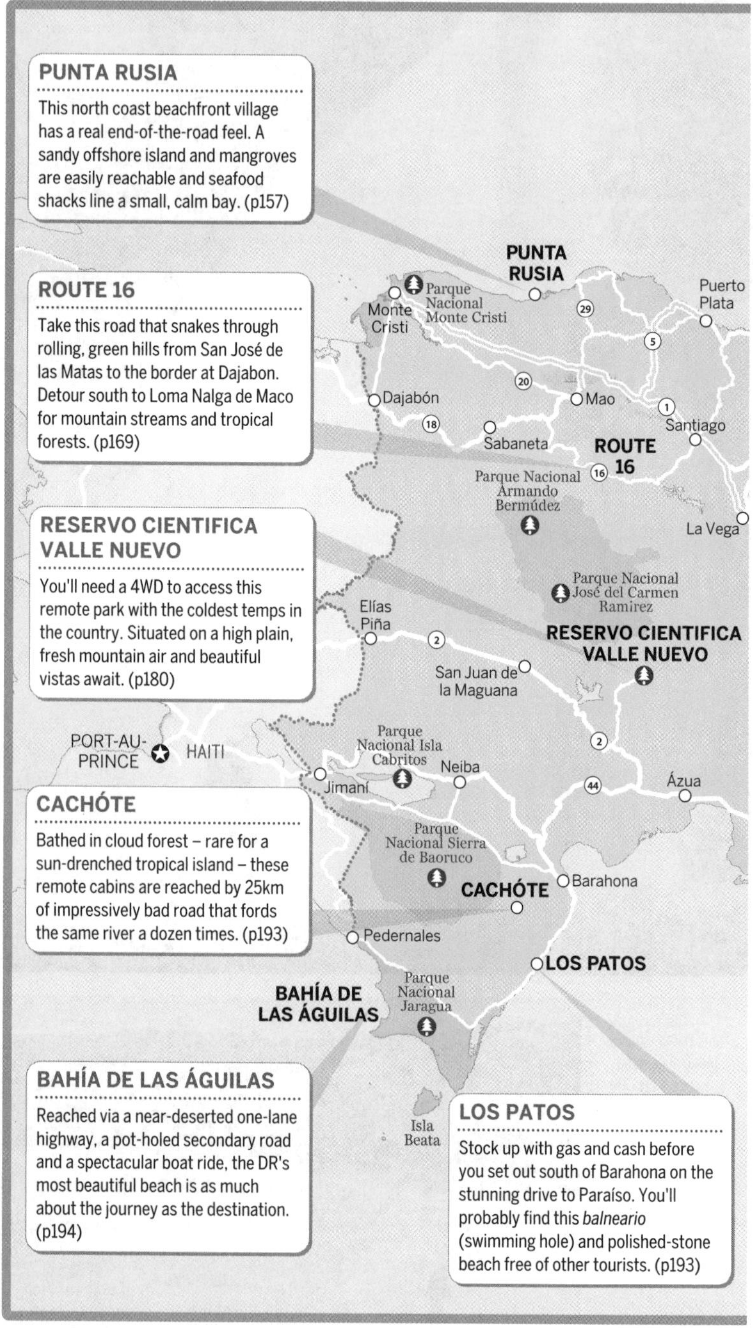

PUNTA RUSIA

This north coast beachfront village has a real end-of-the-road feel. A sandy offshore island and mangroves are easily reachable and seafood shacks line a small, calm bay. (p157)

ROUTE 16

Take this road that snakes through rolling, green hills from San José de las Matas to the border at Dajabon. Detour south to Loma Nalga de Maco for mountain streams and tropical forests. (p169)

RESERVO CIENTIFICA VALLE NUEVO

You'll need a 4WD to access this remote park with the coldest temps in the country. Situated on a high plain, fresh mountain air and beautiful vistas await. (p180)

CACHÓTE

Bathed in cloud forest – rare for a sun-drenched tropical island – these remote cabins are reached by 25km of impressively bad road that fords the same river a dozen times. (p193)

BAHÍA DE LAS ÁGUILAS

Reached via a near-deserted one-lane highway, a pot-holed secondary road and a spectacular boat ride, the DR's most beautiful beach is as much about the journey as the destination. (p194)

LOS PATOS

Stock up with gas and cash before you set out south of Barahona on the stunning drive to Paraíso. You'll probably find this *balneario* (swimming hole) and polished-stone beach free of other tourists. (p193)

CORDILLERA SEPTENTRIONAL

In this dramatic mountain range, Rtes 25 and 233 wind past coursing rivers, jungle-clad escarpments and placid rural settlements. Stop in a village to appreciate Dominican warmth and hospitality. (p170)

CABRERA

This low-key village is a good base to explore a handful of gorgeous beaches and a freshwater lagoon off the highway between the tourist enclaves of the central North Coast and Peninsula de Samana. (p155)

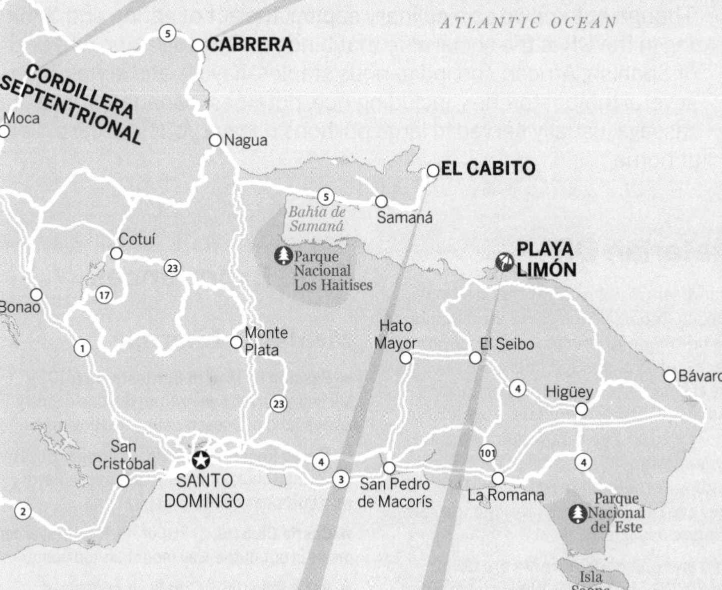

EL CABITO

This rustic restaurant literally hangs over the northeastern edge of the country. Consider the jaw-dropping views your just rewards for tackling the wicked unpaved road that leads here. (p118)

PLAYA LIMÓN

North of Punta Cana, this far-flung beach is the antithesis of the resorts. Pass colorful *colonias* (settlements) and sugar plantations to discover these coconut tree-lined sands. (p104)

CARIBBEAN SEA

Plan Your Trip

Eat & Drink Like a Local

Though not known as a culinary capital, the act of eating and drinking in the DR is the social glue that binds people together. A hybrid of Spanish, African and indigenous staples, flavors and styles, it has several major starches, including rice, potatoes, bananas, yucca and cassava, usually served in large portions – leave your low-carb diet at home.

Vegetarian DR

Vegetarianism is not widely practiced in the Dominican Republic, and there are certainly a large number of Dominicans who view it as downright strange. Still, there are enough nonmeat side dishes in Dominican cuisine – rice, salad, plantains, eggplant, yucca, okra and more – to ensure that vegetarians and even vegans shouldn't have too much problem finding something to eat. Beans are another easy-to-find staple, though they are often made using lard.

Pizza and pasta restaurants are ubiquitous in the DR and there is always at least one vegetarian option on the menu (and if not, it's easy enough to request).

For those vegetarians who make an exception for fish and seafood, there is no problem whatsoever. There is at least one vegetarian restaurant in the DR – Ananda (p67) in Santo Domingo – but virtually all the restaurants listed in this book will have at least some nonmeat alternatives.

Food Experiences

Meals of a Lifetime

- **Passion by Martin Berasategui** (p102) Michelin starred owner from Basque country does a fabulous seven-course tasting menu.
- **Mares Restaurant & Pool Lounge** (p133) Renowned chef combining Dominican flavors with European culinary inspiration.
- **Castle Club** (p151) Elaborate, locally-sourced meals in out-of-the-way mountain-top home.
- **Pat'e Palo** (p66) Creatively conceived dishes in sparkling setting overlooking Santo Domingo's Plaza España.
- **El Cabito** (p118) Fresh seafood in one of the most dramatically beautiful locations in the DR.
- **Mi Corazon** (p124) Inventive tasting menu served in a romantic colonial-style courtyard.
- **La Terrasse** (p124) Sophisticated French bistro on the Las Terrenas beachfront.
- **Rincon Rubi** (p118) Fresh fish grilled to perfection on one of the DR's most stunning beaches.
- **Casa Bonita** (p195) Organic and locally sourced fare in a boutique hotel.
- **Aroma de la Montana** (p176) The DR's only rotating dining room has panoramic views of the Jarabacoa countryside.

CASABE

From ancient Taíno cooking fires to elegant presidential banquets, there is at least one common thread, a starchy bread known as casabe. High in carbs and low in fat, casabe is made from ground cassava roots (also known as manioc and a close relation to yucca). Cassava was one of the Taíno's principal crops, as it was for numerous indigenous peoples throughout the Caribbean and South America. Easy to plant – just bury a piece of the root or stalk into the ground – it's also fast growing. Europeans brought the hardy plant from the Caribbean to their colonies in Africa and Asia, where it was widely adopted. Casabe is still popular today, especially at traditional meals with soups and stews where it's great for soaking up every last drop. Rather tasteless on its own, casabe is best topped with butter, salt, tomato or avocado. A modern variation is the *catibía*, fried cassava flour fritters stuffed with meat.

Staples & Specialties

To Eat

➡ **La Bandera** The most typically Dominican meal consists of white rice, *habichuela* (red beans), stewed meat, salad and fried green plantains, and is usually accompanied by a fresh fruit juice. It's good, cheap, easy to prepare and nutritionally balanced. Red beans are sometimes swapped for small *moros* (black beans), *gandules* (small green beans) or *lentejas* (lentils).

➡ **Guineos** (bananas) A staple of Dominican cuisine and served in a variety of ways, including boiled, stewed and candied, but most commonly boiled and mashed, like mashed potatoes. Prepared the same way, but with plantains, the dish is called *mangú*; with pork rinds mixed in it is called *mofongo*. Both can be served for breakfast, lunch or dinner, either as a side dish or main.

➡ **Seafood** Most commonly a fish fillet, usually *mero* (grouper) or *chillo* (red snapper), served in one of four ways: *al ajillo* (with garlic), *al coco* (in coconut sauce), *al criolla* (with a mild tomato sauce) or *a la diabla* (with a spicy tomato sauce). Other seafood such as *cangrejo* (crab), *calamar* (squid), *camarones* (shrimp), *pulp* (octopus) and *langosta* (lobster) are similarly prepared or *al vinagre* (in vinegar sauce), a variation on ceviche.

➡ **Chivo** Goat meat is popular and presented in many ways. Two of the best are *pierna de chivo asada con ron y cilantro* (roast leg of goat with rum and cilantro) and *chivo guisado en salsa de tomate* (goat stewed in tomato sauce).

➡ **Locrio** The Dominican version of paella – rice is colored with achiote – with a number of different variations, and Dominican sweet bean soup – *habichuela con dulce* – a thick soup with root vegetables.

To Drink

➡ **Ron** (Rum) Known for its smoothness and hearty taste, as well as for being less sweet than its Jamaican counterparts, it's tough to beat the quality of Dominican rum. Dozens of local brands are available, but the big three are Brugal, Barceló and Bermudez. Within these brands, there are many varieties, including *blanco* (clear), *dorado* (golden) and *añejo* (aged). Bermudez, established in 1852, is the oldest of the distilleries. Try a *santo libre* (rum and Sprite), which is just as popular among Dominicans as the more familiar *cuba libre* (rum and Coke). *Ron ponche* (rum punch) – a blend of rum and sweet tropical juices – is more often ordered by foreigners than by locals.

➡ **Beer** Local brews include the ubiquitous Presidente, Quisqueya, Bohemia and Soberante. The most popular way to enjoy a beer is to share a *grande* (large) with a friend or two. A tall 1.1L beer is brought to your table in a sort of insulated sleeve, made from either wood or bamboo or from plastic and Styrofoam, along with a small glass for each of you.

➡ **Whiskey** Popular in the Dominican Republic and a number of familiar brands, plus a few Dominican variations, are available at most bars – purists will want a *trago de etiqueta roja* (Johnny Walker Red Label) or *trago de etiqueta blanca* (Dewar's White Label).

➡ **Mamajuana** The DR's own homemade version of Viagra, is a mixture of herbs, dried bark, rum, wine and honey, which is then steeped for around a month. If you can keep it down, locals believe it can cure various illnesses and, in general, is a substitute for vitamins.

➡ **Coffee** Grown in six different regions by more than 60,000 growers, coffee is a staple of any menu. It's typically served black in an espresso cup with sugar; a *café con leche* is a coffee with hot milk.

PRICE RANGES

The categories for reviews refer to the cost of a main dish with tax.

$ Less than RD$214 (US$5)

$$ RD$214-640 (US$5-15)

$$$ More than RD$640 (US$15)

➡ **Batidas** (smoothies) Made from crushed fruit, water, ice and several tablespoons of sugar. A *batida con leche* contains milk and is slightly more frothy. Popular varieties include *piña* (pineapple), *lechoza* (papaya), *guineo* (banana) and *zapote* (sapote) and *morir soñando* (literally, 'to die dreaming'), made of the refreshing combination of orange juice, milk, sugar and crushed ice.

➡ **Jugos** (juices) Sometimes referred to as *refrescos* (this also means carbonated soda), *jugos* are typically made fresh in front of you. Popular flavors include *chinola* (passionfruit) and *piña* (pineapple peel). Orange juice is commonly called *jugo de china*, although most will understand you if you ask for *jugo de naranja*.

➡ **Coco** Coconut juice from a *cocotero* (a street vendor who hacks out an opening with a machete), is available everywhere.

➡ **Jugo de caña** (sugarcane juice) Sold from vendors, usually on tricycles with a grinder that mashes the cane to liquid.

➡ **Mabí** Delicious drink made from the bark of the tropical liana vine.

Cheap Treats

➡ **Pastelito** Usually beef or chicken, which has first been stewed with onions, olives, tomatoes and a variety of seasonings, and then chopped up and mixed with peas, nuts and raisins – all tucked into a patty of dough and fried in boiling oil.

➡ **Empanada** Similar to pastelitos except typically containing ham or cheese.

➡ **Chimi** Sandwich of seasoned ground meat, cabbage, carrots, red onions and tomatoes.

➡ **Quipe** Afternoon snack of bulger stuffed with ground meat and fresh mint and fried.

➡ **Frituras de batata** Sweet-potato fritters.

➡ **Fritos maduros** Ripe plantain fritters.

➡ **Tostones** Fried plantain slices.

➡ **Yaniqueques** Johnny cakes.

➡ **Frío-frío** Dominican version of snow cone; shaved ice and syrup.

➡ **Agua de coco** Fruits like oranges, bananas and pineapples mixed with sliced coconuts and sugarcane juice.

How to Eat & Drink

When to Eat

Dinner *(cena)* is the biggest meal (except on Sunday when it's generally at midday), though neither breakfast *(desayuno)* nor lunch *(almuerzo)* are exactly light. All three meals usually consist of one main dish – eggs for breakfast, meat for lunch and dinner – served with one or more accompaniments, usually cold cuts, fresh fruit, rice, beans, salad and/or boiled vegetables. Dinner, at restaurants at least, isn't usually eaten until 8 or 9 o'clock.

Menu Decoder

➡ **a la parrilla** (a la pa-ree-ya) broiled

➡ **al carbon** (al car-bone) grilled

➡ **al horno** (al or-no) oven-baked

➡ **al vino** (al vee-no) cooked in wine

➡ **frito** (free-to) fried

➡ **guisada** (gui-sa-da) any stew

➡ **parillada** (pa-ri-yada) barbecue

➡ **sopa** (so-pa) soup

CELEBRATIONS

There are a number of dishes usually reserved for special occasions, such as baptisms, birthdays and weddings: *puerco asado* (roast pork), *asopao de mariscos* (seafood) and the more modest *locrio de pica-pica* (spicy sardines and rice). Dishes such as *sancocho de siete carnes* (seven-meat soup), made with sausage, chicken, beef, goat and several pork parts, all combined with green plantains and avocado into a hearty stew, are sometimes on restaurant menus. Christmas time in the Dominican Republic is associated with a few specialties: *jengibre*, a drink made of cinnamon, fresh ginger root, water and sugar; *pastelitos*; *moro de guandules* (rice with pigeon peas and coconut milk); and *ensalada rusa* (basically, potato salad).

Plan Your Trip

Dominican Republic Outdoors

No doubt, lounging by the pool or on the beach is what draws many visitors to the Dominican Republic. This is certainly an attractive option, but if you want to get the blood flowing, there's a wide range of sports and skill- and stamina-challenging adventures.

Water Sports

If it involves standing on a board, the Dominican Republic's got it in spades – you'll find world-class kitesurfing, windsurfing, surfing and wakeboarding. The undisputed water-sports capital of the DR is Cabarete on the north coast, and Las Terrenas on the Península de Samaná is the runner-up, but the adventurous can find a few other more-isolated spots as well.

Kitesurfing

Kitesurfing (also known as kiteboarding) involves strapping a board to your feet and a powerful kite to your torso, which propels you through the waves at sometimes breakneck speeds. The learning curve to get good enough to enjoy it – not to mention learning the lingo for tricks like 'kitelooping' and 'back-side handle passes' – is steep. On average, it takes a week's worth of lessons to go out solo, and months of practice to get competent. It's also expensive – to make this a regular hobby, you'll end up spending a few thousand dollars on lessons and gear. No wonder, then, around 90% of wannabes who try it out don't generally advance to become regular kitesurfers.

Best Outdoors

Best Mountain Biking

From Jamao near Moca to the isolated Magante Beach near Rio San Juan, country roads in the central highlands, Septentrional range around Cabarete.

Best Month to Go

February for migratory birds in the southwest, whale-watching in Samaná, and wind sports in Cabarete.

Best Adventures to Try for the First Time

Kitesurfing, canyoning, paragliding, white-water rafting and wakeboarding.

Best Base for Active Adventures

Jarabacoa in the central highlands, Cabarete on the North Coast, Las Terrenas in Península de Samaná or Bayahibe in the southeast.

Best Places for More Leisurely Exploration

Parque Nacional Los Haitises, Parque Nacional Jaragua, San José de las Matas, Parque Nacional del Este or Parque Nacional Sierra de Bahoruco.

That said, if you've got the time and the money, and you relish a challenge, the DR is one of the world's leading kitesurfing destinations – so much so that the International Kiteboarding Organization (p145) has its headquarters in Cabarete. Plenty of kitesurfing schools offer instruction in Cabarete or Las Terrenas in Samaná (the wind is lighter and water shallower here); Puerto Plata is another excellent spot to learn the sport. Most people need a minimum of four days of lessons at a cost of around US$350 to US$450. Schools and instructors vary considerably in personality, so spend some time finding one where you feel comfortable.

Surfing

According to many, the very first person to surf in the Dominican Republic was an American Army colonel, part of the US occupying force in Santo Domingo in 1965. Before leaving he sold his board to locals and the sport grew steadily from there. Until the late 1970s, specifically October 31, 1979, when hurricane Daniel struck the southern coast, the waves around Playa Guibia on Santo Domingo's Malecón were some of the best in the country. The exact explanation of the storm's impact is unclear. What is known, Sosua experienced its first tourism boom when surfers began flocking to nearby beach breaks soon after.

The north coast, especially Cabarete's Playa Encuentro, has grown into the capital of surfing in the DR. Of course, with nearly 800 miles of coastline, there's nary a region where adventurous surf gypsies can't find gnarly sets. In addition to the specific breaks listed here, the independent-minded can explore waves in Rio San Juan, Playa Grande, Playa La Preciosa, Cabrera and Nagua along the north coast; Playa Coson and Playa Bonita near Las Terrenas on the Península de Samaná and Punta Cana and Macao in the east. The best season is December through March, when waves can get up to 4m high.

There are a number of surf shops in Cabarete, Playa Encuentro and Las Terrenas where you can rent boards or take surfing lessons. Rentals cost US$25 to US$30 for half a day; courses vary from three-hour introductory sessions (US$45 to US$50) to a full-blown five-day surf camp (US$200 to US$225 per person). Surfboards can be rented at a handful of other beaches including Playa Grande.

- **La Borja** Near Santo Domingo's Las Americas airport and large shipping terminal at Boca Chica. A right, reef break with long lines; not for beginners.
- **Pato** West of Santo Domingo near the town of Nizao. A long, left break near a river mouth good for beginners.
- **Tankline & La Puntillo** Class A breaks, the former a right and the latter a left, both in front of Puerto Plata's fortress along the Malecón. Best time is November to March.
- **Playa Encuentro** This, the epicenter of Dominican surf culture, is just 4km west of Cabarete with five separate breaks.

Diving & Snorkeling

Compared to other Caribbean islands, the DR is not known as a diving destination. That being said, it has some great places for underwater exploring – the offshore area around Bayahibe on the southeast coast is generally considered the best. The warm Caribbean waters around here have pretty fields of coral and myriad tropical fish that make for fun easy dives. Two

BEHOLD LEVIATHAN

Between mid-January and mid-March more than 80% of the reproductively active humpback whales in the North Atlantic – some 10,000 to 12,000 in all – migrate to the waters around the Península de Samaná to mate. The Bahía de Samaná is a favorite haunt of the whales, and one of the best places in the world to observe these massive, curious creatures. Most tours depart from the town of Samaná, and you are all but guaranteed to see numerous whales surfacing for air, lifting their fins or tail, jostling each other in competition, and even breaching – impressive jumps followed by an equally impressive splash. Whale-watching season coincides with Carnaval (every weekend in February) and Independence Day (February 27) – major holidays here – so you should make reservations well in advance.

RESPONSIBLE DIVING

Please consider the following tips when diving and help preserve the ecology and beauty of reefs:

- Avoid touching or standing on living marine organisms or dragging equipment across the reef. Polyps can be damaged by even the gentlest contact. If you must hold on to the reef, only touch exposed rock or dead coral.
- Be conscious of your fins. Even without contact, the surge from fin strokes near the reef can damage delicate organisms. Take care not to kick up clouds of sand, which can smother organisms.
- Take great care in underwater caves. Spend as little time within them as possible as your air bubbles may be caught within the roof and thereby leave organisms high and dry. Take turns to inspect the interior of a small cave.
- Resist the temptation to collect or buy corals or shells or to loot marine archaeological sites (mainly shipwrecks).
- Do not feed fish.

national parks east of Santo Domingo – Parque Nacional Submarino La Caleta and Parque Nacional del Este – can be reached through dive shops in Boca Chica and Bayahibe, respectively.

La Caleta is an underwater preserve covering just 10 sq km but is one of the country's most popular dive destinations. The main attraction is the *Hickory,* a 39m salvage ship with an interesting past that was intentionally sunk in 1994. Parque Nacional del Este has a number of interesting dives, too, including another wreck – a massive 89m cargo ship – and a site ominously called Shark Point.

The DR's north coast provides a very different diving experience. Facing the Atlantic, the water there is cooler and somewhat transparent, but the underwater terrain is more varied, making for challenging dives and unique profiles.

Sosúa is the dive capital here and excursions can be organized to all points along the coast. Divers exploring the waters near the Península de Samaná can sometimes hear humpback whales singing; Las Terrenas and Las Galeras have a few small dive shops.

Other off-the-beaten-track options are two diveable freshwater caves – Dudu Cave, near Río San Juan, and Padre Nuestro, near Bayahibe. Dudu, with two openings, three different tunnels and a spacious stalactite-filled chamber, is one of the most memorable cave dives in the Caribbean (generally needed is an Advanced Diver certificate or at least 20 logged dives in order to come out here). Located within the Parque Nacional del Este, Padre Nuestro is a challenging 290m tunnel that should be attempted only by trained cave divers. With the exception of the cave dives, most of the sites also make for excellent snorkeling.

Dive prices vary from place to place, but average US$30 to US$40 for one tank, plus US$5 to US$10 for equipment rental. Most people buy multidive packages, which can bring the per-dive price down to around US$25. You must have an Open Water certificate; if you're new to the sport, dive shops offer the Discover Scuba and Open Water certification courses. Snorkeling trips cost around US$25 to US$40 per person.

White-Water Rafting

The Dominican Republic has the only navigable white-water river in the Caribbean, the Río Yaque del Norte. It's mostly a Class II and III river, with a couple of serious rapids, and the rest consists of fun little holes and rolls. The river winds through bucolic hilly countryside and makes for a fun half-day tour.

Be aware that the water can be cold – you'll be issued a wetsuit along with your life vest and helmet. While you can make this a day trip from the north coast or Santo Domingo, it's a long journey in a bus – you'll enjoy yourself a great deal more if you spend a couple of nights in Jarabacoa. Trips cost around US$50 per person.

HANDY WEBSITES FOR OUTDOOR ACTIVITIES

www.drpure.com An overview of outdoor adventure activities; good place to start.

www.activecabarete.com Features listings, information and reviews about sporting activities in and around Cabarete.

www.windalert.com Up-to-the-minute wind reports and forecasts to help plan your wind-powered water activities.

www.godominicanrepublic.com Information on outdoor activities, golfing and beach activities.

www.ambiente.gob.do (in Spanish) The home page of the federal Department of the Environment has information on national parks.

Fishing

Like most places in the Caribbean, there is good sport fishing to be had for those so inclined. Blue marlin peaks in the summer months, there's white marlin in springtime, and mahi-mahi, wahoo and sailfish in wintertime.

The best places to go deep-sea fishing are the north-coast region and Punta Cana. Expect to pay around US$70 to US$100 per person (US$60 to US$70 for watchers) for a group half-day excursion. Most captains will also gladly charter their boats for private use; expect to pay upwards of US$700/900 for a half-/full day.

Windsurfing

Cabarete's bay seems almost custom-made for windsurfing, and it's here that the sport is most popular – although you'll also find a small windsurfing school in Las Terrenas. The best time to come is generally in winter, when the wind is strongest – in general, windsurfing requires stronger winds than kitesurfing does.

The beach at Cabarete has a few dedicated outfits renting windsurfing equipment and offering lessons for beginners. Renting a board and sail will cost about US$35/65/300 per hour/day/week. Lessons range from just one hour (US$50) to a complete four-session course (US$200).

In general, windsurfing is much easier to learn than kitesurfing, meaning you can be out on the water enjoying yourself within a few days' time. Lessons and equipment rentals are also significantly cheaper.

Kayaking

The DR holds great potential for both sea and river kayaking. A few scattered shops and hotels rent sea kayaks for a paddle along the beach and gung-ho river kayakers looking for some crazy rapids (and who don't mind traveling with a kayak in their luggage) should head to Jarabacoa, where Class III, IV and V rapids surge past on the Río Yaque del Norte, which flows nearby. Or get in touch with Kayak River Adventures (p147) in Cabarete to customize a trip.

Land Sports

Cascading & Canyoning

Cascading – climbing up through a series of waterfalls, and then jumping and sliding down into the pools of water below – is hugely popular at the 27 waterfalls of Damajagua, on the north coast. For many travelers it's their favorite experience in the DR. You'll be issued a life jacket and safety helmet, and guides will lead you, sometimes pulling you bodily through the force of the water. Some of the jumps down are as much as 8m high. You can visit the waterfalls by yourself – foreigners pay RD$600 per person, and while a guide is mandatory, there's no minimum group size. Alternatively, you can come with a tour group, but all the package 'jeep safari' tours go only to the 7th waterfall – disappointing. Only a very few tour agencies offer the trip to the very top.

Canyoning – often referred to as 'canyoneering' in the US – is cascading's technical, older brother and is even more of an adrenaline rush, involving jumping, rappelling and sliding down a slippery river gorge with a mountain river raging around you. You'll be issued a safety helmet and usually a shorts-length wetsuit. It's becoming more popular in the DR, but there are really only three reliable and experienced companies: Iguana Mama (p147) and Kayak River Adventures (p147) in Cabarete on the north coast and Rancho Baiguate (p177) in Jarabacoa in the mountains. We highly recommend it.

Hiking

Pico Duarte

The most famous hike in the DR is the ascent of Pico Duarte (3087m), the tallest peak in the Caribbean. First climbed in 1944 as part of the 100th anniversary celebration of the Dominican Republic's independence from Haiti, it's a tough multiday hike, but involves no technical climbing, and mules carry supplies and equipment up the mountain (best time to go is December to March). There are two main routes to the summit and several side trips you can take along the way, including hikes through two beautiful alpine valleys and up the Caribbean's second-highest peak, La Pelona, just 100m lower than Pico Duarte.

While the destination – the peak itself and the views – is stunning, the well-traveled walker may be disappointed by the journey required to get there. You pass quickly through the ferns and moss-bound rainforest of the lower elevations, and once you hit 2200m all you see are burnt-out forests of Caribbean Pine, spaced at regular intervals, with no animals and only cawing crows for company. Still, if it's clear at the top when you get there – and you have time to linger at the summit – then the hard work to get there may be worth it.

Shorter Hikes

The DR is not a world-class hiking destination. Still, there are a number of waterfalls and quite a few challenging trails around Jarabacoa. The Península de Samaná has some beautiful hikes near Las Galeras, with picturesque deserted beaches as your reward at the end. In the southwest, there's some decent half-day and full-day hikes just outside Paraíso, although they are best visited as part of a tour.

Lesser-known trails are slowly being developed for organized hikes in the Cordillera Septentrional south of Sosúa. Contact Tubagua Plantation Eco-Village (p170) for customized itineraries. And rising out of flat plains near San Francisco de Macorís, Loma Quita Espuela is surrounded by organic cocoa plantations and swimming holes.

Golf

Known as one of the premier golf destinations in the Caribbean, the DR has more than two dozen courses to choose from. Signature courses from high-profile designers like Tom Fazio, Robert Trent Jones Sr, Pete Dye, Jack Nicklaus, Nick Faldo and Arnold Palmer continue to be built at a steady pace. The majority are affiliated with (or located nearby) the top all-inclusive resorts (the most by far are located along the southeastern coast between La Romana and north of Punta Cana; none are west of an imaginary line that runs south to north from Santo Domingo, to Jarabacoa, Santiago and Puerto Plata), but are open to guests and nonguests alike. Almost all take advantage of their Caribbean setting (of course this means many were built on former mangrove areas) and feature fairways and greens with spectacular ocean views. A few of the best in the country:

➡ **Corales** Tom Fazio–designed course opened in Punta Cana area in 2010.

➡ **La Cana Golf Course** Best in the area; design completed by Pete Dye's son Paul Burke (p98).

➡ **Playa Grande** Last course designed by Robert Trent Jones Sr (p154); due for renovations.

➡ **Punta Espada** One of three Jack Nicklaus Signature courses at Cap Cana (p99).

➡ **Teeth of the Dog** One of four highly-rated Pete Dye–designed courses in Casa de Campo (p85).

Mountain Biking

The Jarabacoa and Constanza areas are the best and most popular areas for mountain-bike riding. The crisp air and cool climate make for ideal cycling and dirt roads and single-track trails offer challenging climbs and thrilling descents through thick forests and a number of waterfalls are within easy reach.

Cabarete also has a number of good rides and is home to the DR's best cycling tour operator, Iguana Mama (p147), and one of it's more passionate advocates/

TIPS FROM MAXIMO

Based in Cabarete, Maximo Martinez has been exploring mountain-bike trails all over the DR for the last 20 years.

➡ A not-to-miss ride for those interested in easy-going terrain is through the sugarcane fields around La Romana in the southeast.

➡ The best times are when you're deep in the mountains and local villagers allow you access to their trails.

➡ The 'Cibao Valley Loop', a wonderful six to seven hours, begins in Cabarete, taking the road to Sabaneta de Yásica, 40km through the mountains down to Moca, heading to the west of Santiago, then north to Puerto Plata and back to Cabarete.

➡ The Septentrional range possesses the most technical rides, especially around Cabarete. The descents are down rocky, shady trails, best during summertime. These are perfect teaching trails.

➡ One of the most demanding rides in the country is Tour del Sufrimiento (the Suffering Tour), from Jarabacoa to Constanza to San José de Ocoa to Santo Domingo.

guides, Maximo Martinez. It offers mountain-bike tours ranging from half-day downhill rides to 12-day cross-country excursions. It can also customize a trip to fit your interests, available time and experience level.

Tour prices vary widely depending on the length of the ride, but begin at around US$45 per person for half-day trips.

Birdwatching

The DR is a popular destination for gung-ho birders looking for the island's endemic bird species – 32 in all (depending on who you ask and how you count). The very best place to go birding is the southwest, especially the north slope of the Sierra de Bahoruco, where you can spot nearly all the endemics, including the high-altitude habitat-loss-threatened La Selle's thrush, western chat-tanager, white-winged warbler, rufous-throated solitaire and Hispaniolan trogon. Lago Enriquillo and Laguna Oviedo are known for populations of wading birds.

The Jardín Botánico Nacional (p59) in Santo Domingo are, surprisingly, also a good spot to look for birds, especially the palm chat, black-crowned palm tanagers, Hispaniolan woodpeckers, vervain hummingbirds and Antillean mangoes. In the Punta Cana area, head to the Indigeneous Eyes Ecological Park; and near Bayahibe, Parque Nacional del Este where 112 species have been recorded.

Parque Nacional Los Haitises is the only place you're likely to see the highly endangered Ridgway's hawk.

While numerous overseas birding groups bring enthusiasts here, there's only one tour company devoted to birdwatching based in the DR.

Paragliding

Head out to Jarabacoa for the thrill of soaring on a thermal with a bird's-eye view of the spectacular mountains surrounding this valley town, with its unusual sights of pine trees and Swiss-type A-frame houses – right in the middle of the Caribbean. There's a great local group of pilots living here year-round.

Horseback Riding

Those equestrian-inclined will find good riding on beaches and in the mountains. You may be somewhat disappointed in the horses, however – Dominicans themselves tend to use mules, and the few horses are principally for tourists and rich Dominicans. Don't expect to ride a thoroughbred, however a handful of well-run, independent operations, especially in the Sosúa and Cabarete region, can be recommended.

A number of stables offer their services through tour agencies and resorts. Expect to pay roughly US$50 to US$70 per person for a half-day ride. You can also ride a mule to the top of Pico Duarte.

The most popular trip is to the waterfalls around Limón on the Península de Samaná.

Regions at a Glance

Santo Domingo

History
Nightlife
Food

Zona Colonial

The heart of the Spanish empire's original seat in the New World is chockablock with museums, sights and plazas surrounded by exquisitely restored 16th-century buildings. However, ordinary life continues apace amid a picturesque backdrop.

Nightlife

Whether it's a modest *colmado* (corner store) or posh nightclubs that wouldn't be out of place in any major world capital, Santo Domingo, the largest city in the Caribbean, is the place to party. Merengue, *bachata* and salsa reverberate on the streets, gritty and posh alike.

Food

This is truly a cosmopolitan dining scene and the country's culinary capital. There's little reason to settle for the *plato del día* when you can feast alfresco on the balcony of a colonial-era building on locally caught seafood with a *haute cuisine* twist.

p46

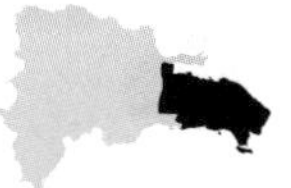

Punta Cana & the Southeast

Beaches
Resorts
Water Sports

Beaches

Planeloads of tourists make a beeline for the stretches of white sand around Baváro and Punta Cana. But there are less-developed patches to the north for the more adventurous.

All-Inclusive Resorts

Much of the country's reputation as a sybaritic holiday land is based on this region. Every stereotype is true; regardless, there's something very intoxicating about having every indulgence, food, drinks, pools and beachfront, close at hand.

Aquatic Adventures

Bayahibe, a fishing village near La Romana, is the center of what's widely regarded as the country's best scuba diving. Snorkelers also have off-shore reefs to choose from.

p78

Península de Samaná

Landscapes
Water Sports
Social Scene

Landscapes

Rolling mountains with hard-to-get-to waterfalls, a sea of hillocks pushing their way to a long coastline of protected beaches and picturesque coves, plus cliffs and hidden lagoons once refuges for pirates.

Water Sports

Be it surfing, kitesurfing, snorkeling or scuba diving, active travelers will find it all here, as well as a community of experienced pros to show beginners how it's done.

Social Scene

A motley crew of mainly European and North Americans have brought a cosmopolitan flavor to the peninsula: Las Terrenas is the center of cafe culture and nightlife, while Las Galeras' sophistication flies under the radar.

p108

North Coast

Beaches
Water Sports
Nightlife

Beaches

Rivaling the southeast in terms of the beauty of its shoreline, the long ocean corridor stretching from Monte Cristi to Cabrera offers seclusion or development, whatever your fancy.

Water Sports

Generally considered the mecca of water-based sports in the DR, the north coast offers virtually every means of propelling yourself across or through liquid. From kitesurfing to wakeboarding to canyoning, the conditions are close to ideal.

Nightlife

Indulge in *la dolce vita* sipping tropical cocktails on Cabarete's beachfront or a leisurely sundowner on Puerto Plata's Malecón. More rowdy Sosúa or resort discos round out your options.

p127

Central Highlands

Adventures
Scenery
Tranquility

Outdoor Activities

Blessed with a roaring river and four of the five highest peaks in the Caribbean, the Cordillera Central is an adventure-sport destination where you can get up high while paragliding or scramble on your hands and knees down a canyon.

Mountain Vistas

Pastoral panoramas of forested slopes are more evocative of the European Alps than the Caribbean, and a drive along one of the winding roads passes from cloud-shrouded jungle to sun-dappled plateaus.

Tranquility

Because it can be relatively challenging to access, tourism is less developed and you're more likely to slow down and rise and shine to the rhythms of the sun.

p161

The Southwest & Península de Pedernales

Landscapes
Nature
Escape

Landscapes

Millennia-old tectonic movements have given the peninsula its unique features: unspoiled sanctuaries, characterized by the beautiful beach along the Bahía de las Águilas and cactus-covered deserts.

Wildlife

An emerging ecotourism destination, this is the best place on the island to go birdwatching: nearly all of the island's endemics are found here. That's to say nothing of the crocodiles, lizards, turtles and marine life.

Tranquility

Get away from the coastal crowds, where any stranger is sure to turn heads. And yet despite this thinly populated region's remoteness, there are still a few luxurious retreats.

p183

On the Road

Santo Domingo

POP 2 MILLION

Includes ➡

Best Places to Eat

- Pat'e Palo (p66)
- Il Cappucino (p67)
- Antica Pizzeria (p66)
- Adrian Tropical (p67)

Best Places to Stay

- Hostal Nicolás de Ovando (p64)
- El Beaterío Guest House (p63)
- Hotel Villa Colonial (p63)
- Hotel Atarazana (p63)

Why Go?

Santo Domingo, or 'La Capital' as it's typically called, is a collage of cultures and neighborhoods. It's where the sounds of life – domino pieces slapped on tables, backfiring mufflers and horns from chaotic traffic, merengue and *bachata* (Dominican music) blasting from corner stores – are most intense. At the heart of the city is the Zona Colonial, where you'll find one of the oldest churches and the oldest surviving European fortress among other New World firsts. Amid the cobblestone streets, it would be easy to forget Santo Domingo is in the Caribbean. But this is an intensely urban city, home not only to colonial-era architecture, but also to hot clubs, vibrant cultural institutions and elegant restaurants. Santo Domingo somehow manages to embody the contradictions central to the Dominican experience: a living museum, a metropolis crossed with a seaside resort, and a business, political and media center with a laid-back, casual spirit.

When to Go

- The city hosts a blowout merengue festival in July and a three-day Latin music event in October. Baseball is played almost five nights a week at Estadio Quisqueya, from the end of October to the end of January. Carnaval, at the end of February and beginning of March, is a big deal in the capital.
- Hurricane season, from August through December, means strong rains and developing storms can be a threat, though sunshine usually prevails. On average September sees the most precipitation and February the least.

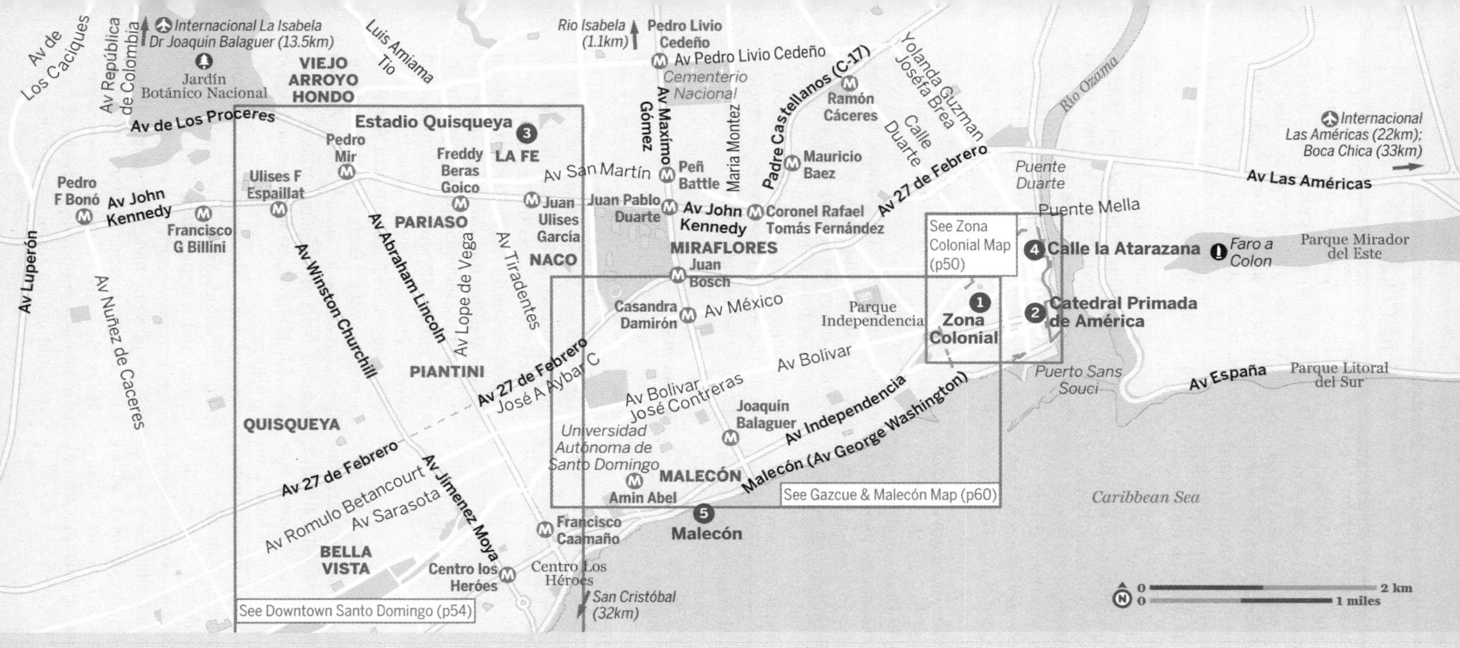

Santo Domingo Highlights

1 Wandering the 500-year-old cobblestone backstreets of the **Zona Colonial** (p48)

2 Entering the **Catedral Primada de América** (p49) – the first church in the New World – and imagining how 16th-century worshippers felt

3 Rooting for the home team at raucous **Estadio Quisqueya** (p70), one of the premier places to watch a baseball game in the Dominican Republic

4 Letting the night slip away after a late dinner along romantic **Calle la Atarazana** (p65), off Plaza España

5 Dancing to **merengue**, **bachata** or **salsa music** (p70) or just plain-old grinding down at one of the capital's vibrant Malecón nightclubs

History

In a way, it can be said that the founding of Santo Domingo was an act of desperation. Columbus' first settlement, Villa La Navidad in present-day Haiti, was burned to the ground and all settlers killed within a year. His second settlement, La Isabela, west of present-day Puerto Plata, lasted only five years and was beset from the beginning by disease and disaster. Columbus' brother Bartolomé, left in charge of La Isabela and facing rebellion from its disgruntled residents, pulled up stakes and moved clear around to the other side of the island. He then founded Nueva Isabela on the east bank of the Río Ozama. The third time, evidently, was the charm for Columbus, and this city – though moved to the west bank and renamed Santo Domingo – has remained the capital to this day.

That's not to say the city hasn't had its fair share of troubles. In 1586 the English buccaneer Sir Francis Drake captured the city and collected a ransom for its return to Spanish control. And in 1655 an English fleet commanded by William Penn attempted to take Santo Domingo but retreated after encountering heavy resistance. A century and a half later a brazen ex-slave and Haitian leader by the name of François Dominique Toussaint Louverture marched into Santo Domingo. Toussaint and his troops took control of the city without any resistance at all; the city's inhabitants knew they were no match for the army of former slaves and wisely didn't try to resist. During the occupation many of the city's residents fled to Venezuela or neighboring islands. It was in Santo Domingo on February 27, 1844, that Juan Pablo Duarte – considered the father of the Dominican Republic (DR) – declared Dominican independence from Haiti, a day still celebrated today.

Sights

The highest concentration of sights are conveniently located within walking distance of one another in the Zona Colonial. Surprisingly, for a city with 15km of Caribbean waterfront, Santo Domingo is more inland-oriented and the Malecón (Esplanade) has been developed haphazardly or neglected. One small spot that has been reclaimed for the public is **Playa Guibia** (Avs George Washington and Maximo Gomez), which has a beach area (packed on weekends), a sandy volleyball court, a kids' playground, gym equipment and free wi-fi access.

Zona Colonial

For those fascinated by the origin of the so-called New World – a dramatic story of the first encounter between native people of the Americas and Europeans – the Zona Colonial, listed as a Unesco World Heritage site, is a great place to explore. It is 11 square blocks, a mix of cobblestone and pavement (the city is going block by block, cordoning off and tearing up streets in an effort to improve drainage and bury electrical cables underground), on the west bank of the Río Ozama, where the deep river meets the Caribbean Sea. **Calle El Conde**, the main commercial artery, is lined with *casas de cambio* (money changers); cafes; restaurants; shoe, clothing and jewelry stores; and vendors hawking cheap souvenirs.

As might be expected, many of the structures in the Zona Colonial that still have their 16th-century walls have more recently altered facades and structural additions like new floors and roofs. Keep your eyes open for the nooks and crannies and street scenes: small pedestrian alleys, men playing dominoes at an aluminum folding-table set on the street. These scenes, as much as the historical sites and buildings, make the Zona Colonial unique.

Museums

Museo de las Casas Reales MUSEUM

(Museum of the Royal Houses; Map p50; ☎809-682-4202; Las Damas; adult/under 12yr RD$100/free; ⏲9am-5pm Tue-Sat, to 4pm Sun) Built in the Renaissance style during the 16th century, this building was the longtime seat of Spanish authority for the entire Caribbean region, housing the governor's office and the powerful Audiencia Real (Royal Court), among others. It showcases colonial-period objects, including many treasures recovered from Spanish galleons that foundered in nearby waters. Each room has been restored according to its original style, and displays range from Taíno artifacts to dozens of hand-blown wine bottles and period furnishings.

Several walls are covered with excellent maps of various voyages of European explorers and conquistadors. Also on display is an impressive antique weaponry collection acquired by dictator/president Trujillo from a Mexican general (ironically, during a 1955 world peace event). You'll see samurai swords, medieval armor, ivory-inlaid crossbows and even a pistol/sword combo. Admission includes an audio guide available in a number of languages including English.

Museo Alcázar de Colón MUSEUM
(Museum Citadel of Columbus; Map p50; ☎809-682-4750; Plaza España; adult/child RD$100/20; ⊙9am-5pm Tue-Sat, to 4pm Sun) Designed in the Gothic-Mudéjar transitional style, this was once the residence of Columbus' son, Diego, and his wife, Doña María de Toledo, during the early 16th century. The magnificent building we see today is the result of three historically authentic restorations: one in 1957, another in 1971 and a third in 1992. The building itself, as well as the household pieces on display (said to have belonged to the Columbus family), are definitely worth a look.

Recalled to Spain in 1523, Diego and Doña Maria left the home to relatives who occupied the handsome building for the next hundred years. It was subsequently allowed to deteriorate, then was used as a prison and a warehouse, before it was finally abandoned. By 1775 it was a vandalized shell of its former self and served as the unofficial city dump. Less than a hundred years later, only two of its walls remained at right angles.

Tickets can be purchased in the standalone building in Plaza España a few steps from the museum's entrance.

Amber World Museum MUSEUM
(Map p50; ☎809-682-3309; www.amberworldmuseum.com; cnr Calle Arzibispo Merino & Restauracion; adult/child RD$50/20; ⊙9am-6pm Mon-Sat, to 1pm Sun) This museum features an impressive collection of amber samples from around the world and excellent exhibits explaining in Spanish and English its prehistoric origins, its use throughout the ages, Dominican mining processes, and its present-day value to the science and art worlds. The 1st-floor shop sells jewelry made from amber, larimar and more ordinary stones.

Larimar Museum MUSEUM
(Map p50; ☎809-689-6605; www.larimarmuseum.com; 2nd fl, Isabel la Católica 54; ⊙8am-6pm Mon-Sat, to 2pm Sun) FREE Thorough exhibits covering larimar from A to Z have signage in Spanish and English. Of course, the museum is meant to inspire you to make a purchase from the strategically located jewelry store on the 1st floor.

Museo de la Familia Dominicana MUSEUM
(Museum of the Dominican Family; Map p50; ☎809-689-5000; cnr Padre Billini & Arzobispo Meriño; adult/under 12yr RD$100/free; ⊙9am-5pm Tue-Sat, to 4pm Sun) This museum is located in the Casa de Tostado – the beautifully restored 16th-century home of writer Francisco Tostado. The museum is interesting as much for its architectural features (it has a double Gothic window over the front door – the only one of its kind in the Americas) as for its exhibits displaying well-restored 19th-century furnishings and household objects. Ask to go up the spiral mahogany staircase for a rooftop view of the Zona Colonial. Admission includes audio guide.

Museo del Ron y la Caña MUSEUM
(Map p50; Isabel la Católica 261; ⊙9am-5pm Mon-Sat) FREE Housed in a restored 16th-century building, exhibits here celebrate rum and sugar cane, two of the country's most important exports. Displays and photographs explain the history of their production and importance to the DR's economy. Of course, you can sample the wares at the small bar or buy some to go.

Museo del Duarte MUSEUM
(Map p50; Isabel la Católica 308; ⊙9am-5pm Tue-Fri, to noon Sat) FREE The birthplace of Juan Pablo Duarte has been converted into a modest museum. Three rooms display documents, artifacts and photos from his life and from La Trinitaria, the underground independence organization he founded.

Quinta Dominica MUSEUM
(Map p50; cnr Padre Billini & 19 de Marzo; ⊙9am-6pm Mon-Sat, to 2pm Sun) FREE This small art gallery, in a renovated 16th-century home, features ever-changing exhibits of colonial and contemporary art. A shady courtyard at the back with tables and chairs provides a great place to just sit and relax. BYO snacks and drinks.

Churches

★**Catedral Primada de América** CHURCH
(Nuestra Senora de la Anunciacion; Map p50; ☎809-685-2302; Parque Colón; adult/child RD$60/free; ⊙8am-5pm Mon-Sat) The first stone of this cathedral, the oldest in operation in the western hemisphere, was set in 1514 by Diego Columbus, son of the great explorer (the ashes of both father and son are said to have once resided in the chapel's crypt). Construction, however, didn't begin in earnest until the arrival of the first bishop, Alejandro Geraldini, in 1521. From then until 1540, numerous architects worked on the church and adjoining buildings, which is why the vault is Gothic, the arches

Zona Colonial

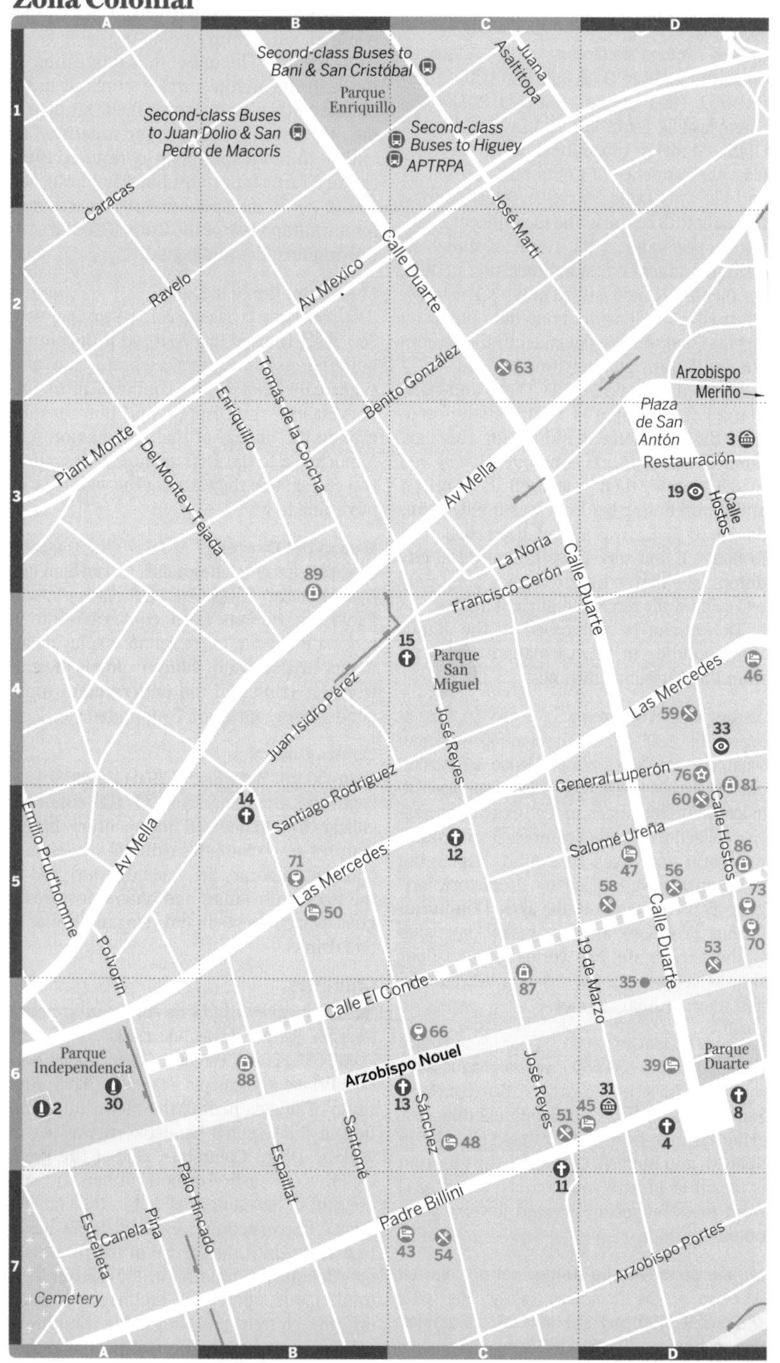

Romanesque and the ornamentation baroque. It's anyone's guess what the planned bell tower would have looked like: a shortage of funds curtailed construction, and the steeple, which undoubtedly would have offered a commanding view of the city, was never built.

The cathedral's current interior is a far cry from the original – thanks to Drake and his crew of pirates, who used the basilica as their headquarters during their 1586 assault on the city. They stole everything of value that they could carry away and extensively vandalized the church before departing.

Among the cathedral's more impressive features are its awesome vaulted ceiling and its 14 interior chapels. Shorts and tank tops are strictly prohibited.

Although Santo Domingo residents like to say their cathedral was the first in the Western hemisphere, in fact one was built in Mexico City between 1524 and 1532; it stood for four decades, until it was knocked down in 1573 and replaced by the imposing Catedral Metropolitano.

Tickets, purchased at the entrance in the southeastern corner of the site, include an audio guide available in a variety of languages (RD$40 without audio guide). Daily mass is at 5pm Monday to Saturday and noon and 5pm Sundays.

Convento de la Orden de los Predicadores — CHURCH

(Convent of the Order of Preachers; Map p50; cnr Calle Duarte & Padre Billini; varies) Built in 1510 by Charles V, this is the first convent of the Dominican order founded in the Americas. It is also where Father Bartolomé de las Casas – the famous chronicler of Spanish atrocities committed against indigenous peoples – did most of his writing. The vault of the chapel, remarkable for its stone zodiac wheel carved with mythological and astrological representations, is worth a look. On the walls are various paintings of religious figures, including Pope Saint Pius V.

Capilla de Nuestra Señora de los Remedios — CHURCH

(Chapel of Our Lady of Remedies; Map p50; cnr Las Damas & Las Mercedes; varies) The Gothic-style chapel was built in the 16th century by alderman Francisco de Avila and was intended to be a private chapel and family mausoleum. Early residents of the city are said to have attended Mass here under its barrel-vaulted ceiling. It was restored in 1884.

Zona Colonial

Top Sights
1 Catedral Primada de América E5

Sights
2 Altar de la Patria A6
3 Amber World Museum D3
4 Capilla de la Tercera Orden Dominica D6
5 Capilla de Nuestra Señora de los Remedios F4
6 Casa de Francia F5
7 Casa del Cordón E3
8 Convento de la Orden de los Predicadores D6
9 Fortaleza Ozama F5
10 Fuerte de Santa Bárbara E1
Hostal Nicolás de Ovando .... (see 42)
11 Iglesia de la Regina Angelorum C6
12 Iglesia de Nuestra Señora de las Mercedes C5
13 Iglesia de Nuestra Señora del Carmen C6
14 Iglesia de San Lázaro B5
15 Iglesia de San Miguel C4
16 Iglesia de Santa Bárbara E2
17 Iglesia de Santa Clara E6
18 Larimar Museum E5
19 Monasterio de San Francisco D3
20 Museo Alcázar de Colón F3
21 Museo de la Familia Dominicana E6
22 Museo de las Casas Reales E4
23 Museo del Duarte E3
24 Museo del Ron y la Caña E3
25 Panteón Nacional E4
26 Parque Colón E5
27 Plaza de María de Toledo E4
28 Plaza España E3
29 Puerta de San Diego F3
30 Puerta del Conde A6
31 Quinta Dominica D6
32 Reloj del Sol F4
33 Ruinas del Hospital San Nicolás de Barí D4

Activities, Courses & Tours
34 Chu Chu Colonial E5
35 Hispaniola Academy D6
Horse-drawn Carriages .... (see 6)
Trikke .... (see 62)

Sleeping
36 Antiguo Hotel Europa E3
37 Bettye's Exclusive Guest House E4
38 Casa Naemie F6
39 El Beatería Guest House D6
40 Hodelpa Caribe Colonial E4
41 Hostal La Colonia E5
42 Hostal Nicolás de Ovando F4
43 Hostal Suite Colonial C7
44 Hotel Atarazana E2
45 Hotel Doña Elvira D6
46 Hotel Francés Santo Domingo D4
47 Hotel Palacio D5
48 Hotel Villa Colonial C6
49 Portes 9 .... F6
50 Residencial La Fonte B5

Eating
51 Antica Pizzeria C6
52 Casa Olivier E7
53 Dajao & Mimosa Restaurant & Bar D5
54 El Rey del Falafel C7
55 El Taquito Don Silvio E3
56 Jumbo Express D5
57 La Bricola E6
58 La Cafetera Colonial D5
59 La Taberna Vasca D4
60 Mesón D'Bari D5
61 Pat'e Palo E3
62 Pizzarelli E5
63 Restaurante Asadero Chino C2
64 Tapati E3
65 Zorro E5

Drinking & Nightlife
66 Cacibajagua C6
67 Canario Patio Lounge E2
68 Double's Bar E6
69 El Conde Restaurant E5
70 El Sarten D5
71 Esedeku B5
72 Faces E3
73 Onno's Bar D5
74 Parada 77 .... E3
75 Segazona Cafe F5

Entertainment
76 Casa de Italia D4
77 Casa de Teatro E6
78 Centro Cultural Español E7

Shopping
Bettye's Galería .... (see 37)
79 Boutique del Fumador E5
80 Choco Museo E5
81 De Soto Galería D4
82 Felipe & Co E5
83 Galería de Arte María del Carmen E5
84 Hombres de las Americas E4
85 La Enoteca E6
86 La Leyenda del Cigarro D5
87 Librería Pichardo C5
88 Mapas Gaar B6
89 Mercado Modelo B3
Pulga de Antigüedades .... (see 37)

Iglesia de Nuestra Señora de las Mercedes CHURCH

(Church of Our Lady of Mercy; Map p50; cnr Las Mercedes & José Reyes; ⏲varies) Constructed during the first half of the 16th century, the church was sacked by Drake and his men and reconstructed on numerous occasions following earthquakes and hurricanes. The church is remarkable for its pulpit, which is sustained by a support in the shape of a serpent demon. The intricate baroque altarpiece is carved from tropical hardwood. Of the group of buildings that pay homage to the Virgin Mary, only the cloister adjacent to the church is in original condition.

Iglesia de Santa Clara CHURCH

(Map p50; cnr Padre Billini & Isabel la Católica; ⏲morning Sun) Home to the first nunnery in the New World built in 1552. Years after being sacked by Drake and his men (who apparently hated all things Catholic), it was rebuilt with funds from the Spanish Crown. This simple, discreet church has a severe Renaissance-style portal with a gable containing a bust of St Claire.

Iglesia de Santa Bárbara CHURCH

(Map p50; cnr Gabino Puello & Isabel la Católica; ⏲varies) This baroque church was built in 1574 to honor the patron saint of the military. After being done over by Drake, however, the church was rebuilt with three arches – two of these are windowless and the third frames a remarkably sturdy door.

Iglesia de la Regina Angelorum CHURCH

(Map p50; cnr Padre Billini & José Reyes; ⏲varies) Paid for by a woman who donated her entire fortune to construct this monument for the cloistered Dominican Sisters, this church was built toward the end of the 16th century. In addition to its imposing facade, the church is known for its elaborate 18th-century baroque altar, which is crowned with the king's coat of arms.

Iglesia de San Lázaro CHURCH

(Map p50; cnr Santomé & Juan Isidro Pérez; ⏲varies) Completed in 1650, but altered several times since, this church was erected beside a hospital that treated people with infectious diseases. The church was constructed to give the patients hope – a commodity that no doubt was in short supply for patients with tuberculosis, leprosy and other common diseases of colonial times.

Iglesia de Nuestra Señora del Carmen CHURCH

(Map p50; cnr Sánchez & Arzobispo Nouel; ⏲varies) Since 1596 this church has served as a hospital, a jail and an inn, but is now famous for its carved-mahogany figure of Jesus, which is worshipped every Holy Wednesday during Easter Week. The small church, originally made of stone, was set aflame by Drake in 1586 and was rebuilt using bricks. During colonial times its small square was used to stage comedies.

Iglesia de San Miguel CHURCH

(Church of Michael the Archangel; Map p50; cnr José Reyes & Juan Isidro Pérez; ⏲varies) In 1784 Spain ordered that the Iglesia de San Miguel be turned into a hospital for slaves. The decree, however, was never followed. Note the appealing juxtaposition of its rectangular stone doorway with the curved shape of the structure's exterior.

Capilla de la Tercera Orden Dominica CHURCH

(Chapel of the Third Dominican Order; Map p50; cnr Calle Duarte & Padre Billini) Built in 1729 and the only colonial structure in Santo Domingo that remains fully intact. These days the building is used by the office of the archbishop of Santo Domingo. It's not open to the general public, but the graceful baroque facade is worth a look.

Historical Sites

Parque Colón PARK

(Map p50; cnr Calle El Conde & Isabel la Católica) Beside the Catedral Primada de América, this historic park contains several shade trees and a large statue of Admiral Columbus himself. It's the meeting place for local residents and is alive with tourists, townsfolk, hawkers, guides, taxi drivers, shoeshine boys, tourist police and thousands of pigeons. El Conde Restaurant (p69), at the corner of Calle El Conde and Arzobispo Meriño, has seating inside and out and is the premier people-watching corner in the Zona Colonial.

Plaza España PLAZA

(Map p50) The large, open area in front of the Alcázar de Colón has been made over many times, most recently during the early 1990s in honor of the 500th anniversary of Christopher Columbus' 'discovery' of the New World. Running along its northwest side is **Calle la Atarazana**, fronted by a half dozen restaurants in buildings that served as warehouses through most of the 16th

Downtown Santo Domingo

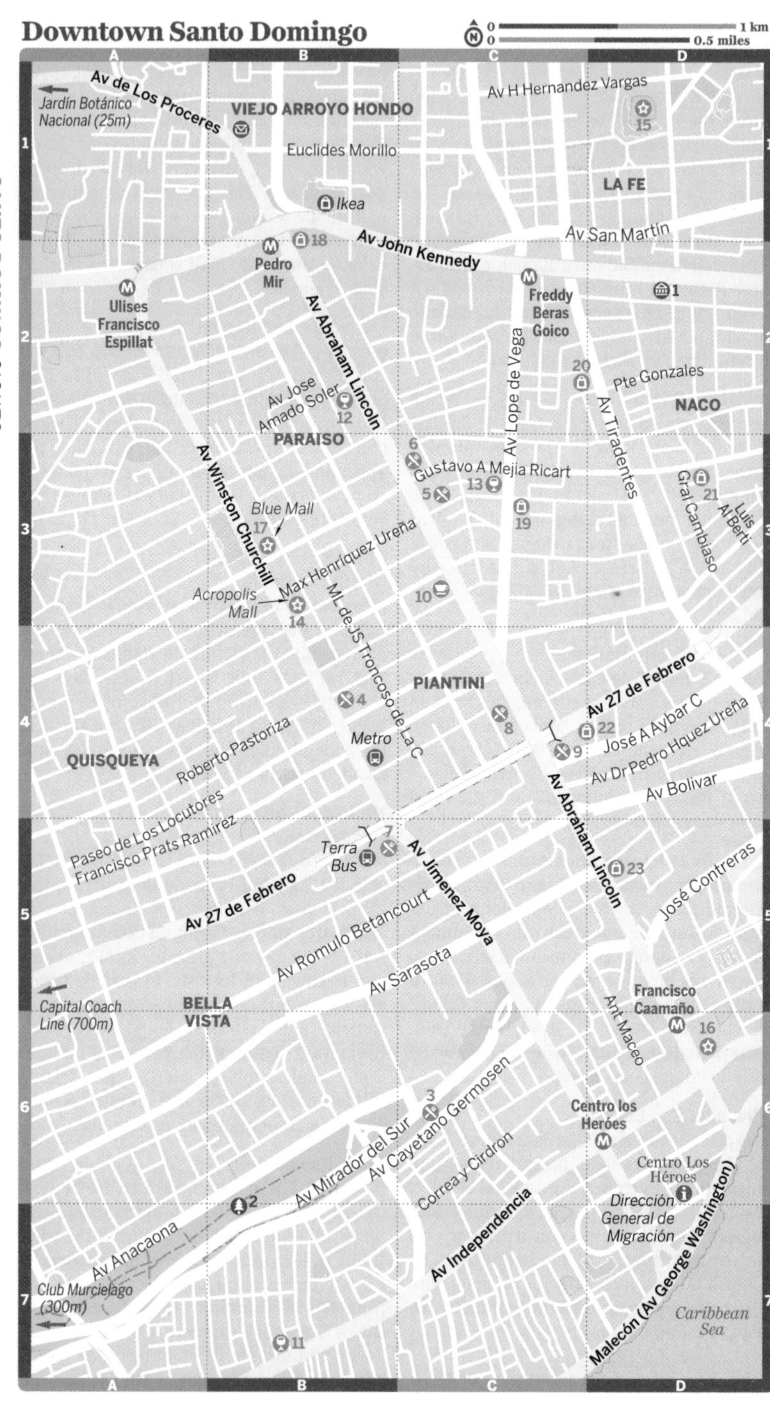

Downtown Santo Domingo

Sights
1 Museo Bellapart D2
2 Parque Mirador del Sur B7

Eating
3 El Mesón de la Cava C6
4 Inpanata B4
5 Mijas Restaurante C3
6 Mitre Restaurant & Wine Bar C3
7 Plaza Lama La Supertienda B5
8 Samurai C4
9 Supermercado Nacional C4

Drinking & Nightlife
10 Haagen-Dazs C3
11 Jet Set B7
12 Monte Cristo B2
13 Praia C3

Entertainment
14 Caribbean Cinemas B3
15 Estadio Quisqueya D1
16 Hispaniola Hotel D6
17 Palacio del Cine B3

Shopping
18 Agora B1
19 El Catador C3
20 Galería de Arte El Greco C2
21 Galería de Arte El Pincel D3
22 Librería Cuesta C4
23 Thesaurus Musica Libros Cafe D5

and 17th centuries. This is a great place for a meal or drink at an outdoor table around sunset.

Fortaleza Ozama HISTORICAL SITE
(Map p50; ☎809-686-0222; Las Damas; admission RD$70; ⏰9am-6:30pm Mon-Sat, to 4pm Sun) This is the oldest colonial military edifice in the New World. The site of the fort – at the meeting of the Río Ozama and the Caribbean – was selected by Fray Nicolás de Ovando. Construction of the fortification began in 1502 under the direction of master builder Gómez García Varela and continued in various stages for the next two centuries. Over the course of its history the fort has flown the flag of Spain, England, France, Haiti, Gran Columbia, the US and the DR. Until the 1970s, when it was opened to the public, it served as a military garrison and prison.

Near the door you'll find several guides (Spanish, English and French spoken, sometimes German and Italian). Be sure to agree on a fee in advance – around US$3.50 per person for a 20-minute tour.

As soon as you walk into the site, you'll see the oldest of the buildings here: the impressive **Torre del Homenaje** (Tower of Homage). Its 2m-thick walls contain dozens of riflemen's embrasures and its roof-top lookout offers 360-degree views of the city. To its right, solid and windowless, stands **El Polvorín** – the Powder House – which was added in the mid-1700s; look for the statue of St Barbara (the patron saint of the artillery) over the door.

Running along the fort's riverside wall are two rows of cannons: the first dates from 1570, the second was added in the mid-1600s. Both served as the first line of defense for the city's port. The living quarters, now almost completely destroyed, were added along the city-side wall in the late 1700s. On the esplanade is a bronze statue of Gonzalo Fernández de Oviedo, perhaps the best-known military chronicler of the New World.

Las Damas STREET
(Calle de las Damas, the Ladies' Street) Heading north and south in front of Fortaleza Ozama is the first paved street in the Americas. Laid in 1502, the street acquired its name from the wife of Diego Columbus and her lady friends, who made a habit of strolling the road every afternoon, weather permitting.

Panteón Nacional MONUMENT
(National Pantheon; Map p50; Las Damas; ⏰9am-5pm Tue-Sun) Originally constructed in 1747 as a Jesuit church, this was also a tobacco warehouse and a theater before dictator Trujillo restored the building in 1958 for its current use as a mausoleum. Today many of the country's most illustrious persons are honored here, their remains sealed behind two marble walls. The entire building, including its neoclassical facade, is built of large limestone blocks. As befits such a place, an armed soldier is ever present at the mausoleum's entrance – along with a powerful fan since it does get hot. Shorts and tank tops are discouraged.

Plaza de María de Toledo PLAZA
(Map p50) Named in honor of Diego Columbus' wife, this plaza connecting Las Damas and Isabel la Católica is remarkable for two arches that were once part of the Jesuits' residence in the 17th century. Note the buttresses that support the Panteón Nacional:

they are original, dating back to the construction of the Jesuit church in 1747, and a likely reason the building has survived the many earthquakes and hurricanes since.

Reloj del Sol MONUMENT

(Map p50; Las Damas) Across from the Museo de las Casas Reales, this sundial was built by Governor Francisco Rubio y Peñaranda in 1753 and positioned so that officials in the Royal Houses could see the time with only a glance from their eastern windows.

Monasterio de San Francisco HISTORICAL SITE

(Map p50; Calle Hostos) The first monastery in the New World belonged to the first order of Franciscan friars who arrived to evangelize the island. Dating from 1508, the monastery originally consisted of three connecting chapels. Today the monastery is a dramatic set of ruins that is occasionally used to stage concerts and artistic performances.

It was set ablaze by Drake in 1586, rebuilt, devastated by an earthquake in 1673, rebuilt, ruined by another earthquake in 1751 and rebuilt again. From 1881 until the 1930s it was used as a mental asylum until a powerful hurricane shut it down – portions of chains used to secure inmates can still be seen.

Ruinas del Hospital San Nicolás de Barí HISTORICAL SITE

(Map p50; Calle Hostos) Standing next to a bright, white Iglesia de la Altagracia are the ruins of the New World's first hospital. They remain as a monument to Governor Nicolás de Ovando, who ordered the hospital built in 1503. So sturdy was the edifice that it survived Drake's invasion and centuries of earthquakes and hurricanes. It remained virtually intact until it was devastated by a hurricane in 1911, and public-works officials ordered much of it knocked down so that it wouldn't pose a threat to pedestrians.

Today visitors can still see several of its high walls and Moorish arches. Note that the hospital's floor plan follows the form of a Latin cross.

Puerta del Conde MONUMENT

(Gate of the Count; Map p50; Calle El Conde) This gate is named for the Count of Peñalba, Bernardo de Meneses y Bracamonte, who led the successful defense of Santo Domingo against an invading force of 13,000 British troops in 1655. It's the supreme symbol of Dominican patriotism because right beside it, in February 1844, a handful of brave Dominicans executed a bloodless coup against occupying Haitian forces; their actions resulted in the creation of a wholly independent Dominican Republic.

It was also atop this gate that the very first Dominican flag was raised. Just west of the gate, inside Parque Independencia, look for the **Altar de la Patria** (Map p50), a mausoleum that holds the remains of three national heroes: Juan Pablo Duarte, Francisco del Rosario Sánchez and Ramón Matías Mella. The park itself has a few benches but little shade.

Puerta de San Diego MONUMENT

(Map p50; Av del Puerto) For a time, this imposing gate, built in 1571 downhill from the Alcázar de Colón, was the main entrance into the city. Beside it you can still see some of the original wall, which was erected to protect the city from assaults launched from the river's edge.

Puerta de la Misericordia MONUMENT

(Gate of Mercy; Map p60; Arzobispo Portes) This gate was erected during the 16th century and for many decades served as the main western entrance to the city. It obtained its name after a major earthquake in 1842, when a large tent was erected beside it to provide temporary shelter for the homeless.

Casa del Cordón NOTABLE BUILDING

(House of the Cord; Map p50; cnr Isabel la Católica & Emiliano Tejera; ⏲8:15am-4pm) Said to be not only one of the first European residences in the Americas, but also one of the first residences in the Western hemisphere with two floors, this was briefly occupied by Diego Columbus and his wife before they moved into their stately home down the street. Today the structure is home to Banco Popular, so visiting the house beyond the main lobby is not permitted.

Named after its impressive stone facade, which is adorned with the chiseled sash-and-cord symbol of the Franciscan order, it is also believed to be the site where Santo Domingo's women lined up to hand over their jewels to Drake during the month he and his men held the city hostage.

Casa de Francia NOTABLE BUILDING

(French House; Map p50; Las Damas 42) This was originally the residence of Hernán Cortés, conqueror of the Aztecs in present-day central Mexico. It was in this building that Cortés is believed to have organized his triumphant – and brutal – expedition. Although the Casa de Francia served as a residence for nearly

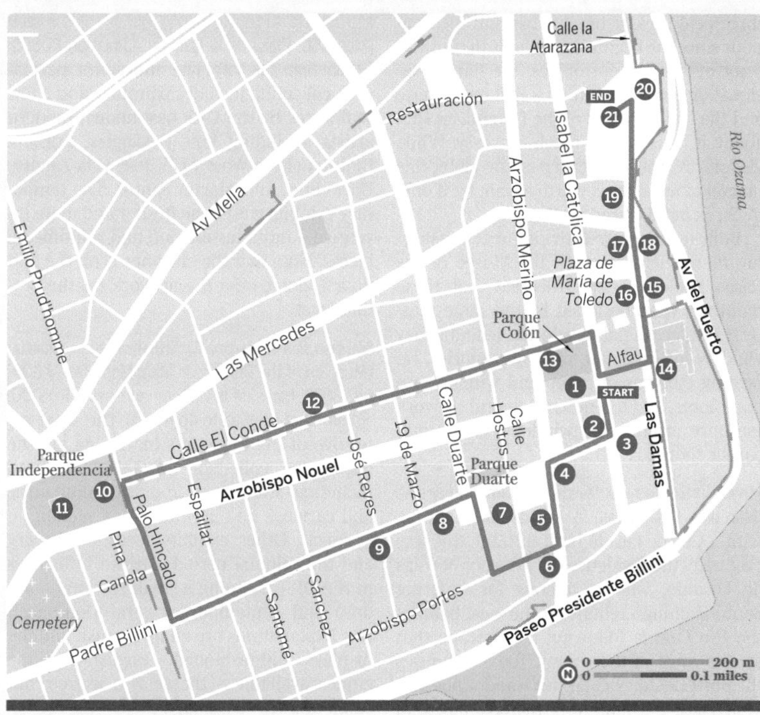

Walking Tour Zona Colonial

START CATEDRAL PRIMADA DE AMÉRICA
END PLAZA ESPAÑA
LENGTH 2.4KM; 2½ HOURS

Start at 1 **Catedral Primada de América** (p49), the New World's oldest working church. Turn south on Isabel la Católica: you'll see the 2 **Larimar Museum** (p49) and the simple 3 **Iglesia de Santa Clara** (p53). Turn west on Padre Billini and walk to the 4 **Museo de la Familia Dominicana** (p49), with its famous Gothic window. Turn south onto Arzobispo Meriño and you'll pass 5 **Casa de Teatro** (p71); ask about upcoming performances. south to the 6 **Centro Cultural** (p71) with a full calendar of events. Head west then turn right onto Calle Duarte, which opens onto a plaza with two churches: the spectacular 7 **Convento de la Orden de los Predicadores** (p51) and the baroque 8 **Capilla de la Tercera Orden Dominica** (p53).

Head west along Padre Billini to the ornate façade of the 9 **Iglesia de la Regina Angelorum** (p53). Continue west before taking Palo Hincado north to the 10 **Puerta del Conde**, the supreme symbol of Dominican patriotism. Inside the gate is Parque Independencia and the 11 **Altar de la Patria** (p56), a mausoleum of three national heroes. Then take 12 **Calle El Conde**, the Zona Colonial's busy commercial walkway, to leafy 13 **Parque Colón** (p53).

From the park take Alfau, a small pedestrian street, to the entrance of 14 **Fortaleza Ozama** (p55), the New World's oldest military structure. Take Las Damas north, checking out the lovely facades of the 15 **Hostal Nicolás de Ovando** (p58) and the 16 **Casa de Francia**. Further up Las Damas, you'll pass the 17 **Panteón Nacional** (p55) and the 18 **Capilla de Nuestra** (p51). Next you'll come upon the interesting 19 **Museo de las Casas Reales** (p48) before reaching 20 **Museo Alcázar de Colón** (p49) in the 21 **Plaza España** (p53), a large plaza overlooking the Río Ozama.

three centuries, it has had several incarnations since the beginning of the 19th century: a set of government offices, the Banco Nacional de Santo Domingo, a civil courthouse and the headquarters of the Dominican IRS. Today it houses the French embassy. While visitors are not permitted past the lobby, this marvel of masonry is worth a walk by, if only to check out its facade.

Built in the early 16th century and sharing many elements with the Museo de las Casas Reales, experts theorize that these buildings were designed by the same master; both have a flat facade and a double bay window in the upper and lower stories, repeating patterns of doors and windows on both floors, and top-notch stone rubblework masonry around the windows, doors and corner shorings.

Hostal Nicolás de Ovando NOTABLE BUILDING
(Map p50; Las Damas) A handsome building with a Gothic facade built in 1509, this was originally the residence of Governor Nicolás de Ovando, who is famous for ordering Santo Domingo rebuilt on the west bank of the Río Ozama following a hurricane that leveled most of the colony. Today it houses the posh Hostal Nicolás de Ovando (p64). To appreciate the building's massive size and solidity, take the steps leading down from the alleyway on El Conde towards Puerto Don Diego.

Fuerte de Santa Bárbara HISTORICAL SITE
(Map p50; cnr Juan Parra & Av Mella) Built during the 1570s, this fort served as one of the city's main points of defense. It proved no match for Drake, however, who along with his fleet of 23 pirate-packed ships captured the fort in 1586. Today the fort lies in ruins at the end of a lonely street. There isn't much to see here anymore, mostly rooftops and occasionally a ship in the distance.

Gazcue

Plaza de la Cultura PLAZA
(Map p60; Av Maxímo Gómez) This large, centrally located park, mostly a sun-baked, fairly unkempt plaza, has three museums (two of which are worth visiting), the national theater (p71) and the national library, plus Il Cappucino (p67) restaurant. The land was once owned by the dictator Trujillo, and was 'donated' to the public after his assassination in 1961.

Museo de Arte Moderno MUSEUM
(Map p60; Plaza de la Cultura; admission RD$50; 9am-5pm Tue-Sat) The museum's permanent collection includes paintings and a few sculptures by the DR's best-known modern artists, including Luís Desangles, Adriana Billini, Celeste Woss y Gil, José Vela Zanetti, Dario Suro and Martín Santos. The temporary exhibits tend to be fresher and more inventive – more installation and multimedia pieces. Note that the entrance is on the 2nd floor – don't miss the artwork on the bottom level.

Museo del Hombre Dominicano MUSEUM
(Museum of the Dominican Man; Map p60; 809-687-3622; Plaza de la Cultura; admission RD$100; 9am-5pm Tue-Sat, to 4pm Sun) The most extensive of the museum's highlights are the impressive collection of Taíno artifacts, including stone axes and intriguing urns and carvings and an interesting section on Carnival. Other exhibits focus on slavery and the colonial period, African influences in the DR (including a small section on Vodou) and contemporary rural Dominican life. Explanations are all in Spanish and the displays old-fashioned. English-speaking guides available – the service is free, but small tips are customary.

Museo Nacional de Historia Natural MUSEUM
(Map p60; 809-686-0106; www.mnhn.gov.do; Plaza de la Cultura; adult/child RD$50/20; 10am-5pm Tue-Sun) This museum includes exhibits on the battles between Haitians and Dominicans; on General Ulises Heureaux, the country's most prominent dictator during the 19th century; and on Trujillo, the country's most prominent dictator during the 20th century – displays include his personal effects such as combs, a razor, a wallet etc.

Palacio Nacional NOTABLE BUILDING
(Map p60; 809-695-8000; Calle Uruguay, btwn Av Pedro Henríquez Ureña & Calle Moisés Garcia) The Dominican seat of government which occupies most of a city block was designed by Italian architect Guido D'Alessandro and inaugurated in 1947. Built of Samaná roseate marble in a neoclassical design, the palace is outfitted in grand style with mahogany furniture, paintings from prominent Dominican artists, magnificent mirrors inlaid with gold, and a proportionate amount of imported crystal.

Primarily used as an executive and administrative office building, it has never been used as the residence of a Dominican president, who is expected to live in a private home. Of special note is the **Room of the Caryatids**, in which 44 sculpted draped women rise like columns in a hall lined with French mirrors and Baccarat chandeliers.

It's not regularly open to the public, nevertheless you may be able to wrangle a tour; free and by appointment only on Monday, Wednesday and Friday. No flip-flops, shorts or T-shirts.

Palacio de Bellas Artes NOTABLE BUILDING

(Palace of Fine Arts; Map p60; ☎809-687-9131; Av Máximo Gómez) This huge recently renovated neoclassical building was used infrequently in the past for exhibitions and performances. Check the weekend edition of local papers for events.

Outlying Neighborhoods

Some of these places are worth a visit as much for the taxi ride there and back as for the sights themselves. A visit allows you to catch a glimpse of the Santo Domingo where ordinary people live and work. The shantytowns that ring much of the city are known as Zona Apache – an allusion to the forbidden territory of the Old West in the US.

Faro a Colón MONUMENT

(Columbus Lighthouse; ☎ext 251 809-592-1492; Parque Mirador del Este; admission RD$65; 9am-5:15pm Tue-Sun) Resembling a cross between a Soviet-era apartment block and a Las Vegas version of an ancient Mayan ruin, this massive monument is worth visiting for its controversial and complicated history. Located on the east side of the Río Ozama, the Faro's massive cement flanks stand some 10 stories high, forming the shape of a cross. At the intersection of the cross' arms is a tomb, guarded by stern white-uniformed soldiers, that purportedly contains Columbus' remains. Spain and Italy dispute that claim, however, both saying *they* have the Admiral's bones.

Inside the monument a long series of exhibition halls display documents (mostly reproductions) related to Columbus' voyages and the exploration and conquest of the Americas. The most interesting (though deeply ironic) displays are those sent by numerous Latin American countries containing photos and artifacts from their respective indigenous communities.

High-power lights on the roof can project a blinding white cross in the sky, but are rarely turned on because doing so causes blackouts in surrounding neighborhoods.

Jardín Botánico Nacional GARDEN

(National Botanic Garden; ☎809-385-2611; Av República de Colombia; adult/child RD$50/40; 9am-6pm, ticket booth 9am-5pm, open-air trolley every 30min until 4:30pm;) The lush grounds span 2 sq km and include vast areas devoted to aquatic plants, orchids, bromeliads, ferns, endemic plants, palm trees, a Japanese garden and much more. The grounds are spotless and the plants well tended, and it's easy to forget you're in the middle of a city with a metropolitan area of over two million people. The exhibits in the on-site **Ecological Museum** (9am-4pm, ticket booth 9am-5pm) explain the country's major ecosystems, including mangroves and cloud forests, plus a special display on Parque Nacional Los Haitises.

An open-air trolley takes passengers on a pleasant half-hour turn about the park and is especially enjoyable for children. The garden hosts a variety of events, including an orchid exhibition and competition in March and a bonsai exhibition in April. A taxi from the Zona Colonial costs around RD$300.

Los Tres Ojos CAVES

(The Three Eyes; Parque Mirador del Este; admission RD$50; 8am-5pm) Consisting of three very humid caverns with still, dark lagoons inside and connected by stalactite-filled passages, this is a mildly interesting site frequented by organized tours. The caves are limestone sinkholes, carved by water erosion over thousands of years. Unfortunately, the tranquility of the setting is usually upset by guides aplenty (who are unnecessary) and vendors aggressively hawking their services and wares at the entrance.

The entrance is a long stairway down a narrow tunnel in the rock; once at the bottom, cement paths lead you through the caves or you can visit them by boat for another RD$20.

Parque Mirador del Sur PARK

(Southern Lookout Park; Map p54; Av Mirador del Sur) A long tree-filled corridor atop an enormous limestone ridge, this park is riddled with caves, some as big as airplane hangars. One of the caves has been converted into a restaurant, another into a dance club. The park's seemingly endless paths are a popular

Gazcue & Malecón

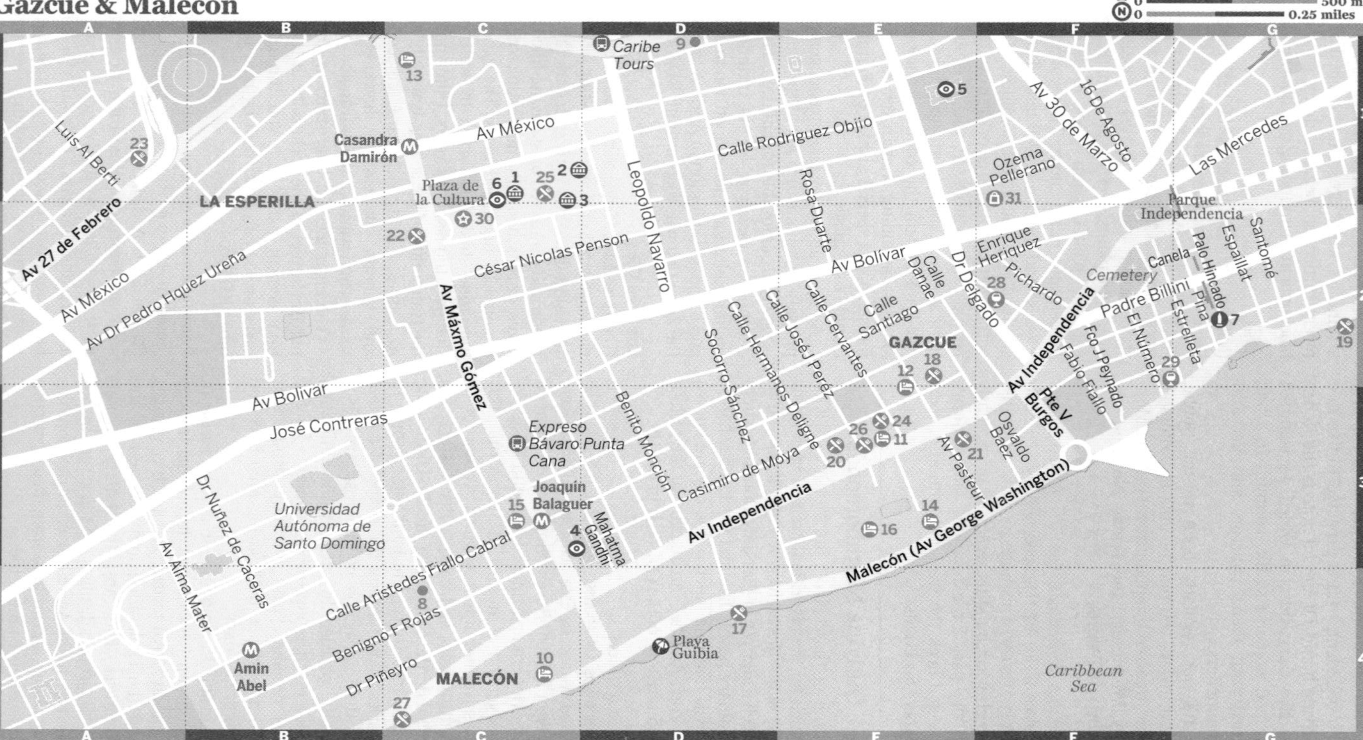

Gazcue & Malecón

Sights

1 Museo de Arte Moderno C1
2 Museo del Hombre Dominicano C1
3 Museo Nacional de Historia Natural C1
4 Palacio de Bellas Artes C3
5 Palacio Nacional E1
6 Plaza de la Cultura C1
7 Puerta de la Misericordia G2

Activities, Courses & Tours

8 Instituto Intercultural del Caribe C4
9 Prieto Tours D1

Sleeping

10 Hilton Hotel C4
11 Hostal Riazor E3
12 Hostal San Francisco De Asis E3
13 Hotel Barcelo Santo Domingo C1
14 Hotel Magna 365 .... E3
15 Hotel San Marco C3
16 Renaissance Jaragua Hotel E3

Eating

17 Adrian Tropical D4
18 Ananda E2
19 D'Luis Parrillada G2
20 El Conuco E3
21 Hermanos Villar E3
22 Il Cappucino C2
23 Kogi Grill A1
24 La Cadena E3
25 Maniqui Restaurant & Lounge C1
26 Manolo E3
27 Vesuvio Malecón C4

Drinking & Nightlife

28 Discoteca Amazonia F2
Jubilee .... (see 16)
29 Mint F2

Entertainment

30 El Teatro Nacional Eduardo Brito C2

Shopping

31 Galeria de Arte Candido Bido F1

jogging spot for 30-something professionals, many of whom live in the middle- and upper-class neighborhoods north of the park.

Museo Bellapart MUSEUM
(Map p54; ☎809-541-7721; www.museobellapart.com; Av JF Kennedy & Dr Peguero; ⏰9am-6pm Mon-Fri, to 12:30pm Sat) FREE Incongruously located on the 5th floor of the Honda building, which looks like a parking garage, is this significant private collection of Dominican painting and sculpture from the late 19th century to the 1960s.

Courses

Instituto Intercultural del Caribe LANGUAGE COURSE
(Map p60; ☎809-571-3185; www.edase.com; Aristides Fiallo Cabral 456, Zona Universitaria) More than a dozen price combinations are offered here, depending on the length and intensity of instruction and whether or not accommodations are included. It also offers merengue dance lessons (eight hours of private lessons US$75) and maintains a language school in Sosúa.

Hispaniola Academy LANGUAGE COURSE
(Map p50; ☎809-688-9192; www.hispaniola.org; Arzobispo Nouel 103) Offering six levels of Spanish-language instruction, this the only language school in the Zona Colonial. A week-long course consists of 20 lessons per week (four 50-minute classes per day). Prices begin at US$140, and accommodations, from homestays to hotels, can be arranged. Cooking (private US$48) and dance classes are also offered.

Tours

Interesting and informative walking tours of the Zona Colonial are offered on a daily basis by a number of official guides – look for men dressed in khakis and light-blue dress shirts, but always ask to see their official tourism license. Walks typically last 2½ hours and cost US$20 to US$30 depending on the language that the tour is given in (Spanish and English are less expensive). To find a guide, head to Parque Colón – you'll find a number of them under the trees. Be sure to agree upon a fee before setting out.

Motorized scooters, sort of a cross between Segways and skateboards, are available for rent through **Trikke** (Map p50; ☎809-221-8077; www.trikke.do; Calle el Conde; 1hr US$35; ⏰9am-6pm), a new business on Parque Colon; audio guides included. A more leisurely option is a **horse-drawn carriage tour** (Map p50; with/without guide US$50/30). Look for the carriages pulled to the side of the road near the corner of Las Damas and El Conde. Or for a cross between the two, you can hop aboard the **Chu Chu Colonial** (Map p50; ☎809-686-2303; www.chuchucolonial.com; child/adult US$7/12; ⏰ 9am-5pm), a bunch of little 'train cars' hooked together that leaves from the corner of El Conde and Isabel la Catolica every 45 minutes. It'll give you the lay of the land and a broad overview; however, the guides and translation are of questionable quality and walking is a better bet.

If you want to hook up with a bus tour that may include outlying sights in addition to the Zona Colonial, try one of the local agencies that provide city tours to guests of all-inclusive resorts. A few popular ones include **Prieto Tours** (Map p60; ☎809-685-0102; Av Francia 125), **Ecodotours** (☎809-526-2937; www.ecodotours.com) and **Turinter** (☎809-686-4020; www.turinter.com). This isn't a bad option if you're short on time.

Festivals & Events

Carnival CARNIVAL

Carnaval (in Spanish) is celebrated throughout the country every Sunday in February, culminating in a huge blowout in Santo Domingo during the last weekend of the month or first weekend of March. Av George Washington (the Malecón) becomes an enormous party scene all day and night. Central to the celebration are the competitions of floats, and costumes and masks representing traditional Carnival characters.

Merengue Festival MUSIC

(late Jul-early Aug) The largest in the country, this two-week celebration of the DR's favorite music is held yearly. Most of the activity is on the Malecón, but there are related events across the city.

Festival Presidente MUSIC

(3-5 Oct) Held at the Estadio Olímpico (Olympic Stadium), this huge three-day event attracts the top names in Latin music – jazz, salsa, merengue and *bachata* (popular guitar music based on bolero rhythms). Jennifer Lopez and Marc Anthony have performed in the past.

Sleeping

The Zona Colonial is the most distinctive part of the city and therefore where most travelers prefer to stay. Sights and restaurants are within walking distance and there's an excellent choice of midrange and top-end hotels to choose from, including several European-owned boutique-style places in restored colonial-era buildings. Budget travelers have fewer options. Gazcue, a quiet residential area southwest of Parque Independencia, has several hotels in the midrange category, though there are far fewer eating options and you're likely to have to rely on taxis, especially at night. The high-rise hotels on the Malecón are best if you're looking for resort-style amenities like swimming pools and tennis courts, and on-site nightclubs and casinos.

Zona Colonial

Portes 9 B&B $

(Map p50; ☎849-943-2039; info@portes9.com; Calle Arzobispo Portes 9; r incl breakfast from US$55;) Four tastefully furnished all-white wood-floored rooms with high ceilings make up this Spanish-owned B&B fronting a quiet plaza in the neighborhood's southeast corner. It's an intimate spot where guests socialize over breakfast. Plans were for four more rooms to be added in the adjoining home.

Casa Naemie HOTEL $

(Map p50; ☎809-689-2215; www.casanaemie.com; Isabel la Católica 11; s/d incl breakfast RD$2000/3000;) This charming oasis only a few blocks from the oldest cathedral in the Americas feels like a European pension. Surrounding a narrow central courtyard are three floors of cozy, clean rooms with large modern bathrooms. An elegant lobby with a vaulted entranceway and brick flooring does double duty in the morning when the excellent breakfast is served.

Bettye's Exclusive Guest House GUESTHOUSE $

(Map p50; ☎809-688-7649; marshallbettye@hotmail.com; Plaza de María de Toledo, Isabel la Católica 163; dm per person US$22, r US$45;) Look for the nondescript iron doorway opening onto Plaza de María de Toledo; don't be discouraged by the messy art-gallery space. There are several dorm rooms (one has a fan) with five to six beds, and while the spaces are hectic, they get good light and there's access to a common kitchen and bathroom.

For privacy but not quiet, a private room opens directly onto Isabel la Católica – the bathroom is extremely small. If no one answers Bettye's door, taxi drivers lounging around the plaza may be able to help; she often leaves the key.

Residencial La Fonte APARTMENTS $

(Map p50; ☎809-686-3265; www.residencial-lafonte.net; Calle Las Mercedes 364; r with fan/aircon US$30/40;) Worth considering for the self-sufficient and long-term deal seekers (discounts for weekly and monthly stays) are the large apartment-style units (all have kitchens) in this multistory pink pastel building, a block off El Conde. There's no front desk per se and the basic furnishings are run down and the paint peeling.

★ **El Beaterío Guest House** GUESTHOUSE $$
(Map p50; ☎809-687-8657; www.elbeaterio.com; Calle Duarte 8; s/d incl breakfast US$75/100;) Take thee to this nunnery – if you're looking for austere elegance. Each of the 11 large rooms is sparsely furnished, but the wood-beamed ceilings and stone floors are truly special; the tile-floored bathrooms are modern and well-maintained.

It's easy to imagine the former function of this 16th-century building, the heavy stone facade, the dark and vaulted front room – now a beautiful reading room and dining area with classical music playing softly – giving way to a lush and sunny inner courtyard, all inspiring peace and tranquility.

★ **Hotel Villa Colonial** HOTEL $$
(Map p50; ☎809-221-1049; www.villacolonial.net; Calle Sánchez 157; s/d incl breakfast US$75/85;) The French owner has created an idyllic oasis, an exceptionally sophisticated combination of European elegance with a colonial-era facade and an art-deco design. The rooms lining the narrow garden and pool area all have high ceilings and four-poster beds, as well as flatscreen TVs and bathrooms with ceramic-tile floors.

Rocking chairs and a Balinese-style lounge bed provide plenty of character and comfort for those wishing to socialize. A few studios set in back, past the open-air breakast area, are more basic but have stovetops and sinks and reduced weekly and monthly rates.

Hotel Atarazana BOUTIQUE HOTEL $$
(Map p50; ☎809-688-3693; www.hotel-atarazana.com; Calle Vicente Celestino Duarte 19; s/d incl breakfast US$80/100;) A boutique hotel for the design-conscious only a few meters away from Plaza España. Housed in a beautifully renovated building from the 1860s, all six rooms sport custom-made furniture from native materials to high-concept fixtures and textiles. Each of the whitewashed, light and airy rooms has a balcony, and breakfast is served in a secret garden-like patio shaded by lush vegetation.

There's even a small plunge pool-Jacuzzi to relax in. Another option is the rooftop, which has lounge chairs and fabulous views of the Zona Colonial and river. An attractive faux-marble floor runs throughout the public spaces.

Hotel Doña Elvira HOTEL $$
(Map p50; ☎809-221-7415; www.dona-elvira.com; Padre Billini 209; s/d incl breakfast from US$64/89; P@) Housed in a renovated colonial building, Doña Elvira is a friendly place geared toward travelers; you can hang out in the inner courtyard, take a dip in the pool (it's too small for swimming), lounge on the rooftop solarium or read in the lobby/dining area. For such a pretty building, it's unfortunate the 13 rooms are a somewhat haphazard amalgam of mostly plain styles and furnishings.

Hotel Palacio HOTEL $$
(Map p50; ☎809-682-4730; www.hotel-palacio.com; Calle Duarte 106; s/d incl breakfast from US$70/90; P) Cross colonial with a touch of medieval and you have the Palacio, a maze-like hotel occupying a 17th-century mansion only a block north of El Conde. Service is exceptional and you'll need it to find your way past the charming nooks and crannies, which include reading areas, a gym, a small bar, a lush interior courtyard and stone-walled walkways.

First-floor rooms are German conquistador minimalist while the larger 2nd-floor rooms are more modern and generic. Though it lacks shade, the small rooftop pool is a big plus, as is the gym.

Hodelpa Caribe Colonial HOTEL $$
(Map p50; ☎809-688-7799; www.hodelpa.com; Isabel la Católica 159; r incl breakfast US$85; P@) Only a block from Parque Colón, the Hodelpa Caribe is a convenient choice for those seeking modern comforts without the colonial ambience. There are some curiously discordant design touches, but the beds are comfortable and service is attentive. A rooftop solarium has several lounge chairs and good views.

Hostal Suite Colonial HOTEL $$
(Map p50; ☎809-685-1082; www.suitecolonial.net; Calle Padre Billini 362; s/d incl breakfast US$53/64;) A solid, extremely friendly midrange choice with an exterior that blends in with the facades of the neighboring colonial-era buildings. However, once past an attractive high-ceilinged lounge area, some of the charm fades. Heavy couches and linoleum-floored hallways lead to rooms with relatively basic furnishings and some haphazard choices. Breakfast is served in a small backyard patio.

Antiguo Hotel Europa HOTEL **$$**
(Map p50; ☎809-285-0005; www.antiguohoteleuropa.com; cnr Arzobispo Meriño & Emiliano Tejera; r incl breakfast US$65; P ❄ @) Considering the impressive-looking facade, spacious lobby and uniformed bellboys of this hotel only two blocks west of Plaza España, the rooms are a letdown. Ask for one with a balcony to ensure your room receives light. Continental breakfast is served in a classy rooftop restaurant with a spectacular view of the Zona Colonial.

Hostal La Colonia HOTEL **$$**
(Map p50; ☎809-221-0084; hostallacolonia@yahoo.com; Isabel la Católica 110A; s/d US$50/60; ❄) Ideally located around the corner from Parque Colón, La Colonia is a good option if character is not an issue. In addition to shiny, polished floors and large rooms, each of the floors has its own spacious street-side sitting area and balcony. Rooms are mostly shielded from the noise on this lively block.

★ **Hostal Nicolás de Ovando** HISTORIC HOTEL **$$$**
(Map p50; ☎809-685-9955; www.mgallery.com; Las Damas; s US$220-336, d US$238-354, restaurant mains US$17-35; P ❄ 🛜 ≋) Even heads of state must get a thrill when they learn they're sleeping in the former home of the first governor of the Americas. Oozing character, old-world charm and historic pedigree, the Nicolás de Ovando is as far from a chain hotel as you can get. Indisputably one of the nicest hotels in the city, it features 97 rooms packed with 21st-century amenities.

There's a variety of room types, some have four-poster beds, exposed-timber ceilings and 500-year-old walls with views of the port and river. The split-level contemporary-style rooms are more basic. Cobblestone walkways run through lushly shaded courtyards and the fabulous pool has commanding views of the Río Ozama. An excellent buffet breakfast is included in the rate; La Residence, the hotel's superb and elegant restaurant, has a separate entrance down the street and opens for lunch and dinner.

Hotel Francés Santo Domingo HOTEL **$$$**
(Map p50; ☎809-685-9331; www.mgallery.com; cnr Las Mercedes & Arzobispo Meriño; s/d incl breakfast US$150/170; P ❄ 🛜) A charming throwback to a bygone era, Francés is housed in a large colonial mansion near Plaza España. Rooms with high ceilings, stucco walls and tasteful decor surround a handsome stone patio. The restaurant here, which serves French fare, is one of the city's more romantic spots. Some of the rooms are larger and quieter than others, so ask for layout specifics (guests can access the pool at sister-hotel Nicolás de Ovando on Las Damas).

Gazcue

Just west of the Zona Colonial this residential area of quiet, tree-lined streets has a number of hotels, restaurants and some services; it's a short walk from the Malecón.

Hostal San Francisco De Asis HOTEL **$$**
(Map p60; ☎809-685-0101; www.hostalsanfranciscodeasis.com; Av Luis Pasteur 102; s/d US$40/60; P ❄ 🛜) Despite chintzy bed linens and little natural light, the sparkling clean rooms with flatscreen TVs at this modern multistory hotel can be recommended. A miniature snack bar is attached to the lobby; breakfast here is US$6.

Hotel Barcelo Santo Domingo HOTEL **$$**
(Map p60; ☎809-563-5000; www.barcelo.com; cnr Maximo Gomez & 27 de Febrero; r from US$75; P ❄ @ 🛜 ≋) Still known to locals as Barcelo Lina, this outpost of the Spanish chain is within walking distance of the Plaza de la Cultura (and is only steps away from the main east-west artery through the city). The spacious rooms have all of the contemporary touches and features of a business-class hotel. The bathrooms are especially nice.

The inner courtyard pool and lounge area is equal to any of the Malecón hotels (though the gym is decrepit). A casino, bakery, cigar lounge, piano bar and two restaurants – one Japanese and the other a recommended buffet (open 24 hours) – mean some guests never leave the property. The biggest downside is pricey wi-fi.

Hotel San Marco HOTEL **$$**
(Map p60; ☎809-686-2876; hotelsanmarco@codetel.net.do; Calle Santiago 752; s/d incl breakfast US$72/81; P ❄ 🛜 ≋) Housed in an old colonial-style home, San Marco's *pièce de résistance* is the shady, inner courtyard pool area furnished with hammocks and lounge chairs. Rooms are simply but tastefully furnished, as you'd expect from the owners of the recommended restaurant Il Cappucino (p67).

The San Marco is located around the corner from a metro stop and the stop for Expreso Bávaro buses. It's also within walking distance of the Malecón, while the campus of the Universidad Autonoma de Santo Domingo is a few blocks west.

Hostal Riazor HOTEL **$$**
(Map p60; ☎809-685-5566; hostal_riazor@hotmail.com; Av Independencia 457; s/d incl breakfast US$65/75; P ❄) The Riazor boasts professional English-speaking front-desk staff and extremely well-kept rooms (some of the nicest in this price range) with faux-wood floors and flatscreen TVs. An elevator means you don't have to lug your bags to whatever floor you're on. Breakfast is served in Manolo, the recommended next-door restaurant.

Malecón

Less appealing than you might otherwise expect considering its waterfront Caribbean setting, Santo Domingo's Malecón, a long expanse of baking concrete, has several high-rise hotels. The upside is that many rooms have views; the downside is that you'll have to take a taxi almost everywhere – you'll sweat just walking from the street to the hotel entrance. A Crowne Plaza opened up on the site of the former Hotel V Centenario Intercontinental, the closest of the Malecón hotels to the Zona Colonial, and at the time of our visit the **Hotel Magna 365** (Map p60; ☎809-221-6666; www.hotelmagna365.com; 365 George Washington Ave; P ❄ @), formerly the Melia, was being converted into a Sheraton.

Hilton Hotel HOTEL **$$$**
(Map p60; ☎809-685-0000; www.hiltoncaribbean.com/santodomingo; Av George Washington 500; r from US$130; P ❄ @) Easily the nicest of the luxury hotels on the Malecón, the Hilton is part of a huge, though mostly abandoned, complex (a casino and movie theaters remain). The highest of the high-rises, it's a long elevator ride from the atrium to the top. Rooms are nicer and newer than its nearby competitors, and it has a bar and restaurant with stunning ocean views.

Renaissance Jaragua Hotel RESORT **$$$**
(Map p60; ☎809-221-2222; www.marriott.com; Av George Washington 367; r from US$90; P ❄ @) Under the Marriott brand, the spacious rooms in the 10-story tower and low-slung annex have been upgraded, though furnishings are still dated. It's generally good value considering the resort-style facilities; there's a popular nightclub, a sports bar and a large casino on the premises.

Eating

Unsurprisingly, Santo Domingo is the culinary capital of the country. It offers the full range of Dominican cuisine, from *pastelitos* (pastries with meat, vegetable or seafood fillings) sold from the back of street-vendors' carts to extravagantly prepared meals in picturesque colonial-era buildings. The Zona Colonial has some of the best restaurants and is most convenient for the majority of travelers. Gazcue, only a short walk from the Malecón, has a number of good choices; the downtown area north and west of Gazcue, between Av Tiradentes and Av Winston Churchill, is another fine area for dining, with a large number of restaurants.

Zona Colonial

A handful of Chinese restaurants serve inexpensive Cantonese-style meals in the small Chinatown neighborhood just north of Av Mella and Calle Duarte; typical of the bunch is **Restaurante Asadero Chino** (Map p50; Calle Duarte; mains RD$160; ⏰10am-4pm Mon-Fri, to 11pm Sat & Sun) with good fried rice and lo mein but reheated frozen egg rolls. For a meal full of ambience choose from Pura Tasca, Harry's, Pat'e Palo, Angelo and Mamajuana Cafe on Plaza Espana's Calle la Atarazana. And of course, Calle El Conde has its fair share of cafes (Cafe Paco Cabana can be especially recommended) and eateries, though primarily fast food.

Jumbo Express (Map p50; cnr Calles El Conde & Duarte; ⏰8am-8pm Mon-Sat 8:30am-3pm Sun) is the largest grocery store in the Zona Colonial – the place to load up on cheap water, soda, alcohol and juice.

La Cafetera Colonial DINER **$**
(Map p50; ☎809-682-7122; Calle El Conde; RD$85; ⏰7am-9pm Mon-Sat, to 7pm Sun) Once a well-known hangout for artists, intellectuals and journalists, this long and narrow greasy spoon still caters to a regular clientele. Pull up a stool at the counter for an egg sandwich, burger or a strong espresso (RD$65).

El Taquito Don Silvio FAST FOOD **$**
(Map p50; ☎809-687-1958; Emiliano Tejera 105; mains RD$50; ⏰9am-1am Mon-Thu, 9am-3am Fri & Sat, 5pm-1am Sun) Head over to this stamp-sized restaurant, really a stall, for tacos, burgers or sandwiches. It's especially good for a late-night snack.

★Antica Pizzeria ITALIAN $$
(Map p50; ☎809-689-4040; cnr Billini & José Reyes; mains RD$350; ⊙5-11pm Mon, Wed & Thu, noon-midnight Fri-Sun) Sophisticated and stylish, with oversized framed poster reproductions of European Renaissance paintings decorating the triple-height ceilings, Antica wouldn't be out of place in a fashionable district of Rome. The Italian owner keeps a watchful eye on the kitchen and the exposed-brick pizza oven, which does excellent pies and a handful of pasta dishes.

Mesón D'Bari DOMINICAN $$
(Map p50; ☎809-687-4091; cnr Calle Hostos & Salomé Ureña; mains RD$350; ⊙lunch & dinner) A Zona Colonial institution popular with tourists and sophisticated *capitaleños* on weekends, Mesón D'Bari occupies a charmingly decaying colonial home covered with large, bright paintings by local artists. The menu has Dominican and international standards, and different versions of grilled meats and fish; the long attractive bar is equally appealing. Live music on some weekend nights.

Tapati INTERNATIONAL $$
(Map p50; ☎809-689-1118; Calle Emiliano Tejera 101; mains RD$460; ⊙11am-midnight) Not the place for solo diners (nor informal dressers), Tapati is where groups of young, well-heeled Dominicans head to celebrate the good (and trendy) life. Sure, the front-door vibe is snooty, but if you pass muster and gain entry, you'll be rewarded with a menu featuring creations like mini foie-gras burgers and two-way duck risotto. Reservations recommended.

El Rey del Falafel MIDDLE EASTERN $$
(Map p50; cnr Sánchez & Padre Billini; mains RD$320; ⊙4:40pm-midnight) This restaurant's stunning open-air dining room is the courtyard of a ruined building lit by shimmering candles, which makes it at least as good a place for a drink as a meal. The kitchen has stepped up its game and now the food, fare like falafel and juicy shwarma platters, lives up to the ambience.

Zorro MEXICAN $$
(Map p50; ☎809-685-9569; Calle El Conde 54; mains RD$325; ⊙8:30am-1am) Awash in bold primary colors like a Mondrian painting, this casual Mexican place with indoor and outdoor seating adds some spice to the alleyway just east of Parque Colon. Quality tacos, enchiladas and quesadillas, plus churros with chocolate and flan for dessert, and tequila and margarita round out the offerings.

D'Luis Parrillada DOMINICAN $$
(Map p60; Paseo Presidente Billini; RD$350; ⊙11am-late) This casual open-air restaurant perched over the ocean only a few blocks from the Zona Colonial is one of only a few restaurants to take advantage of the Malecón's setting. The large menu includes fajitas, grilled and barbecue meats, sandwiches, seafood *cazuela* (RD$400) and little-found *pulpofongo* (*mofongo* with Creole-style cuttlefish; RD$330). It's a wonderful place for a drink as well.

Casa Olivier DOMINICAN, INTERNATIONAL $$
(Map p50; ☎809-682-0836; Calle Arzobispo Portes 151; mains RD$250-500) As homey as you can get, Casa Olivier feels like you've stumbled upon a set: an upper-middle-class, mid-20th-century Dominican living and dining room. Traditionally furnished and intimate, it also has a tiny stage and a piano and offers live music some nights. It has a small menu of lovingly prepared meat and pasta dishes. Service can be very slow.

Dajao & Mimosa Restaurant & Bar DOMINICAN $$
(Map p50; ☎809-686-0712; Arzobispo Nouel 51; mains RD$300; ⊙11am-4pm Mon-Sat) These two restaurants – Dajao, a sleek, modern side resembling a European cafe, and Mimosa, a fan-cooled side much like an ordinary *comedor* (eatery) – share a kitchen and you can order from either menu regardless of where you sit. The former has mains like rib eye (RD$675) and fish in coconut soup (RD$375), while the latter does a filling *plato del dia* (dish of the day; RD$275).

Pizzarelli ITALIAN $$
(Map p50; cnr Calle el Conde & Isabel Catolica; mains RD$285; ⊙11am-11pm Mon-Thu, to midnight Fri & Sat) A diminutive version of Pizza Hut, and a step up in quality, Pizzarelli anchors a strategic Zona Colonial intersection. It sells pizza by the slice (RD$125) and personal pizzas (RD$265), plus less than stellar strombolis, calzones and pasta. A spot for gelato is attached.

★Pat'e Palo SPANISH, MEDITERRANEAN $$$
(Map p50; ☎809-687-8089; Calle la Atarazana 25; mains RD$650-1200; ⊙noon-midnight) The most happening and deservedly longest surviving of Plaza España's restaurant row, Pat'e Palo is for anyone tired of the same old bland

pasta and chicken. Large, both physically and in terms of its selection, the menu includes creatively designed dishes like foie gras with dark beer jam and risotto in squid ink and shrimp *brunoise* with lobster tail and roasted arugula. The lobster ravioli (RD$630), one of the least expensive items on the menu, is excellent. Stick around for dessert – crème brûlée is the speciality – and an extensive wine and cigar list are for those who want to spend an extra hour or two hanging out in the candlelight.

Because of its popularity (or maybe a reason for it), there's something of a prepackaged vibe to the efficiently professional waitstaff's service; pirate-like headscarves are part of the uniform. English and French menus available.

La Bricola ITALIAN **$$$**
(Map p50; ☎809-688-5055; Arzobispo Meriño 152; mains RD$850; ⏲noon-3pm & 6pm-midnight Mon-Sat) From the candlelit open-air patio to the soft melodic piano, La Bricola embodies romance – a meal here is the perfect place to pop the question. Set in a restored colonial-era palace, the ambience can't help but trump the food, which is international- and Italian-inspired mains, including fresh fish specials. Despite the almost regal, fairytale setting, service is more welcoming than stuffy.

La Taberna Vasca MEDITERRANEAN **$$$**
(Map p50; ☎809-221-0079; cnr Calle Hostos & Las Mercedes; mains RD$650; ⏲noon-3pm & 7pm-midnight Tue-Sat, from 7pm Mon) Now housed in a beautifully restored 500-year-old building, this charming bistro's intimate dining room and lush patio ooze romance. The kitchen turns out well-prepared seafood and meat dishes inspired by French and Basque cuisine; we recommend the duck confit and paella.

Gazcue & Malecón

The grocery **La Cadena** (Map p60; cnr Calle Cervantes & Casimiro de Moya; ⏲7:30am-10pm Mon-Sat, 9am-2:30pm Sun) carries produce, meats and everything you should need.

★**Adrian Tropical** DOMINICAN **$**
(Map p60; Av George Washington; mains RD$200; ⏲8am-11pm Mon-Fri, 24hr Sat & Sun; 👪) This popular family-friendly chain occupies a spectacular location overlooking the Caribbean. Waiters scurry throughout the two floors and outdoor dining area doling out Dominican specialities like yucca or plantain *mofongo* as well as standard meat dishes. An inexpensive buffet (RD$200) is another option and the fruit drinks hit the spot. There are three other outposts in Santo Domingo.

Ananda VEGETARIAN **$**
(Map p60; ☎809-682-7153; Casimiro de Moya 7; mains RD$70; ⏲11am-9pm Mon-Fri, to 4pm Sat & Sun; 🌱) Vegetarians will want to try out this pleasant cafeteria-style restaurant and yoga center (hatha classes 6pm to 7pm Monday, Wednesday and Thursday) run by the 'International Society of Divine Realization.' Dominican dishes like brown rice and roast beans outnumber the Indian offerings.

Hermanos Villar DOMINICAN **$**
(Map p60; ☎809-682-1433; cnr Avs Independencia & Pasteur; mains RD$175; ⏲7am-11pm) Occupying almost an entire city block, Hermanos Villar has two parts: the bustling Dominican-style diner serving cafeteria food and hot, grilled deli sandwiches, and a large outdoor garden restaurant that is slightly more upscale in terms of menu. Finding an empty table inside during the heavy lunchtime traffic is a challenge, so getting things to go is always an option.

★**Il Cappucino** ITALIAN **$$**
(Map p60; ☎809-682-8006; Máximo Gómez 60; mains RD$400; ⏲8am-11:30pm; 📶) You might leave this oasis of comfort and sophistication (on an otherwise gritty stretch) feeling envious of the regulars who are welcomed like family. It's the sort of place where the Italian owner bustles around, doling out pats and quips. Nearly three-dozen types of really top-notch pizza and pasta, plus fish and meat dishes round out the menu.

Great-looking pastries, cakes, gelato and wine are on display in the bright and welcoming cafe side. The larger dining room is a dreamy fantasyscape of papier-mâché trees and structures like canopied beds.

El Conuco DOMINICAN **$$**
(Map p60; ☎809-686-0129; Casimiro de Moya 152; mains RD$350; ⏲11:30am-midnight) Unashamedly touristy, El Conuco is stereotypically Dominican in the same way the Hard Rock Café is authentically American. Nevertheless, Dominicans as well as tour groups come here to get traditionally prepared dishes while taking in traditional dancers – the real highlight – in a dining room covered with traditional decorations.

Manolo DOMINICAN $$

(Map p60; Av Independencia; mains RD$200-600; ⏲24hr) Owned by next-door Hotel Riazor, Manolo has an indoor dining room and an elevated outdoor terrace that is great for a leisurely meal or drink. The menu runs the gamut from basic sandwiches to elaborately prepared lobster and steaks.

Vesuvio Malecón ITALIAN $$$

(Map p60; ☎809-221-1954; Av George Washington 521; mains RD$700; ⏲10am-midnight Sun-Thu, 11am-1am Fri & Sat) A Malecón institution only a few blocks from the Hilton and one of the city's better restaurants since 1954, Vesuvio is elegant without being snooty. Expect refined Neapolitan-style seafood and meat dishes; lobster and shellfish are featured in beautifully plated antipasti.

Maniqui Restaurant & Lounge INTERNATIONAL $$$

(Map p60; ☎809-689-3030; Av Pedro Henríquez Ureña, Plaza de la Cultura; mains RD$700; ⏲noon-midnight Mon-Thu & Sun, to 2am Fri & Sat; P) Decked out like the boudoir of a burlesque club, this lavishly and curiously decorated space, seemingly inspired by modeling, is in the middle of the Plaza de la Cultura. Pizza and pasta dishes are identified as a 'model's nightmare' on the menu; other choices include beef carpaccio, crepes and croquettes. Live music Friday nights; karaoke and even stand-up comedy other nights.

Downtown

West of Gazcue between Avs Tiradentes and Winston Churchill is a fairly high-end area of businesses, restaurants, apartment buildings, homes and shopping malls (restaurants and food courts in many of the latter).

Plaza Lama La Supertienda (Map p54; cnr Avs Jímenez Moya & 27 de Febrero) and **Supermercado Nacional** (Map p54; cnr Avs Abraham Lincoln & 27 de Febrero; ⏲9am-9pm Mon-Sat, 10am-8pm Sun) live up to their names, the latter (an enormous megastore occupying several city blocks) especially so; it's located at one of the busiest intersections in the city. There's another branch in Gazcue.

Inpanata SOUTH AMERICAN $

(Map p54; Calle Roberto Pastoriza; mains RD$100; ⏲11am-10pm Mon-Fri, from 8am Sat; Wi-Fi) A pocket-sized spot with an appealing menu featuring empanadas and their equivalents from around the world (ie, egg rolls listed under China and *salchichas* for Germany); the Columbian *arepas* are especially tasty. Located in a small shopping plaza only a few blocks from the Metro bus terminal.

Kogi Grill KOREAN $$

(Map p60; ☎809-227-5577; Av 27 de Febrero 195; mains RD$385; ⏲noon-4pm & 6-10pm Mon-Thu, to 11pm Fri & Sat) The mod design of colored mirror tiles and the informal vibe match the somewhat playful menu. Groups can choose to grill at their table, but regardless of the number of diners, every meal comes with a half-dozen delicious *banchan* (Korean side dishes). Not easily reached on foot, it's on a busy roadway at the corner of Ortega y Gasset.

Mitre Restaurant & Wine Bar FUSION $$$

(Map p54; ☎809-472-1787; cnr Gustavo A Mejía Ricart 1001 & Av Abraham Lincoln 1005; mains RD$850; ⏲noon-1am) This sleek restaurant, located in a nondescript building in an upscale business and residential district, serves a creative fusion of Asian, Italian and Dominican cuisines. The results are satisfying to both the eye and stomach; an outdoor patio and 2nd-floor wine and cigar bar are more casual than the stylish white-tableclothed dining room.

El Mesón de la Cava DOMINICAN $$$

(Map p54; ☎809-533-2818; www.elmesondelacava.com; Av Mirador del Sur; mains RD$850; ⏲noon-1am) This is where Batman would take a date – this craggy stalactite-filled limestone cave is home to a unique and romantic restaurant. Formally clad waiters and soft merengue and salsa music add to the atmosphere, though the food, primarily grilled meats and fish, is ordinary. Live music some nights in the leafy terrace.

Samurai JAPANESE $$$

(Map p54; ☎809-565-1621; Calle Seminario 57; mains RD$850; ⏲noon-4pm & 6:30pm-midnight Tue-Thu, noon-midnight Fri-Sun) One of the best Japanese restaurants in the city, with *yakinuku*-style tables (grill the meat and seafood at your table), a sushi bar and a large dining room.

Mijas Restaurante SPANISH $$$

(Map p54; ☎809-567-5040; Max Henríquez Ureña 47; mains RD$900; ⏲noon-2am) Upscale and trendy restaurant serving some of the best tapas in the city. There is live music on Saturday nights.

Drinking & Nightlife

Santo Domingo has the country's best nightlife scene, from glitzy hotel nightclubs and casinos to small bars and dance spots, much of it conveniently located in the Zona Colonial. Restaurants and cafes along Plaza España and the eastern end of Calle El Conde are happening spots at night; that being said, most restaurants tend to be good places to linger with a few drinks. Otherwise many of the nicer bars are in strip malls around the city and you can always strap on a few Presidentes at a *colmado* (combination corner store and bar). The big, bright one at the corner of Sanchez and Arzobispo Nouel in the Zona Colonial is worth checking out.

And lest you scoff, hotel nightclubs, especially those along the Malecón, are hugely popular, especially among Santo Domingo's rich, young and restless. Merengue and *bachata* are omnipresent, but house, techno, reggaeton and American and Latin rock are popular as well. A number of clubs in town cater to gays and lesbians, or at least offer a welcoming mixed atmosphere; check out www.monaga.net for the latest. Newspapers are a good place to find out about upcoming concerts and shows, and if your Spanish is good, radio stations hype the capital's big events.

Only a 10-minute ride or so from the Zona Colonial on the eastern side of the Río Ozama is Av Venezuela, where more than half-a-dozen bars and clubs are concentrated in the span of only three or so blocks; a taxi is recommended there and back.

Some of the venues attract the wealthiest and hippest in Santo Domingo, but wherever you go, expect people to be dressed to the nines, so definitely no T-shirts, sneakers or sandals. Admission is up to RD$250 when there's a DJ (most nights) and RD$350 when there's a band.

Zona Colonial

★El Conde Restaurant CAFE

(Map p50; Hotel Conde de Peñalba, cnr Calle El Conde & Arzobispo Meriño; 8am-midnight) Hands down, the best place for an afternoon drink. As much a restaurant as a cafe, El Conde's appeal isn't its varied menu of decent but overpriced food (pasta RD$350), but its commanding location at the busiest corner in the Zona Colonial, crowded with tourists and locals alike. Try cooling off with a *morir sonado* (RD$108).

Segazona Cafe CAFE, BAR

(Map p50; 809-685-9569; Calle El Conde 54; 9am-1am Mon-Thu, to 3am Fri & Sat) Occupying separate spaces on either side of a cobblestoned alleyway, Segazona operates as an Italian-style cafe during the day and an Ibiza-like club on weekend nights, when DJs spin and dancers get off their feet and onto one of the day beds in the hangar-like backyard. Crepes, paninis and other morsels are also served inside and out.

Double's Bar BAR

(Map p50; Arzobispo Meriño; 6pm-late) Good-looking 20-somethings grind away to loud pop and Latin music on weekend nights. Otherwise, groups can lounge around one of the couches or sidle up to the classic long wood bar.

Canario Patio Lounge BAR, NIGHTCLUB

(Map p50; Calle la Atarazana 1; 7pm-3am Tue-Sun) Owned by a Dominican salsa star, this bar, whose walls are covered in graffiti, is for grown-ups; if the salsa and merengue music gets too loud, step out into the beautiful courtyard. Quiet on weekday nights.

El Sarten NIGHTCLUB, BAR

(Map p50; Calle Hostos 153; 7pm-late) A diverse mix of *capitalenos* get down to *son* (Afro-Cuban percussion), *bachata* and merengue at this old-school space.

Onno's Bar BAR

(Map p50; Hostos btwn Calle El Conde & Arzobispo Nouel; 5pm-1am Sun-Thu, to 3am Fri & Sat) There's always something going on at this fashionable hot spot just off El Conde: several flatscreen TVs, lasers, an illuminated bar, DJs and a smoke machine...

Parada 77 BAR

(Map p50; Isabel la Católica 255; 8pm-1am Sun-Thu, to 3am Fri & Sat) Thankfully, there's no dress code at this laid-back, sort of grungy place with graffiti-covered walls and live merengue on weekend nights.

Faces NIGHTCLUB, BAR

(Map p50; Calle la Atarazana 9; 8pm-late Wed-Sun) This two-story bar and strobe-lit dance club just off Plaza España doesn't get started until after 10pm. Dress to impress, especially in terms of footwear, or else the beefy bouncers will likely turn you away.

Cacibajagua BAR

(Map p50; Sánchez 201; 8pm-1am Sun-Thu, to 3am Fri & Sat) Also known as 'La Cueva' (the

Cave), this small and dark spot favors good ol' rock music such as Pink Floyd and Led Zeppelin.

Esedeku GAY BAR
(Map p50; ☎809-869-6322; Las Mercedes 341; ⊙9pm-late Wed-Sun) Only a block from Calle El Conde, Esedeku is an intimate bar with a huge selection of cocktails. It's popular with local professionals; not for hustlers.

Gazcue & Malecón

Jubilee NIGHTCLUB
(Map p60; ☎809-221-2222; Renaissance Jaragua Hotel, Av George Washington 367; ⊙9pm-4am Tue-Sat) A long-standing hot spot, this nightclub in the Jaragua Hotel continues to draw in good-looking, well-heeled and well-dressed hordes looking to get down to live merengue music; most nights it doesn't get hopping until around midnight. Drink bills can be pretty steep at the end of a long evening.

Mint NIGHTCLUB
(Map p60; ☎809-687-1131; www.napolitanohotel.com; Av George Washington 51; admission RD$150; ⊙10pm-morning, closed Mon) A smaller and less-glamorous version of the Jubilee is the nightclub at this fairly rundown hotel. But because of its proximity to the Zona Colonial and its more reasonable drink prices, it still gets packed on weekends.

Discoteca Amazonia GAY BAR
(Map p60; ☎809-412-7629; Dr Delgado 71; ⊙8pm-late Thu-Sun) The oldest (mostly) lesbian bar in Santo Domingo; located in Gazcue.

Downtown

Jet Set NIGHTCLUB
(Map p54; ☎809-535-4145; Av Independencia 2253; admission US$7; ⊙9pm-late) A trendy, good-looking crowd flocks to this 7th-floor disco where Justin Bieber's entourage tussled their way into the tabloids in late 2013. Besides offering great views of the city, there's live music – salsa, merengue – most nights of the week and *bachata* on Mondays. Happy hour is from 5pm to 9pm.

Praia NIGHTCLUB
(Map p54; ☎809-732-0230; Gustavo A Mejia Ricart 74, Naco; ⊙10pm-2am) Replete with an upstairs VIP area and a transparent wine cellar, this ultramodern bar and club is a little bit Soho with a dash of Miami Beach. The drinks are expensive, though maybe not for the well-heeled Dominican clientele, and the music runs the gamut from electronica to reggaeton.

Monte Cristo NIGHTCLUB, BAR
(Map p54; ☎809-542-5000; Av Jose Amado Soler; ⊙6pm-5am) This sophisticated club doubles as a cigar lounge with good wine and mixed drinks thrown in as well. It has a dance floor for merengue and salsa and live music on Wednesday. Weekends tend to be a hodgepodge of salsa, merengue, reggaeton and Latin rock.

Club Murcielago NIGHTCLUB
(☎809-533-1051; www.guacarataina.net; Av Mirador del Sur 655; admission RD$300; ⊙9pm-close Tue-Sun) Formerly Guácara Taína, a somewhat legendary nightclub, now maybe at least as popular with foreign tourists as Dominicans, this is still an interesting place to party. Located inside a huge underground cave in the Parque Mirador del Sur, this club hosts everything from raves to live merengue and hip-hop acts.

Haagen-Dazs CAFE
(Map p54; ☎809-566-4950; Av Abraham Lincoln; ⊙11am-11pm; 📶👪) This modern, sleek and (most importantly) air-conditioned place is an oasis for families and those foolhardy enough to walk along this sun-baked stretch of asphalt. Shakes (RD$175), ice-cream sodas (RD$135), iced coffees (RD$100) and, of course, plain old ice cream are available.

☆ Entertainment

Baseball

★**Estadio Quisqueya** SPORTS
(Map p54; ☎809-540-5772; www.estadioquisqueya.com.do; cnr Avs Tiradentes & San Cristóbal; tickets RD$250-1000; ⊙games 5pm Sun, 8pm Tue, Wed, Fri & Sat) One of the best places to experience Dominican baseball is at the home field of two of the DR's six professional teams, **Licey** (www.licey.com) and **Escogido** (www.escogido). You can get tickets to most games by arriving shortly before the first inning; games between the hometown rivals or Licey and Aguilas sell out more quickly. Asking for the best seats available at the box office is likely to cost RD$1000 and put you within meters of the ballplayers and the between-innings dancers.

Scalpers also congregate along the road to the stadium and at the entrance. A taxi back to the Zona Colonial should run around RD$170. The stadium has been the site of big-name concerts like Justin Bieber in 2013.

Cinemas

There are no cinemas in the Zona Colonial. Centro Cultural Español periodically showcases alternative films, mostly by Spanish and Dominican filmmakers. The theater is actually a gallery with a big white wall where DVDs are projected. Stop by for a current schedule.

Palacio del Cine (Map p54; Blue Mall, Av Winston Churchill) and **Caribbean Cinemas** (Map p54; Acropolis Mall, Av Winston Churchill) screen Hollywood films as well as a smattering of Dominican and other films; all of the malls mentioned in the Shopping section, as well as a handful of others, have multiplex cinemas. Tickets on average are child/adult RD$175/250. Check www.cine.com.do for current listings.

Cultural Centers

Casa de Italia CULTURAL CENTER
(Italian House; Map p50; ☎809-688-1497; cnr Calle Hostos & General Luperón; ⏰9:30am-9pm Mon-Thu, to 6pm Sat) FREE Hosts art exhibits in its 1st-floor gallery; also doubles as an Italian-language institute.

Casa de Teatro CULTURAL CENTER
(Map p50; ☎809-689-3430; www.casadeteatro.com; Arzobispo Meriño 110; admission varies; ⏰9am-6pm & 8pm-3am Mon-Sat) Housed in a renovated colonial building, this fantastic arts complex features a gallery with rotating exhibits by Dominican artists, an open-air bar, and a performance space and theater that regularly host dance and stage productions.

Centro Cultural Español CULTURAL CENTER
(Spanish Cultural Center; Map p50; ☎809-686-8212; www.ccesd.org; cnr Arzobispo Meriño & Arzobispo Portes; ⏰10am-9pm Tue-Sun) A cultural space run by the Spanish embassy, this institute regularly hosts art exhibits, film festivals and music concerts, all with a Spanish bent. It also has 15,000 items in its lending library.

Theaters

El Teatro Nacional Eduardo Brito THEATER
(National Theater; Map p60; ☎809-687-3191; Plaza de la Cultura; tickets RD$150-500) Hosts opera, ballet and musical performances, from classical to Latin pop stars. Tickets for performances at this grandly ornate 1700-seat theater can be purchased in advance at the box office from 9:30am to 12:30pm and 3:30pm to 6:30pm daily. For show dates and times, call or check the weekend editions of local newspapers.

Casinos

After baseball, cockfighting and playing the lottery, gambling is one of the DR's favorite pastimes. Casinos generally open at 4pm and close at 4am. Bets may be placed in Dominican pesos or US dollars. Las Vegas odds and rules generally apply, though there are some variations. All of the large hotels on the Malecón have casinos, as do the Barcelo Santo Domingo (p64), Hotel Santo Domingo and **Hispaniola Hotel** (Map p54; ☎809-221-7111; cnr Avs Independencia & Abraham Lincoln), and all the dealers speak English.

Shopping

More than anywhere else in the country, shopping in Santo Domingo runs the gamut from cheap tourist kitsch to high-end quality collectibles. The easiest – and best – neighborhood to shop in is the Zona Colonial, where you'll find rows of shops offering locally made products at decent prices.

Large, American-style malls are scattered around the city, especially in the adjoining downtown neighborhoods of Paraiso, Piantini, Naco and Miraflores. They include Novocentro, Blue Mall, Acropolis, Plaza Naco, Diamond Mall and Agora and Sambil, the two newest and possibly nicest.

If you're considering buying something in amber or larimar, shop around, since these stones, considered national treasures, are ubiquitous in Santo Domingo. Typically they're presented as jewelry, but occasionally you'll find figurines, rosaries and other small objects. Quality and price vary greatly, and fakes aren't uncommon. In Zona Colonial, the most recommended places are Amber World Museum (p49) and Larimar Museum (p49).

Dominican cigars are widely respected by aficionados around the world, so much so that the DR is one of the leading exporters. To try one for yourself, stop in at one of the many cigar stores around Santo Domingo – you'll see several while strolling down Calle El Conde. Typically, prices vary from US$2 to US$6 per cigar, and boxes can run as high as US$110.

Felipe & Co HANDICRAFTS
(Map p50; ☎809-689-5812; Calle El Conde 105; ⏰9am-8pm Mon-Sat, 10am-6pm Sun) This shop on Parque Colón, easily one of the best in the Zona Colonial, is stocked with charming high-quality handicrafts, like ceramics,

ART GALLERIES

Walking around Santo Domingo, you'll see sidewalk displays of simple, colorful canvases of rural life and landscapes. This so-called Haitian or 'primitive art' is so prevalent that it's understandable if you mistake it for the country's de facto wallpaper. Most of what you see on the street is mass-produced, low-quality amateur pieces with little value.

For unique and interesting Dominican pieces, there are a number of formal galleries in Santo Domingo, such as the **Galería de Arte María del Carmen** (Map p50; ☎809-682-7609; Arzobispo Meriño 207; ⏰9am-7pm Mon-Sat, 10am-1pm Sun), which has been selling art long enough to attract a wide range of talented Dominican painters. The **Galeria de Arte Candido Bido** (Map p60; Calle Dr Baez 5, Gazcue; ⏰9:30am-12:30pm & 3pm-6:30 Mon-Fri, to 12:30pm Sat) displays the intensely colorful and exuberant works reflecting this well-known painter's affection for the rural people of his native Cibao region. Every square inch of the small **De Soto Galería** (Map p50; ☎809-689-6109; Calle Hostos 215; ⏰9am-5pm Mon-Fri) is filled with an array of antiques and paintings by Dominican and Haitian artists.

Outside the Zona Colonial are dozens of other galleries that feature Haitian and Dominican art. **Galería de Arte El Greco** (Map p54; ☎809-562-5921; Av Tiradentes 16, Naco; ⏰8am-noon & 2-6pm Mon-Fri) and **Galería de Arte El Pincel** (Map p54; ☎809-544-4295; Gustavo Mejía Ricart 24, Naco; ⏰8am-noon & 2-6pm Mon-Fri) are good options.

jewelry and handbags, and also a good selection of paintings.

Hombres de las Americas CLOTHING
(Map p50; ☎809-686-2479; hombresdelamericas@gmail.com; Arzobispo Meriño 255; ⏰10am-6pm Mon-Sat) A high-end boutique selling Panama hats and guayabera (also known as *chacabana*), traditionally white shirts worn on formal occasions. The former start at around RD$2300.

Choco Museo CHOCOLATE
(Map p50; ☎809-221-8222; www.chocomuseo.com; Calle Arzobispo Meriño 254; ⏰10am-7pm) More a shop than museum, Choco Museo nonetheless has signs in Spanish and English that explain the history of chocolate and manufacturing processes in the DR. It has a small cafe and shop, as well as workshops where you can make your own bars (organic and fair-trade bars for sale US$6).

La Leyenda del Cigarro CIGARS
(Map p50; ☎809-682-9932; Calle El Conde 161; ⏰9am-7pm Mon-Sat & 10am-6pm Sun) A good selection of premium cigars, but equally importantly, the helpful staff are more than willing to answer the naive questions of cigar novices. Another location is several blocks away at the corner of Calle Hostos and Mercedes.

El Catador WINE
(Map p54; ☎809-540-1644; www.elcatador.com; cnr Av Lope de Vega & Enrique Urena; ⏰10am-11pm Mon-Fri, to 7pm Sat) If in Piantini, this is the place to stock up on quality wine from around the world, as well as whiskey, gin, champagne and more. The elegant brick-walled space has a back room with comfy couches where regular tastings are held.

Mercado Modelo MARKET
(Map p50; Av Mella; ⏰9am-5pm Mon-Sat, to noon Sun) Bargain hard at this crowded market, which sells everything from love potions to woodcarvings, jewelry and, of course, the ubiquitous 'Haitian style' paintings. The more you look like a tourist, the higher the asking price. The market is housed in an aging two-story building just north of the Zona Colonial in a neighborhood of fairly run-down stores and souvenir shops.

Librería Cuesta BOOKSTORE
(Map p54; ☎809-473-4020; www.cuestalibros.com; cnr Av 27 de Febrero & Abraham Lincoln; ⏰9am-9pm Mon-Sat, 10am-8pm Sun; wi-fi) This modern, two-story Dominican version of Barnes & Noble is easily the nicest and largest bookstore in the city, and has an upstairs cafe with wi-fi. It's attached to the Supermercado Nacional.

La Enoteca WINE
(Map p50; cnr Calle Padre Billini & Arzobispo Meriño; ⏰noon-2am) The only high-end wine shop in the Zona Colonial. It offers free tastings on Tuesdays (6pm to 8pm). Bottles run from RD$425 to RD$17,000, and a bottle of the priciest rum, Siglo de Oro, is RD$2900.

Thesaurus Musica Libros Cafe BOOKSTORE
(Map p54; cnr Sarasota & Abraham Lincoln; ⌚9am-9pm Mon-Sat, 10am-3pm Sun) Rivals Librería Cuesta for nicest bookstore; upstairs cafe.

Boutique del Fumador CIGARS
(Map p50; ☎809-685-6425; Calle El Conde 109; ⌚9am-7pm Mon-Sat, 10am-3:30pm Sun) A small boutique shop selling Cohibas (a box of hand-rolled for as little as RD$430) as well as other brands; also organic Dominican chocolate (RD$200), coffee (RD$160) and rum (RD$140). Staff explain the cigar-making process from start to finish, and you can see *tabacos* being rolled in the upstairs workshop.

Bettye's Galería HANDICRAFTS
(Map p50; Plaza de María de Toledo, Isabel la Católica 163; ⌚9am-6pm Wed-Mon) Browse through this gallery, connected to the guesthouse of the same name, if you like antiques, jewelry, and quirky souvenirs and paintings.

Pulga de Antigüedades MARKET
(Map p50; Plaza de María de Toledo, Calle General Luperón; ⌚9am-4pm Sun) Poke around the clothes, shoes, handicrafts and antiques at this open-air flea market, held every Sunday on a small plaza a block north of Parque Colón.

Libreria de Cultura BOOKSTORE
(Calle La Atarazana 2; ⌚9am-5pm Mon-Fri) An intellectual's collection of poetry, non-fiction and fiction, all in Spanish.

Librería Pichardo BOOKSTORE
(Map p50; cnr José Reyes & Calle El Conde; ⌚8am-7pm Mon-Thu, to 5:30pm Fri, to 1pm Sun) This store is squeezed into a cave-like space below a parking garage. You can bargain for good prices on early and antique Spanish-language books, mostly on colonial history and Latin American literature and poetry, plus some curios.

Mapas Gaar MAPS
(Map p50; ☎809-688-8004; www.mapasgaar.com.do; 3rd fl, cnr Calle El Conde & Espaillat; ⌚8am-5:30pm Mon-Fri, to 2:30pm Sat) Located on the 3rd floor of an aging office building, Mapas Gaar has the best variety and the largest number of maps in the Dominican Republic. Maps are designated by city or region and include a country map, as well as several city maps on the back of each (RD$250).

ℹ Information

DANGERS & ANNOYANCES

Pick-pocketing, especially on buses or in clubs, is the main concern for visitors to Santo Domingo. Being alert to the people around you and being careful with your wallet or purse (or even leaving them in the safety deposit box back at the hotel) is the best defense. Muggings are less common, especially of tourists, but they do happen occasionally. The Zona Colonial is generally very safe to walk around, day or night. The Malecón is safe as well, but be extra cautious if you've been drinking or you're leaving a club or casino especially late. Gazcue is a mellow residential area, but street lights are few and far between. If you're unsure of the neighborhood, play it safe and call or hail a taxi.

EMERGENCY

Policia Nacional (☎809-682-2000) Or dial 911 for police, fire department and Red Cross.

Politur (☎809-682-2151; cnr Calle El Conde & José Reyes; ⌚8am-5pm) The Tourist Police can handle most situations; for general police, ambulance and fire dial 911.

INTERNET ACCESS & TELEPHONE

Internet cafes are scarce, whereas wi-fi is common at cafes and restaurants.

Centro de Internet (☎809-238-5149; Av Independencia 201; ⌚8:30am-9pm Mon-Sat, 8:30am-3pm Sun) Internet and call center in Gazcue.

Internet & Llamadas (Calle El Conde; RD$20 per 30min; ⌚9am-9pm Mon-Sat, 10am-6pm Sun) Inside small plaza.

INTERNET RESOURCES

Colonial Zone (www.dr-colonialzone.com) A detailed site with information and reviews on everything – historical sites, hotels, restaurants, bars – as well as discussions on Dominican history, superstitions and more.

MEDICAL SERVICES

Centro de Obsetetricía y Ginecología (☎809-221-7322; cnr Av Independencia & José Joaquín Pérez; ⌚24hr) Equipped to handle all emergencies.

Clínica Abreu (☎809-687-4922; cnr Av Independencia & Beller; ⌚24hr) Widely regarded as the best hospital in the city.

Farmacia San Judas (☎809-685-8165; cnr Av Independencia & Pichardo; ⌚24hr) Pharmacy that offers free delivery.

Farmax (☎809-333-4000; cnr Av Independencia & Dr Delgado; ⌚24hr) Pharmacy that offers free delivery.

Hospital Padre Billini (☎809-221-8272; Sánchez; ⌚24hr) The closest public hospital to the Zona Colonial, service is free but expect long waits.

MONEY

There are several major banks (Banco de Reserves, Banco Popular, Banco Leon, Banco Progreso and Scotiabank) with ATMs in the Zona Colonial. Gazcue also has a number of banks and others are scattered throughout the city, especially around major thoroughfares like Av 27 de Febrero and Av Abraham Lincoln. Large hotels, particularly those on the Malecón, all have at least one ATM.

POST

Both Caribe and Metro bus companies have package-delivery services based in their respective terminals; these are the best options for mailing anything within the country.

Federal Express (Map p54; ☎809-565-3636; www.fedex.com; cnr Av de los Próceres & Camino del Oeste, Arroyo Hondo)

Post Office (Map p50; Isabel la Católica; ⌚8am-5pm Mon-Fri, 9am-noon Sat) Facing Parque Colón in the Zona Colonial.

TOURIST INFORMATION

Tourist Office (Map p50; ☎809-686-3858; Isabel la Católica 103; ⌚9am-7pm Mon-Sat) Located beside Parque Colón, this office has a handful of brochures and maps for Santo Domingo and elsewhere in the country, as well as a half-dozen ones with a variety of Zona Colonial walking tours. Some English and French spoken.

TRAVEL AGENCIES

Colonial Tour & Travel (☎809-688-5285; www.colonialtours.com.do; Arzobispo Meriño 209) This long-running professional outfit is good for booking flights, hotel rooms, and any and all excursions from mountain biking to rafting to whale-watching. English, Italian and French spoken.

Explora Eco Tours (☎809-567-1852; www.exploraecotour.com; Gustavo A Mejia Ricart 43, Naco) Specializes in organizing customized tours, from a single day to a week long, of national parks, nature preserves and rural communities. Website announces regularly scheduled trips open to general public.

Giada Tours & Travel (☎809-682-4525; www.giadatours.com; Hostal Duque de Wellington, Av Independencia 304) Friendly professional outfit arranges domestic and international plane tickets, and also conducts area tours.

Tody Tours (☎809-686-0882; www.todytours.com) Former Peace Corps volunteer who specializes in tropical birding tours all over the country (US$200 per day).

Getting There & Away

AIR

Santo Domingo has two airports: the main one, Aeropuerto Internacional Las Américas (p236), is 22km east of the city. The smaller Aeropuerto Internacional La Isabela Dr Joaquin Balaguer (p236), around 20km north of the Zona Colonial, handles mostly domestic carriers and air-taxi companies.

AeroDomca (www.aerodomca.com), Air Century (www.aircentury.com), Dominican Shuttles (www.dominicanshuttles.com) and Aerolineas MAS (www.aerolineasmas.com) connect Santo Domingo, primarily Aeropuerto La Isabela, to Punta Cana, Samaná, Santiago and La Romana. Aerolineas MAS and Dominican Shuttles also fly to Port-au-Prince in Haiti and to Aruba.

Most international flights use Las Américas. Direct connections include Antigua, Atlanta, Caracas, Havana, Miami, Newark, New York (JFK), Orlanda, Pointpitre (Guadeloupe), Panama, San Juan (Puerto Rico) and St Maarten. The 3rd-floor food court and the one past arrivals are better bets than the limited, overpriced options beyond security by the gates. There are several ATMs in the arrivals area. Watch your bags. Cigar shops, cafes, pharmacy and gift shops are in the departures terminal. Major carriers include:

Air Antilles Express (☎809-688-6661; www.flyairantilles.com) Flights to Fort de France, Lamentin; Pointe a Pitre; and St Maarten.

Air Europa (☎at airport 809-549-1110; www.aireuropa.com) Direct flights to Madrid and New York (JFK).

Air France Airport (☎809-549-0309); Central Santo Domingo (☎809-686-8432; Plaza El Faro, Av Máximo Gómez 15) The city branch shares its office with KLM.

American Airlines (☎809-542-5151; Bella Vista Mall, Av Sarasota 6) Direct flights from Miami.

Continental Airlines (☎809-262-1060; Suite 104, cnr Max Henríquez Ureña & Winston Churchill)

Copa (☎airport 809-549-0757, reservations 809-472-2233)

Delta (☎809-955-1500; Plaza Comercial Acropolis Center, cnr Winston Churchill & Andres Julio Aybar)

Iberia Airport (☎809-950-6050); Santo Domingo (☎809-227-0188; Av Lope de Vega 63)

Insel Air (☎809-621-7777, in US 855-493-6004; www.fly-inselair.com) Flights to Curaçao and St Maarten in the Netherlands Antilles.

Jet Blue (☎at airport 809-947-2297; cnr Av Winston Churchill & Paseo de los Locutores, Plaza Las Americas) Ticket office located next to Metro bus terminal.

Lufthansa/Condor (☎809-689-9625; Av George Washington 353)

US Airways (☎809-540-0505; Gustavo Mejía Ricart 54)

BOAT

The DR's only international ferry service, *Caribbean Fantasy*, run by **America Cruise Ferries** (☎Mayagüez, Puerto Rico 787-832-4800, San Juan, Puerto Rico 787-622-4800, Santo Domingo 809-688-4400; www.acferries.com) connects Santo Domingo with San Juan and Mayagüez, Puerto Rico. The ticket office and boarding area are in the **Puerto Don Diego** (Map p50) on Av del Puerto, opposite Fortaleza Ozama in the Zona Colonial.

The ferry departs Santo Domingo at 7pm on Sunday and 8pm Tuesday and Thursday, before returning from San Juan at 7pm Monday and Friday and Mayagüez at 8pm on Wednesday. The trip from Santo Domingo takes 12 hours (eight hours in the other direction; difference is because of prevailing currents) and costs around US$200 round-trip.

The other major terminal that handles cruise ships is the **Puerto Sans Souci** (www.sanssouci.com.do) on the eastern bank of the Rio Ozama, directly across from the Zona Colonial.

BUS

First-Class Buses

The country's two main bus companies – Caribe Tours (p239) and **Metro** (Map p54; ☎809-227-0101; www.metrotours.com.do; Calle Francisco Prats Ramírez) – have individual depots west of the Zona Colonial. Caribe Tours has the most departures, and covers more of the smaller towns than Metro does. In any case, all but a few destinations are less than four hours from Santo Domingo. Caribe Tours has a much larger terminal with a gift shop, though both have ATMs and a limited food selection.

It's a good idea to call ahead to confirm the schedule and always arrive at least 30 minutes before the stated departure time. Both bus lines publish brochures (available at all terminals) with up-to-date schedules and fares, plus the address and telephone number of their terminals throughout the country.

Expreso Bávaro Punta Cana (Map p60; ☎in Santo Domingo 809-682-9670; Juan Sánchez Ramirez 31) has a direct service between the Gazcue neighborhood (just off Av Máximo Gómez) in the capital and Bávaro, with a stop in La Romana. Departure times in both directions are 7am, 9am, 11am, 1pm, 3pm and 4pm (RD$400, three hours). Some drivers are flexible and let passengers off at other stops in the city.

Another option is **APTRPA** (Map p50; ☎809-686-0637; www.aptpra.com.do; Calle Ravelo), located amid the chaos of Parque Enriquillo, which services Higuey (RD$250), Bávaro and Punta Cana; there are six daily departures (on the hour) from 7am to 4pm for the latter two (RD$400).

> **SANTO DOMINGO–SAMANÁ HWY**
>
> Considering its importance, it's strange that the turnoff to the two-lane, 102km Santo Domingo–Samaná Hwy (aka Juan Pablo II or DR-7; toll RD$412) is difficult to spot. To find it coming from Santo Domingo, drive east on the coastal road and past the toll booth for the airport; make a U-turn and continue slowly in the far right lane until you spot the small sign for Samaná.

Second-Class Buses

Four informal depots surround the smelly, exhaust-fume-filled Parque Enriquillo on the northern edge of the Zona Colonial. All buses make numerous stops en route. Because the buses tend to be small, there can be a scrum for seats. Since Metro and Caribe service the major destinations, especially those over several hours away, these should be avoided in the interest of comfort and sanity. *Caliente*, literally 'hot' buses, refer to those generally without air-con; *expreso* buses stop less often.

Buses to Haiti

Capital Coach Line (☎809-530-8266; www.capitalcoachline.com; Av 27 de Febrero 455) and Caribe Tours offer daily services in comfortable, air-con buses to Port-au-Prince (US$40, six to eight hours). Capital Coach Line has one 8am departure daily that stops in Tabarre and ends in Petion Ville, a neighborhood of Port-au-Prince, and another at 10am that goes only to Tabarre. Caribe Tours has daily departures at 9am and 11am to Petion Ville; tickets are sold in a separate office marked Atlantic Travel Agency, at the entrance to the downtown terminal (p239). If possible, make a reservation at least two days in advance.

CAR

Numerous international and domestic car-rental companies have more than one office in Santo Domingo proper and at Las Américas International Airport, including **Avis** (☎809-535-7191; Av George Washington 517), **Dollar** (☎809-221-7368; Av Independencia 366), **Europcar** (☎809-688-2121; Av Independencia 354) and **Hertz** (☎809-221-5333; Av José Ma Heredia 1). All are open daily roughly from 7am to 6pm in Santo Domingo (sometimes later) and from 7am to 11:30pm at the airport.

Getting Around

TO/FROM THE AIRPORT

There are no buses that connect directly to either of Santo Domingo's airports. From Las Américas, a taxi into the city costs US$40, with little room for negotiation – **Taxi Sichala** (809-549-0245; www.taxisichala.com) is the controlling syndicate (credit cards accepted). The trip is a solid half-hour (26km). If other

BUSES FROM SANTO DOMINGO

First-Class

DESTINATION	FARE (RD$)	DURATION (HR)	DISTANCE (KM)	FREQUENCY (PER DAY)
Ázua	190	1¼	120	8
Barahona	270	3½	200	4
Dajabón	350	5	305	4
Jarabacoa	280	3	155	4
La Vega	210	1½	125	every 30min 6am-8pm
Las Matas de Santa Cruz	350	2½	250	4
Monte Cristi	350	4	270	6
Nagua	330	3½	180	11
Puerto Plata	330	4	215	hourly 7am-7pm
Río San Juan	330	4½	215	5
Samaná	320	2½	245	6
San Francisco de Macorís	260	2½	135	every 30-60min 7am-6pm
San Juan de la Maguana	270	2½	163	4
Sánchez	320	4	211	6
Santiago	280	2½	155	hourly 7am-8pm
Sosúa	330	5	240	hourly 7am-7pm

Second-Class

DESTINATION	FARE (RD$)	DURATION (HR)	FREQUENCY
Baní	120	1½	every 15min 5am-10pm
Boca Chica	50	½	every 15min 6am-8pm
Higüey	210	2½	every 30min 6am-7pm
Juan Dolio	75	1	every 30min 6am-9:30pm
La Romana	180	1½	every 20min 5am-9pm
Las Galeras	350	3	3
Las Terrenas	350	2½	5
Paraiso	350	4	2
Pedernales	400	6	2
San Cristóbal	50	1	every 15-30min 6am to 10pm
San Pedro de Macorís	80	1	every 30min 6am-9:30pm
Santiago	200	2½	take any Sosúa bus

travelers arrive when you do, try sharing a ride. If flexible, carrying a light pack and prioritizing cost over comfort, you can walk around 100m to the right of baggage claim and grab a *motoconcho* (RD$100) to take you to a *guagua* (minivan) stop on the highway.

Some taxis may be willing to take you from the city to the airport for less. Or grab any eastbound *guagua* from the city and get off at the airport turnoff (it's a regular stop on these routes); a pack of *motoconchos* will be waiting to ferry you the remaining kilometer or two.

The fare from La Isabela is more reasonable at US$15. There's no permanent taxi stand there, but at least one or two taxis meet every flight.

CAR

Driving in Santo Domingo can challenge the nerves and test the skills of the most battle-hardened driver. Heavy traffic, aggressive drivers, especially taxis and buses, and little attention to, or enforcement of, rules means it's a free-for-all. Many of the city's major avenues are gridlocked during rush hour and you're better off walking.

Finding parking is not typically a problem, though if you are leaving your car overnight, ask around for a parking lot. Many midrange and top-end hotels have parking with 24-hour guards. In any case, be sure not to leave any valuables inside your car.

PUBLIC TRANSPORTATION

Bus

The cost of a bus ride from one end of the city to the other is around RD$12 (6:30am to 9:30pm). Most stops are marked with a sign and the word *parada* (stop). The routes tend to follow major thoroughfares – in the Zona Colonial, Parque Independencia is where Av Bolivar (the main westbound avenue) begins and Av Independencia (the main eastbound avenue) ends. If you're trying to get across town, just look at a map and note the major intersections along the way and plan your transfers accordingly.

Metro

Caribbean islands and underground metros usually don't appear to go together, but in January 2009 Santo Domingo joined San Juan, Puerto Rico, as the second city in the region to have a commuter train system. Line 1 from La Feria (Centro de los Héroes) near the Malecón to the far northern suburb of Villa Mella is a 14.5km route with 16 stations running primarily north-south above and below ground along Av Máximo Gómez. In April 2013, Line 2 which runs east-west for 10.3km (entirely underground) along Av John F Kennedy, Expreso V Centenario and Av Padre Castellanos began operating. The master plan calls for six lines.

It's worth a trip for travelers to get a sense of Santo Domingo's size and sprawl, and on Line 1 for the rather stunning views over the rooftops, and scattered palm trees and mountains in the distance. The entrances, stations and subway cars are modern and clean, certainly a world away from New York City subways. The fact that stations are named after well-known Dominicans (and foreigners like John F Kennedy and Abraham Lincoln) rather than streets may be inconvenient, but it may also lead some to brush up on their history.

Each ride costs RD$20; however, it's best to purchase a card at one of the ticket booths for RD$50, which can then be refilled when needed. Place the card on top of the turnstile to enter the station (6:30am to 11:30pm Monday to Friday, to 10pm Saturday).

Públicos

Even more numerous than buses are the *públicos* – mostly beaten-up minivans and private cars that follow the same main routes but stop wherever someone flags them down. They are supposed to have *público* on their license plates, but drivers will beep and wave at you long before you can make out the writing. Any sort of hand waving will get the driver to stop, though the preferred gesture is to hold out your arm and point down at the curb in front of you. The fare is RD$12 – pay when you get in. Be prepared for a tight squeeze.

Taxi

Taxis in Santo Domingo don't have meters, so you should always agree on the price before climbing in. The standard fare is around RD$200 from one side of the city to another; rates tend to be higher in the evening. Within the Zona Colonial it should be even cheaper. Taxi drivers don't typically cruise the streets looking for rides; they park at various major points and wait for customers to come to them. In the Zona Colonial, Parque Colón and Parque Duarte are the best spots.

You can also call for a taxi or ask the receptionist at your hotel to do so. Service is usually quick, the fare should be the same, and you don't have to lug your bags anywhere. Many of the top hotels have taxis waiting at the ready outside, but expect to pay significantly more for those. Reputable taxi agencies with 24-hour dispatches include **Apolo Taxi** (✆809-537-7771), **Super Taxi** (✆809-536-7014) and **Amarillo Taxi** (✆809-368-3333, 809-620-6363).

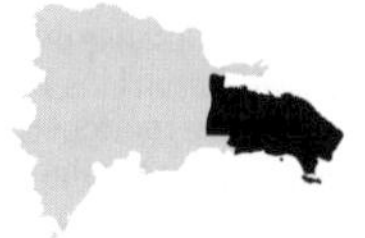

Punta Cana & the Southeast

Includes ➡

Best Places to Eat

- Passion by Martín Berasategui (p102)
- Restaurante Playa Blanca (p102)
- Ñam Ñam (p102)
- Ristorante El Sueño (p83)
- Balicana (p102)

Best Places to Stay

- Paraíso Caño Hondo (p107)
- Paradisus Punta Cana (p100)
- Tortuga Bay (p101)
- Casa de Campo (p85)
- Bávaro Hostel (p100)

Why Go?

A Caribbean workhorse of sun and sand, the southeast is synonymous with go-big-or-go-home tourism and carries the weight of the Dominican Republic's most dramatic beaches and turquoise seas on its deeply-tanned shoulders. Sprawling resort developments, some like city-states unto themselves, line much of the beachfront from Punta Cana to Bávaro, offering families, couples and the young and restless alike a hassle-free Caribbean holiday on some of the most idyllic environs in the region. But there is life beyond Punta Cana. Less-crowded beach towns such as Bayahibe and Juan Dolio offer only slightly less dramatic seascapes but sands that go unshared with the masses; and isolated getaways such as Playa Limón, beyond the sugar plantations and inland mountains to the north, showcase a different and worthwhile side of the southeast if you can tear yourself away from the buffets long enough to take the rewarding journeys required to make their acquaintance.

When to Go

- **January & February** If you can hold off just past the winter holidays, January and February offer the same sun and sand as Christmas and New Year's Eve – but a whole lot less people.
- **March** If you're looking for a fiesta, join North American Spring Breakers descending upon Punta Cana. If you're not on Spring Break, this is probably a bad time for that leisurely family vacation.
- **October** For those pinching pesos, October bridges the gap between hurricane season and the preholiday onslaught. *¡Salud!*

History

Before sugar, it was cattle ranching and the cutting and exporting of hardwoods that drove the region's economy. But Cuban planters, fleeing war in their country, began to arrive in the southeast in the 1870s and established sugar mills with the Dominican government's assistance (this migration also explains baseball's popularity and importance in the region). Rail lines were built and La Romana and San Pedro de Macorís, formerly sleepy backwaters, began to prosper as busy ports almost immediately when world sugar prices soared. Hundreds of families from the interior migrated to the area in search of jobs. In 1920, after peasants were dispossessed of their land during the US occupation, many fought a guerrilla war against the marines in the area around Hato Mayor and El Seibo. Until the 1960s, the economy in the southeast was still strictly driven by sugar, despite fluctuations in the world market and agriculture in general. However, when the US company Gulf & Western Industries bought La Romana's sugar mill, invested heavily in the cattle and cement industries and, perhaps most importantly, built the Casa de Campo resort, tourism became the financial engine of the southeast, and remains so today.

Getting There & Around

The majority of international visitors to this region fly directly to the airport in Punta Cana and then are whisked away in private vehicles to their respective resorts. Otherwise, it's anywhere from a two- to four-hour drive, depending on your destination, from Aeropuerto Internacional Las Américas in Santo Domingo. La Romana has an airport as well, though it mostly handles charter flights.

Traffic between the resort centers can be surprisingly heavy and it's difficult to navigate much of the road system, which is being revamped and expanded. Though the distances aren't great, travel in the region, especially along the coast north of Bávaro all the way to Sabana de la Mar, can be slow and unreliable because of the poor condition of the roads. It's now possible to fly between Punta Cana and the Península de Samaná.

EAST OF SANTO DOMINGO

Cross Río Ozama, the eastern border of the Zona Colonial in Santo Domingo, and the claustrophobia fades, the horizon opens and you remember that you're in the Caribbean. The highway hugs the coast for some time with promising views but then retreats inland once again, passing service stations and shops hugging the roadside until the turnoff for the beach resorts of Boca Chica and Juan Dolio a little further on.

Juan Dolio

The recession hasn't been kind to parts of Juan Dolio, a tranquil beach town about 20km east of rambunctious Boca Chica. Once tipped as the Caribbean's next hot spot, real estate speculation and investors flocked here since development began in earnest in the late 1980s, but these days, you'll see more 'For Sale' signs and half-finished condos on the west side than smiles and sunshine. Of course, the news isn't all bad: Juan Dolio is one of the few beach towns in the area that caters somewhat to independent budget travelers and the laid-back feel around town makes losing a few days here far from difficult.

The public beach itself on the west side of town is fairly small and cramped (especially on weekends), but the area in front of the resorts to the more prosperous east side of town is wider and softer than in nearby Boca Chica. Most tourists stay at one of the several all-inclusive resorts on the east side, however there's enough of a trickle of guests, independent travelers, loyal expats (mainly retired Germans and Italians) and Dominicans to keep a handful of bars and restaurants on the more free-spirited west side of town in business.

Sights & Activities

Los Delfines Water & Entertainment Park WATER PARK
(809-476-0477; www.losdelfinespark.com; Autovia del Este; adult/child US$49/39; 10am-6pm Wed-Sun;) This new water park between Boca Chica and Juan Dolio claims to be the Caribbean's biggest. With its 17 water slides and nine pools, it's easy to get lost in here.

Cigua Tours ADVENTURE, CULTURAL TOUR
(809-396-8441; www.erika-cigua-tours.com; Playa Real; 9am-11pm) This small travel agency is located just east of Talanquera Beach Resort on the old Decameron Resort property. It organizes day trips to Santo Domingo (per person US$35), Isla Saona (per person US$55), Isla Catalina (per person US$55), Parque Nacional Los Haitises (per person US$70)

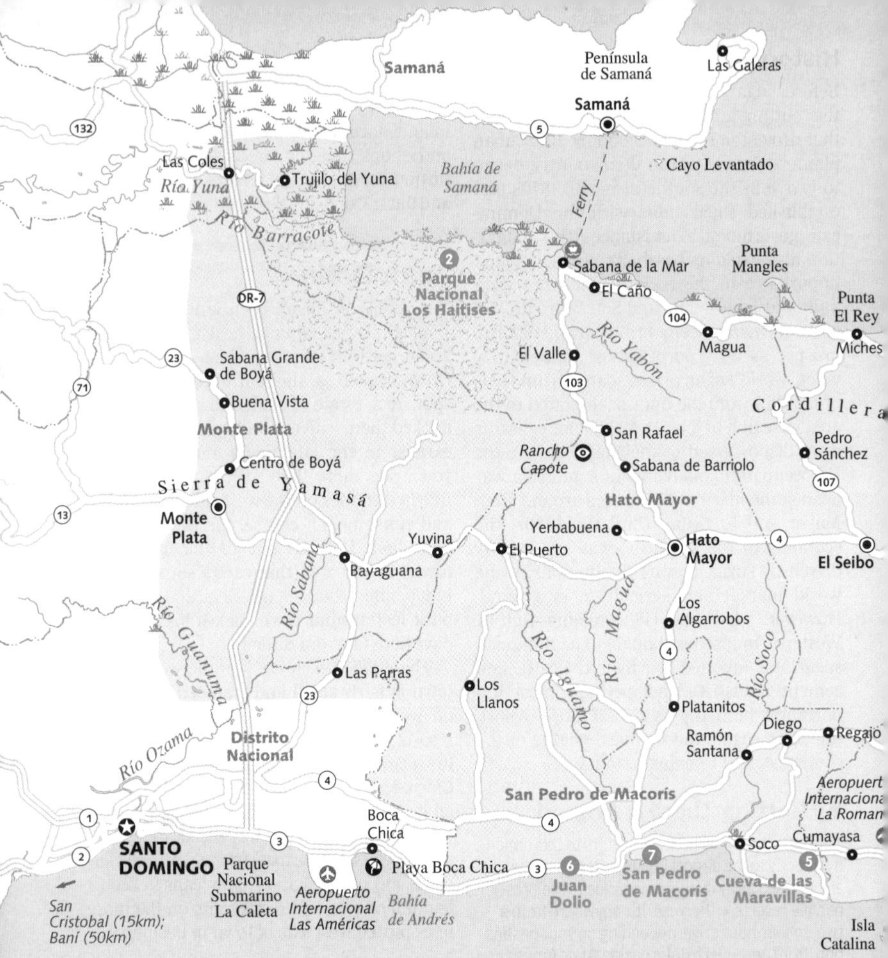

Punta Cana & the Southeast Highlights

1 Tucking yourself away on an all-inclusive binge of beaches and buffets around **Bávaro** and **Punta Cana** (p96)

2 Ogling the mangrove-infested forests of **Parque Nacional Los Haitises** (p106) on a tranquil kayak excursion

3 Dunking into crystal-clear waters on a snorkeling or diving trip around **Parque Nacional del Este** (p88)

4 Journeying through colorful Caribbean *colonias* and lush mountains to wild **Playa Limón** (p104)

5 Plunging yourself into the fascinating illuminated

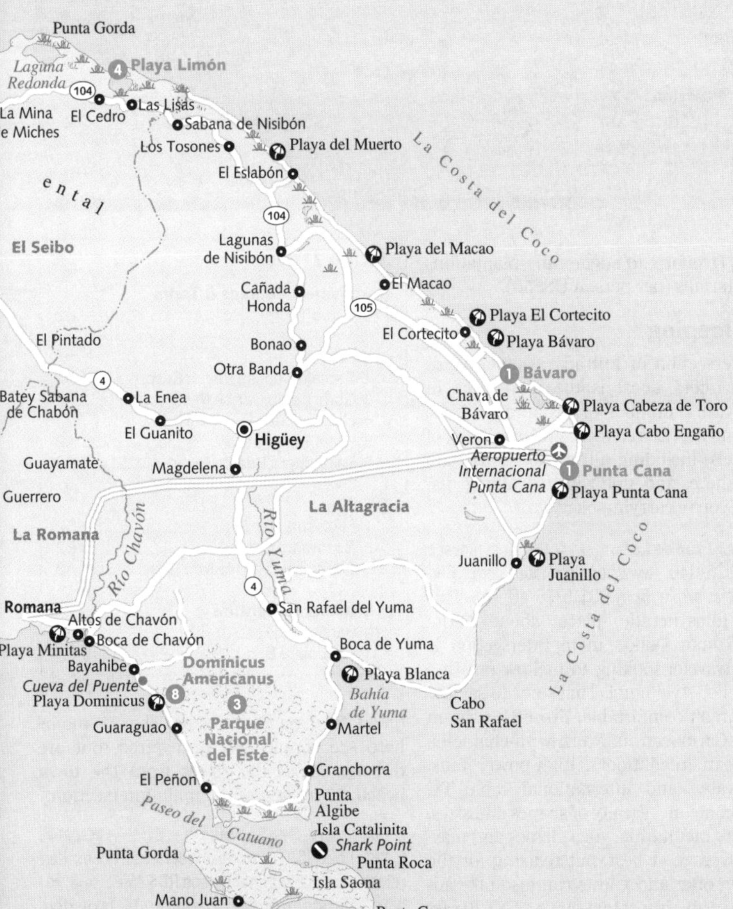

underworld at **Cueva de las Maravillas** (p88)

6 Hiding out for a few days on the tranquil sands of **Juan Dolio** (p79), the best beach near Santo Domingo

7 Taking in the 7th inning stretch at **Estadio Tetelo Vargas** (p85) in San Pedro de Macorís, the DR's baseball capital

8 Gorging on fresh lobster in **Dominicus Americanus** (p88)

Juan Dolio

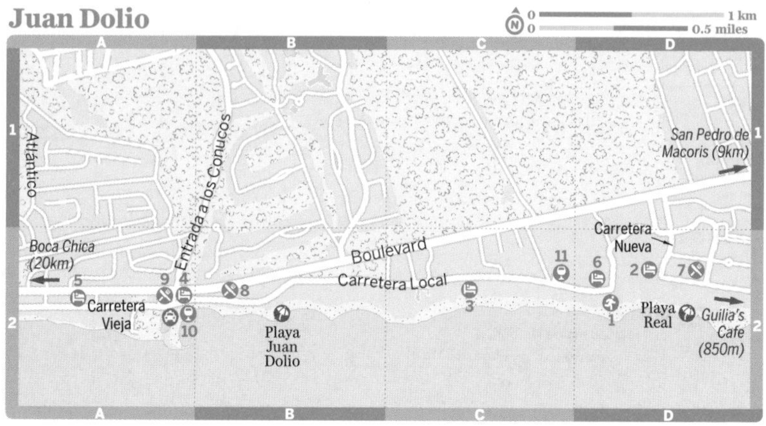

and 4WD safaris to sugar cane plantations and waterfalls (per person US$50).

Sleeping

The intersection of Entrada a los Conucos and Carretera Local is the main area in town, with a number of restaurants, bars, shops and services clustered nearby. Most of the hotels, including all of the resorts, are east of here, and not within walking distance if you're carrying baggage.

★ Hotel Fior di Loto GUESTHOUSE $
(809-526-1146; www.fiordilotohotels.com; Carretera Vieja; s/d/tr from US$15/25/40;) This small, idiosyncratic place about 500m west of Juan Dolio's main intersection is for the traveler looking to mellow out in a backpacker-style hotel. That's not to say the rooms aren't comfortable; this little ashram in the Caribbean is worn-with-character, with clean, tiled floors, high-power fans, tepid water, and international cable TV. Rooms come in a variety of shapes and sizes.

There's meditation, yoga classes and massages (average at best, but relaxing for the price) on offer and guests can also take advantage of an airport taxi that's a US$20 savings on the street rate. Some proceeds from the hotel go to supporting a girl's foundation in India, where the good-hearted Italian owner, Mara, spends half the year.

Habitaciones Don Pedro GUESTHOUSE $
(809-526-2147; juandolioarq@gmail.com; Carretera Local; r with fan/air-con RD$1000/1200;) This well-located, simple guesthouse is run by Antonio, who can usually be found across the street at the family's beach bar (good food on the cheap). The 22 rooms here are simple and uninspired, but are directly across the street from the town beach, 200m east of the main intersection.

Juan Dolio

Activities, Courses & Tours
1 Cigua Tours D2

Sleeping
2 Barceló Capella Beach Resort D2
3 Coral Costa Caribe Resort C2
4 Habitaciones Don Pedro A2
5 Hotel Fior di Loto A2
6 Talanquera Beach Resort D2

Eating
7 El Mesón D2
8 Ristorante El Sueño B2
9 Supermercado Naito A2

Drinking & Nightlife
10 Bar Cacique A2
11 Chocolate Bar C2

Talanquera Beach Resort RESORT $$
(809-526-1510; www.talanqueraresort.com; Carretera Local; all-incl r per person RD$2595;) The Talanquera never seems to be crowded, but perfectly acceptable rooms here are a stunning deal – half the price of much of the competition.

Barceló Capella Beach Resort RESORT $$$
(809-526-1080; www.barcelo.com; Carretera Nueva; all-incl s/d from RD$2868/4780;) One of Juan Dolio's more glamorous choices, the rooms at the Capella are spread out around lush grounds with reflecting pools. Inevitably for a resort this size, room quality is a bit

uneven – the best are in the 4000 block just steps from the shady palmed beach. The pool area is a little small considering the number of guests, but it's generally a more tranquil scene than some others in town.

Coral Costa Caribe Resort RESORT **$$$**
(809-526-2244; www.coralcostacaribe.com; Carretera Local; all-incl s/d/tr US$125/190/245;) Action at Juan Dolio's liveliest all-inclusive centers around the pool area, where a variety of sizes and professions mingle over bottomless cocktails and fist-pumping reggaeton. It's probably worth splurging an extra US$50 per night for newly renovated superior category rooms here, a more modern escape from the nice but potentially crowded beach. Three signature restaurants (Dominican, Italian and Mexican), a watersport/diving center and five bars and a disco round out a lively atmosphere. If you're staying further west and want to imbibe here, a full-day pass is a painful US$50, but if you're a fast drinker, the US$25 afternoon-only pass might easily be washed down your gullet.

Eating & Drinking

Don't worry if you're staying at an all-inclusive with less-than-stellar buffet food – Juan Dolio has several decent restaurants, both near the main intersection and strung out along Carretera Nueva east of the main resort area.

★ **Ristorante El Sueño** ITALIAN **$$**
(Carretera Local; pizza RD$280-425, pasta RD$255-425; noon-11pm Tue-Sun;) Italian owners and their Azurri cohorts sit around this casual open-air eatery *Godfather*-style, giving it a nod of authenticity it doesn't need – the real-deal pizzas do the job on their own. The lobster fettuccine also stands out, a favorite of local expats, as does the *all'amatriciana*, as does anything *alla criolla*, as does the whole menu. It's rare that you eat in an Italian restaurant outside of Italy and think to yourself, "Bam! This must be how it is in Italy!" This is *that* restaurant – one of this coast's most consistently great spots.

El Mesón SPANISH, ITALIAN **$$**
(Carretera Nueva , across from Club Hemmingway; mains RD$250-490; lunch & dinner) If the waft of fresh-off-the-grill whole lobster doesn't suck you in, go for the spot-on paella at this perennially popular Spanish restaurant. You'll also find smoked chorizo, lamb, *morcilla* (blood sausage) and heaps of the usual suspects, all excellently prepared with little regard for your waistline. There's live music on Friday evenings.

El Lobo y La Sal SEAFOOD **$$**
(Calle Principal 570; mains RD$550-675; 11am-11pm Wed-Mon;) This classy seafooder on the beach represents what Juan Dolio aspires to be. The most pleasant atmosphere in the old side of town serves a serious seven-ingredient fried fish, grilled lobster and much more ambitious dishes like Korean ribs and Vietnamese-style wings. It's walking distance from the main intersection.

Guilia's Café BURGERS **$$**
(Carretera Nueva; meals RD$100-460; 7:30am-5:30pm Wed-Mon;) Juan Dolio's interpretation of a sports bar, Guilia's offers a flat-screen TV and pool table and serves up homemade burgers (RD$200) and freshly cut fries. It's popular with foreigners.

Supermercado Naito MARKET
(cnr Carretera Local & Entrada a los Conucos; 8am-8pm) This is the largest market in the center of town, with basic groceries and supplies.

Bar Cacique BAR
(Carretera Local; to midnight Sun-Thu, to 2am Fri & Sat) A quintessential dive popular with expats and Dominicans alike. Solo men may get more attention than they bargained for, however; respond to unwanted attention with a polite "*no, gracias*".

Chocolate Bar BAR
(Plaza Chocolate, Carretera Local; 9am-late) Convivial outdoor bar catering to all-inclusive escapists near Coral Costa Caribe Resort. There's live rock on Thursdays and DJs spinning house through the weekend.

Information

The Shell gas station on the boulevard west of Entrada a los Conucos has a Banco León ATM available between 7am and 10pm. There is also an ATM on the property of the Coral Costa Caribe Resort.

Banco Popular (Carretera Nueva) With 24-hour ATM, located 200m north of Barceló Capella Beach Resort.

Farmacia La Formula (Plaza Colonial Tropical, Carretera Nueva; 8am-9pm Mon-Sat, to 6pm Sun) Small pharmacy and sundries.

Galmedical Internacional (809-526-2044; off Carretera Nueva; 24hr) Serious matters should be seen in San Pedro de Macorís, but the good doc here speaks English, German, French and Italian. It's off Carretera Nueva just north of Guilia's.

LAYOVER: BOCA CHICA

Boca Chica, just 10km from Aeropuerto Internacional Las Américas, ends up being a good final stop for those wanting to take one last dip in the Caribbean before catching their flights home. Aside from its proximity to the capital and the airport, there's not a lot to recommend as it caters to a weathered crowd and is marred by in-your-face sex tourism.

There are over 25 dive sites in the area, including the shipwreck *Catuan*, a 33m-long troller sunk in 2006. The most recommended dive shop in town is **Caribbean Divers Asobuca** (☎809-854-3483; www.caribbeandivers.de; enter at Av Duarte 28; ⌚8:30am-5pm).

Sichoproboch *guaguas* service Santo Domingo (RD$70, 30 minutes, every 15 minutes from 6am to 11pm), departing on the north side of Parque Central and along Av San Rafael. If you're heading east, *guaguas* stop at the intersection of the highway and Av Caracol. You can often find taxis near the intersection of Av San Rafael and Av Caracol, or you can get door-to-door service with **Taxi Turístico Boca Chica** (☎809-523-4946).

Politur (☎809-526-3211; www.politur.gob.do; Av Boulevard; ⌚24hr) Tourist police for emergencies; next to the National Police building.

Getting There & Around

Guaguas pass through Juan Dolio all day every day, going westward to Boca Chica (RD$35) and Santo Domingo (RD$120), and east to San Pedro de Macorís (RD$40) and La Romana (RD$120), among others. No buses originate here, so there is no fixed schedule, but they pass roughly every 15 minutes from 6am to 7pm – stand on the Boulevard at the corner of Entrada a los Conucos and flag down any one that passes.

Taxis can be found in front of any of the resorts in town. One-way fares for one to four people include Aeropuerto Internacional Las Américas (US$50), Santo Domingo (US$60), Bayahibe (US$90), Bávaro (US$140) and points further afield like Las Galeras (US$300) and Lago Enriquillo (US$350). You can also call **Sitraguza Taxi Service** (☎809-526-3507) for door-to-door service. When driving from Santo Domingo on Hwy 3, take the turnoff marked Playa Guayacanes.

LA ROMANA TO HIGÜEY

La Romana

POP 130,426

This bustling city is a convenient stop for those traveling between Santo Domingo, 131km to the west, and the beach resorts further east. Surrounded by vast sugar plantations, and the enormous Casa de Campo resort to the east, La Romana feels slightly more prosperous than neighboring cities. There isn't much beyond Casa de Campo other than some great restaurants to refuel on cuisines and dishes you don't see on every other menu between here and Santo Domingo – nearly worth a stop alone.

Sights & Activities

Altos de Chavón LANDMARK

(☎809-523-3333; admission US$25; ⌚8am-5:45pm) While a trip to a faux 15th-century southern Italian–Spanish village created by a Paramount movie-set designer won't exactly give you a window into Dominican culture, Altos de Chavón has some redeeming qualities, especially the excellent views of the Río Chavón (a scene from the film *Apocalypse Now* was filmed here). There's a church, a small pre-Columbian museum and a 5000-seat amphitheater, which attracts big names – Frank Sinatra did the inaugural gig here.

Created in the 1970s, most tourists visit Altos de Chavón by the busload in the morning and early afternoon as part of a tour from resorts around Bayahibe and Bávaro/Punta Cana, but it can be visited independently.

Motoconchos (motorcycle taxis) are prohibited from entering the area. If you're driving from La Romana, take the main road past the gated entrance to Casa de Campo and continue for 5km until the turnoff on your right, marked with a small 'Altos de Chavón' sign. A cab from La Romana costs around US$40 round-trip with an hour's wait. Others arrive at the end of a group tour to Isla Catalina; the 250 steps from the pier to the top of the bluff can be challenging for some.

El Obelisco MONUMENT

(Av Libertad, btwn Calles Márquez & Ducoudrey) Modeled after the George Washington monument in Washington, DC, the Obelisk is a much smaller version in central La Romana, painted on all four sides with contemporary and historical depictions of Dominican life.

Isla Catalina NATURE RESERVE

In the 15th century, pirates including Francis Drake would lurk around Isla Catalina waiting to pounce on Spanish ships on their way to and from Santo Domingo. Today, this island ringed by fine coral reefs teeming with fish in shallow water is a popular destination for groups from nearby Casa de Campo; the resort has frequent shuttles making the 2km trip, as do large cruise ships.

Most groups spend a couple of hours for snorkeling and lunch, and divers head to a steep drop-off called The Wall. With enough people or cash it's possible to charter a boat (most tour companies in the area, from Bayahibe to Romana to Punta Cana and Bávaro, would probably be open to this for the right price) to an infrequently visited beach on the far side of the island. In order to camp on the island you must gain permission from the Parque Nacional del Este office (p88) in Bayahibe – Isla Catalina is officially part of the park protected area.

Golf GOLF

(www.casadecampo.com.do) Within the grounds of the Casa de Campo are four Pete Dye–designed golf courses, including 'The Teeth of the Dog,' open since 1971, which has seven seaside holes; and 'Dye Fore.' Green fees for both courses in high season are US$218 and US$295 for guests and nonguests, respectively. 'Links' (green fees guests/nonguests US$182/206 in high season) also comes highly recommended. You should make reservations as far in advance as possible. Tee times can be reserved by email.

Sleeping

Hotel River View HOTEL $$

(809-556-1181; hotelriverview@gmail.com; Calle Restauración 17; s/d/tr incl breakfast & dinner RD$1650/1950/2775;) One of La Romana's few hotels that has both a pleasant enough location and the right price, this multistory place is perched a block from the Río Dulce and is a solid choice for independent travelers. Don't expect a lot of smiles or faultless rooms, but you can have a coffee in the tiny patio area overlooking...the parking lot. Rates include dinner, but you can negotiate out of that, which is the way to go – you're walking distance from better choices.

★**Casa de Campo** RESORT $$$

(800-877-3643; www.casadecampo.com.do; Av Libertad; r from US$570, villas from US$2144, all-incl supplement per adult/child US$275/150;) Known as much for its celebrity guests (LeBron James, Kanye West) and villa owners (Shakira, Sammy Sosa) as for its facilities, Casa de Campo is an all-inclusive, supersized place that remains discerning despite its enormity. The 285 or so hotel rooms have hardwood furnishings, wonderful local art, 42-inch LCD televisions, Nespresso machines and a golf cart for all. The 28-sq-km complex is home to 16 restaurants, an equestrian center, polo fields, an exclusive beach, a shooting range – the list goes on and on. It truly resembles a city-state, albeit one with G8 conference security and a disproportionate amount of 'beautiful people' per capita.

DON'T MISS

PLAY BALL!

Baseball is king in the Dominican Republic, so it would be a travesty not to take in the national pastime live if you're visiting during the winter baseball season from mid-November to February. A great spot to do so is in San Pedro de Macorís, located 70km east from Santo Domingo between Juan Dolio and La Romana. The city's most prominent building, **Estadio Tetelo Vargas** on the north side of Hwy 3, is home to the **Estrellas Orientales** (www.estrellasorientales.com.do) or the Eastern Stars. During big games you'll get cheerleaders and marching bands through the stands – quite a contrast for those used to Major League Baseball in the USA!

Despite being ridiculed as the Chicago Cubs of the six-team Dominican Winter Baseball League due to their prolonged drought without a championship (their last was 1968), San Pedro is a baseball prodigy factory, a centerpiece of a country that has given birth to more Major League Baseball players than any other country outside the US (perhaps explaining their sad track record – all the great players bolt for the big leagues).

To attend a game, pre-order tickets from the **ticket hotline** (809-529-3618; admission RD$450-400) or at the box office before the game.

In other baseball news, the New York Yankees announced in 2013 the construction of a US$120 million 'Latino Baseball Town,' a tourism complex that will include the Major League Baseball–quality Latin Center Stadium in Benerito, 20km east of La Romana.

La Romana

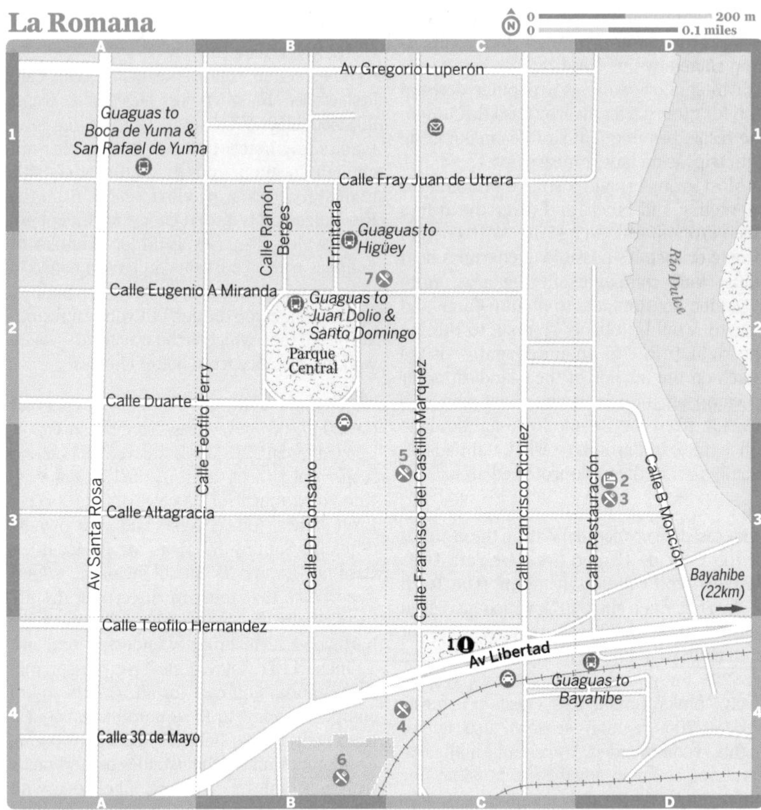

La Romana

Sights
1 El Obelisco C4

Sleeping
2 Hotel River View D3

Eating
3 Cinco D3
4 Punto Italia C4
5 Shish Kabab Restaurant C3
6 Supermercado Jumbo B4
7 Trigo de Oro B2

Catering mostly to celebrities, golfers and families, Casa de Campo feels less like a resort than a tropical Beverly Hills, mainly due to the independent design of the 2000 or so extravagant villas. All-inclusive rates include unlimited horseback riding, tennis, one round of skeet/trap shooting and nonmotorized water sports at the beach. Other available activities include kayak trips down the Río Chavón (per person US$30) and buggy tours through sugarcane country (per person US$87). Four Pete Dye–designed golf courses and Altos de Chavón, a Tuscan-style 'village' and a Mediterranean-style piazza overlooking a massive marina round out the resort's offerings.

Day passes (US$75) are available for nonguests and can be purchased at the information office on the right before the entrance gates. Whether this is good value is debatable: you are allowed to enter the property, access the beach (towel included) and have a meal and one alcoholic drink at the beachside restaurant. A property tour pass (US$25) includes a visit to Altos de Chavón and the marina – no lunch or beach access.

Most guests arrive at the resort by air, either at the private landing strip or the airport that serves La Romana, and are then driven onto the property. If arriving by private vehicle, follow Av Libertad east across the river, and stay in the right lane for 4km until you see the entrance on your right.

All of the resort's restaurants – the best in the region – are open to nonguests. You must email the **concierge** (a.concierge@ccampo.com.do) for a reservation and be prepared to show identification at the security gate.

Eating & Drinking

Cinco CAFE $

(Calle Restauración 15; gelato RD$100-270; noon-8pm Mon-Wed, from 10am Thu, 10am-10pm Fri & Sat, to 9pm Sun) Cinco does Illy espresso, delicious beat-the-heat gelato and creative sandwiches (RD$190 to RD$295).

Trigo de Oro BAKERY $

(Calle Eugenio A Miranda 9; mains RD$60-350; 7am-9pm Mon-Sat, to 1pm Sun;) Though it (oddly) had most of its shady courtyard renovated away in favor of a more modern look, this French bakery and cafe remains a welcome respite from *motoconcho* fumes. Located inside an historic mansion, the bakery side has freshly made pastries like mini-lime tarts and cheesecake, while the cafe does great sandwiches served on crusty baguettes.

★ **Da Lucas** ITALIAN $$

(809-550-3401; Plaza Buena Vista, Av Los Robles; mains RD$220-750, pizza RD$200-300; 6-11pm Tue-Sat, 11am-11pm Sun) Harder to find than the Holy Grail, this local's secret is buried inside a residential complex less than 2km from *centro*. Delectable fresh pastas (ravioli, tagliatelle and gnocchi are made in-house) are served on an atmospheric patio under a giant fig tree. The jovial owner, from Liguria, greets everyone with his Italian enthusiasm. Try the black tagliatelle with lobster and tomato sauce. Take note of the number, you'll need a taxi to find it. And even then...

Shish Kabab Restaurant MEDITERRANEAN $$

(Calle Francisco del Castillo Marquéz 32; mains RD$300-695; 11am-11pm Tue-Sun) The wall beside the bar is covered with photos of famous guests, attesting to the popularity of this local *institución*. The Palestinian owners dish out limited Middle Eastern dishes such as hummus, baba ganoush and delectable shish kebabs (one should hope), but the menu also includes everything else, including perhaps the DR's coldest *Presidentes* beer, served nearly frozen.

Punto Italia MARKET, ITALIAN $$

(Av Libertad; mains RD$180-500; 9am-9pm Mon-Sat) Imports gourmet Italian and European brands; stocks fresh meat and cheeses and serves quick-fire pastas.

Supermercado Jumbo SUPERMARKET

(Av Libertad; 8am-10pm Mon-Sat, 9am-8pm Sun) Occupying a full city block, this massive grocery sells everything imaginable.

Information

La Romana has a main town square (Parque Central) from which you can easily walk to most hotels, restaurants, internet cafes, post office and more.

Banco León (Calle Duarte) Located at southeast corner of the main park; ATM.

Banco Popular (Calle Dr Gonsalvo) Has an ATM.

Clínica Canela (www.clinicacanela.com; cnr Av Libertad 44 & Calle Restauración) A private clinic with 24-hour pharmacy and emergency room.

Farmacia Dinorah (Calle Duarte; 8am-9pm Mon-Sat, to 12:30pm Sun) Free delivery available.

InposDom (www.inposdom.gob.do; Calle Francisco del Castillo Marquéz, near Av Gregorio Luperón; 9am-3pm Mon-Fri)

Politur (Tourist Police; 809-754-5080; www.politur.gob.do; Calle Francisco del Castillo Marquéz, near Av Gregorio Luperón; 24hr) Inside the Secretary of Tourism office across from Supermarket Jumbo.

Getting There & Away

AIR

Aeropuerto La Romana (LRM) is 8km east of town. There are a few regularly scheduled flights, but most of the traffic here is chartered. Commercial carriers include **American Airlines** (809-200-5151; www.aa.com) with flights from Miami; and **JetBlue** (809-200-9898; www.jetblue.com) from New York City. Year-round charters include **Blue Panorama** (www.blue-panorama.com) and **Neos** (www.neosair.it) from Italy, while **Air Berlin** (www.airberlin.com) and **Condor** (www.condor.com) from Germany and **Canjet** (www.canjet.com), **Westjet** (www.westjet.com) and **Air Transat** (www.airtransat.ca) from Canada fly seasonal charters, among others.

BUS

Guaguas to Bayahibe (RD$60, 20 minutes, every 20 minutes from 6am to 7pm) depart from a stop on Av Libertad at Restauración. *Guaguas* for other destinations leave from stops near or on Parque Central.

Boca de Yuma (RD$110, 1¼ hours, every 45 minutes from 7am to 7pm)

Higüey (*caliente/expreso* RD$100/110, 1¼ hours, every 30 minutes from 6am to 10pm)

Juan Dolio (RD$80, one hour, every 20 minutes from 5am to 9pm)

WORTH A TRIP

CUEVA DE LAS MARAVILLAS

More than 500 pictographs and petroglyphs can be seen on a tour of **Cueva de las Maravillas** (Cave of Wonders; adult/child RD$300/50; 9am-5:15pm Tue-Sun), an enormous cavern complex discovered in 1926 on the highway some 20km west between San Pedro de Macorís and La Romana. Extending for 840m between Río Cumayasa and Río Soco, this massive underground museum is well marked and beautifully illuminated with motion-sensing lights. As far as caves go, it's pretty stunning. The entrance fee includes a 45-minute guided tour (some English is spoken as well as French, Italian and German). There is also an equestrian center (horseback riding RD$400 per hour) and a small iguana exhibit.

Coming from San Pedro de Macorís, look for the entrance on your left not far past the Playa Nueva Romana resort complex. Best way to get here is to take your own car, though taxis are also an option (round trip from La Romana including wait time US$60).

San Rafael del Yuma (RD$100, 45 minutes, every 45 minutes from 7am to 7pm)

Santo Domingo (*caliente/expreso* RD$175/180, 1½ hours, every 20 minutes from 5am to 9:30pm)

Getting Around

Motoconchos and taxis are typically found near the southeast corner of Parque Central. *Motoconcho* rides within the city normally cost RD$50; taxis within town are RD$100. You can call **Santa Rosa Taxi** (809-556-5313; Calle Duarte) or **Sichotaxi** (809-550-2222) for a pickup, or wait for the latter at a stop across the street from El Obelisco on Av Libertad. A taxi to or from the airport costs US$15.

To rent a car, try **Avis** (809-550-0600; www.avis.com.do; cnr Calles Francisco del Castillo Márquez & Duarte).

Bayahibe & Dominicus Americanus

POP 2260

Bayahibe, 22km east of La Romana, was originally founded by fishermen from Puerto Rico in the 19th century. Today, it's a tranquil beach village caught in a schizophrenic power play. In the morning it's the proverbial tourist gateway, when busloads of tourists from resorts further east hop into boats bound for Isla Saona. Once this morning rush hour is over it turns back into a sleepy village. There's another buzz of activity when the resort tourists return, and then after sunset another transformation. What sets Bayahibe apart is that it manages to maintain its character despite the continued encroachment of big tourism.

A short drive from Bayahibe is Dominicus Americanus, an upscale Potemkin village of resorts, hotels and several shops and services centered on a terrific public beach.

Sights & Activities

One advantage of staying in Bayahibe is that virtually every water-related activity is right outside your front door, so you avoid the long commute that most travelers make here daily from resorts further east.

Parque Nacional del Este NATURE RESERVE
(admission RD$100) More than simply Isla Saona, which is all that most people see on a group tour, the Parque Nacional del Este includes eight emerged reef terraces, 400 or so caverns, some with pictographs and ceramic remains, and Islas Catalinita and Catalina, in addition to Saona. Designated a national park in 1975, it stretches over 310 sq km of territory, the majority of which is semihumid forest. The park is also home to 539 species of flora, 55 of which are endemic. There is also a good variety of fauna: 112 species of birds, 250 types of insects and arachnids, and 120 species of fish. There are occasional sightings of West Indian manatees and bottlenose dolphins, and the much rarer Haitian solenodon, a small bony animal with a long snout and tiny eyes.

There's a **park office** (Map p89; 809-833-0022; 8am-3pm) in the parking lot in Bayahibe, where you must pay your entrance free and obtain a mandatory wristband. One entrance is at Guaraguao, a ranger post 5km past Dominicus Americanus. The other entrance is in the town of Boca de Yuma, on the eastern side of the park. There is a ranger station there but no formal services. A road leads along the coast for several kilometers and has a number of nice vista points.

Isla Saona NATURE RESERVE

There's a reason why boatloads of tourists descend upon this island daily. The powdery, white-sand beach doesn't seem real from afar, and a dip in the aquamarine surf is a gentle restorative, like the waters of the most luxurious spa; palm trees provide a natural awning from the intense sun. All of this would be perfect if it weren't for the fact that ear-splitting dance music is blasted from competing sound systems and vendors wander the beach in search of buyers in need of hair braiding, shells and other knickknacks. There isn't much coral to speak of, much of it damaged by heavy boat traffic and inexperienced snorkelers. Most of this 12km by 5km island is taken over by various companies and all-inclusive resorts that have set up lounge chairs, small dance floors, bars and buffets. **Mano Juan** (population 500) is the only established community on the island which is separated from the mainland by the narrow Paseo del Catuano.

The majority of visitors are ferried to Bayahibe early in the morning from resorts further east expecting a booze-cruise-like experience, and they usually aren't disappointed. Most trips include a catamaran ride out to the island and then a speedier motorboat trip back, or vice versa. A stop at the **piscina natural**, a shallow sandbank that extends far from the shore and has crystal-clear water, often includes young Dominican men and women wading through the water serving up glasses of rum and soda to tourists in need of a drink. The buffet lunch tends to be large and quite good. Unless you specifically request a trip that avoids the standard stops, don't expect a peaceful paradise, much less a protected national park. The dive shops in Bayahibe tend to offer more-rewarding trips that stop for lunch at Isla Saona, but only after visiting other spots for hiking, snorkeling or both. Every hotel, restaurant and shop advertises Saona trips with little variation in quality and price (US$65 to US$80).

Isla Catalinita NATURE RESERVE

This tiny uninhabited island on the eastern edge of the park is a common stop on snorkeling and diving tours. Arriving on the island's western (leeward) side, it's about a half-hour hike to the other side, where a lookout affords dramatic views of the powerful open-ocean waves crashing on the shore. There is a coral reef in about 2m of water that makes for great snorkeling, and a good

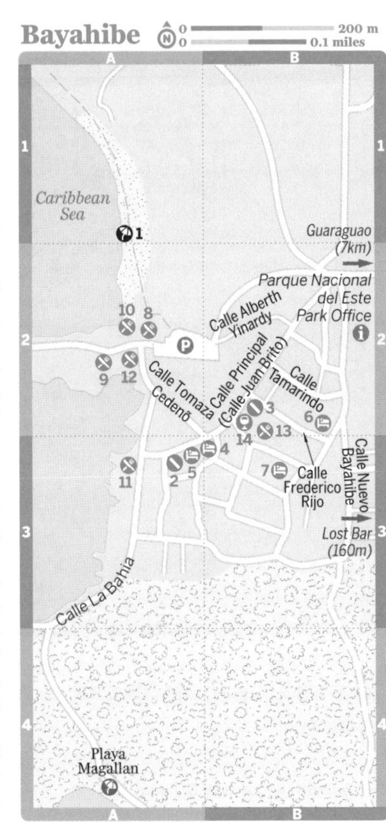

Bayahibe

Sights

1 Playa Bayahibe ... A1

Activities, Courses & Tours

2 Casa Daniel ... A3
3 Scubafun ... B2

Sleeping

4 Cabañas Taíno ... B3
5 Hotel Bayahibe ... A3
6 Villa Baya ... B2
7 Villa Iguana ... B3

Eating

8 Cafecito de la Cubana ... A2
9 Chikyblu ... A2
10 Mama Mia ... A2
11 Mare Nuestro ... A3
12 Saona Cafe ... A2
13 Supermercado La Defensa ... B2

Drinking & Nightlife

14 Super Colmado Bayahibe ... B2

Dominicus Americanus

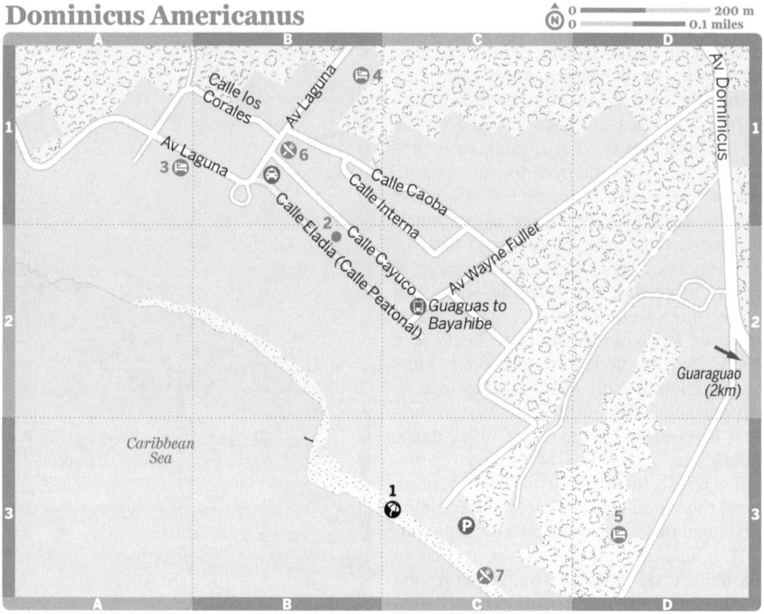

0 — 200 m
0 — 0.1 miles

Calle los Corales
Av Laguna
Calle Caoba
Calle Interna
Calle Eladia (Calle Peatonal)
Calle Cayuco
Av Wayne Fuller
Av Dominicus
Guaguas to Bayahibe
Guaraguao (2km)
Caribbean Sea

Dominicus Americanus

Sights
1 Playa Dominicus C3

Activities, Courses & Tours
2 Max Tours B2

Sleeping
3 Cabaña Elke A1
4 Hotel Eden B1
5 Iberostar Hacienda Dominicus D3

Eating
6 L'Angelo di Liz B1
7 Las Palmas C3

dive site called Shark Point, where sharks are in fact often seen.

Cueva del Puente CAVE

Parque Nacional del Este also has more than 400 caves, many of which contain Taíno pictographs (cave paintings) and petroglyphs (rock carvings). Archaeologists have found several structures and artifacts in and around the caves, including what appears to be the remains of a large Taíno city (perhaps the largest) and the site of a notorious massacre of indigenous people by Spanish soldiers.

Only one of the caves that contain Taíno pictographs, **Cueva del Puente**, can be easily visited. It is partially collapsed, but has a modest number of Taíno pictures, mostly depicting animals and human-like figures that may represent people or deities. The cave also has some impressive stalagmites and stalactites.

To visit Cueva del Puente, you must drive to the national park entrance at Guaraguao, 5km past Dominicus Americanus (turn right 350m down a dirt road after the Cadaques Caribe Resort). There you will pay the RD$100 entrance fee and the guard will guide you to the cave – it's a little over 3km, about a 40-minute walk; you'll need a flashlight and good shoes. South of here is **Cueva Penon Gordo**, a smaller cave but with more pictographs.

La Punta de Bayahibe NATURE WALK

This short, pleasant walk (10 minutes) follows a path beginning just past the Bamboo Beach Bar. It passes by the attractive Iglesia de Bayahibe, a small green, wooden structure, and signs in both English and Spanish outline interesting facts about the town's history and flora and fauna.

Snorkeling & Diving

Bayahibe is arguably the best place in the country to dive or snorkel, featuring warm Caribbean water, healthy reefs and plenty of fish and other sea life. The diving tends to be 'easier' (and therefore ideal for beginners) than it is on the DR's north coast, where the underwater terrain is less flat, the water cooler and the visibility somewhat diminished.

There are about 20 open-water dive sites; some favorites include **Catalina Wall** and an impressive 85m ship in 18m to 44m of water, known as **St Georges Wreck** after Hurricane Georges. Deep in the national park, **Padre Nuestro** is a weaving 290m tunnel flooded with freshwater that can be dived, but only by those with cave certification.

Scubafun DIVING
(Map p89; ☎809-833-0003; www.scubafun.info; Calle Principal/Calle Juan Brito 28, Bayahibe; ⏲8am-6pm) In operation for more than 12 years and located on the main strip in the middle of town, this American-run PADI dive center offers two-tank dives in nearby reefs (with/without equipment US$90/80) and day trips to Isla Catalina (US$69) and Isla Saona (US$69). Beginner and advanced PADI courses are also offered.

Casa Daniel DIVING
(Map p89; ☎809-833-0050; www.casa-daniel.com; Calle Principal/Calle Juan Brito, Bayahibe; ⏲8am-6pm Mon-Sat, to 4pm Sun) This German-run operator offers one-tank dives with/without equipment rental for US$54/47. Packages of six dives are US$290/243, 10-dive packages are US$445/365. PADI certification courses are available. Ask about accommodations packages. Day tours to Isla Saona come with lobster (US$74) or without (US$68). Half day tours to Isla Catalina run US$47.

Beaches

Playa Bayahibe BEACH
(Map p89) Much of Playa Bayahibe, the town beach to the right of the parking lot, is occupied by dozens of motorboats waiting to ferry tourists to Isla Saona. There's a relatively small, uninviting and narrow stretch of sand between the last of these and the start of the all-inclusive Dreams La Romana – the beach here is restricted to guests of the resort.

Playa Dominicus BEACH
(Map p90) The advantage of staying in Dominicus Americanus is being able to walk to Playa Dominicus, a beautiful stretch of thick, nearly-white sand, and good water for swimming. It does tend to get crowded, especially because there's easy public access via a parking lot at the far eastern end of the enclave, which means no cutting through hotels or restaurants to get to the beach.

Tours

Virtually every hotel in Dominicus Americanus offers a wide variety of tours. Most are more expensive than those arranged through one of the two dive shops in Bayahibe, or from Max Tours. The two major dive shops have multilingual guides and instructors, with Spanish, English, German, French and Italian spoken, and can accommodate groups of both snorkelers and divers.

One of the more enjoyable ways of spending a few hours exploring the coastline is to take a **sail** on a local's fishing boat. No doubt you wouldn't have to ask many people before finding a taker; one particularly nice man who can read the winds like a soothsayer is **Hector Julio Brito** (☎829-285-4368), who charges US$130 for one to three people for a half-day trip. A longer outing, from 9am to 4pm to the *piscina natural*, will run around US$200.

Max Tours DIVING
(Map p90; ☎809-399-0225; www.maxtours-dominicus.com; Calle Eladia, Dominicus Americanus; ⏲8am-noon & 5-10pm) A friendly tour company in Dominicus Americanus. Full-day snorkel and beach trips to Isla Saona are USD$75, including a lobster feast on the more secluded beach in Mano Juan, away from the Spring Break mayhem of the hotel tour groups. Isla Catalina trips with snorkeling and snacks on the beach are US$47.

Festivals & Events

Every year on the Saturday of Semana Santa (late March/early April), Bayahibe hosts a **regatta** of handmade fishing boats. The race runs from the town cove to Catalina Island and back.

Sleeping

Bayahibe proper has several good budget hotels all within walking distance of one another; locals can point you in the direction of a family willing to take on temporary boarders. A stay here affords you excellent eating options and the chance to experience the rhythms of the town away from the masses. The enclave of Dominicus Americanus has several midrange and top-end options – the advantage here is that it's a short walk to an excellent beach. There is a string of all-inclusive resorts in Dominicus

Americanus and along the road between there and Bayahibe; only Dreams La Romana is within walking distance of town.

★Villa Baya HOTEL $
(Map p89; ☎809-833-0048; www.hotelvillabaya.com; Calle Tamarindo 1, Bayahibe; r without/with air-con from US$40/60; ❄📶) With its shaded palapa, floral-draped fringes and large rooms, this is Bayahibe's best bang for the buck. The Italian-owned villas all come with patios and stone flooring while the air-con rooms have kitchens and living room spaces. Room 5 is a steal for US$50, featuring top-floor views and a wrap-around terrace. The hotel's residential location *might* equal quieter.

Cabañas Taíno CABAÑAS $
(Map p89; ☎829-924-9409; centralmico@yahoo.com; Calle Principal/Calle Juan Brito, Bayahibe; r without/with air-con RD$900/1200; ❄📶) Cabañas Taíno, under new ownership, is a perfectly doable budget choice located in the center of the action in town. Pop your head in before making a decision. It has simple rooms with basic furnishings, minibars, small porches, private bathrooms with hot water (hopeless pressure) and working wi-fi in the rooms – the big advantage here over similarly-priced options.

Bring earplugs: rooms with fans are extremely loud due to the blasting music coming from the nearby bar.

Hotel Bayahibe HOTEL $$
(Map p89; ☎809-833-0159; www.hotelbayahibe.net; Bayahibe; s/d/tr incl breakfast US$40/80/100; ❄📶) The staff is cute, friendly and not particularly service-oriented, but what you get for your money here means the Bayahibe has the some of best value rooms in town. This three-story modern building is easily noticeable, since it's the biggest around. Large, colorful rooms are very comfortable with cable TV, balconies, small bathtubs and some even boast good views. Breakfast is served on the seafront at Restaurante Doña Clara. One bummer is wi-fi is restricted to common areas only.

Villa Iguana GUESTHOUSE $$
(Map p89; ☎809-757-1059; www.villaiguana.de; Calle 8, Bayahibe; r without/with air-con US$49/59, 1-bedroom apt without/with air-con US$69/79, penthouse US$120; ❄📶) This friendly German-owned hotel has 14 well-kept rooms and apartments, the former a bit cramped but colorful, while some of the newer apartments in the modern annex next door are a wonderfully comfortable deal for the price. A simple US$5 breakfast is served in a covered-over indoor patio area for all rooms without kitchens. The penthouse, with its own small pool, is a little rooftop oasis that beckons longer stays.

Hotel Eden HOTEL $$
(Map p90; ☎809-833-0856; www.santodomingovacanze.com; Av La Laguna 10, Dominicus Americanus; r/tr US$71/90; ❄📶🏊) A good choice for those seeking hotel-style comfort, amenities and service alongside peace and quiet (there are birds chirping here). Because it's located on the access road to the resort area, you might confuse the Eden for a hotel somewhere in Arizona or Florida, just not necessarily on a Caribbean beach. The pool area and grounds are attractive and all rooms come with a king-sized bed.

Cabaña Elke HOTEL $$
(Map p90; ☎809-833-0024; www.viwi.it; Av Eladia, Dominicus Americanus; s/d RD$3000/5000; ❄📶🏊) Sandwiched between the road and a high fence marking the boundary of the Viva Wyndham Dominicus Beach property, Elke's rooms are arranged in two long narrow rows. Rooms are airy, especially the split-level doubles, but the furnishings are aging. There's a nice pool area with lounge chairs, but unfortunately no view.

★Iberostar Hacienda Dominicus RESORT $$$
(Map p90; ☎809-688-3600; www.iberostar.com; Playa Dominicus; all-incl s/d from US$220/360; ❄@📶🏊) An impeccably maintained resort doused in soothing pastels, the Iberostar Hacienda Dominicus has beautifully landscaped grounds – most of the buildings surround quiet interior courtyards with beautiful historic Spanish tiles and there are duck-strewn ponds and tranquility-inducing fountains throughout. Some big, gaudy art means the whole thing teeters precariously on the fortunate side of Vegas flamboyance, but it wins points for restraint in the end. Standard rooms aren't as grandiose as the common areas – they're even cramped – but the awesome pool (with its Jacuzzi island), huge beach (with a picturesque lighthouse bar) and newly renovated spa is where you'll be spending your time, anyway.

Bayahibe has a surprising number of good restaurants for a town of its size. Most offer relaxing waterfront seating and fresh seafood, with Italians running the show in most cases. Dominicus Americanus has a number of modern tourist-ready restaurants serving a mix of international standards and fish, though few have views.

L'Angelo di Liz ICE CREAM **$**
(Map p90; Calle La Laguna, Dominicus Americanus; gelato RD$80-150; ⏲8am-12:30pm & 3:30-10:30pm) The good Italian gelato here helps ward off heatstroke. Illy espresso as well.

★**Mama Mia** ITALIAN **$**
(Map p89; Plaza La Punta, Bayahibe; mains RD$150-250; ⏲noon-3:30pm & 7-10:30pm Tue-Sun) It's hard to eat this well for these prices in the DR, but this place specializes in classic pasta recipes like *all'amatriciana* (tomato sauce, bacon and chilli – our fave), carbonara, *all'arrabiata* and *aglio, olio e peperoncino* (garlic, olive oil and chilli powder), as well as local adaptations *(lambi*, or conch, in fresh tomato sauce). It's an endlessly charming dive near Bayahibe Beach, overseen by a one-woman-show in the kitchen. Dishes are simple – concentrating on flavor nuance rather than huge portions or other bells and whistles – and priced to please.

Mare Nuestro ITALIAN **$$**
(Map p89; www.marenuestro.com; cnr Calle Principal/Calle Juan Brito & Calle La Bahia, Bayahibe; mains RD$250-700; ⏲11am-2am Tue-Sun; 📶) Freezing red wine aside, this is the classiest restaurant in Bayahibe, a breezy, 2nd-story patio affair overlooking beautiful views day and night of the turquoise sea. Lanterns and tablecloths add a romantic ambiance and the food is equally impressive, offering excellent homemade pastas, pages of salads, scrumptious fish dishes and melt-in-your-mouth risottos, among others. There is a small but trendy lounge on the ground floor.

Chikyblu SUSHI, ITALIAN **$$**
(Map p89; www.chikyblu.com; Bayahibe; mains RD$300-700; ⏲11:30am-11pm Wed-Mon; 📶) It's normally a bad idea to recommend a place that does pizza and sushi, but Chikyblu pulls it off. It's equally popular for thin-crust pies (RD$150 to RD$400) as its creative sushi rolls (RD$270 to RD$285). Give the Caribe Roll a try: shrimp tempura, jalapeño and avocado, reminiscent of some of Los Angeles' best sushi creations. If you're a connoisseur, it might not cut it, but considering your environs, it shouldn't make you angry. It's as cute as can be, too, decked out in knick-knacks, and is right next to the sea.

Saona Cafe CAFE **$$**
(Map p89; www.saonacafe.com; Calle La Bahia, Bayahibe; mains RD$50-895; ⏲11am-midnight Tue-Sat, 8am-6pm Sun; 📶) The French-Canadian owners of this Bayahibe hotspot surely scoured the coast to see what everyone else *wasn't* serving, then put it on their menu: bagels, French toast, *poutine*, excellent fries, fried chicken burgers – you can even try lionfish. It's also wildly popular for burgers and beers.

Unfortunately on our visit, the owners were vacationing and service was slower than the light breeze and our cheeseburger tasted distinctly like overcooked McDonald's. Still, local North Americans and Europeans swear by it.

Cafecito de la Cubana CAFE **$$**
(Map p89; Playa Bayahibe; mains RD$140-600; ⏲11am-11pm Wed-Mon) One of several little kiosks set up around the parking lot and beach area in town, la Cubana is particularly charming and serves a well-rounded menu that includes authentic Cuban dishes such as those famous sandwiches (RD$170), *ropa vieja* (shredded meat in tomato sauce; RD$320) and Cuban-style coffee.

★**Las Palmas** SEAFOOD **$$$**
(Map p90; Playa Dominicus Americanus; Prix-fixe from US$40; ⏲dinner by reservation) This 2013 newcomer has quickly made waves for its made-to-order fresh lobster – you need reservations so they know to send a fisherman out to catch them for you! The prix-fixe menu includes fresh fish, drinks and desserts and as far as experiences go around here, it pretty much tops the list. It's sandwiched between the Wyndham and Iberostar resorts, next to the public beach parking lot.

Supermercado La Defensa SELF-CATERING
(Map p89; off Calle Principal/Calle Juan Brito, Bayahibe; ⏲8am-9pm) To stock up on your own rations, Supermercado La Defensa is the biggest market in town.

Drinking

★**Lost Bar** BAR
(Calle Flor de Bayahibe, Bayahibe) One of the best bars this side of the DR sits hidden in a residential neighborhood less than five minutes walk from the water. A local expat favorite – they thought tourists would never find it. Guess again! A gaggle of hipster Italian waitresses oversee the dark and sexy, multiroom space with picnic and pool tables and a swing!

WORTH A TRIP

BOCA DE YUMA

The antithesis of big DR tourism, the ramshackle little town of Boca de Yuma plays the role of the end-of-the-road like a seasoned actor in an indie film festival flick that only the critics love. Off the beaten track in terms of mass tourism, the town sits at the southeast end of Hwy 4 and offers rough, unpaved roads and half-finished buildings leading to a quiet seaside promontory where waves crash dramatically into the rocky shore. Like a town forgotten, Boca de Yuma's slow-pace, near-apocalyptic crowdless feel is its appeal, along with cinematic sunrises and a wealth of fresh seafood, and makes for a great little getaway from the grandiose resorts that are encroaching on the town in all directions.

Several kilometers west of town on the way toward the entrance of the national park is **Cueva de Berna**, a large cave with scattered Taíno pictographs (and graffiti) and stalactite and stalagmite formations. A caretaker usually sits outside the entrance and will gladly accompany you up the rickety ladder and deep into the cave (a small gratuity is appreciated). To find the cave, follow the paved road that runs along the ocean wall west (away from the mouth of the river) past the cemetery and follow the sign; you need no more than 15 minutes inside. There is suppose to be an admissions charge but it was deserted when we came through.

A few kilometers further west down the same road (4WD only), past several ranches with grazing cows and horses, is the eastern entrance of **Parque Nacional del Este** (admission RD$100). A park ranger sleeps at the small cabin just past the gate, and should be around for much of the day, but there's little formality or information as few people enter here. A long, easy-to-follow road hugs the coast for many kilometers and involves some hiking up a moderately steep slope to make it to the top of the rugged bluffs with beautiful views of the ocean. There is good birdwatching here if you're out early enough.

While **Playa Blanca** is a pretty, mostly deserted beach about 2km east of town on the other side of the river, the hassles of getting here may not make the trip worth it. The easiest and most expensive option is to hire a boat from one of the boatmen congregated at the mouth of the river at the east side of town (round trip RD$1200). One alternative is to have them ferry you to the other side of the river and walk to the beach; however, the path is hard to find and follow, and the sharp rocks are a hazard.

Should you stay the night, bed down at **El Viejo Pirata** (☎809-780-3236; hotelelviejopirata@hotmail.com; Calle Duarte 1; r RD$1200; ❄ 🏊). Both forlorn and inviting at the same time, this Italian-owned hotel with eight clean, modern rooms produces these contradictory feelings. It could stand to be friendlier as well, but its appeal lies in its off-the-beaten-path ethos, just the same as Boca de Yuma itself.

Almost a dozen restaurants are lined up along the road overlooking the ocean. Try **Restaurant La Bahia** (mains RD$200-500; ⊙8am-10pm), owned and operated by a friendly Dominican family.

To find it, head south on Calle Nuevo Bayahibe and hang a left at the third street on the left – there should be a boat on the corner – it's about 300m on the left.

Super Colmado Bayahibe BAR

(Map p89; Bayahibe) Town square, town bar and town radio station (whether you want it or not) rolled into one, this *colmado* is where locals gather to talk, drink and listen to music all day long.

Information

BanReservas Offers ATMs in both its Bayahibe (Calle Juan Brito) and Domincus Americanus (Calle Eladia) branches.

Centro Clinico Bayahibe (Calle El Tamarindo 15, Bayahibe; ⊙24hr) English and Italian are spoken at this small home clinic run by friendly Dr Gustavo Brito Morel.

El Mundo (Calle Eladia, Dominicus Americanus; ⊙9am-8pm Mon-Sat, 9am-1pm & 4:30-8pm Sun) Can arrange day-old editions of world newspapers like the *New York Times*, *Le Monde and Corriere della Sera* with a day's notice, plus souvenirs, snacks and sundries. It's also a bar, restaurant (mains RD$150 to RD$700) and social gathering point.

Farmacia Job (Calle La Bahia, Bayahibe; ⊙8am-9pm Mon-Sat, 8am-6pm Sun) Pharmacy across from Restaurant La Bahia de Capitan William Kidd.

Lavandaría da Franco (Calle Cayuco, Dominicus Americanus; per piece RD$50-90; ⏲9am-6pm Mon-Sat) Independent laundry facility.

Politur (☎809-833-0019; Calle Principal/Calle Juan Brito, Bayahibe; ⏲24hr) Tourist police at the entrance to Bayahibe.

Getting There & Away

A single road of 7km or so connects the coastal highway with Bayahibe. The road splits about 1km south: the right fork heads to Bayahibe, the left on to Dominicus Americanus.

Guaguas are the only means of public transportation to and from Bayahibe. Servicio de Transporte Romana–Bayahibe *guaguas* leave from a stand of trees across from Super Colmado Bayahibe in the center of town, a block north of the Hotel Bayahibe. Services run to La Romana (RD$60, 20 minutes, every 20 minutes from 7:20am to 7:40pm). You can also catch a ride over to Dominicus Americanus (RD$25, five minutes, every 20 minutes). For Higüey, it's best to connect in La Romana.

Sichotuhbared (Map p90; ☎809-833-0059) is the local taxi union, with a stop next to the Viva Wyndham Dominicus Beach. One-way rates for one to five people include La Romana airport (US$35), Casa de Campo (US$35), Higüey (US$45), and Bávaro resorts (US$110). Be sure to agree upon a price before you get in the car.

To rent a car, look for **MTM** (☎809-949-8162; Calle Cayuco, Dominicus Americanus) in Dominicus Americanus or **D&M** (☎809-833-0047; Nuevo Bayahibe) in Bayahibe.

Higüey

POP 168,501

Higüey is a hectic, working-class hub kept in line by its giant concrete basilica, famous around the country and the lone needle worth visiting in this massive concrete haystack surrounded by sugarcane fields in all directions. The basilica, rising from the center of town like an arched stone rocket set to launch, is both odd and beautiful and well worth a day trip or pit stop while passing through – in fact, you're bound to end up here at some point traveling around the southeast. If not, its prominence on the RD$50 note will have to do.

Sights

Basilica de Nuestra Señora de la Altagracia CHURCH

(admission RD$40; ⏲6am-7pm) From the outside, this is a strange mixture of the sacred and profane. A utilitarian concrete facade, not far removed from a military bunker, is topped by an elongated arch reaching high into the sky. But it's one of the most famous cathedrals in the country because of the glass-encased image of the Virgin of Altagracia housed inside.

According to the story, a sick child in Higüey was healed when an old man thought to be an Apostle asked for a meal and shelter at the city's original church, the Iglesia San Dionisio. On departing the following day, he left a small print of Our Lady of Grace in a modest frame. Since that day the 16th-century image has been revered by countless devotees, upon whom the Virgin is said to have bestowed miraculous cures. Originally housed in the handsome Iglesia San Dionisio, the image of the Virgin has been venerated in the basilica since the mid-1950s. Designed by Frenchmen Pierre Dupré and Dovnoyer de Segonzac, and completed in 1956, the long interior walls consist mostly of bare concrete and approach each other as they rise, connecting at a rounded point directly over the center aisle. The entire wall opposite the front door consists of stained glass and is quite beautiful, especially in the late afternoon when the sunshine casts honey-colored shadows across the floor.

The new **Museo de la Altagracia** (Calle Arzobispo Nouel; Dominicans/foreigners RD$400/US$5; ⏲9am-5pm Tue-Sun) is an extremely well-done and modern museum tracing the history of religion and culture in the DR back to the 18th century. It is on the grounds of the basilica, surrounded by an impressive sea of palm trees, and well worth a pop in.

Festivals & Events

Thousands of people travel to Basilica de Nuestra Señora de la Altagracia in a moving and intense homage to the Virgin every January 21. Pilgrims, dressed in their finest, file past the Virgin's image, seeking miracles and giving thanks. The church's bells chime loudly throughout the day. In August, the city's streets fill up with cowboys on horseback who ride in from all directions for the **Fiesta Patronal** (Festival of the Bulls).

Sleeping & Eating

Hotel Don Carlos HOTEL $

(☎809-554-2344; cnr Calle Juan Ponce de León at Sánchez; r old/new bldg RD$1250/1490; ❄📶) Only a block west from the basilica, Don Carlos is a maze of rooms. It's friendly and professional, but deserving of only a night when passing through. Ask to stay in the newer annex, with

DON'T MISS

CASA PONCE DE LEÓN

Outside the town of San Rafael del Yuma, east of the two-lane highway linking Higüey to Boca de Yuma, is a fine rural Dominican town surrounded by fields in all directions, with dirt roads. Spanish explorer Juan Ponce de León had a second residence built in the countryside near San Rafael del Yuma during the time he governed Higüey for the Spanish crown. Still standing nearly 500 years later, **Casa Ponce de León** (Ponce de León House; admission RD$50; ⏲9am-5pm) is now a museum to this notorious character of the Spanish conquest.

Born in 1460, Ponce de León accompanied Christopher Columbus on his second voyage to the New World in 1494. In 1508 he conquered Boriquén (present-day Puerto Rico) and served as governor there from 1510 to 1512. While there, he heard rumors of an island north of Cuba called Bimini, which had a spring whose waters could reverse the aging process – the fabled fountain of youth. Setting off from Puerto Rico, Ponce de León reached the eastern coast of present-day Florida on April 2 1513, Palm Sunday, and named it Pascua Florida (literally 'Flowery Easter'). He tried to sail around the peninsula, believing it to be an island, but after realizing his mistake he returned to Puerto Rico. When he resumed his quest eight years later, landing on Florida's western coast, he and his party were attacked by Indians. Wounded by an arrow, Ponce de León withdrew to Cuba, where he died shortly after landing.

The residence-turned-museum is sparse but contains many original items belonging to Ponce de León, including his armor and much of his furniture. Also original are the candelabra and his bed; his coat of arms is carved into the headboard. Limited signs are bilingual.

If you have a car and are entering from the north, you'll encounter a fork in the road right past the police station. Bear left and then turn left onto a dirt road just before the cemetery (it's surrounded by a tall white wall and there's a sign). After 1.2km, you'll see a set of gates leading to a long access road on your right with a boxy stone building at the end, which is the museum.

modern and larger rooms; rooms in the older building are cramped and aged. Conveniences include an attached restaurant (mains RD$100 to RD$500; open for breakfast, lunch and dinner) – best to eat here due to Higüey's uninspiring dining scene – while the biggest inconvenience is the lobby-only wi-fi.

ℹ Information

Banco Leon (Av La Altagracia) ATM along the median.

BanReservas (Av La Altagracia) Has an ATM on the western end of the Av La Altagracia's median.

ℹ Getting There & Away

Air-con coaches to Santo Domingo (RD$250, two hours, every 15 minutes from 5am to 7pm) leave from the large **Aptpra** (☎829-537-5342; www.aptpra.com.do; Av Laguna Llana at Colón) terminal. There are at least two *expressos* per hour.

Guaguas to La Romana (RD$110, 45 minutes, every 30 minutes from 5am to 10pm) leave from the small **Sitraihr** (☎809-550-0880; Av la Altagracia) station on Av La Altagracia just west of Av Laguna Llana. For Samaná, walk a few meters east to **Asotraihs** (☎809-554-1177; Av la Altagracia 91) (it's hard to notice but the stop is in front of Banco Eden Henriquez) and take a bus or *guagua* to Hato Mayor (RD$130, 1¼ hours, every hour from 4:45am to 8:10pm) or El Seibo (RD$110, one hour, every 30 minutes from 5am to 7:30pm) and transfer to the bus for Sabana de la Mar, where there are ferries across the bay. Be sure to tell the driver that you are planning to connect to another bus, as they will often drop you right at the next terminal.

Guaguas and buses to Bávaro and Punta Cana (RD$130, one hour, every 15 minutes from 4:55am to 8:30pm) leave from the **Sitrabapu** (☎829-554-0452; Av La Libertad 60) terminal 1.2km east of the basilica.

PUNTA CANA TO SABANA DE LA MAR

Bávaro & Punta Cana

It wouldn't be out of line to equate the eastern coast of the Dominican Republic as a sort of sea and sun Disneyland – after all, it is here where the megalomaniacal all-inclusive resorts snatch up broad swaths of cinematic beaches faster than the real estate agents can get the sun-soaked sands on the market.

There are more than 40,000 hotel rooms from Punta Cana to El Macao, with more on the way, and for good reason: its beaches do rival those anywhere else in the Caribbean, both in terms of their soft, white texture and their warm aquamarine waters. Despite a lack of restraint on development in the area, the resorts and beaches here still manage to offer an idyllic Caribbean seascape for a seemingly endless crowd of sunseekers. But it's not all resorts and condos – the municipality has done a commendable job recently in either re-doing or paving all the main roads and adding sidewalks as well.

Punta Cana, shorthand for the region as a whole, is actually somewhat of a misnomer. The majority of resorts are scattered around the beaches of Bávaro, really nothing more than a series of small commercial plazas, and El Cortecito, a short strip of shops along a 'town beach'. Punta Cana (Grey-Haired Point), the easternmost tip of the country and where the airport is located, has some of the more luxurious resorts and Caribbean-hugging golf courses.

Sights

Indigenous Eyes Ecological Park & Reserve NATURE RESERVE
(829-470-1368; www.puntacana.org; admission adult/child US$25/12, with guided tour US$50/25; 8:30am-5pm) Though development may eventually cover every inch of the Dominican coastline, for now there are still large areas of pristine coastal plains and mangrove forests. About 500m south of (and part of) the Puntacana Resort and Club, this ecological park covers more than 6 sq km of protected coastal and inland habitat and is home to some 100 bird species (27 of which are indigenous species native only to the DR), 160 insect species and 500 plant species.

Visitors can take very worthwhile three-hour **guided tours** in English, French, German or Spanish through a lush 30-hectare portion of the reserve with 11 freshwater lagoons all fed by an underground river that flows into the ocean. The tour also includes a visit to the park's botanical and fruit gardens, iguana farm (part of a conservation program) and a farm-animal petting zoo.

The visitor center has a great collection of insects that was compiled by entomology students from Harvard, and interesting maps and photos of the area. The park is operated by the Puntacana Ecological Foundation, a nonprofit foundation created in 1994 that works to protect the area's ecosystems – including 8km of coral reef along the reserve's shoreline – and to promote sustainable tourism and hotel practices. Nearly 4 hectares of the reserve are dedicated to the Center for Sustainability, a joint project with Cornell and other American universities to survey and study native plants, birds and insects. Unfortunately, there is no hotel pickup service and only invited guests or guests of Puntacana Resort and Club can do self-guided tours; a roundtrip cab here including two to three hours waiting will cost around US$90 from Bávaro or El Cortecito.

Beaches

Superlatives describing the beaches here are bandied about like free drinks at a pool bar, but they're mostly deserved; keep in mind, however, that the best pieces of property have been claimed by developers and are either already occupied by all-inclusives and condos or will be in the near future. This means you will not be alone. In fact, you will be part of a beach-lounging crowd.

Public access is protected by the law, so you can stroll from less-exclusive parts like **Playa El Cortecito**, which tends to be crowded with vendors, to nicer spots in front of resorts – but without the proper color wrist bracelet you won't be able to get a towel or chair.

North of El Cortecito is **Playa Arena Gorda**, lined with all-inclusive resorts and their guests, many topless, riding around on banana boats, parasailing or just soaking in the sun. A further 9km north of here is the best accessible surf beach, **Playa del Macao**, a gorgeous stretch of sand best reached by car. It's also a stop-off for a slew of ATV (All-Terrain Vehicle) tours that tear up and down the beach every day – there's less noise at the far northern end of the beach.

In the other direction, south of Bávaro and El Cortecito, is **Playa Cabo Engaño**, an isolated beach that you'll need a car, preferably a 4WD, to reach.

Activities

Water Sports

Virtually every water activity is available but some involve a long commute to the actual site. Every hotel has a tour desk offering snorkeling, diving and boat trips to destinations such as Isla Saona (p89). Parasailing is done from the beach all over Punta Cana and Bávaro.

Bávaro & Punta Cana

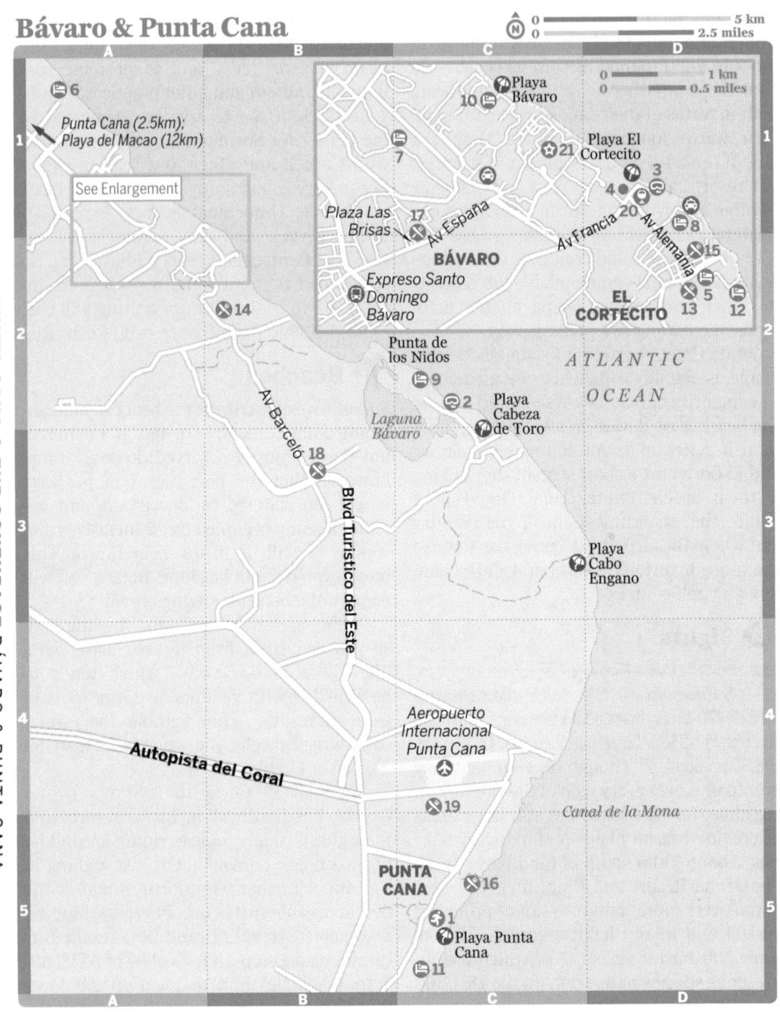

Marinarium SNORKELING

(www.marinarium.com; adult/3-12yr US$99/49.50) A popular family outing is a snorkeling trip to the Marinarium, a natural offshore pool near Cabeza de Toro, which is arguably more ecofriendly than other excursions. Rays, nurse sharks, tropical fish and patches of coral are all on hand.

Power Adventures SNORKELING, DIVING

(809-552-1597; www.power-adventures.com; El Cortecito; adult/child $79/39.50; tours 9am & 2pm;) Offers a 3½-hour snorkeling tour combined with power snorkeling (using a motorized propellent) and hooka diving, where you are attached to a leash-like breathing apparatus that allows you to reach depths of up to 4m. It's a great family option, though everyone digs it. Fruit and an open bar (after diving!) are bonuses.

Golf

La Cana Golf Course GOLF

(809-959-4653; www.puntacana.com; Punta Cana Resort & Club, Punta Cana; 7:30am-6pm) Punta Cana's top golf course is located at the area's top resort. The 18-hole course, designed by Pete Dye, has several long par fives and stunning ocean views. Green fees

Bávaro & Punta Cana

Activities, Courses & Tours

1 La Cana Golf Course C5
2 Marinarium C2
3 Power Adventures D1
4 RH Tours & Excursions D1

Sleeping

5 Bávaro Hostel D2
6 Hard Rock Hotel Punta Cana A1
7 Hostel Punta Cana C1
8 Hotel Cortecito Inn D1
9 NaturaPark Beach Ecoresort & Spa C2
10 Paradisus Punta Cana C1
11 Puntacana Resort & Club C5
12 Villas Los Corales D2

Eating

Balicana .... (see 12)
Brot .... (see 19)
13 Chickeeta Bonita's D2
14 El Burrito Taqueria B2
El Burrito Taqueria .... (see 19)
15 La Posada de Gladys D2
Ñam Ñam .... (see 5)
Passion by Martín Berasategui .... (see 10)
16 Restaurante Playa Blanca C5
17 Solo Pollo C1
18 Super Mercado Pola B3
19 Super Mercados Nacional C4

Drinking & Nightlife

20 Onno's D1

Entertainment

21 Mangú C1

are US$135/175 (including cart) for guests/nonguests for 18 holes or US$80 (guests only) for nine. Club rental is US$50 for 18 holes or US$25 for nine. Tee times may be booked online. Also part of the Punta Cana Resort is the Tom Fazio–designed **Corales Golf Course**, exclusive to Puntacana homeowners and Tortuga Bay guests; and **Hacienda**, also designed by Pete Dye.

Cap Canа GOLF
(☎809-469-7767; www.capcana.com; Punta Cana) Near La Cana is the site of a huge development project in the works, which has one Jack Nicklaus Signature golf course already complete and open for play (nonguest greens fees May to October US$275, November to May US$375) and two more on the way.

Tours

Every resort has a separate tour desk that can arrange all manner of trips, from snorkeling and deep-sea fishing to the popular Isla Soana trip. A handful of locals set up on El Cortecito beach offer one-hour **snorkel trips** (per person US$25) and two-hour **glass-bottom boat rides** (per person US$35) to a nearby reef and **parasailing** (15min US$85). Most also offer **deep-sea fishing trips** (minimum 4 people, 4 hours, per person US$75) for marlin, tuna, wahoo and barracuda. There are a few pushy kiosks near the north end of the beach, although the odds are that you'll be approached by touts as soon as you set foot in town and on the beach. The most popular day tour by far is the day trip to Isla Saona (p89).

RH Tours & Excursions DAY TOUR
(☎809-552-1425; www.rhtours.com; El Cortecito; ⏰9am-5pm Mon-Sat) If you're looking to explore the region, this tour operator offers a number of decent day trips for tourists. Popular excursions include exploring Parque Nacional Los Haitises (US$128), boat trips to Isla Saona (US$92 to US$118) and tours of Santo Domingo's Zona Colonial (US$77). All trips include lunch and drinks. English, German and Spanish are spoken.

Bávaro Runners DAY TOUR
(☎809-455-1135; www.bavarorunners.com) Well-established outfitter offering a range of tours, including all-day trips taking in a sugarcane plantation, cigar museum, beach and horseback riding.

X Bike MOUNTAIN BIKING
(☎809-758-0113; jhsmfb71@yahoo.com) Need to shed some all-inclusive calories? The friendly Joaquin can get you out of the resorts and into the mountains, with half-day mountain-bike trips to Miches and Constanza and overnight trips to Jarabacoa. Prices start from US$50 per person.

Sleeping

For resorts in the area, walk-in-guests are about as common as snowstorms; if you can convince the suspicious security guards that your intentions are innocent and make it to the front desk, you'll be quoted rates that absolutely nobody staying at the resort is paying. Book all-inclusive vacations online or through a travel agent, as they can offer discounts of up to 50% off rack rates. Bear in mind that most resorts cater to a particular

WORTH A TRIP

DOWN UNDER IN THE DR

For something down'n'dirty, check out **Cueva Fun Fun** (809-553-2656; www.cuevafunfun.com; Rancho Capote, Calle Duarte 12, Barrio Puerto Rico, Hato Mayor; adult/child US$155/110), which runs spelunking trips to one of the largest cave systems in the entire Caribbean. The day includes a horseback ride, a walk through a lush forest, a 20m abseil and 2km walk through the cave, which involves a good deal of sploshing and splashing in the underground river. Breakfast is provided, as is the equipment, including boots, harness, crash helmet and colorful jumper outfits – the overall effect is of a group of disposable extras for a James Bond baddie in a missile silo. Trips are generally booked as groups from hotels in the Bávaro/Punta Cana area, a 2½-hour drive away, but singles or small groups can piggyback on with enough advance notice.

niche, whether it's families, honeymooners, golfers or the Spring Break crowd.

There is finally a blossoming hostel scene in Bávaro, a refreshing alternative for independent travelers.

Bávaro

★Bávaro Hostel HOSTEL $
(809-931-6767; www.bavarohostel.com; Av Alemania, Edificio Carimar 4A, Bávaro; dm US$22, r US$40-45;) This new hostel, mere meters from the beach, occupies several rooms in a four-story building in the heart of Los Corales and is run by an immensely friendly half-Dominican, half-English brother-sister team. Given the dearth of independent lodgings in Punta Cana, it has quickly positioned itself as the much-needed traveler hub in the area. Choose between four- and six-bed mixed dorms and eight private rooms divided within various apartments that each share a common kitchen. Everything can be arranged here, including a gaggle of new friends to hit the bars with.

Hostel Punta Cana HOSTEL $
(809-505-8090; www.hostalpuntacana.com; Calle Italia, Residencial Nautilus, Bávaro; dm US$20-25, r US$50; @) A pretty remarkable deal for a hostel, this newcomer occupies three buildings inside a residential condominium complex, complete with a pool, gym, restaurant and spa. Air-conditioned dorms come in four- and six-bed versions, but its the private rooms – basically luxury apartments with marble floors, large kitchens and terraces, that are the true steal.

The only bummer about staying here is you are a bit isolated from the action, but it's a 10-minute walk to White Sands beach or hop on a free bike. If you arrange with the hostel, they'll fetch you from the bus station (US$5) or airport (US$25).

Villas Los Corales APARTMENT $$
(809-552-1262; www.los-corales-villas.com; Playa Bávaro; r US$90-300;) This small Italian-owned development has none of the grandiose ambitions of the nearby all-inclusives to be all things to all people. For those seeking more-modest surroundings and a community feel, Los Corales will do. Of the 50 or so apartments, all have small private patios and balconies, and private kitchenettes; some have oceanfront views.

Some of the cheapest options are a bit musty – it's worth dropping an extra US$30 to their US$120 category. In addition to the excellent Balicana (p102), there's an Italian restaurant, as well as a bar, holistic spa, small fitness center and swimming pool.

Hotel Cortecito Inn HOTEL $$
(809-552-0639; www.hotelcortecitoinn.net; El Cortecito; r incl breakfast US$60;) One of the few independent, reasonably priced choices in the area. Smileless service, confrontational staff and uninspiring breakfasts are the rule, but the rooms can be spacious and the pool and renovated grounds pleasant enough. Expect to leave your ID at reception.

★Paradisus Punta Cana RESORT $$$
(809-687-9923; www.melia.com; Playa Bávaro; all-incl d from US$446; @) Almost jungly and discerningly quiet, this resort feels nothing like most in the area. It attracts singles and families alike and takes appreciated steps to keep them separate where desired. The madeover standard rooms feel more urban arthouse than Caribbean and the 190 newer Reserve rooms feature lush courtyards, modern art, patios and Jacuzzi tubs for two.

Both the large and winding main pool and the beach (full of day beds) are gorgeous, and the separate Royal Services pool feels like a Roman bath. Kids get batting cages and a climbing wall, adults 12 restaurants, including Passion by Martín Berasategui (p102), considered by most to be Punta Cana's top restaurant. Everybody wins.

NaturaPark Beach Ecoresort & Spa HOTEL **$$$**
(809-221-2626; www.blau-hotels.com; Cabeza de Toro; d from US$218;) NaturaPark has a narrow beach outside the village of Cabeza de Toro, halfway between Bávaro and Punta Cana. From the Lincoln Logs–style recycled coconut wood lobby furniture to the beautiful free-growing mangroves on the property, it's all got a sustainable edge and the resort has won awards for reducing its environmental impact.

It's extra popular with Canadians and those who care more about reducing their carbon footprint than hopping in and out of bars and clubs at night. The pool is a bit small, but the beach is quite nice. Free-range swans, geese and flamingos and the Laguna Bávaro creeping on its doorstep means nature is never too far away.

Hard Rock Hotel Punta Cana RESORT **$$$**
(809-731-0099; www.hardrockhotelpuntacana.com; Playa Macao; all-incl d from US$559;) Imagine Las Vegas with a Caribbean sea. This den of decadence and cool sits atop Punta Cana's list of bold and beautiful resorts. The lobby feels like a rock-and-roll hall of fame, with memorabilia galore, including Madonna's sequined-covered limo. It caters to a diverse hipster crowd.

The gorgeous casino is the DR's largest and there are 13 pools (seven oceanfront), 17 restaurants and 10 bars, so you're never far from the party on the sprawling grounds. But why not party in your room? They feature party-size Jacuzzis at the foot of the beds. The latest bells and whistles include the revamped 18-hole Cana Bay Palace Punta Cana Golf Club and chef's Kerry Simon's Simon Mansion & Supper Club (mains US$18 to US$35; no beach attire) – definitely one of the trendiest restaurants in Punta Cana.

Punta Cana

Even though it's commonly used as shorthand for the vacation area of the southeast, Punta Cana actually refers to the area just east and south of the airport.

Puntacana Resort & Club RESORT **$$$**
(809-959-2714; www.puntacana.com; Punta Cana; d incl breakfast from US$382;) Famous for its part-time residents like Julio Iglesias, Oscar de la Renta and Mikhail Baryshnikov, this discerning and huge resort is also notable for its environmental efforts, especially the associated ecological park across the street from the entrance to the resort. Unlike all-inclusives, however, lunch, dinner and drinks aren't included in the rates.

The resort's previous centerpiece property, the Puntacana Hotel, has closed in favor of its brand new 200-room Westin near Playa Blanca (doubles from US$558), opened in late 2013, where every room has at least a partial ocean view. The complex also includes the 124-room Four Points Sheraton (doubles from US$382), a 2012 opener, poised as a modern business hotel at Puntacana Village. But the real coup here is the luxurious and discerning Tortuga Bay (designed by de la Renta; doubles from US$1285), a small enclave of one-, two- and three-bedroom luxury villas that sets the bar for luxury in Punta Cana. There are nine restaurants to choose from within the 60-sq-km complex, a Six Senses Spa, a modern PADI dive facility and a kiteboarding school, among numerous other distractions.

Eating

Resort buffets ensure most folks keep hunger pains at bay, but there are enough condos and villas and locals to support numerous independent eateries. Most are in various shopping centers in the area, easily reached by *motoconcho* or taxi.

The excellent **Super Mercados Nacional** (Puntacana Village, Punta Cana; 8am-9pm Mon-Sat, 9am-6pm Sun) is the best in Punta Cana. In Bávaro, the best option is the new and huge **Super Pola** (San Juan Shopping Center, Bávaro; 8am-10pm Mon-Sat, 9am-8pm Sun) near Cruce de Cocoloco. You'll find smaller supermarkets with daily essentials spread about many of Bávaro's plazas.

Solo Pollo DOMINICAN **$**
(Plaza Brisas de Bávaro, Bávaro; meals RD$250-300; 8am-1pm) A legion of locals flock to this simple *comida criolla* restaurant serving – as the name implies – only chicken. Juicy, perfectly-seasoned *pollo horneado* (baked

chicken) is the specialty of a menu that is scribbled out on a paper receipt each day.

Meals include rice, beans and salad and you can get out of here for under RD$300 even if you tack on a fresh *tamarindo* juice.

La Posada de Gladys DOMINICAN **$**
(Av Alemania, Bávaro; meals RD$130-500; ⏲7am-10pm) Get down with Dominicans at this pleasant, open-air palapa where the RD$175 plate of the day is the working man's staple in Bávaro. It's simple: a meat or fish dish accompanied by rice, beans and plantains, and made with local love.

Chickeeta Bonita's CAFE **$**
(Plaza Arenal Caribe, Bávaro; mains RD$130-300; ⏲8am-10pm; 📶) It's a far cry from Italian-style gelato, so we'll call it Canadian gelato based on the owner's citizenship. Popular flavors here include caramel brownie and chocolate orange, but all the house-made wares here go down easy in this heat. The gelato is available from noon but there's breakfast, sandwiches and nachos before and after that. Good book exchange, too.

★ **Ñam Ñam** CAFE **$$**
(www.nam-nams.com; Plaza Sol Caribe, Bávaro; mains RD$119-549; ⏲11am-3pm & 6-11pm Tue-Sun; ✎) Ñam Ñam means 'yummy' in Serbian: That ain't no lie. The friendly Belgradian couple behind this tiny Los Corales kitchen – they do it all themselves – know a thing or two about making your belly happy. The now-famous burgers, in regular, gourmet (minced with bacon and chili) and stuffed (with ham, cheese and mushrooms) versions are superb. But the menu of international comfort food doesn't stop there. There's also crepes, sandwiches, a wealth of veggie options and even Serbian *chevap*, a type of minced meat kebab from the Motherland. You can't go wrong dousing anything on the menu in the house-made pureed habanero-carrot hot sauce (serious burn) or the home-spun mayo with parsley. You're welcome.

Balicana ASIAN FUSION **$$**
(Villas Los Corales, Bávaro; mains RD$350-400; ⏲noon-3pm & 7-11pm Mon-Sat; 📶) Give your taste buds a shock: this pleasurable spot to eat offers all the Asian recipes normally missing in action in the DR. There's Thai (green curries, pad Thai), Indonesian (nasi goreng) and Malayasian (coconut curries), all devourable under a fan-cooled poolside palapa inside Villas Los Corales.

Brot CAFE **$$**
(Puntacana Village, Punta Cana; breakfast RD$85-325; ⏲8am-10pm Mon-Sat, 8am-5pm Sun; 📶) Slammed at breakfast, this is where Punta Cana comes for its bagel fix. Fab *bagelwiches* (also available on baguettes) are the call, in such rarely seen flavors as Hummus Supreme and Montecristo, among others. There's a wealth of salads and wraps, too. Homesickness cured!

El Burrito Taqueria MEXICAN **$$**
(Galerías Comerciales, Punta Cana; burritos RD$280-380; ⏲11am-4pm & 7-11pm; 📶) First sign of a great Mexican place is fresh chips and salsa, and our instincts proved correct at this small and festive *taqueria*. Excellent shoebox-sized burritos and a wide-range of tacos, enchiladas and margaritas should quell your cravings when you tire of ubiquitous fish and pasta choices. There's also a branch in **Bávaro** (Palmareal Shopping Village; ⏲11am-11pm Mon-Thu, to midnight Fri-Sun; 📶).

★ **Passion by Martín Berasategui** BASQUE **$$$**
(Paradisus Punta Cana, Bávaro ; 7-course prix-fixe guest/nonguest US$45/65; ⏲6:30-10pm) Chef Martín Berasategui hails from San Sebastián in Spanish Basque country – not a bad place to eat for those who might not know – and he packed a few recipes in his gastro-luggage on his way to overseeing what is easily Punta Cana's most memorable dining experience.

The seven-course tasting menu is the way to go, where you might encounter dishes such as *ajo blanco* (a cold, almond-based soup), a fabulous herb-crusted white tuna over creamy onions, a decadent pork confit and a vanilla-poached banana dessert that will leave your taste buds dancing to a different ditty in each bite. With six Michelin stars amid three restaurants to Berasategui's name, a meal here – even though he isn't over the stove – is priced in your favor; and the chef and line cooks have all worked under Berasategui's watch in Spain.

Restaurante Playa Blanca FUSION **$$$**
(Puntacana Resort, Punta Cana; mains US$12-29; ⏲11am-10:30pm; 📶) Flanked by an army of palms, this atmospheric, open-air restaurant is within the Puntacana Resort complex but open to the public and worth the trip. The beach here (Playa Blanca) is spectacular, and you can eat on the sand for lunch.

The hip, white-on-white space reeks of cool, but the Dominican comfort menu is highlighted by some wild cards such as spicy Dominican goat (US$14) and criolla-style *lambi* (conch; US$12) as well as staples like the wonderful grouper *al ajillo*. It's atmospheric at night, but its hard to skip the swirl of turquoise across your plate at lunchtime.

 Drinking & Entertainment

Nightlife is big business in Bávaro. Many resorts have nightclubs and there is a slew of independent bars in and around the beaches near Los Corales and El Cortecito. The hottest clubs of the moment change like baby's diapers – best to check the ground running.

Onno's — BAR

(www.onnosbar.com; Calle Pedro Mir, Bávaro) This open-air bar right on El Cortecito beach is without question the best independent spot to catch a cocktail, which you can down to DJs spinning Haitian Creole jams one minute, 'Gangnam Style' the next. Cool people, cool atmosphere.

Mangú — NIGHTCLUB

(www.mangudiscobar.com; Occidental Grand Flamenco, Bávaro; ⏲11pm-late) While most discos in Punta Cana come and go, Mangú perseveres; after over a decade in, locals still tout it as the best club in town. In high season, it's *merengue*, *bachata* and hip-hop on the bottom floor and EDM up the stairs. There is a sex tourism component at work here, but everyone else happily mixes in.

Information

Most of Bávaro's services are located in one of several outdoor plazas (malls) just north of El Cortecito, the small one-road enclave where there's another cluster of shops and tour companies.

Almost every major Dominican bank has at least one branch in the Bávaro area. The banks listed here have ATMs. You'll also find BanReservas/Banco Progresso ATMs at Plaza Estrella and a Banco Popular ATM at Barceló Dominican Beach Resort between El Cortecito and Los Corales.

All-inclusive hotels have small on-site clinics and medical staff, who can provide first aid and basic care. Head to one of several good private hospitals in the area for more serious issues.

Banco Popular (Av España, btwn Plaza Brisas de Bávaro and Plaza Estrella)

Centro Médico Punta Cana (www.grupo-rescue.com; Av España, Bávaro) Name notwithstanding, this is the main private hospital in Bávaro, with a multilingual staff, 24-hour emergency room and in-house pharmacy.

Farmacia Estrella (☎809-552-0344; Plaza Estrella, Bávaro; ⏲7:45am-midnight) This pharmacy offers delivery.

Hospitén Bávaro (www.hospiten.es; Carretera Higüey-Punta Cana) Best private hospital in Punta Cana, with English-, French- and German-speaking doctors and a 24-hour emergency room. The hospital is located on the old Hwy 106 to Punta Cana, 500m from Cruce de Verón.

Laundromat Punta Cana (Plaza Arenal Caribe, Bávaro; wash/dry RD$100/200; ⏲7am-8:30pm) Do-it-yourself laundry facility near Los Corales.

Pharmacana (Puntacana Village, Punta Cana; ⏲7am-10pm Mon-Sat, 8am-9pm Sun) Punta Cana's main pharmacy.

Politur (Tourist Police; ☎809-754-3082; www.politur.gob.do; Av Estados Unidos, Bávaro) The main Politur station is in Friusa, next to the bus terminal in Bávaro, with additional stations at the Punta Cana airport, Cabeza de Toro and and Uvero Alto.

Scotiabank Bávaro (Plaza Las Brisas); Punta Cana (Puntacana Village)

 Getting There & Away

From the small village of El Cortecito, the road follows an endless cluster of strip malls to a Texaco gas station, where you'll find the bus station and the route to resorts further north and Higüey to the southwest.

AIR

Several massive thatched-roof huts make up the complex of the **Aeropuerto Internacional Punta Cana** (PUJ; www.puntacanainternationalairport.com; Carretera Higuey-Punta Cana Km 45), located on the road to Punta Cana about 9km east of the turnoff to Bávaro. The arrival process, including immigration, purchase of a tourist card (US$10), baggage claim and customs, moves briskly.

Several airlines have offices here, including **Aeroflot** (☎809-959-3014; www.aeroflot.com), **Air France** (☎809-686-8432; www.airfrance.com), **American Airlines** (☎809-959-2420; www.aa.com), **British Airways** (☎in Santo Domingo 800-247-9297; www.ba.com), **Copa** (☎809-959-8021; www.copaair.com), **Delta** (☎809-959-2009; www.delta.com), **Gol** (☎809-959-3014; www.voegol.com.br), **Frontier** (☎809-959-3014; www.flyfrontier.com), **JetBlue** (☎809-959-1490; www.jetblue.com), and **United** (☎809-959-2039; www.united.com), but they are tucked away behind the scenes and hard to find. Other airlines serving the Punta Cana airport include Airtran, US Airways, Air Canada, Avianca, KLM, Spirit and Westjet, among a wide-range of charter carriers.

For domestic air connections, **Dominican Shuttles** (☎in Santo Domingo 809-738-3014; www.dominicanshuttles.com) has direct domestic flights on five- and 19-seat planes between

Punta Cana and Samaná's Aeropuerto Internacional Arroyo Barril (one way $159, 8am Monday, Wednesday, Thursday, Friday and Sunday).

There are Banco Popular ATMs located in the arrivals area in both terminals and an internet facility in Terminal A. Several car agencies have small booths near baggage claim, including **Avis** (☎809-688-1354; www.avis.com.do; Aeropuerto Internacional Punta Cana), **Budget** (☎809-959-1005; www.budget.com), **Hertz** (☎809-959-0365; www.hertz.com) and **Sixt** (☎829-576-4700; www.sixt.com).

Resort minivans transport the majority of tourists to nearby resorts, but taxis are plentiful. Fares between the airport and area resorts and hotels range between US$30 and US$80 depending on the destination.

BUS

The new 70km Autopista del Coral, from La Romana to Punta Cana, opened in 2012 to great fanfare, cutting drive time from Santo Domingo to Punta Cana by two hours. The toll charge runs RD$150.

The **bus terminal** is located on Av Estados Unidos in Friusa, near the main intersection in Bávaro, almost 2km inland from El Cortecito.

Expreso Santo Domingo Bávaro (☎809-552-1678; Av Estados Unidos) has direct 1st-class service between Bávaro and the capital (RD$400, three hours). Departure times in both directions are 7am, 9am, 11am, 1pm, 3pm and 4pm.

From the same terminal, **Sitrabapu** (☎809-552-0771; Av Estados Unidos), more or less the same company, has departures to La Romana at 6am, 8:20am, 10:50am, 1:20pm, 3:50pm and 6:20pm (RD$225, 1¼ hours); and to Higüey (RD$130, one hour, every 15 minutes, 3am to 10:30pm). To all other destinations, head for Higüey and transfer there. You can also get to/from Santo Domingo this way, but it's much slower than the direct bus.

Getting Around

Local buses start at the main bus terminal, passing all the outdoor malls on the way to El Cortecito, then turn down the coastal road past the large hotels to Cruce de Cocoloco, where they turn around and return the same way. Buses have the drivers' union acronym – Sitrabapu – printed in front and cost between RD$30 and RD$40 depending on distance. They generally pass every 30 minutes between 5am and 8pm, but can sometimes take up to an hour.

It is possible to take a local bus to the airport from Bávaro, but you will need to give yourself *at least* an extra hour to do so and you must change buses at Cruce de Cocoloco and/or Veron. Tell the driver you are going to the airport and he will drop you at the spot to switch buses. From the airport, don't count on any *guaguas* after 6pm.

Daytime traffic is sometimes gridlocked between the resorts clustered just north of Bávaro and El Cortecito. Despite the stop-and-go pace of driving, renting a car for a day or two is recommended if you prefer to see the surrounding area independently. Consider paying more for extra insurance coverage, especially if you'll be driving north toward Playa Limón, Miches and Sabana de la Mar. Some agencies allow you to drop off the car in Santo Domingo, usually for an extra charge, but check in advance. Rental agencies include **Thrifty** (☎809-466-2026; www.thrifty.com; Puntacana Village), **Europcar** (☎809-459-0177; www.europcar.com; Puntacana Village), **Avis** (☎809-954-0534; www.avis.com.do; Puntacana Village) and **Budget** (☎809-466-2028; www.budget.com; Puntacana Village), all conveniently together in the Car Rental Center at Puntacana Village; and **Budget** (☎809-466-2028; www.budget.com; Carr Bávaro (Av Barceló) Km 6.5), **Hertz** (☎809-466-0105; www.hertz.com; Carr Bávaro/Av Barcelo Km 5), **Europcar** (☎809-688-2121; www.europcar.com; near Plaza Punta Cana, Bávaro)and **National/Alamo** (☎809-466-1083; Carr Bávaro/Av Barceló Km 5) in Bávaro.

Otherwise, there are numerous taxis in the area – look for stands at El Cortecito, Plaza Bávaro and at the entrance of most all-inclusive places. You can also call a cab – try **Siutratural** (☎809-552-0617; www.taxibavaropuntacana.com). Fares vary depending on distance, but some examples include US$8 (pretty much minimum charge on a short trip within Bávaro), US$35 to the airport and US$40 to Playa Blanca. **Asobapuma** (☎809-820-5507; El Cortecito) water taxis also can be found on El Cortecito beach and cost between US$10 and US$50 per ride. *Motoconchos* congregate around Plaza Punta Cana in Bávaro and along the beach road in El Cortecito, and you can generally find one or two parked in front of the entrance to most resorts. Fares run around RD$500 to RD$100 within the El Cortecito/Bávaro area.

Playa Limón

Playa Limón, about 20km east of Miches and just outside the hamlet of El Cedro, is a 3km-long, isolated Atlantic beach lined with coconut trees leaning into the ocean – coveted property that you're likely to have to yourself for much of the time. Horseback-riding tours descend upon it a few hours a day, generally from late morning to early afternoon.

The rugged area surrounding Playa Limón has two important wetland areas, including Laguna Limón, a serene freshwater body of water surrounded by grassy wetlands and coastal mangroves. The lagoon feeds into the ocean on the eastern end of Playa Limón and is known for bird-watching; tours are organized by Rancho La Cueva. The other lagoon – **Laguna Redonda** – is just 5km away, but is more commonly visited from Punta El Rey.

At time of writing, the new Carretera Miches, a modern highway from Bávaro, was set to make Playa Limón a whole lot more accessible.

Sleeping & Eating

There is a second hotel tucked away next to Rancho La Cueva, Hotel Limón, but the Swiss owners had closed it during our research and its future was unclear. Check ahead to see if it has re-opened.

Rancho La Cueva HOTEL $
(809-519-7251; www.rancholacueva.com; s/d/tr with fan US$30/40/45;) Horses and pigs roam this out-of-the-way property that feels like a true find. The 10 large spick-and-span rooms are sparsely furnished and what furniture there is tends to be aged. An open-air restaurant hosts daily tour groups for a seafood buffet, but breakfast and dinner are taken from the restaurant, which sources mostly local seafood (mains RD$240 to RD$650).

The Austrian owner can arrange a trip that includes a visit to a coffee plantation, a ride in the mountains, a seafood buffet and a boat ride across the lagoon for US$65 per person (warning: includes brief cockfighting *gallera* stop) and he is building a small beach bar to provide minimal services for guests and locals at the beach.

Getting There & Away

The new highway from Bávaro to Miches, an extension of the Autopista del Coral, will cut the drive time to Miches from Bávaro to under one hour when finished. The new road passes within a few hundred meters of the turnoff to Playa Limón on the the very eastern edge of El Cedro. From the turnoff (there are several signs, though none are easy to see or read), head north on a rough dirt road (a normal car can make it if it's dry; otherwise a 4WD is recommended). Rancho La Cueva is about 3km down this road and the beach only another 500m. Keep in mind that the only gas stations between Otra Banda (the start of old Hwy 104) and Miches are in the town of Lagunas de Nisibón and El Cedro. From Playa Limón it's only 27km to Miches, about a 35-minute drive in your own vehicle – much faster when the highway is finished.

Guaguas running between Higüey (RD$135, two hours) and Miches (RD$80, 30 minutes) can be flagged down from the main road during daylight hours – just make sure you are on the right side of the street for where you want to go. If arriving, be sure to let the driver know that you want to get off in El Cedro; it's easy to miss. Then catch a *motoconcho* for the remaining 3km or so (RD$150).

Miches

POP 10,152

From the surrounding hills, Miches, on the southern shore of the Bahía de Samaná, is fairly picturesque. A slim 50m-high radio tower marks the geographic center of what appear to be well-ordered streets, and Playa Miches, just east of the town proper, looks inviting. Upon closer inspection, however, it's a fairly tumbledown place and the beach, though long and wide, is not very attractive. The water isn't good for swimming, mainly because the Rió Yaguada empties into the ocean here. Miches sometimes makes national headlines as the launching point for Dominicans hoping to enter the USA illegally, via the Mona Passage to Puerto Rico.

Sleeping & Eating

Hotel La Loma HOTEL $$
(809-553-5562; hotel.laloma@yahoo.es; Miches; r/tr RD$1600/1900;) Perched atop a hill at the end of a rather steep driveway, rooms here have commanding views of the city and bay to the north and sweeping mountaintops to the south. It's a comfortable place to stop for the night on your way to Sabana de la Mar, and it's the best place to stay in town. Rooms are sparse but large and clean and have equally spectacular views – the real draw here. Open for breakfast, lunch and dinner, the restaurant (mains RD$140 to RD$460) serves good food and huge portions.

Information

BanReservas (cnr Calle Fernando Deligne & Gral Santana) is at the western end of town, one block south of Calle Mella; there's a 24-hour ATM.

Getting There & Away

Keep in mind, the new Carretera Miches from Bávaro will cut drive times to Higüey from those mentioned here upon its completion.

Sitrahimi *guaguas* to Higüey (RD$180, three hours, every 30 minutes from 4:10am to 5:40pm) leave from a terminal at the Isla gas station at the east end of town just before the bridge. **Asochosin** *guaguas* going to and from Sabana de la Mar (RD$130, 1½ hours, every 30 minutes from 6:45am to 6pm) leave from the corner of Calle Mella and Calle 16 de Agosto.

PARQUE NACIONAL LOS HAITISES

Eight kilometers west of Sabana de la Mar, **Parque Nacional Los Haitises** (admission RD$100; ⊙7am-8pm) is certainly the best reason to visit this small bayside town. Its name means 'land of the mountains', and this 1375-sq-km park at the southwestern end of the Bahía de Samaná indeed contains scores of lush hills jutting some 30m to 50m from the water and coastal wetlands. The knolls were formed one to two million years ago, when tectonic drift buckled the thick limestone shelf that had formed underwater. The turnoff to the park is near the crossroads of Hwys 104 and 103, at the south end of town (near the bus stop). The road is passable in a normal car but pretty rough. The western side of the park is accessed via the new DR-7 highway to Samaná, about 75km north of Santo Domingo.

Los Haitises contains over 700 species of flora, including four types of mangrove, making it one of the most highly biodiverse regions in the Caribbean. Los Haitises is also home to 110 species of birds, 13 of which are endemic to the island. Those seen most frequently include the brown pelican, the American frigate bird, the blue heron, the roseate tern and the northern jacana. If you're lucky, you may even spot the rare Hispaniolan parakeet, notable for its light-green and red feathers.

The park also contains a series of limestone caves, some of which contain intriguing Taíno pictographs. Drawn by the native inhabitants of Hispaniola using mangrove shoots, the pictures depict faces, hunting scenes, whales and other animals. Several petroglyphs can also be seen at the entrance of some caves and are thought to represent divine guardians. **Las Cuevas de la Arena**, **La Cueva del Templo** and **La Cueva de San Gabriel** are three of the more interesting caves and shouldn't be missed.

The most intimate way to see the park is on a kayak excursion. Whale Samaná (p111) is an excellent outfitter offering trips outside whale season (April to December).

There is talk of extending the new highway to Sabana de la Mar, but that's still a few years off.

If you're passing through town, let the driver know you want to catch an onward bus and he will most likely drop you at the next terminal, saving you a *motoconcho* or taxi ride between the two.

Sabana de la Mar

POP 13,723

The literal and figurative end of the road, this small, ramshackle and largely forgotten town is the gateway to Parque Nacional Los Haitises. However, until the roadways in the area are improved, especially Hwy 104 east to Miches, Sabana will continue to miss out on sharing a slice of the economic pie from the growing number of tourists visiting the bay for whale-watching and Los Haitises tours. Sabana is the departure point for the passenger ferry across the bay to Samaná, as well as for the dangerous Mona Passage crossing to Puerto Rico, the first stop for many Dominicans hoping to make their way to the USA.

Tours

The **Paraíso Caño Hondo** (☎809-248-5995; www.paraisocanohondo.com) is a highly recommended hotel 9km west of town and 1km past the park entrance, and offers good tours inside Parque Los Haitises as well. Boat excursions range between RD$1250 and RD$4400 for groups of two to four depending on the extent of the tour, and hiking trips (RD$500 per guide) through the park's *bosque humedo* (humid forest) also can be arranged. During the humpback season, Paraíso organizes whale-watching tours (US$56 per person) in the waters near Samaná.

The **local guide association** has whale-watching tours in season (per person US$120), trips to Los Haitises (per person US$60) and Cayo Levantado (per person US$90). There are four or so that speak basic English. You'll find them in the small blue 'Tourist Information' office near the pier; or at the **Parque Nacional Los Haitises office** one block west of the town plaza. Both are on Calle Elupina Cordero, which parallels the seafront.

At the entrance to Los Haitises, **boatmen Joel** (☎809-225-0517) and **Tin** (☎809-225-0535) also offer to take visitors on tours of the park (RD$500 per person for groups of three to 10, RD$400 for 10 to 25). Groups of less than three people will pay RD$1500 for the boat. While the excursions are similar to those offered by the tour operators, background information on the sights is often less detailed and English is scarce.

Sleeping & Eating

The turnoff to Caño Hondo and Parque Nacional Los Haitises is a short distance north of the Miches intersection – look for a Brugal rum sign saying 'Caño Hondo'. There's a Texaco gas station at the entrance to town on the road to Hato Mayor as well as a La Isla 2km south.

★**Paraíso Caño Hondo** HOTEL **$$**
(809-248-5995; www.paraisocanohondo.com; s/d/tr incl breakfast RD$2040/3212/4437;) Nothing good comes easy and this quirky and rustic retreat, one of the more special places to stay anywhere in the DR and the antithesis of the all-inclusives for which the country is famous, won't persuade you otherwise. Coming upon Paraíso Caño Hondo so far out of the way after a long and rough road feels like an epiphany.

The Río Jivales, which runs through the 28-room property, has been channeled into 10 magical waterfall-fed pools, perfect for a soak any time of the day. Rooms are large and rustic, made mostly of wood, though extremely comfortable. Bathroom ceilings are made of aged dried palm fronds and energy-saving light fixtures are used throughout, giving the whole place a sustainable edge. Newer rooms in the hilltop annex (US$10 supplement) have spectacular views but are less sustainable than their older counterparts below. The *criolla* restaurant here is the best place to eat in the area any time of day (the hotel offers all-inclusive packages but it's cheaper to order from the menu á la carte). To find it, follow the 'Parque Nacional Los Haitises' sign toward Caño Hondo one block south of the intersection of Hwys 103 and 104 in town for around 9km down a nasty road.

Hotel Riverside HOTEL **$**
(809-556-7465; Av de los Héroes 75; r without/with air-con RD$400/600;) A block south of the *guagua* station is this place where you can lay your head for the night; a family rents out 14 or so large rooms next door to their home.

Restaurant Jhonson SEAFOOD **$**
(Calle Paseo Elupina Cordero 5; mains RD$220-550; 8:30am-midnight) Great seafood on the cheap. It's a simple Dominican place on the town square, walkable from the ferry pier.

Information

Sabana de la Mar is a small town with relatively few services. **BanReservas** (Calle Duarte) is three blocks south of the ferry pier and has an ATM.

Getting There & Away

Hwy 103, from Hato Mayor, which was being worked on at the time of research, descends from the hills straight into Sabana de la Mar, turning into Av de los Héroes before reaching a roundabout that leads to Av Duarte and Av Eliseo Demorizi (Calle Diego de Lira) to the east, the two one-way main streets, and eventually bumping right into the pier where the Samaná ferry leaves and arrives. Hwy 104 northeast from Miches intersects with the Higüey highway just outside (south) of town, but remains in awfully bad shape and is best avoided. *Guaguas* to Miches, Hato Mayor, El Seibo, Higüey and Santo Domingo all congregate at or near that intersection.

If you are coming from Miches in your own vehicle, you are better off going the long way round via El Seibo and Hato Mayor – it takes the same amount of time and is way less stressful – at least until the Carretera Miches becomes the Carretera Sabana de la Mar!

Guaguas leave from the entrance of town on Av de los Héroes, near the crossroads of Hwy 104 and Hwy 103. **Asotrasamar** *guaguas* headed to Santo Domingo (RD$250, 3½ hours, every 40 minutes from 4:15am to 5pm) stop along the way in Hato Mayor (RD$100, one hour) and San Pedro de Macorís (RD$160, two hours). **Asochosin** *guaguas* also provide service to Miches (RD$120, two hours, every 20 minutes from 6:35am to 5pm).

Passenger ferries across the Bahía de Samaná to Samaná depart from the town pier (RD$200, 1¼ hours, 9am, 11am, 3pm and 5pm). From there you can catch *guaguas* to Las Galeras, Las Terrenas or puddle-jump to other destinations on the north coast. Bad weather means rough seas and frequent cancellations, and some of the boats are rickety, making even a voyage under sunny skies a potentially seasickening experience for those with sensitive stomachs. Buy your ticket on the boat.

Taxis (809-479-3425) for up to three passengers head to Santo Domingo (US$200) and Punta Cana (US$200), among others.

CAR OR 4WD?

A regular car can continue west to Sabana de la Mar but it's a slow, painstaking journey – a 4WD is recommended. The road is particularly bad until Las Cañitas, from where it's then paved the remaining 13km, although that's not much of a reprieve in some parts. Eventually, the new highway should extend this far west. Until then, it's faster for regular cars to go around via El Seibo and Hato Mayor.

Península de Samaná

Includes ➡

Best Places to Eat

- El Cabito (p118)
- Mi Corazon (p124)
- La Terrasse (p124)
- Le Taínos (p118)
- Rincón Rubi (p118)

Best Places to Stay

- Peninsula House (p126)
- Chalet Tropical (p118)
- Eva Luna (p123)
- Casa Por Qué No? (p117)
- Hotel Atlantis (p126)

Why Go?

This small slither of land is the antithesis of the Dominican-Caribbean dream in the southeast, where resorts rule and patches of sand come at a first-class premium. Far more laid-back and, in certain senses, more cosmopolitan, Samaná offers a European vibe as strong as espresso; it's where escape is the operative word, and where French and Italian are at least as useful as Spanish. The majority come to gasp at the North Atlantic humpback whales doing their migratory song and dance from mid-January to mid-March, but the peninsula is no one-trick pony. Sophisticated Las Terrenas is the place for those who crave a lively social scene, and sleepy Las Galeras boasts several of the best and most secluded beaches in the Dominican Republic (DR).

When to Go

- **Mid-January to late March** Over 10,000 North Atlantic humpback whales put on a show of monstrous proportions in the Bahía de Samaná. February is the best month.
- **April** Bypass the whale-watching frenzy and have the peninsula to yourself. Crowds have thinned out considerably but weather remains pleasant before the summer heats up.
- **December** Enjoy drier days in early December, after the autumn rains have thinned-out significantly but the flood of domestic holidaymakers haven't yet descended.

History

Because of Bahía de Samaná's fortuitous geography – its deep channel, eastward orientation and easy-to-defend mouth, perfect for a naval installation – the Península de Samaná has been coveted, fought over and bought several times over. At least six different countries, including Haiti, France, Spain, the US and Germany, have either occupied the Samaná area or sought to do so.

Founded as a Spanish outpost in 1756, Samaná was first settled by émigrés from the Canary Islands. It was deemed a prize as early as 1807, during the brief French possession of Hispaniola. France's commander in Santo Domingo, an ambitious leader no doubt, proposed building a city named Port Napoleon in Samaná, but France lost the island before the plan could move forward.

After its independence from Spain, the DR was taken over by Haiti, which controlled Hispaniola from 1822 to 1844. During this period Haiti invited more than 5000 freed and escaped slaves from the US to settle on the island. About half moved to the Samaná area. Today, a community of their descendents still speaks a form of English.

During Haitian rule, France pressured its former colony to cede the Península de Samaná in return for a reduction in the debt Haiti owed it. Incredibly, Haiti had been forced to pay restitution to France for land taken from French colonists in order to gain international recognition. Of course, France never paid restitution to former slaves for their ordeal.

After independence from Haiti in 1844, the new Dominican government feared its neighbor would reinvade, so sought foreign

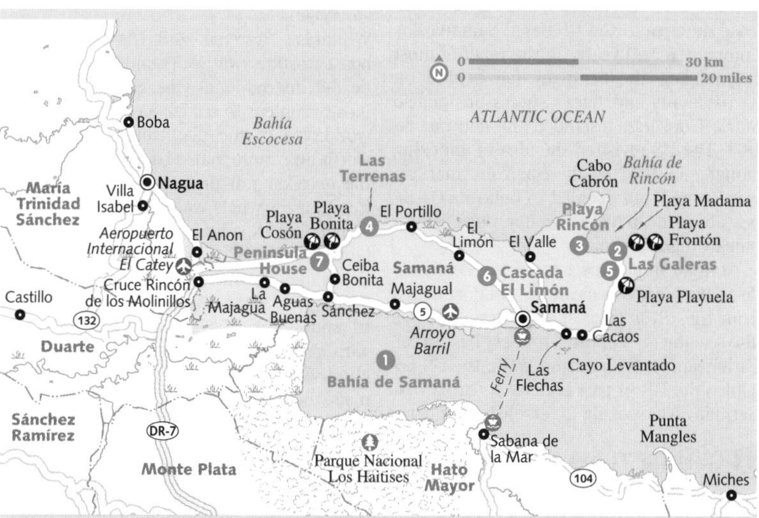

Península de Samaná Highlights

1. Taking in the spectacular sight of majestic humpbacks breaching and diving on a whale-watching trip in the **Bahía de Samaná** (p111)
2. Dining precariously above crashing waves on the edge of the Dominican Republic at **El Cabito** (p118) in Las Galeras
3. Losing yourself for hours on the gorgeous sands of **Playa Rincón** (p116)
4. Enjoying the sophisticated European atmosphere in the bars and restaurants of **Las Terrenas** (p123)
5. Lounging, snorkeling and lazing about the isolated beaches in end-of-the-road **Las Galeras** (p115), one of the few independent-traveler-friendly locales in the DR
6. Navigating the rugged and wet mountain scenery of Samaná's interior on the trip to 52m-high **Cascada El Limón** (p122)
7. Showering yourself in discerning luxury at **Peninsula House** (p126), one of the Caribbean's most distinguishing properties

assistance from France, Britain and Spain. The DR eventually resubmitted to Spanish rule in 1861, and Spain immediately sent a contingent of settlers to the Samaná area and reinforced the military installations on Cayo Levantado, a large island (and site of a luxury all-inclusive resort today) near the mouth of the bay.

Even after independence in 1864, the Península de Samaná remained a tempting prize for other countries. Beginning in 1868, the US, under President Ulysses S Grant, sought to purchase the peninsula from the DR in order to build a naval base there. Dominican president and strongman Buenaventura Báez agreed to the sale in order to obtain the money and weapons he needed to stay in power. However, the US Senate, under pressure from Dominican exile groups and strong opposition from France and the UK, rejected the proposal in 1871. A year later, Báez arranged to lease the area to the US-based Samaná Bay Company for 99 years. To the relief of most Dominicans, the company fell behind on its payments and Baez's successor, Ignacio María González, rescinded the contract in 1874. The US revisited the idea of annexing Samaná in 1897 as the Spanish-American war loomed, but decided to build its Caribbean base in Guantánamo Bay, Cuba after it quickly defeated Spain.

German intentions toward the Península de Samaná are less clear, but US documents from the 1870s suggest that Germany was also seeking to establish a military base in the Caribbean. In 1916, during WWI, the US occupied the DR in part because it feared that Germany was seeking to establish itself here.

Getting There & Around

Península de Samaná is accessible by air at Aeropuerto Internacional El Catey (AZS; otherwise known as Aeropuerto Internacional Presidente Juan Bosch; p236), on the highway between Nagua and Sánchez. It receives international flights from New York on **JetBlue** (☎809-200-9898; www.jetblue.com), London-Gatwick on **Thomson Airways** (www.flights.thomson.co.uk) and Toronto on **Air Canada** (www.aircanada.com) and **Westjet** (www.westjet.com). In high season, more cities in the US, Canada and Europe are serviced through charter flights.

One other airport – 'international' by name only – serves the peninsula. Domestic charter airlines serve Aeropuerto Internacional Arroyo Barril near Samaná, especially during whale-watching season.

Other than arriving by cruise ship, the only sea option is the regular ferry service between Samaná and Sabana de la Mar in the southeast. Cars are not allowed and the schedule is subject to the weather.

Journey time by car along the DR-7 highway from Santo Domingo to Samaná is less than two hours. The 102km or so stretch of highway begins at Autopista Las Américas DR-3 (30km east of Santo Domingo near the international airport) and ends at the Cruce Rincón de Molinillos, 18km west of Sánchez. The toll road – practically an autobahn compared to most other roads in the country – costs RD$412 for the entire journey.

EASTERN PENÍNSULA DE SAMANÁ

Samaná

POP 33,196

While Las Terrenas and Las Galeras can boast pristine swaths of sand and a sophisticated international vibe, Samaná town is mostly content to trudge along as the gritty workhorse of the peninsula. It would be worth little more than a backwards glance in the rearview mirror for most tourists were it not for the whale-watching on offer here.

The first expedition to see the North Atlantic humpback whales that pass through the waters off the town was in 1985, and every year since then, from mid-January to mid-March, the town springs into life with the influx of tourists coming to catch glimpses of these magnificent aquatic mammals. Because North Atlantic humpbacks find the bay water particularly suitable for their annual version of speed dating, the commercialization of this natural spectacle has single-handedly catapulted the town's tourism status – for a few months each year at least – to world-renowned.

Attempts are being made to inject some class and cash into the place, including recently paved streets, some waterfront renovation, and controversial plans for a new cruise ship terminal/water park. Despite this, Samaná – officially Santa Bárbara de Samaná – maintains a somnolent air for most of the year.

Sights

Cayo Levantado ISLAND

A gorgeous public beach lies on the western third of this lush island, 7km from Samaná, the only section that's open to the public (a five-star hotel occupies the rest). Boatmen at the pier make the trip for RD$250 per person round-trip; groups up to 15 people can negotiate a private full-day boat round-trip for RD$3000.

Note that the idyll can be somewhat marred by the commercialisation of the experience. Touts wander the sands looking for tourists wanting to have their photographs taken with exotic animals, some endangered and on leashes, such as parrots, boa constrictors, monkeys and even sea lions. Large cruise ships dock here regularly, and the facilities, including a few restaurants and bars, don't offer much peace and quiet. If you choose to visit, try going mid-to-late afternoon, when most of the activity is winding down.

Playa las Flechas BEACH

This small beach, around 5km east of Samaná, is easily accessible from town and quieter than the one on Cayo Levantado. It's thought by many historians to be the site of a small and short battle between Columbus' crew and the Ciguayos, a Taíno *cacique* (chiefdom), in which the Spaniards were driven back to their ship. A week later, their differences somehow reconciled, they formed an alliance against the rival *caciques*.

Taíno Park MUSEUM

(www.tainopark.com; Los Róbalos; adult/child RD$500/free; 9am-5.30pm) This new museum, 15 minutes west of Samaná on the road to Sánchez, offers a well-done recreation of the history of the Americas and the indigenous Taíno people via a series of more than 25 outdoor fiberglass scenes, narrated in numerous languages via MP3 players.

Some 200 pieces of Taíno art made from clay, stone and wood are showcased, and a nearby shop offers locally made products with profits going towards developing the area.

Activities

For sheer awe-inspiring, 'the natural world is an amazing thing' impact, a whale-watching trip is hard to beat. Samaná is considered to be one of the top 10 destinations in the world for whale-watching. Around 45,000 people travel here every year between January 15 and March 25 to see the majestic acrobatics of these massive creatures. February is peak season for humpback whales, but try to avoid the weekend of February 27 – the Independence Day holiday 'Carnaval' for Dominicans makes it the busiest weekend of the winter and Samaná is packed.

Most of the whale-watching companies have a morning and afternoon trip. There's little difference in terms of your likelihood of seeing whales, and although the water may be slightly rougher in the afternoon, it also tends to be less busy, with fewer boats out. There are 43 vessels with legal permits: eight companies, two of which are foreign-owned (Canadian and Spanish) and the rest owned by Dominicans from Samaná, and around 12 independent operators. A co-management and self-regulation agreement was established in 1994 between the boat owners and various departments of the Dominican government, including the Ministry of Tourism and the Ministry of the Environment. A manual of rules and responsible behavior was created and every year all the stakeholders sign it to renew their commitment. One of the more important objectives is ensuring a minimum boat size of 8.7m: in big seas small boats are low to the water and sometimes aren't aware of the whales until they're too close.

Private vessels are strictly prohibited from whale-watching; this applies to yachts and boats of any size. They can only transit into or out of the bay. Additionally, do your part by not frequenting illegal operators. Your vessel should have a registration number and a yellow flag issued by the Ministry of Environment.

Whale Samaná WHALE-WATCHING

(809-538-2494; www.whalesamana.com; cnr Calle Mella & Av La Marina; adult/under 5yr/5-10yr RD$2500/free/RD$1250; office 9am-1pm & 3-6pm Jan-Mar, 9am-1pm Mon-Fri Apr-Dec) Samaná's most recommended whale-watching outfit is owned and operated by Canadian marine mammal specialist Kim Beddall, the first person to recognize the scientific and economic importance of Samaná's whales back in 1985. The company uses a two-deck boat with capacity for 60 people. The daily tour leaves at 9am and lasts three to four hours.

There is also a 1:30pm trip when demand is high, and tours can include a stop at Cayo Levantado on the way back. The skilled captains religiously observe the local boat-to-whale distance and other regulations – most of which Beddall helped create – while on-board guides offer interesting facts and information in five languages over the boat's sound system. Sodas and water are provided free of charge. The price does not

Samaná

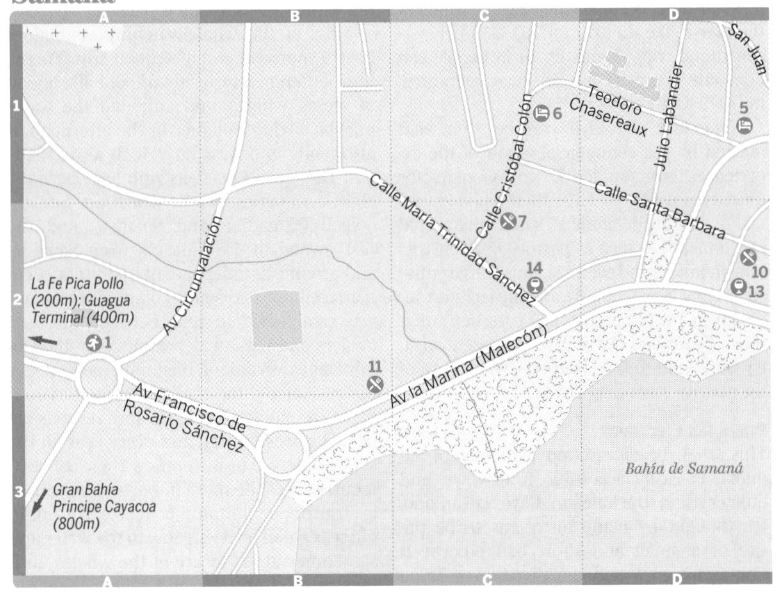

Samaná

Activities, Courses & Tours

	Moto Marina	(see 2)
1	Tour Samaná with Terry	A2
2	Whale Samaná	F2

Sleeping

3	Aire y Mar	F2
4	Hotel Chino	E1
5	Hotel Docia Backpackers Samaná	D1
6	Samaná Spring Hotel	C1

Eating

7	El Rancho Du'Vagabond	C2
8	La Mata Rosada	E2
9	Le Royal Snack	E2
10	L'Hacienda Restaurant	D2
11	Mini-Market	B2
12	Taberna Mediterranea	F2

Drinking & Nightlife

13	Cafe del Paris	D2
14	Sunset Garden Cafe	C2

include admission fees to the marine sanctuary (RD$100, with a price hike consistently threatened). As an added bonus, Whale Samaná allows you to reuse your ticket for a second trip if you don't see any whales – there is no expiration date for this offer. Off-season, this is the only outfitter taking kayaks into Parque Nacional Los Haitises – a definite highlight. Reserve in advance.

Tours

In addition to Whale Samaná (p111), several other agencies also offer whale-watching excursions, as well as trips to Cascada El Limón and Parque Nacional Los Haitises, both hovering around RD$2600 per person. For larger groups, most of these companies generally include a tour guide who can often answer basic questions, but there are no permanent naturalists associated with these operators.

Tour Samaná with Terry ADVENTURE TOUR
(809-538-3179; www.toursamanawithterry.com; Av La Marina; 9am-4pm Mon-Sat) Offers recommended day trips to El Limón as well as more adventurous horseback riding/zip-line and quad bike/zip-line combos starting from RD$2730.

Moto Marina BOAT TOURS
(809-538-2302; www.motomarinatours-excursionsamana.com; Av la Marina 3; 8am-noon & 2-6pm Mon-Sat, 8am-noon Sun) This is a long-standing, dependable option for getting to Los Haitises.

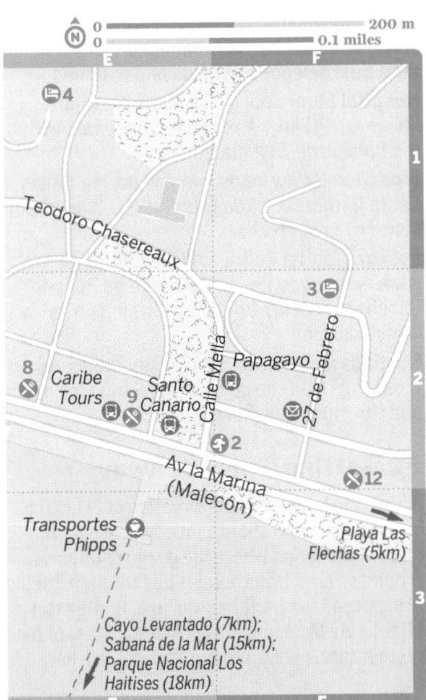

Sleeping

There's little reason to stay in Samaná proper and most people booking whale-watching or Los Haitises trips do so from Las Terrenas, Las Galeras or further out. Hotels don't generally include breakfast, though coffee and tea are usually available. If you're looking for luxury, the **Gran Bahía Principe Cayacoa** (809-538-3131; www.bahiaprincipe.com; all-incl d per person RD$4100;) in town, and **Gran Bahía Principe Cayo Levantado** (809-538-3232; www.bahia-principe.com; Cayo Levantado; all-incl r from RD$6400;) on Cayo Levantado, are the places to head. Keep an eye out for an ecotourism project/ lodge called Dominican Tree House Village, which was in the works 10-minutes' drive northeast of the Malecón when we visited.

Aire y Mar GUESTHOUSE $
(809-538-2913; aparthotel-aireymar@hotmail.com; Calle 27 de Febrero 4; r with fan RD$1200-1600;) This relative newcomer ups the budget stakes in town. The six rooms are simple but clean; there's a nice communal kitchen; and the owner, Noelia, looks after guests with motherly care. But the real highlight, and reward for climbing the street from the Malecón followed by a steep staircase, is the view from the hammock-strewn patio.

Hotel Docia Backpackers Samaná HOSTEL $
(809-538-2497; www.backpackers-samana.com; Calle Teodoro Chasereaux 30; dm US$10, r without/ with air-con US$30/20;) This veteran budget hotel's new American/Dominican owners have given it a makeover, trading no frills and concrete for a backpacker-friendly hostel – just what Samaná so badly needed – with a swimming pool and bar on the way. The pleasant 2nd-floor patio overlooking the bay is an additional bonus.

Hotel Chino HOTEL $$
(809-538-2215; hotelchino.samana@hotmail.com; Calle San Juan 1; r/tr from RD$2200/4200;) Located above a nice international/Chinese restaurant (mains RD$150 to RD$800) on top of a hill, Hotel Chino's rooms have balconies with fantastic views of town and the waterfront. The rooms are shiny and clean, with cable TV, air-con and mini-bars, though aging bathtubs aren't all that inviting. The restaurant is popular for its outstanding views.

Samaná Spring Hotel HOTEL $$
(809-538-2946; samanaspring@hotmail.com; Calle Cristobal Colón 6; s/d RD$1700/2200;) Clean and extra-friendly, Samaná Spring's rooms are basic but well-maintained and come with cable TV and hot water.

Eating & Drinking

The majority of restaurants are located along Av Malecón, while cheaper eats can be found in converted wooden kiosks along the waterfront and along Av Francisco Rosario Sánchez. The most colorful nightlife is along Av Malecón near Calle María Trinidad Sánchez, where locals gather in the evening at a line of makeshift bars pumping reggaeton and *merengue*. Nicer spots nearby for cocktails include **Cafe del Paris** (Av Malecón 6;) and **Sunset Garden Cafe** (www.sunsetgardencafe.com; Av Malecón 10; 7:20am-midnight;).

The expensive **mini-market** (Av Malecón; 10am-1pm & 2-7pm) in the faux Caribbean village that dominates the western end of the Malecón is ok for basic sundries, wine, cigars and kitsch souvenirs.

Le Royal Snack CAFE $
(Av Malecón 4; breakfast RD$80-150; 7:30am-10pm) Across from the ferry dock, this simple French-run cafe is your best bet for espresso, *pain au chocolat* and other early-morning sustenance.

La Fe Pica Pollo DOMINICAN $
(Av Francisco de Rosario Sánchez 15; meals RD$120-150; 7am-11pm) A hole in the wall close to the *guagua* terminal serving tasty fried chicken plus a few other Dominican dishes.

Taberna Mediterranea SPANISH $$
(Av Malecón 1; mains RD$280-650; 10am-11pm Tue-Sun;) Probably the nicest eating option in town, this stone-walled Spanish tavern dishes up tapas, fresh seafood and massive meat and fish *tablas* big enough for three or more (RD$750 to RD$1470), all served by adorable staff.

El Rancho Du'Vagabond ITALIAN $$
(Calle Cristobal Colón 4A; pizzas RD$295-405; noon-2pm & 6-11pm Aug-Sep & Dec-Mar, 4-11pm Apr-Jul & Nov) Though it hasn't aged as well as we would have liked, you'll be pleasantly surprised as you walk past the nondescript entrance to the charming back room, where you'll find no views whatsoever, just an intimate dining spot that's all about pizza and pasta. Their best pie (La Roberto: prosciutto, fresh tomatoes, arugula, freshly grated Grano parmesan and truffle oil) disappointed us on our most recent visit, but it's still better than any of the other Italian options in town.

L'Hacienda Restaurant STEAKHOUSE, SEAFOOD $$
(Calle Santa Barbara; mains RD$440-680; 5pm-midnight Tue-Thu, closed Jun-Jul) A friendly French chef-owner with a Spanish name (José) has been running this intimate French-Caribbean spot since 1996. It's a small and simple menu whose highlights are the meat and seafood grills.

La Mata Rosada DOMINICAN $$
(Av Malecón 5; mains RD$280-700; 10am-3pm & 6:30pm-11pm, closed Wed) A reliable Malecón mainstay, La Mata Rosada has a more extensive menu of seafood and grills than others in its price range. The sophisticated front patio is the town's most formal, but that doesn't mean it's immune to *motoconcho* exhaust. The small bar is one of the classier in town.

Information

Banco Popular (Av Malecón 4; 8am-4pm Mon-Fri, 9am-1pm Sat) Located on the Malecón across from the ferry dock.

BanReservas (Calle Santa Barbara; 8am-4pm Mon-Fri, 9am-1pm Sat) Bank situated one block north of the Malecón.

Clinic Assist (809-538-2426; Av Francisco de Rosario Sánchez; 24hr) Doctors on call 24 hours. Located in the faux Caribbean village.

Farmacia Giselle (cnr Calles Santa Barbara & Julio Labandier; 8am-9pm Mon-Sat, to 1pm Sun) Best selection of meds and toiletries.

Hospital Municipal (Calle María Trinidad Sánchez; 24hr) A very basic hospital near the Palacio de Justicia.

InposDom (www.inposdom.gob.do; cnr Calles Santa Barbara & 27 de Febrero; 8:30am-5pm Mon-Fri) Post office.

Politur (Tourist Police; 809-754-2556; www.politur.gob.do; Av Francisco de Rosario Sánchez; 24hr) On the traffic circle near Av Circunvalación.

Scotiabank (Av Francisco Rosario Sánchez) Closest ATM to the *guagua* (local bus) terminal and the municipal market.

Getting There & Away

Arriving in town from the direction of El Limón or Sánchez, head about 1km downhill past the municipal market where the *guagua* station is, around several traffic circles and through Pueblo Principe, a faux Caribbean village, to the main street – Av Malecón or Av la Marina. Most of the restaurants, banks and bus stations are here.

AIR

Aeropuerto Internacional El Catey (p236), 40km west of Samaná, receives international flights. The closest airstrip to Samaná, Aeropuerto Internacional Arroyo Barril, receives mostly domestic charter flights only.

BUS

Facing the pier, **Caribe Tours** (809-538-2229; www.caribetours.com.do; Av Malecón 6) offers the fastest services to Santo Domingo on the new highway leaving at 8am, 10am, 2pm and 4pm (RD$320, 2½ hours). Oddly, for the same price you can choose the slow road at 7am, 9am, 1pm and 3pm (RD$320, 4½ hours).

For direct services to Puerto Plata, 210km to the west, **Santo Canario** (829-658-3282) minivans leave at 11am beside the Banco Popular. **Papagayo** (ask for Salvador 809-749-6415) has a service at 1:30pm from under the mango tree on the eastern side of the little park next to Banco Popular on the Malecón. If you miss him there, he waits at the municipal market until 2pm. Both charge RD$300 and the trip takes about 3½ to four hours. Call ahead to double-check the day's departure. Locals say the latter is a safer, though slightly slower, ride. Arrive 30 to 45 minutes early to reserve a seat.

For service to towns nearby, head to the **guagua terminal** (Av Francisco de Rosario Sánchez) at the *mercado municipal*, 200m west of the Politur station, near Angel Mesina street. From here, minivans head to Las Galeras (RD$100, one hour, every 15 minutes from 6:30am to 6pm), El Limón (RD$70, 50 minutes, every 15 minutes from 6:30am to 4:45pm) and Las Terrenas (RD$100, 1¼ hours, hourly from 6:30am to 4:45pm). Destinations further afield also leave from the same block: Santo Domingo (RD$300, 2½ hours, every 45 minutes from 4:30am to 4:45pm), Puerta Plata (RD$300, 2½ hours, 8am) and Santiago (RD$300, three hours, hourly from 4:45pm to 2:30pm).

FERRY

Transportes Phipps provides the only ferry service – passengers only, no vehicles – across the Bahía de Samaná to Sabana de la Mar (RD$200, one hour plus, daily at 7am, 9am, and 3pm, sometimes 11am as well). Buy tickets on board. From there, it's possible to catch *guaguas* to several destinations in the southeast and then on to Santo Domingo, though the road network in this part of the country is rough and public transportation is not so comfortable.

Getting Around

Samaná is walkable, but if you're carrying luggage, catch a *motoconcho* (motorcycle taxi) – they're everywhere. 4WD vehicles are your only option in terms of car rental – roads on the peninsula are bad enough to warrant the extra expense. Rates average around RD$2500 per day (tax and insurance included) and discounts are typically given for rentals of a week or longer. Try **Xamaná Rent Motors** (809-834-7841; Av Malecón; 8am-6pm Mon-Sat, to noon Sun).

Las Galeras

POP 6,929

The road to this small fishing community 28km northeast of Samaná ends at a fish shack on the beach. So does everything else, metaphorically speaking. One of the great pleasures of a stay here is losing all perspective on the world beyond; even a trip to one of the beautiful outlying beaches seems far away. But Las Galeras, as much as anywhere else on the peninsula, offers land- and water-based activities for those with a will strong enough to ignore the temptation to do nothing more than lie around their bungalow or while away the day at a restaurant. The town's laid-back charms have not gone unnoticed, drawing a mix of European and North American visitors who make it a more eclectic global village than other more touristy spots on the peninsula; and it's one of the few independent-traveler-minded locales in the DR – there's barely an all-inclusive resort in sight.

Sights

Las Galeras has a number of natural attractions that can be visited by boat, foot, car or horseback. All can be reached on your own, provided you're in decent shape or have a sturdy vehicle.

Playas Frontón & Madama — BEACH

Preferred by some locals over Playa Rincón, Playa Frontón boasts some of the area's best snorkeling. Apparently it's also popular with drug smugglers, Dominicans braving the Mona Passage on their way to Puerto Rico, and reality show contestants – in 2002 *Expedición Robinson,* Colombia's version of the reality show *Survivor,* was filmed here. Playa Madama is a small beach framed by high bluffs; keep in mind there's not much sunlight here in the afternoon.

Trails lead to both beaches but it's easy to get lost, so hire a local guide (contact Karin at La Hacienda Hostel (p117) or, preferably, get to them by boat. Asociación de Lancheros de Las Galeras have now installed fixed prices: RD$2200 to Playa Madama (RD$700 per person with four or more people) and RD$2500 to Playa Frontón (RD$800 per person with four or more). A full-day boat excursion to all the beaches, including Rincón, is RD$5000 (RD$1500 per person with four or more). All prices are roundtrip.

Playita — BEACH

Better than the beach in town, Playita (Little Beach) is easy to get to on foot or by *motoconcho*. It's a stretch of tannish sand, with mellow surf, backed by tall, dramatically leaning palm trees. On the main road just south of Las Galeras, look for signs for Hotel La Playita pointing down a dirt road headed west. Beach chairs rent for RD$100 for the day.

Boca del Diablo — LANDMARK

'Mouth of the Devil' is an impressive vent or blowhole, where waves rush up a natural channel and blast out of a hole in the rocks. Car or motorcycle is the best way to get here – look for an unmarked dirt road 7km south of town and about 100m beyond the turnoff to Playa Rincón. Follow the road eastward for about 8km, then walk the last 100m or so.

ROBBERIES

Tourists visiting Boca del Diablo and Playas Madama and Frontón on their own have frequently been targets of robberies, especially in high season. Leave your valuables at your hotel or go with a local guide.

DON'T MISS

PLAYA RINCÓN

For connoisseurs of such things, Playa Rincón is a pitch-perfect beach. Stretching uninterrupted for almost 3km, it offers nearly white, soft sand for stretching out on and multicolored water that's good for swimming – there's even a small stream at the far western end for a quick freshwater dip at the end of a long, sunny day. A thick palm forest provides the backdrop. Some historians claim that it's here, not Playa las Flechas, where Columbus and his crew landed. One downside: an awful lot of flotsam and jetsam lies uncollected along the sands.

Several small restaurants serve mostly seafood dishes and rent beach chairs, making this a great place to spend the entire day. Most people arrive by boat; the standard option is to leave Las Galeras around 9am and be picked up at 4pm – it's around 20 minutes each way. **Asociación de Lancheros de Las Galeras** (☎809-916-7591) runs fixed-price return boat trips for RD$2000 (RD$600 per person with four or more people).

All but the last 2km of the road to the beach have been recently resurfaced, but even the unpaved section is passable in any vehicle, except after particularly heavy rain. The turnoff to Playa Rincón is 7km south of Las Galeras on the road to Samaná. A round-trip taxi to Rincón, including wait time (9am to 5pm), is RD$1500.

Activities

Water Sports

For experienced divers, **Cabo Cabrón** (Bastard Point) is one of the North Coast's best dive sites. After an easy boat ride from Las Galeras, you're dropped into a churning channel with a giant coral formation that you can swim around; you may see dolphins here. Other popular sites include **Piedra Bonita**, a 50m stone tower good for spotting jacks, barracudas and sea turtles; **Cathedral**, an enormous underwater cave opening to sunlight; and a sunken 55m container ship haunted by big morays. Several large, shallow coral patches, including **Los Carriles**, a series of underwater hills, are good for beginner divers.

Scubalibre Diving Center DIVING
(☎809-958-9119; www.divingscubalibre.com; Grand Paradise Samaná resort; ⏲8:30am-5pm) Scubalibre Diving Center is located at the far end of Grand Paradise Samaná's beach. In addition to diving, it also offers snorkeling trips (RD$1200) and windsurfer and catamaran rental and instruction (RD$1000 per hour), all available to guests and nonguests alike. It's easy enough to walk to the dive shop here by following the path along the beach from town; resort security will let you through. If you try to drive up, they won't let you in.

Las Galeras Divers DIVING
(☎809-538-0220; www.las-galeras-divers.com; Plaza Lusitania; ⏲8:30am-7pm) This is a well-respected, French-run dive shop at the main intersection. One-/two-tank dives including all equipment cost US$2200/3400 (RD$400 less if you have your own). A 10-dive package brings the rate down to RD$1300 per dive, including gear. PADI certification courses can also be arranged.

The Dive Academy DIVING
(☎829-577-5548; www.diveacademy.co; Calle Principal; ⏲8am-9pm) The newest dive operator in town, this English-run NAUI outfitter offers a 10% discount for online bookings.

Hiking

The spectacular **El Punto** lookout is a 5km walk from La Rancheta. To get there, simply continue past the turnoffs to Playas Madam and Frontón and keep climbing up, up and up. Allow at least an hour to get to the top.

Horseback Riding

Karin, the Belgian owner of La Hacienda Hostel, leads well-recommended horseback riding tours to various spots around Las Galeras, including El Punto lookout, Playas Madama, Frontón and Rincón, and the surrounding hills. Her trips cater to all skill levels and range from two-hour excursions (RD$1450 per person) to half day (RD$2280 per person) to full-day (RD$2900) and all-inclusive overnight (RD$8300) trips.

Tours

It's possible to book all of the peninsula's standard tours with Las Galeras-based operators – day-trips include whale-watching in Bahía de Samaná (RD$2500 with lunch) and boat excursions through Parque Nacional Los Haitises (RD$2600 per person) –

but you are better off making your way to Samaná, where Whale Samaná (p111) and Tour Samaná with Terry (p112) have better reputations for eco-awareness and consistently churn out happy campers. Boat tours to isolated beaches around Las Galeras itself can be arranged from the town beach with the Asociación de Lancheros de Las Galeras (from RD$2000 or RD$600 per person with four or more people).

Sleeping

Most of the hotels and bungalows located in Las Galeras are within walking distance of the main intersection. The unimpressive Grand Paradise Samaná is the only resort in town.

Sol Azul BUNGALOWS $
(829-882-8790; www.elsolazul.com; s/d incl breakfast from RD$1800/2000;) A fun Swiss couple run these four earthy, natural-hued and spacious bungalows, all set around a pristinely manicured garden and pleasant pool area just 50m from the main intersection. Two of the bungalows feature mezzanine levels – good for children – and the breakfast buffet gets high marks from travelers. If Casa Por Qué No? is full, it's the best alternative around this price range.

La Hacienda Hostel GUESTHOUSE $
(829-939-8285; www.lahaciendahostel.com; dm/s/d RD$580/1160/1450;) Some three kilometers from the town intersection on the trail/rough road to Playas Madama/Frontón, Belgian expat Karin runs a one-woman show offering five rustic rooms, a communal kitchen, and a pleasant open-air porch with sea and mountain views. It's fairly basic though – expect cold showers and don't be surprised if there's a frog in your toilet.

Guests can help themselves from the fruit and vegetable garden, and collect fresh eggs for RD$10. Those who don't want to cook for themselves often take meals down at La Rancheta. The big reason to stay here is to take advantage of Karin, an expert tour guide, who leads fabulous day and overnight hiking and horseback riding trips to out-of-the-way beaches and mountaintops.

La Rancheta BUNGALOWS $
(829-889-4727; www.larancheta.com; r/bungalow RD$1400/1800-2000) Buried in the lush jungle, 2.5km from the main intersection, this hotel has a number of simple but funky two-storied bungalows that can accommodate between four and six people comfortably. Semi-outdoor rustic kitchens lend an eclectic cabin-in-the-woods feel to this *very* laid-back traveler favorite. Breakfast is an extra RD$175 to RD$225.

The Belgian owner, Ronald, offers a godsend after too many intimate evenings with Presidente – Belgian brews from the motherland, served in the restaurant (a favorite for those not wanting to traipse all the way into town).

★ **Casa Por Qué No?** B&B $$
(809-712-5631; casaporqueno@live.com; s/d incl breakfast US$45/55; closed May-Oct;) Pierre and Monick, the charming French-Canadian owners of this B&B, are consummate hosts and rent out two rooms on either side of their cozy home – each room has a separate entrance and hammock – only 25m or so north of the main intersection on your right as you're walking toward the beach.

The house is fronted by a long, well-maintained garden where tasty breakfasts (including delicious homemade bread) are served (RD$350 for nonguests). When you tire of DR's ubiquitous restaurant offerings, Monick can whip up a Thai dinner for you. It's definitely not the fanciest spot in town, but it offers the warmest hospitality.

★ **Todo Blanco** BOUTIQUE HOTEL $$
(809-538-0201; www.hoteltodoblanco.com; r with/without air-con RD$3800/3700;) Living up to its 'All White' name, this whitewashed, well-established inn sits atop a small hillock a short walk from the end of the main drag in Las Galeras. Rooms are large and airy, with high ceilings, private terraces overlooking the sea, and pastel headboards, while the multilevel grounds are nicely appointed with gardens and a gazebo.

Cheerful owner Maurizio is a fun guy to sip an espresso with, and he makes dedicated fresh-fruit runs to Samaná to provide guests' breakfasts (an extra RD$300).

Casa Dorado B&B $$
(829-933-8678; www.casadoradodr.com; r RD$2800-3400;) This beautiful house, a kilometer from both the main intersection and Playita, is decked out in Mexican-style interiors by the American-Dominican owners. Four rooms are available; the largest and most expensive comes with a Jacuzzi.

There are ample spots for relaxing, from expansive hammock-strung terraces to cozy living rooms – if the weather turns sour, this is where you want to be. Breakfast in the gorgeous kitchen is the real deal and guests from other hotels often find their way here, happy to fork over US$8 for the privilege.

Casa Calliope VILLA **$$**
(☎829-929-8506; www.casacalliope.com; d/q incl breakfast RD$3600/4000; @📶) Around 4km east of town, this two-bedroom hilltop Mexican-style villa offers funky luxury in beautiful surroundings. Each of the two large bedrooms has a full bathroom and terrace, and there's also a fully equipped kitchen for guests' use – vegetarian and healthy meals can be ordered up as well. The owners, a friendly couple from Boston, are a great source of information on the area. Two-night minimum stay generally required.

Chalet Tropical CHALETS **$$$**
(☎809-901-0738; www.chalettropical.com; Calle por La Playita; chalets from US$185; ❄📶) An Italian stylist is the big personality behind these rustic-chic A-frame chalets. Each boasts a range of colors and unique interior details like stone showers, coconut and bamboo wood accents, and all manner of creative combinations – everything here looks like a beautiful indigenous handicraft made to wow you. All the huge chalets are split-level, with full kitchens and ample living space; and security on the private premises is a priority. They're tucked away down a residential street across from BanReservas, a 10-minute walk from both Playita beach and the center of town.

Plaza Lusitania Hotel HOTEL **$$$**
(☎809-538-0178; www.plazalusitania.com; Plaza Lusitania, Calle Principal; r with/without air-con incl breakfast from RD$4880/3800; ❄📶) Situated at the main intersection, on the 2nd floor of a tiny mall, complete with a good Italian restaurant and pleasant open-air atrium. Rooms are large and extremely comfortable, but steer clear if you don't like cats.

Eating

For a town of its size, Las Galeras has an abundance of fantastic food outlets, with many restaurants located at the single intersection on the main street. Several hotels also offer meals when ordered in advance. Note that many restaurants close outside of the high season. For self-caterers, the largest grocery store is **Supermercado No 1** (Calle Principal; ⏲7am-9:30pm).

End of the Road FAST FOOD **$**
(Calle Principal; mains RD$50-190; ⏲8am-9pm; 📶) Right at the town intersection, this small traveler's hub serves gourmet Angus beef burgers and massive burritos (including an awesome breakfast version) cooked by the French chef from Le Taínos, the town's chicest eatery. It has an internet cafe (per hour RD$40).

★**Rincón Rubi** CARIBBEAN, SEAFOOD **$$**
(☎809-380-7295; Playa Rincón; mains RD$300-650; ⏲9am-4pm Dec-Mar, with reservation Apr-Nov) This dressed-up beach shack justifies the trip to long and beautiful Playa Rincón on whose eastern end it sits. Picnic-table-style seating is juiced up with bright tablecloths, and a single chalkboard relays the offerings: fresh fish, *langosta* (lobster), grilled chicken etc, all cooked up on a massive, open-air grill. The whole fish in coco sauce melts off the bone and again in your mouth; and don't forget to douse your coconut rice in the excellent salsa. Not only is it a perfect meal on a dreamy beach, but it's also a great place to give some of your money to actual Dominicans.

★**El Cabito** SEAFOOD **$$**
(☎829-697-9506; mains RD$250-900; ⏲4-10pm Tue-Sun) Clinging spectacularly onto the edge of the DR, this rustic, postcard-perfect restaurant and its amazing cliff-hugging views offer the peninsula's most dramatic dining. The best time to go is sunset, when a kaleidoscopic flurry of hues melts into the sea as you sip on Belgian beers. In terms of food, go for the excellent grilled calamari (RD$550) or dorado (RD$650) if they're on the menu. Staff may offer a pick-up/drop-off service anywhere in Las Galeras; otherwise take a taxi (RD$800 return with waiting). Reservations are usually essential.

★**Le Taínos** FUSION **$$**
(Calle Principal; mains RD$360-640; ⏲6-11pm Nov-Apr) The focal point of the center of town, this atmospheric eatery is the town's most cosmopolitan, with a small but exciting menu of all sorts of scrumptious dishes you don't see elsewhere, beautifully presented on massive plates fit for a king.

The honey-oregano pork mignon is a real treat, as is the key lime chicken and fish in a banana leaf, all served in a candlelit alfresco space with a designer thatched-roof. The bar is the most sociable around, too, and the cocktails are huge, adding a level of value uncommon on the peninsula.

El Pescador SPANISH **$$**
(www.restaurantpescador.com; Calle Principal; mains RD$420-950; ⏲10am-11pm Wed-Mon) Located across from BanReservas on the main road, this is an excellent seafood option, notably for its *paella* (the owner is Spanish). They even serve it for one person (solo travelers rejoice!) and, truth be told, it's better than any *paella* we ever had in Spain.

Locals give the pizza (RD$280 to RD$550) high marks too, and the coconut flan is a nice way to end a meal.

Il Nodo del Pirata ITALIAN, SEAFOOD **$$**
(Plaza Lusitania, Calle Principal; pasta RD$180-520, pizza RD$200-520; ⏲3-11pm Dec-Apr, 5-10pm May-Nov) This long-time staple serves a varied menu of Italian dishes, including homemade pasta (tagliatelle with gorgonzola or fresh tomatoes), large thin-crust individual pizzas, meat and fish dishes, followed by an extensive list of Italian and American desserts and artisanal ice cream (coconut gets a round of applause).

Despite the fact that the decor consists of little more than lawn chairs, it's still one of the town's most popular options.

Drinking & Nightlife

Much of the nightlife involves drinks at one of the restaurants in town – the bar at Le Taínos is the best for cocktails. Further up the road is **L'Aventura** (Calle Principal), which also has a healthy bar scene.

Information

The paved road coming from Samaná winds along the coast and through lovely, often-forested countryside before reaching the outskirts of Las Galeras. There's one main intersection in town (about 50m before the highway dead-ends at the beach) and most hotels, restaurants and services are within walking distance from there.

BanReservas (Calle Principal; ⏲9am-5pm Mon-Fri) The most convenient ATM, though can be fussy. There is another at Grand Paradise Samaná resort.

Centro Medico Asistencial (☎809-963-1633; Calle Principle; ⏲24hr) A small on-call clinic; no English spoken.

Farmacia Las Galeras (Calle Principal; ⏲9am-8:30pm) Basic meds and supplies near the main intersection.

Grand Paradise Samaná (www.grandparadisesamana.com; ⏲24hr) Has a small clinic that nonguests can use in emergencies.

Politur (Tourist Police; ☎809-754-2987; www.politur.gob.do; Calle Principal; ⏲24hr) Tourist police.

RP Motors (☎829-729-8727; Calle Principal; ⏲9:30am-6pm Mon-Sat) Exchanges cash dollars and euros; also rents cars.

Getting There & Around

Guaguas head to Samaná (RD$100, one hour, every 15 minutes from 6:30am to 5:45pm) from the beach end of Calle Principal, and also pick up passengers as they cruise slowly out of town. There are also three daily buses to Santo Domingo (RD$350, three hours, 5:30am, 1:15pm & 3:15pm).

You can walk pretty much everywhere in Las Galeras. **Taxis** (☎809-481-8526) are available at a stand just in front of the main town beach. Sample one-way fares include: Aeropuerto Catey (RD$3000); Las Terrenas (RD$2500); Samaná (RD$1000); and Santo Domingo (RD$7000). You may be able to negotiate cheaper fares, especially to Samaná.

Renting a car is an excellent way to explore the peninsula on your own. Prices are generally around RD$3000 per day with insurance.

WESTERN PENÍNSULA DE SAMANÁ

Las Terrenas

POP 18,829

Once a rustic fishing village, Las Terrenas today is a cosmopolitan town and seems as much French (approaching a colony) and Italian as Dominican. Fashionable-looking European women in designer sunglasses ride their personal ATVs with a bag of baguettes in tow, battling on roads with way too many *motos*. The balancing act between locals and expats has produced a lively mix of styles and a social scene more vibrant than anywhere else on the peninsula. Walking in either direction along the beach road leads to a beachfront scattered with hotels, tall palm trees and calm aquamarine waters.

Las Terrenas is independent-traveler-friendly and a good place to hook up with fellow nomads.

Sights

Parque Nacional Los Haitises NATURE RESERVE
(US$60) Las Terrenas might not be that close to the Parque Nacional Los Haitises, but since so few independent travelers make it

Las Terrenas

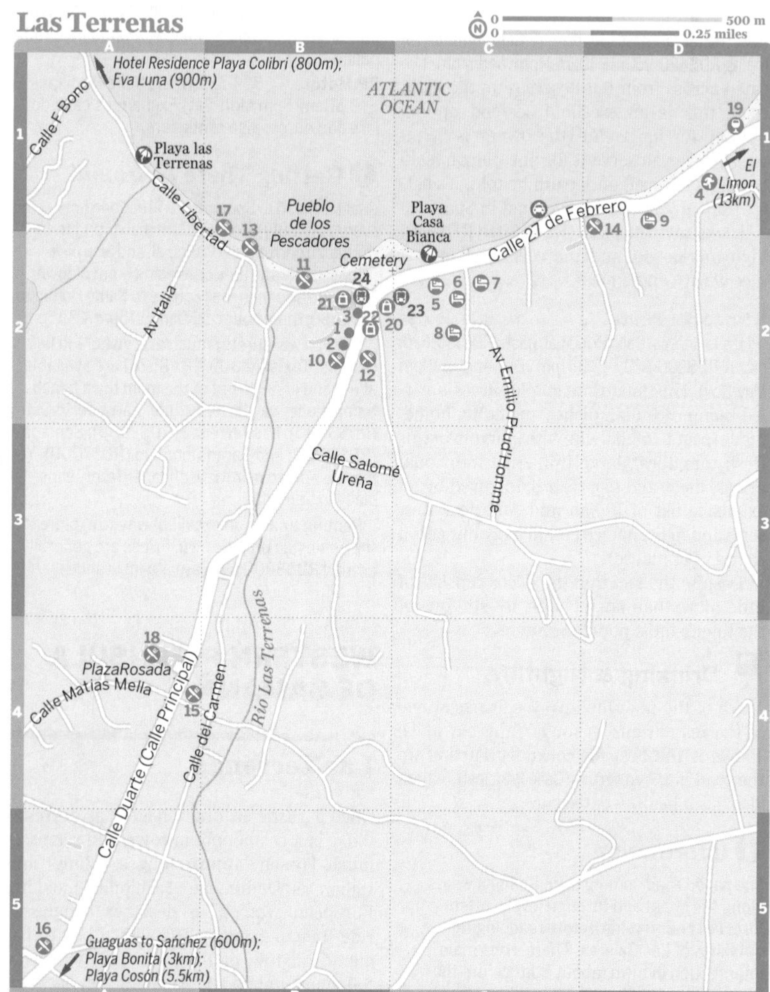

to Sabana de la Mar, the closest entrance to the park, Las Terrenas has become a popular place to book trips there.

Flora Tours is a recommended operator, but virtually every company in town offers excursions to Los Haitises, though generally only twice a week unless you're part of a group of six or more, in which case you can arrange trips at your own convenience. There should be at least one company with a tour on offer five days a week, but schedules change, so it's best to book as soon as you arrive in town.

Activities

Diving & Snorkeling

Las Terrenas has reasonably good diving and snorkeling and at least three shops in town to take you out. Favorite dive spots include a wreck in 28m of water and Isla Las Ballenas, visible from shore, with a large underwater cave. Most operators also offer special trips to Cabo Cabrón near Las Galeras and Dudu Cave near Río San Juan. Standard one-tank dives average US$60 with equipment. Four-, 10- and 12-dive packages will save you about US$10 to US$20 per dive. Two-tank diving day-trips to Cabo Cabrón

Las Terrenas

Activities, Courses & Tours
1 Casa de las Terrenas ... B2
2 Flora Tours ... B2
3 Fun Rental ... B2
4 LTK ... D1
Turtle Dive Center ... (see 21)

Sleeping
5 Albachiara Hotel ... C2
6 Casa del Mar Neptunia ... C2
7 Casa Robinson ... C2
8 El Rincon de Abi ... C2
9 La Dolce Vita ... D1

Eating
10 Big Dan's Polar Bar ... B2
Boulangerie Française ... (see 22)
11 La Casa Azul ... B2
12 La Serviette ... B2
13 La Terrasse ... B2
14 Le Tre Caravelle ... D1
15 Mar y Tierra ... A4
16 Mi Corazon ... A5
Mini-Market Plaza Taína ... (see 22)
17 One Love Surfshack ... B1
18 Supermercado Lindo ... A4

Drinking & Nightlife
La Cave Au Vin ... (see 21)
19 Mojitos ... D1

Shopping
20 Casa Linda ... B2
21 El Paseo ... B2
Haitian Caraibes Art Gallery ... (see 22)
22 Plaza Taína ... B2
Prensa International ... (see 21)

Transport
23 Guaguas to Samaná & El Limón ... C2
24 Las Terrenas Transportes ... B2

are US$160, including gear, lunch and transportation; and one-tank day-trips to Dudu Caves are US$130, also including gear, lunch and transportation. Open Water courses average around US$430 all in.

A popular full-day snorkel trip is to Playa Jackson, several kilometers west of town, reached by boat.

Turtle Dive Center DIVING
(829-903-0659; www.turtledivecenter.com; El Paseo shopping center; 10am-12:30pm & 4-7pm) A highly recommended SSI-affiliated shop, run by a safety-first Frenchman. Also runs snorkeling trips to Playa Jackson (half-/full-day US$55/80) and Isla Las Ballenas (US$45).

Kitesurfing & Windsurfing

Second only to Cabarete, Las Terrenas is a good place to try out a windsport in the DR. The beach at Punta Popy, only 1km or so east of the main intersection, is a popular place for kitesurfers and windsurfers. Be on the lookout for the new **Centro Nautico** (829-286-4735; ltsailingclub@gmail.com; Playa Las Ballenas), which will offer rental equipment for windsurfing, sailing, catamarans and Stand Up Paddle in Playa Las Ballenas.

LTK WATER SPORTS
(809-801-5671; www.lasterrenas-kitesurf.com; Calle 27 de Febrero) Recommended kitesurfing school run by a friendly Frenchman who speaks Spanish and English as well. It rents surfboards (per day US$15) and kitesurfing equipment (per day US$70) and provides lessons for both these activities. Six hours of kitesurfing lessons (really the minimum needed to have a sporting chance of making it work) cost US$300; a two-hour surfing lesson is US$40.

Tours

Flora Tours ECOTOURS
(809-923-2792; www.flora-tours.net; Calle Principal 278; 8:30am-12:30pm & 3:30-6:30pm Mon-Sat) This French-run agency takes top honors in town for eco-sensitive tours to Parque Nacional Los Haitises and hard-to-access beaches, as well as more tranquil catamaran trips, culturally-sensitive quad tours to remote villages and mountain bike excursions of varying levels. Kayak tours are in the works.

Casa de las Terrenas ADVENTURE TOURS
(809-666-0306; www.lasterrenas-excursions.com; Calle Principal 280; 8:30am-12:30pm & 3:30-6:30pm Mon-Sat) Small, friendly, French-run operation run out of a little kiosk in front of Plaza Taína.

Fun Rental QUAD/SCOOTER RENTAL
(809-713-6666; funrental@hotmail.fr; Calle Principal) Rents quad bikes (US$55 per day) and scooters (US$25).

Sleeping

The majority of accommodations options are located along the beachfront roads to the east and west of the main intersection.

WORTH A TRIP

CASCADA EL LIMÓN

Tucked away in surprisingly rough landscape, surrounded by peaks covered in lush greenery, is the 52m-high El Limón waterfall. A beautiful swimming hole at the bottom can be a perfect spot to wash off the sweat and mud from the trip here, though it's often too deep and cold for a dip. The departure point is the small town of El Limón, only a half-hour from Las Terrenas. Just about everyone who visits does so on horseback, and almost a dozen *paradas* (horseback-riding operations) in town and on the highway toward Samaná offer tours (though it is not recommended to hire someone off the street, as there's little saving and the service is consistently substandard). All outfits offer essentially the same thing: a 30- to 60-minute ride up the hill to the waterfalls, 30 to 60 minutes to take a dip and enjoy the scene, and a 30- to 60-minute return trip, with lunch at the end. Your guide – who you should tip – will be walking, not riding, which can feel a little weird but is the custom. Walking or on horseback, you will get wet as there are several river crossings along the way – rubber sandals are a good idea.

Spanish-owned Santí, at the main intersection in El Limón, is a good choice but also the most expensive. The lunch is excellent and the guides and staff (all adults) are better paid than elsewhere (though that doesn't make them any more professional). If you book with a tour company in Las Terrenas, transportation to/from El Limón is often not included (*guagua* RD$50). Typically the tour (horse, guide and lunch) costs per person from US$35 to US$50. Most other operators charge around RD$650/300 with/without lunch; try Parada la Manzana, 5km east of El Limón toward Samaná, which has the added advantage – depending on your perspective – of being much closer to the falls as well as offering a pleasant new bar for cocktails, Apple Bar.

Tours may also be booked from Las Terrenas, some of which include transportation to El Limón by quad bikes, followed by the standard horseback ride and lunch (US$55); try Casa de las Terrenas. Otherwise, it's a minimum 40-minute walk (from the main intersection in El Limón it's roughly 5.6km), up a sometimes very steep trail over rough terrain and with even a river or two to ford. It's not difficult to follow the path once you find it, though, especially if there are groups out on the trail. If you do make the trip independently you'll need to pay the entrance fee (RD$50).

Those to the east are across from the beach on the paved highway, while the newly cobblestoned road to the west means the area is somewhat quieter and feels more secluded. Prices drop dramatically in the low season, but at any time of the year discounts are negotiable for long-term stays.

★El Rincon de Abi HOTEL **$**
(☎809-240-6639; www.el-rincon-de-abi.com; Av Emilio Prud'Homme; d/tr incl breakfast from RD$1500/2000, bungalow without/with air-con RD$2000/2500, apt RD$4000-5000; ❄📶🏊) This French-owned hotel is well maintained and full of cute colors and character. Even better, there's a somewhat established independent traveler vibe here. There's a nice communal outdoor kitchen, a Jacuzzi and a small pool. Rooms are either in the main two-storey building topped with a thatched roof (a tad sterile, but high-pressure showers) or the bungalows that are more vibrant. Bonus points for high security: the owners have 24-hour video surveillance beamed to their iPhones.

Casa del Mar Neptunia HOTEL **$**
(☎809-240-6884; www.casasdelmarneptunia.com; Av Emilio Prud'Homme; s/d incl breakfast RD$1600/1900; 📶) New hands-on Canadian owners have whipped this humble abode into a charming little oasis of hospitality and calm. Homey and quiet with 12 large, airy rooms, it lacks some of the privacy of others on the same street, but makes up for it in value – your pesos will rarely go this far in Las Terrenas.

Casa Robinson HOTEL **$**
(☎809-240-6496; www.casarobinson.it; Av Emilio Prud'Homme; s/d/tr RD$1300/1400/2000; 📶) Set in leafy grounds down a side street a block from the beach, this hotel offers privacy on the cheap. Fan-cooled rooms in the all-wood buildings are simple and clean and have little balconies and patios. Though Italian-owned, it's run with a smile by Dominicans. It's a family-run place where any type of debauchery is not appreciated.

Hotel Residence Playa Colibrí HOTEL **$$**
(809-240-6434; www.hotelplayacolibri.com; Playa Las Ballenas; apt for 2/4/6 incl breakfast from US$89/179/269;) One of the last hotels along this stretch of Playa Las Ballenas, Playa Colibrí is a good option for those seeking peace and quiet. Regardless of the room layout you choose, all 45 apartments are spacious and good value with fully equipped kitchens. Split-level apartments are especially good for families. Each has a terrace that overlooks a pool area and meticulously manicured gardens; breakfast can be served on the tranquil stretch of beach across the road.

La Dolce Vita APARTMENT HOTEL **$$**
(809-240-5069; www.ladolcevitaresidence.com; Calle 27 de Febrero; r per night/month US$90/$1610;) The apartments at this aqua-trimmed Caribbean plantation-style seafront complex are good long-term rentals.

★ **Eva Luna** VILLAS **$$$**
(809-978-5611; www.villa-evaluna.com; Calle Marico, Playa Las Ballenas; villas for 2/4 people US$120/220;) A paragon of understated luxury, these five Mexican-style villas come with fully equipped kitchens, gorgeously painted living rooms, and terraces where a delicious gourmet breakfast is served. The bedrooms are a bit cramped, but the serenity and exquisite decor more than make up for it. The romantic villas all face a quiet pool and a garden area and the whole show is overseen by the adorable Aude and her partner, Jérôme, a trained chef who has been known to throw a fish or two on the grill for guests. It's west of town, tucked away in a residential neighborhood 300m from Playa Las Ballenas. Doubles are a steal in low season at US$80.

Albachiara Hotel APARTMENT HOTEL **$$$**
(809-240-5240; www.albachiarahotel.com; Calle 27 de Febrero; apt incl breakfast from US$115;) It suffers from a bit of street noise, but this 46-apartment hotel is well located, close to the beach and center of Las Terrenas. It offers extra large options with king-sized beds, big kitchens and cozy patios that look out on the grand columns that are a feature of the hotel's architecture.

Eating

The most atmospheric restaurants in Las Terrenas are in Pueblo de los Pescadores, a cluster of fishermen's shacks-cum-waterfront restaurants recently devastated by fire but rebuilt just west of the river on what was the original site of the town. Virtually every restaurant has an entrance facing the road and an open-air dining or bar area out back, overlooking the ocean and narrow beach.

Mini-Market Plaza Taína (7:30am-8:30pm Mon-Sat, 8am-noon Sun) has snacks and basic necessities, while the largest and best supermarket in town, **Supermercado Lindo** (Plaza Rosada, Calle Principal; 8:30am-1pm & 3-8pm Mon-Sat, 9am-1pm Sun), is the place to go for canned foods, pasta, produce, snacks, decent imported wine and other supplies.

Boulangerie Française BAKERY **$**
(Plaza Taína; items RD$40-150; 7am-7:30pm Mon-Sat, to 7pm Sun) Transport yourself to Paris at this pleasant bakery serving fresh *pain au chocolat*, croissants, *beignets* and other traditional French pastries and desserts. The streetside patio practically feels like Montmartre and they serve the best espresso on the peninsula by a long shot.

One Love Surfshack BURGERS, BREAKFAST **$**
(Pueblo de los Pescadores; burgers RD$200-250, breakfast RD$100-200; 7am-1am Wed-Mon;) North American breakfasts and decent burgers are One Love's calling. Equally as popular for food as for a great place to down a few cold ones to the tune of crashing waves, you could swing your life away here on the oceanside back porch. The hands-on Quebecois owners even take a tasty stab at *poutine*, improvising with local cheese instead of curds.

Mar y Tierra DOMINICAN **$**
(Calle Principal; meals RD$150-370; 11:30am-6pm) Dead simple affair but a good choice for cheap Dominican *comida criolla*. With its shaded patio, it's a step up from the average shack, too.

Big Dan's Polar Bar AMERICAN, BAR **$**
(Calle Principal; mains RD$100-385; noon-11pm Mon-Sat, 12 to 4pm Sun;) You'll be hard-pressed to find a better RD$100 burger than Dan's, an American expat doing prescriptions for the homesick in the shape of burgers, fish and chips, chili con carne and more.

TOUTS

If you are driving yourself to El Limón, beware of *motoconcho* touts who will pull up alongside your vehicle and try to persuade you to go to a *parada* that pays them a commission. Keep driving.

★La Terrasse FRENCH $$
(Pueblo de los Pescadores; mains RD$380-750; ⏲11:30am-2:30pm & 6:30-11pm) The Dominican chef at this sophisticated French bistro deserves a few Michelin stars for his steak *au poivre* (RD$500) – you'll be genuflecting at his kitchen's door after it graces your lips – one of the most perfect meals in the entire Dominican Republic. The menu continues with lovely seafood like red snapper in garlic and parsley (RD$530), spicy creole calamari (RD$430) and lobster with tarragon butter sauce (RD$580). Like most spots along this gourmet promenade, the sea nearly steals back its wares every time a wave comes crashing in. But the best part of all might just be eating this for well under US$15 – a tall order anywhere in the world.

La Serviette FRENCH $$
(Plaza Taína; mains RD$310-770; ⏲6pm-midnight Mon, 10am-3pm & 6pm-midnight Tue-Sat; 🛜) This hidden jewel, tucked away at the back of Plaza Taína, brings a touch of Lyonais pizzazz to Las Terrenas. *Cassoulet, entrecôte*, escargots – they're all here and all done extremely well. The house-specialty steak tartare (RD$520) and pastis-flambéed shrimp (RD$490) do not disappoint, and the friendly couple do their hardest to ensure satisfaction. (Except for the smoking).

Le Tre Caravelle ITALIAN $$
(Calle 27 de Febrero ; mains RD$270-490; ⏲noon-11:30am; 🛜) The local's pick for best Italian is indeed a great little spot for risotto and fresh seafood, though the ambience won't floor you – waitresses in sailor hats (overly cutesy but extra friendly) and a questionable maritime tiki motif might raise eyebrows. A rundown of the daily recommendations is given via a traveling chalkboard.

La Casa Azul ITALIAN $$
(Calle Libertad; pizzas RD$210-350; ⏲6pm-midnight Wed-Mon) Service leaves *mucho* to be desired but the Italian owners turn out the best pizza in town, with a few tables right on the sand.

★Mi Corazon FUSION $$$
(☎809-240-5329; www.micorazon.com; Calle Duarte 7; mains RD$780-1040; ⏲7-11pm Tue-Sun; 🛜) Las Terrenas may feel like a Franco-Italian enclave, but it's a Swiss-German trio that offers the area's top dining experience. Daniel, Lilo and Flo ensure your culinary ride here is a doozy: everything is made fresh on the premises and served in a romantic white-washed colonial-style courtyard, open to the stars and complete with a trickling fountain.

Some molecular gastronomy creeps into the food here (Angus beef with olive oil foam, for example) but it's really all about fresh, simple flavors seasoned perfectly. A variety of tasting menus are available to suit all appetites. The weekly-changing chef's menu (three/four-course RD$1650/2150) is the way to go.

Drinking

Most of the restaurants have bars and stay open well after the kitchen has closed. Barhopping could scarcely be easier, as it takes about 45 seconds to walk from one end of Pueblo de los Pescadores to the other. There are a few notable spots outside of Pueblo de los Pescadores as well.

Mojitos BAR, RESTAURANT
(Calle 27 de Febrero; ⏲9am-10pm; 🛜) The problem with mojitos is that they go down too fast. The ones at this upscale beach shack at Punta Popy are made by Cubans in 14 flavors (with Cuban rum for an extra RD$50) in traditional, *chinola* (passion fruit) and *tamarindo* varieties (RD$200). They aren't cheap, but couldn't be any better if Fidel Castro himself were tending the bar. There's great seafood as well (try the vinaigrette octopus), plus wonderful sunset views.

La Cave Au Vin WINE BAR
(El Paseo shopping center, Calle Principal; ⏲8am-2pm & 6-10pm; 🛜) When you tire of the Dominican propensity for serving Presidente beer and freezing red wine, this small but knowledgable wine shop and deli is the place to head. It dishes out (very) French tapas (RD$50 to RD$400) and 10 or so properly chilled French, Spanish, Chilean and Argentinian wines by the glass.

Shopping

Calle Duarte (aka Calle Principal) and around are virtually wallpapered with the typical Haitian art found everywhere in the DR. The three shopping centers a stone's throw away from one another on Calle Duarte – Plaza Taína, Casa Linda and El Paseo – have high-end boutiques, eating options and a few shops selling basic tourist kitsch.

Haitian Caraibes Art Gallery GALLERY
(Calle Principal 159; ⏲9am-1pm & 4-7:45pm Mon-Sat) For a better selection of paintings than the ubiquitous cookie-cutter mass-produced

ones, stop by this art gallery. It also sells crafts, jewelry and typical batiks and sarongs.

Prensa International ACCESSORIES
(El Paseo shopping center, Calle Duarte; ⏰9am-7:30pm Mon-Sat, to 1pm Sun) Toward the rear of the El Paseo shopping mall, it sells a variety of international newspapers and magazines, the majority in French and English.

Information

Most hotels and restaurants have wi-fi (always ask at restaurants – nobody seems to name their networks in any logical way after the name of the establishment). If you are without a device, there are a few places along Calle Principal for internet access.

EMERGENCY

Politur (Tourist Police; ☎809-754-3062; Av Emilio Prud'Homme; ⏰24hr)

LAUNDRY

Lavanderia Las Terrenas (☎809-240-5500; per lb RD$60; ⏰8am-7pm Mon-Thu, to 6pm Fri, to 4pm Sat-Sun) The most convenient laundry service, with 24-hour turnaround.

MEDICAL SERVICES

Clínica Especializada Internacional (☎809-240-6701; Calle Fabio Abreu) This new private hospital, run by Cuban doctors, is the peninsula's most modern.

Super Farmacia del Paseo (El Paseo, Calle Principal; ⏰9am-7pm Mon-Sat, to 1pm Sun) Well-stocked pharmacy.

MONEY

There are ATMs at El Paseo shopping center, Pueblo de los Pescadores and Plaza Rosada.

BanReservas (Calle Duarte 254; ⏰8am-5pm Mon-Fri, Sat 9am-1pm)

Banco Popular (Av Juan Pablo Duarte/Calle Duarte 52; ⏰9am-4pm Mon-Fri, 9am-1pm Sat)

TRAVEL AGENCIES

Colonial Tours (☎809-240-6822; www.colonialtours.com.do; Plaza Rosada; ⏰9am-1pm & 3-7pm Mon-Fri, to 12:30pm Sat) The town's main full-service travel agency.

Getting There & Away

AIR

International flights arrive at Aeropuerto Internacional El Catey (p236), located 8km west of Sánchez and a 35-minute taxi ride (US$70) to Las Terrenas. **Air Canada** (☎888-760-0020) and **Westjet** (☎in Puerto Plata 809-586-0217) offer direct flights from El Catey to Montreal and Toronto, respectively. There are also a handful of charter flights.

Aerodomca (☎in Santo Domingo 809-826-4141; www.aerodomca.com) offers sporadic, often cancelled, services to Aeropuerto Internacional Arroyo Barril near Samaná from Punta Cana daily, departing at 2pm.

BUS

For Santo Domingo, **Las Terrenas Transportes** (☎809-240-5302) operates coaches to Santo Domingo (RD$350, 2½ hours, 5am, 7am, 9am, 2pm and 3:30pm), Puerto Plata (RD$300, three hours, 6:30am), Santiago (RD$300, three hours, 6am, 8am and 12:30pm) and Nagua (RD$150, 1¼ hours, 7:20am). Buses leave from in front of El Paseo shopping center.

Las Terrenas has two *guagua* stops at opposite ends of Calle Principal. *Guaguas* to Samaná leave in front of Casa Linda on the corner of Calle Principal and the coastal road eight times daily (RD$100, 1¼ hours) between 7:15am and 5pm. For those going to El Limón, 14km away, trucks and *guaguas* leave from the same stop at Casa Linda (RD$50, 35 minutes, every 15 minutes from 7:15am to 6:15pm).

CAR

Las Terrenas is easily accessible by road if you're motoring on your own. A portion of the new highway, Boulevard Turístico del Atlántico, connects Las Terrenas with Aeropuerto Internacional El Catey, 24km to the west, bypassing the former need to transit first through Sánchez. The toll charges are high, relative to kilometers (RD$484), and it hasn't exactly been embraced by locals, but it's a beautiful drive all the same.

TAXI

The local **taxi consortium** (☎809-240-6339) offers rides for one to six passengers to just about everywhere. Some sample one-way fares are Playa Cosón (US$30), El Limón (US$25), Samaná (US$70), Las Galeras (US$100), Santo Domingo (US$200) and Punta Cana (US$400).

Getting Around

The two main roads in town, Calle Duarte (also known as Calle Principal in town, and Av Juan Pablo Duarte or Av Duarte as it exits town) and the parallel Calle del Carmen, form a figure eight of sorts, crisscrossing in the middle.

You can walk to and from most places in Las Terrenas, though getting from one end to the other can take a half-hour or more. Taxis charge US$15 each way to Playa Bonita, US$50 round-trip to Playa Cosón and US$40 round-trip to El Limón. *Motoconchos* are cheaper – RD$100 to Playa Bonita and RD$200 to Playa Cosón – but are less comfortable. There are taxi and *motoconcho* stops in front of El Paseo shopping center and *motoconchos* are plentiful on Calle

Principal and around Pueblo de los Pescadores – and are incessantly in your face practically everywhere else.

There are several local rental-car agencies in town. Rates go from painful during the week (US$50) to highway robbery on the weekends (US$300). One of the more established and reliable ones is **ADA Rental Car** (809-685-7515; www.ada-santodomingo.com; Plaza Taína; 9am-1pm & 2-7pm Mon-Sat). At Aeropuerto El Catey, **Sixt** (809-338-0107; www.do.sixt.com) is the lone option.

Playa Bonita

A getaway from a getaway, this appropriately named beach only a few kilometers west of Las Terrenas is a better alternative for those seeking a more peaceful, reclusive vacation. Playa Bonita (Pretty Beach) is not without its imperfections – the half-moon-shaped beach is fairly steep and narrow, and parts are strewn with palm-tree detritus. However, backed by a small handful of pleasant hotels, this is an enticing spot.

Sights & Activities

Surfers and bodyboarders hit the waves around the eastern part of Playa Bonita near Calle Van der Horst. Just around the southwestern bend is the secluded, 6km-long **Playa Cosón**. The sand here is tan, not white, and the water greenish, not blue, but nevertheless it's a good place to pack a lunch and lose yourself for the day. There are two small rivers that run through the thick palm-tree forest and open into the ocean; the easternmost is said to contain agricultural runoff.

Sleeping & Eating

★ **Hotel Atlantis** HOTEL $$
(809-240-6111; www.atlantis-hotel.com.do; Calle F Peña Gomez; s/d/tr from $85/100/150;) This rambling and charming hotel is straight out of a children's fairy tale – all twisting staircases, covered walkways and odd-shaped rooms. The furnishings are comfortable, not luxurious, and each of the 18 rooms is different – some have balconies and fine ocean views. There's a palm-tree-covered patio and the ex-private chef of French president François Mitterrand handles the kitchen at the restaurant. Have him whip you up some lunch in the hotel's beach kiosk.

Hotel Acaya HOTEL $$
(809-240-6161; www.acaya-hotel-fr.com; Calle F Peña Gomez; r US$75, with air-con US$95;) Evocative of a more genteel era, the Acaya's two-story colonial building sits back from the beach on a finely manicured lawn. It's a French-owned, tastefully furnished place, with a relaxing lounge-restaurant, a small spa, a surf school and a half-hearted playground for kids. Rates include breakfast.

Coyamar HOTEL $$
(809-240-5130; www.coyamar.com; cnr Calles F Peña Gomez & Van der Horst; s/d/tr incl breakfast US$45/55/75;) Located at Calle Van der Horst and the beach road, Coyamar is the least luxurious of the Playa Bonita hotels. The vibe is casual and friendly, especially good for families, and the restaurant occasionally dishes out Asian and Mexican dishes. Bright colors and good-value rule the day here and the fan-cooled rooms are simple, spacious and comfortable. The pool is no bigger than a Jacuzzi.

★ **Peninsula House** BOUTIQUE GUESTHOUSE $$$
(809-962-7447; www.thepeninsulahouse.com; Playa Cosón; r US$832;) One of the Caribbean's most exquisite hotels, this discerning Victorian B&B perched high on a hill overlooking Playa Cosón is the choice for utmost exclusivity and service. Six rooms grace the mansion, each different and dressed up French Chateau-style (a Franco-American couple are your hosts). A Mexican husband-wife team runs the kitchen (three-course dinner US$80), focusing on simple preparations sourced locally and from their organic vegetable garden. Rooms are dressed head-to-toe in exquisite antiques, romantic four-poster beds and deep bathtubs, making the prospect of checking out agonizing – the average stay is five days, but you'll want to move in permanently.

Getting There & Away

By car, Playa Bonita is reachable along a single paved road that turns off from Calle Fabio Abreu in Las Terrenas. In theory it's possible to walk from Playa Bonita to Las Terrenas via a coastal dirt/mud trail, but it requires clambering over a steep pitch, and some water wading. A taxi ride here is US$15, a *motoconcho* is RD$100. There are usually a few *motoconchos* there in high season when you're ready to return, but it's best to set out before nightfall and/or make other arrangements in low season.

North Coast

Includes ➡

Best Places to Eat

- Otra Cosa (p152)
- Mares Restaurant (p133)
- Castle Club (p151)
- Beach Shack Seafood Grill (p154)
- Baia Lounge (p142)

Best Places to Stay

- Casa Colonial Beach & Spa (p136)
- Casita Mariposa (p158)
- Swell Surf Camp (p149)
- El Morro Eco Adventure Hotel (p159)
- Casa Veintiuno (p141)

Why Go?

From east to west on the Dominican Republic's north coast, you'll find world-class beaches, some of the best water sports in the country and out-of-the-way locales evocative of timeless rural life. This long coastal corridor stretching from Monte Cristi and the Haitian border in the west to Cabrera in the east has enclaves of condo-dwelling expat communities that have endowed some towns with a cosmopolitan air. There are forested hills, dry desert scrub, and jungly nature preserves. There are waterfalls to climb, sleepy little Dominican towns where it's possible to escape and mile after mile of sandy beaches. In the middle is Puerto Plata's international airport; nearby is the city itself and where most of the coast's all-inclusive resorts are located. Independent travelers will find plenty of accommodations to suit a variety of tastes and several good places to base themselves for explorations further afield, especially to Cabarete, where you can kitesurf, surf or just plain bodysurf.

When to Go

- Winds on the north coast pick up from late December to March, making this an ideal time to try surfing and kitesurfing; check out some of the best exponents in the Master of the Ocean competition in the last week of February.
- Puerto Plata's week-long June Cultural Festival brings the party to this coastal city's streets, while a jazz festival takes over Sosúa and Cabarete on the last weekend of October.
- The north is generally wetter from October to January and spectacularly sunny from June to September.

North Coast Highlights

1. Learning how to kitesurf or windsurf with the pros in **Cabarete** (p143), and afterwards digging your toes into the sand, and your fork into some great grub while dining on the beach
2. Jumping and sliding down the thrilling **27 Waterfalls of Damajagua** (p135)
3. Worshipping the sun as the waves roll onto beautiful **Playa Grande** (p154)
4. Going to school to learn how to **kitesurf** (p143) or **windsurf** (p146) from the pros
5. Exploring the underwater marine life around **Sosúa** (p139)
6. Finding tranquillity in the typical small-town Dominican atmosphere of **Río San Juan** (p153)

Getting There & Around

Aeropuerto Internacional Gregorío Luperón (p134) at Puerto Plata is within two hours' driving distance of almost everywhere on the north coast. It's also the best place to rent a car, although an SUV might be preferred if you're traveling to smaller communities inland or along the coast to the west of Puerto Plata. Cibao airport at Santiago and El Catey airport at Samana are secondary options worth considering.

Buses and *guaguas* (minivans) offer frequent service, although you may find the cost of the fare to be inversely proportional to your Spanish-language ability. Keep in mind the relatively small size of the country – Puerto Plata is only 215km from Santo Domingo.

PUERTO PLATA

POP 158,800

Squeezed between a towering mountain and the ocean is this working port town, the oldest city on the north coast. Wander the Malecón or the downtown streets surrounding the Parque Central and you'll see that small-scale revitalization efforts have replaced what was until recently a palpable feeling of neglect. Intermingled with run-of-the-mill shops are the fading, once-opulent homes built by wealthy German tobacco merchants in the 1870s. Several restaurants are worth a visit, as are a few interesting museums, and the cable car ride to the nearby bluff, if not clouded over, offers panoramic views.

History

As Columbus approached the bay in 1493, the sunlight reflected off the water so brilliantly it resembled a sea of sparkling silver coins and so he named it Puerto Plata (Silver Port). He also named the mountain that looms over the city Pico Isabel de Torres (799m), in honor of the Spanish queen who sponsored his voyages. In 1496 his brother Bartolomé Colon founded the city.

An important port for the fertile north coast, Puerto Plata – and, indeed, the entire north coast – was plagued by pirates. It eventually became more lucrative for colonists to trade with the pirates (who were supported by Spain's enemies, England and France) rather than risk losing their goods on Spanish galleons. Such trade was forbidden and enraged the Spanish crown. In 1605 the crown ordered the evacuation of Puerto Plata – as well as the trading centers of Monte Cristi, La Yaguana and Bayajá – rather than have its subjects trading with the enemy.

The north coast remained virtually abandoned for more than a century, until the Spanish crown decided to repopulate the area to prevent settlers from other countries from moving in. Puerto Plata slowly regained importance, suffering during the Trujillo period, but eventually reinventing itself as a tourist destination. The early 1990s were golden years for the city, and for the first time tourism revenues surpassed those of its three main industries – sugar, tobacco and cattle hides – combined.

Sights

Teleférico CABLE CAR

(☎809-586-2122; www.telefericopuertoplata.com; Camino a los Dominguez; round trip RD$400; ⏰8am-5pm) A cable car takes visitors to the top of the enormous flat-topped Pico Isabel de Torres. On clear days there are spectacular views of the city and coastline – go early, before the mountain clouds up. The botanical gardens at the top are good for an hour's stroll. You'll also find a large statue of Christ the Redeemer (similar to but smaller than its counterpart in Rio de Janeiro), an overpriced restaurant and aggressive knick-knack sellers.

Board the *teleférico* at its base at the southern end of Camino a los Dominguez, 800m uphill from Av José Ginebra (near the entrance to the campus for Universidad Tecnologica de Santiago, aka UTESA). A *motoconcho* (motorcycle taxi) here costs RD$75, a taxi RD$150. The ride is notorious for opening late or closing early. Officially licensed guides will no doubt try to coax any independent travelers to use their services, though they really aren't necessary.

In theory, you can also walk up (or down) the mountain, paying only a one-way fare to return (the trail begins under the cable car). However, this can't really be recommended, in part because it's a strenuous two- to three-hour walk (about 7km) and certainly impossible to do without a guide (in part because of safety issues). It is, however, a good warm-up for Pico Duarte. On weekends, local guides (RD$1000) hang out in the ticket office parking lot. Alternatively, Iguana Mama offers this tour.

Casa Museo General Gregorio Luperón MUSEUM

(☎809-261-8661; museogregorioluperon@claro.net.do; Calle 12 de Julio 54; adult/child RD$200/100; ⏰8:30am-6:30pm Tue-Sun) The life and times

Puerto Plata

of native-born son and independence leader, Gregorio Luperón are impressively fleshed out inside this beautifully restored pale-green Victorian-era building. Photographs and period artifacts trace Luperón's life, from humble beginnings to his role as provisional president during the 'Restoration', as well as tell Puerto Plata's story during the late 19th century.

Dominicans and Spanish speakers are charged only RD$100/50 per adult/child. The charming cafe, which serves pastries, tapas and sandwiches (RD$175), is open until 10:30pm.

Museo del Ambar Dominicano MUSEUM, SHOP

(☎809-586-3910; www.ambermuseum.com; Calle Duarte 61; admission RD$50; ⏰9am-5pm Mon-Sat) The colonial-era building houses a collection of amber exhibits. These exhibits include valuable pieces with such rare inclusions as a small lizard and a 30cm-long feather (the longest one found to date). Tours are offered in English and Spanish. A gift shop on the ground floor has a large selection of jewelry, rum, cigars, handicrafts and souvenirs.

Galería de Ambar MUSEUM, SHOP

(☎809-586-6467; www.ambercollection.itgo.com; Calle 12 de Julio; admission RD$25; ⏰8:30am-6pm Mon-Fri, 9am-1pm Sat) Despite its unfortunate location, housed in a rundown office-like building, there are museum-quality exhibits on the history of amber mining in the DR as well as on rum, sugar, tobacco and coffee. Multilingual guides are on hand to answer questions. Of course, the *raison d'etre* of the tour is the soft-sell pitch to buy the gallery's own proprietary cigar brand, as well as jewelry and other gifts in the ground-floor shop.

Fuerte de San Felipe HISTORICAL SITE

(San Felipe Fort; admission RD$100; ⏰9am-5pm Sun-Fri) Located right on the bay, at the western end of the Malecón, the fort is the

Puerto Plata

Sights

1 Casa de la Cultura........B2
2 Casa Museo General Gregorio Luperón........B2
3 Fuerte de San Felipe........A1
4 Galería de Ambar........B2
5 Iglesia San Felipe........B2
6 La Sala de Arte Camilo Carrau........B2
7 Museo del Ambar Dominicano........B2

Sleeping

8 Hotel Kevin........B2
9 Villa Carolina........C3

Eating

10 El Barco........B1
11 Jamvi's........C1
12 La Sirena........D1
13 Mares Restaurant & Pool Lounge........D2
14 Mercado Municipal........C3
15 Tam Tam Café........B1
Tostacos & Sushito........(see 13)

Shopping

16 La Canoa........B2

only remnant of Puerto Plata's early colonial days. Built in the mid-16th century to prevent pirates from seizing one of the only protected bays on the entire north coast, San Felipe never saw any action. For much of its life its massive walls and interior moat were used as a prison.

Included in the price of admission is an audio tour (English, French, German and Spanish); however, it's disappointingly thin in terms of historical breadth and depth. There are short explanations of the objects displayed in the small museum – a few rusty handcuffs, a handful of bayonets and a stack of cannonballs. The views of the bay are impressive, though, and a large grassy area in front of the fort makes for a restful stop.

Also at the fort is Puerto Plata's **lighthouse**, which first lit up on September 9, 1879, and was restored in 2000. The white-and-yellow tower – 24.4m tall, 6.2m in diameter – is a melding of neoclassical style with industrial construction.

Iglesia San Felipe CHURCH
(Parque Central, Calle Duarte; 8am-noon & 2-4pm Mon-Sat, 7am-8pm Sun) This twin-steepled church has been completely renovated since Hurricane George devastated the town in 1988. Check out the small but beautiful Italian stained-glass windows donated by local families during the renovation. It's on the southern side of the refurbished Parque Central, which is distinguished by a large gazebo in the center.

Malecón STREET
The completely paved Malecón (also known as Av General Luperón and Av Circunvalación Norte) runs along the shore. There are a handful of restaurants, as well as a half-dozen beachside shacks selling food and drinks on **Long Beach**, the main city beach around 2km east of downtown. A few experienced kitesurfers launch themselves into the waves here on windy days.

Casa de la Cultura CULTURAL CENTER
(809-261-2731; Parque Central, Separación; 9am-noon & 3-5pm Mon-Fri) FREE In addition to dance and music workshops, the center often showcases work by Dominican artists in its 1st-floor gallery.

La Sala de Arte Camilo Carrau CULTURAL CENTER
(809-457-7876; Calle Duarte 40) Next to the Casa de la Cultura on the Parque Central is this arts center, which holds theater, ceramic and painting classes (Spanish, English and Italian spoken).

Activities

All the nearby all-inclusive resorts organize tours for their guests. For independent travelers, Mark Fernandez, the hardworking and personable owner of several interlocking tour companies under the banner of **Caribbean Ocean Adventures** (809-586-6668, 809-586-1239; www.caribbeanoceanadventures.com) is the man to go to. **Freestyle catamaran boat trips** with snorkeling stops near Sosúa leave from Playa Dorada, the entrance to which is about 4km east of Puerto Plata; these are a fun way to spend a half-day, especially because of the crew's comedic shtick and all-you-can-drink bar. And finally, scuba divers looking to explore the north coast's reefs can contact **Sea Pro Divers** (www.seaprodivers.com).

For big-game fishing trips contact **Gone Fishing** (809-586-1239; www.caribbeanoceanadventures.com), run by experienced expat fisherman Barry Terry; you'll pay around US$100/US$165 (US$70 for watchers) per half-day/full day in larger groups, or you can charter a boat for US$550/800 per half-/full day.

Though less renowned than Cabarete's, Puerto Plata's own Kite Beach has close to ideal conditions for **kitesurfing**: year-round

WHALE'S-EYE VIEW

Only a day's sail north of Puerto Plata is Silver Bank, part of a protected migratory area that extends all the way from the Bahamas to Banco de la Navidad, and one of only two places in the world (the other is Tonga) where you can snorkel with humpback whales, some 60ft long. These 'soft water encounters' are both intimidating and exhilarating. However, because of the trip's costly price tag (US$4000 per person including sanctuary, port and fuel fees), it remains under the radar to most. **Tom Conlin** (☎in US 954-382-0024; www.acquaticadventures.com), an American naturalist who has been running week-long live-aboard trips here for 20 years, is the preeminent guide; the season is from the end of January to April and boats depart from Puerto Plata. Mini-seminars are conducted on board every night, in which the ins and outs of the species are explained as well as safety precautions – for the whales' benefit and your own.

flat water, cross-shore winds (so you won't end up blown out to sea) and a beach break, and it's relatively uncongested. For lessons, contact **Fernando Subero** (☎829-552-2200; fernandosubero@gmail.com; lesson per hr incl gear US$50), a young English-speaking Dominican guy and the only International Kiteboarding Organization (IKO) certified instructor in Puerto Plata.

Brugal Rum Plant TOUR
(☎809-261-1888; www.brugal.com.do; Carretera a Playa Dorada; ⏲8am-4pm Mon-Fri) FREE Some package tours come through this rum distillery and bottling facility, but it's an underwhelming 15-minute tour from a 2nd-floor gangway. Complimentary rum-based cocktails provided at the end.

Festivals & Events

Cultural Festival CULTURAL
(⏲3rd week of Jun) This festival sees merengue, blues, jazz and folk concerts held at Fuerte de San Felipe. Troupes from Santo Domingo perform traditional dances that range from African spirituals to sexy salsa tunes and local artisans gather for an arts-and-crafts fair at Parque Central.

Merengue Festival MERENGUE
(⏲early Nov) The entire length of the Malecón is closed to vehicular traffic, food stalls are set up on both sides of the oceanside boulevard and a stage is erected for merengue performances.

Sleeping

Unless you're after budget accommodations there's no real reason to spend more than a night in Puerto Plata, considering that there are better options nearby.

Villa Carolina GUESTHOUSE $
(☎809-586-2817; www.villacarolina.hostel.com; Av Virginia Elena Ortea 9; s/d incl breakfast RD$1200/1600; @ 🛜 🏊) This rambling old house with a leafy courtyard is easily the best place for independent travelers in Puerto Plata. Beyond the security gate at the end of a long driveway, several old cars, the family-occupied front house and the vine-covered pergola and pool area is the carriage house-cum-villa where the tastefully furnished rooms are located.

The colored tile floors add a touch of colonial elegance, both in the rooms and the large front lounge area. An old kitchen is available for guest use.

Hotel Kevin HOTEL $
(☎829-263-5182, 809-244-4159; hotel-kevin1@hotmail.fr; JF Kennedy, btwn Separación & Castellanos; s/d with fan RD$900/1000, with air-con RD$1000/1200; ❄ 🛜) Only a block from the Parque Central and housed in a building with Victorian-era facade and structure, this is a good-value choice. The basic rooms are clean and relatively well furnished, with cable TV and comfortable bathrooms. Wi-fi is accessible from the sunny front lobby.

Eating & Drinking

All the restaurants are also good places for a drink, with or without a meal. Along Kite Beach on the eastern end of the Malecón are around a half-dozen informal kiosks serving food and drinks, including **Kite Bar** (Malecón 32; ⏲lunch & dinner) and La Carihuela. Regulars, both expats and Dominicans, head here for sundowners and simple meals (RD$200 to RD$300). National flags hang from a few kiosks, announcing the country of origin of their owners.

Av Luis Ginebra, from the intersection with Av Hermanas Mirabal until it turns into Av 12 de Julio, has close to a dozen restaurants (Weng Yeng for inexpensive Chinese cuisine) and bars popular with the city's middle class. Topaci and El Furgon are recommended for drinks (dancing at the latter as well).

The enormous **La Sirena** (Malecón; ⌚8am-10pm Mon-Sat, 9am-8pm Sun) is the best place for groceries; several fast-food options, a pharmacy, dry cleaners (RD$650 per load of machine wash and dry) and banks are also inside. At the **Mercado Municipal** (cnr Calles 2 & López; ⌚7am-3pm Mon-Sat) you'll find meat and vegetables and tourist knick-knacks in what looks like an enormous, crown-shaped concrete gas station from the 1960s.

Tostacos & Sushito MEXICAN, JAPANESE **$$**
(☎809-261-3330; cnr Presidente Vasquez & Francisco Peynardo; mains RD$280; ⌚4-11pm, closed Mon) Offering tacos, burritos, sushi, sashimi and a few Dominican (tasty *mofongo*) and American options in between, this casual, outdoor eatery will appeal to a variety of tastes. And everything is above average, as you'd expect from the owner, Rafael Vasquez-Heinsen.

Kilometro Zero DOMINICAN, ITALIAN **$$**
(☎809-244-4346; Av Luis Ginebra; mains RD$350; ⌚10am-11:30pm, closed Wed; 📶) A friendly open-air place where you can pull a seat up at the bar or chow down on pasta (close to 20 varieties), surf and turf (RD$1300), plus burgers and crepes at a picnic table. Several flatscreen TVs are usually tuned to sports.

El Manguito Restaurant & Liquor Store SEAFOOD **$$**
(☎809-586-4392; mains RD$350; ⌚11am-11pm) Nestled at the side of the highway just east of the Costa Dorada complex (and just west of Playa Dorada) is this good-value seafood joint. Beers here are only US$2, and the lobster (US$14) is great value. Service is excellent, and there's also a variety of desserts.

Jamvi's PIZZERIA **$$**
(☎809-320-7265; cnr Malecón & Calle López; pizzas RD$275; ⌚10am-late) This gargantuan open-air pizza joint sits above street level on the Malecón, offering a pleasant sea breeze and great views. Good for a pizza and wine fix (there's a decent wine list); from 10pm onward it pumps merengue and reggaeton till late. Also delivers.

Terraza Las Almendras DOMINICAN **$$**
(☎809-854-0092; cnr Malecón & Calle A Brugal Montañez; mains RD$250; ⌚8am-late) With pleasant outdoor seating under bright umbrellas, this sea-facing restaurant is a good place for an inexpensive breakfast or a couple of beers. The food consists almost entirely of *pinchos* (snacks) – if it once roamed the earth (or sea), you can get it here served on a stick.

El Barco DOMINICAN, INTERNATIONAL **$$**
(Malecón; mains from RD$250; ⌚8am-late) At the northern end of the Malecón, El Barco is primarily an expat hangout. The menu includes standard Dominican fare such as grilled fish, with 'international' dishes such as pasta.

Tam Tam Café DOMINICAN, INTERNATIONAL **$$**
(Malecón; mains from RD$250; ⌚8am-late) Lots of expats eat here. The food is a combination of international and Dominican.

★ **Mares Restaurant & Pool Lounge** DOMINICAN **$$$**
(☎809-261-3330; Francisco Peynado 6; mains RD$700; ⌚6pm-midnight Wed-Sat) Distinguished chef Rafael Vasquez-Heinsen has converted his elegant home into a candlelit destination for foodies. *Top Chef* and food channel fans won't be disappointed. The kitchen turns out what elsewhere might be defined as haute fusion cuisine – dishes that creatively combine Dominican ingredients with other culinary traditions: try Dominican goat marinated with rum (RD$600). Reservations recommended.

Shopping

La Canoa JEWELRY, SOUVENIRS
(☎809-586-3604; Av Beller 18; ⌚9am-6pm Mon-Sat, to 1pm Sun) La Canoa is a large, rambling store with a mini amber museum and work spaces where amber and larimar stones are polished and set in jewelry. It also sells cigars (some are rolled on the premises), the usual acrylic Haitian paintings, postcards and other souvenirs.

Information

There are a few banks with ATMs in the blocks surrounding the Parque Central.

Banco BHD (JF Kennedy; ⌚9am-4:30pm Mon-Fri, to 1pm Sat)

Banco León (JF Kennedy; ⌚9am-4:30pm Mon-Fri, to 1pm Sat)

Centro Médico Bournigal (☎809-586-2342; www.bournigal-hospital.com; Calle Antera Mota; ⏰24hr) OK for minor things.

Melosa Clínica Brugal (☎809-586-2519; José del Carmen Ariza 15; ⏰24hr)

Discover Puerto Plata (www.discoverpuerto-plata.com) Official tourism website with general information for visitors.

Dot Com (☎809-261-6165; Calle 12 de Julio 69; internet per hr RD$30)

Farmacia Carmen (☎809-586-2525; Calle 12 de Julio; ⏰ 8am-5pm Mon-Fri) Pharmacy offering free delivery.

Politur (☎809-320-0365)

Puerto Plata Report (www.popreport.com) Regional news and travel information from the north coast of the DR.

Getting There & Away

AIR

Puerto Plata is served by **Aeropuerto Internacional Gregorío Luperón** (POP; ☎809-586-0107; www.puerto-plata-airport.com), 18km east of town along the coastal highway (past Playa Dorada), and just a few kilometers west of Sosúa. Numerous charter airlines, including several Canadian ones use the airport, mostly in conjunction with the all-inclusive resorts. A taxi to or from the airport costs US$30 to US$35. Or walk 500m from the terminal to the main highway to flag down a *guagua* to Puerto Plata (RD$55, 45 minutes) or Sosúa (RD$15, 10 minutes).

Airlines with international service here:

Air Berlin (www.airberlin.com) Direct flights to Berlin.

Air Canada (☎809-541-5151; www.aircanada.com) Direct flights to Montreal.

Air Turks & Caicos (☎in Turks & Caicos 649-946-4999, in US 954-323-4949; www.flyairtc.com) Daily flights to Turks and Caicos and to San Juan, Puerto Rico.

American Airlines (☎809-200-5151; www.aa.com)

Continental (☎809-200-1062; www.continental.com)

Delta (☎809-586-0973; www.delta.com)

Jet Blue (☎809-200-9898; www.jetblue.com)

Lufthansa (☎809-200-1133; www.lufthansa.com)

Martinair (☎809-200-1200; www.martinair.com)

Thomson (www.thomson.co.uk) This charter travel company flies from Gatwick, London and Manchester once weekly.

West Jet (www.westjet.com) Direct flights from Toronto.

BUS

Caribe Tours (☎809-586-4544; cnr Camino Real & Kounhart) and **Metro** (☎809-586-6063; cnr 16 de Agosto & Beller) run services from Puerto Plata to Santo Domingo (RD$350, four hours, hourly) and Sosúa (RD$50, 30 minutes, hourly 6am to 7pm). For Santiago (RD$110, 1¼ hours) get on the Santo Domingo–bound bus.

EASTBOUND GUAGUA

These leave from a stop on the north side of Parque Central, passing by the entrance of Playa Dorada and through Sosúa (RD$35, 30 minutes), Cabarete (RD$50, 45 minutes) and Río San Juan (RD$100, two hours). **Transporte Papagayo** (☎809-749-6415) buses leave daily for Samaná (RD$300, 3½ to four hours) at 6:30am from in front of the public hospital and Las Terrenas Transporte travels five times daily to Las Terrenas (RD$300, three hours).

SOUTH & WESTBOUND GUAGUA

Javilla Tours (☎809-970-2412; cnr Camino Real & Av Colón; ⏰every 15min 5am-7:30pm) serves Santiago (RD$120, 1½ hours) with stops along the way at Imbert (RD$40, 20 minutes) and Navarrete (RD$80, 50 minutes). To get to Monte Cristi, take Javilla's bus to Navarrete and tell the driver to let you off at the junction, where you can change for the Expreso Linieros bus (RD$140, 1½ hours).

CAR

Avis (☎809-586-4436, airport 809-586-0214; www.avis.com.do; Carretera Luperon Km 4½; ⏰8am-6pm), **Budget** (☎airport 809-586-0284; www.budget.com.do; Playa Dorada Plaza; has an office in Playa Dorada), **Europcar** (☎809-586-7979; www.europcar.com.do; cnr Av Luis Ginebra & Hermans Mirabal) and **National** (☎809-586-1366, airport 809-586-0285; www.nationalcar.com.do; Carretera Luperon Km 2½; ⏰8am-5pm) all have offices at the airport (the first two also have off-airport sites), where they are open 7am to 10pm and are usually on call overnight, but charge extra for late pickup or delivery.

Getting Around

The old town and parts of the Malecón are walkable. Otherwise, you'll need to get comfortable taking *motoconchos* (motorcycle taxis), rent a car or shell out cash for taxis.

Officially licensed *motoconcho* drivers wear numbered, colored vests and tend to be only slightly more cautious in traffic than their unlicensed brethren. The in-town fare is RD$25 and RD$60 to Playa Dorada.

You'll find taxi fares priced almost exclusively for tourists – the in-town fare is around RD$150 to RD$200. Taxis don't generally cruise the streets looking for customers, so try **Taxi Puerto Plata** (☎809-558-7682) with several taxi stands, including along the Parque Central and across from the Caribe Tours office.

TWENTY-SEVEN WATERFALLS

Travelers routinely describe the tour of the waterfalls at Damajagua as 'the coolest thing I did in the DR.' We agree. Guides lead you up, swimming and climbing through the waterfalls. To get down you jump – as much as 8m – into the sparkling pools below. These days, with the construction of a suspension bridge and a safer pathway up (no longer in view of the river), it's a less 'wild' experience for better or worse.

It's mandatory to go with a guide, but there's no minimum group size, so you can go solo if you wish. You can go up to the seventh, 12th or 27th waterfall, though most 'jeep safari' package tours only go to the 7th. You should be in good shape and over the age of 12. Foreigners pay RD$600 to the highest waterfall and less to reach the lower ones (US$1 of every entrance fee goes to a community development fund). Tour companies in Puerto Plata, Sosúa and Cabarete organize trips here for between US$80 and US$100. The falls are open from 8:30am to 4pm, but go early before the crowds arrive. A **visitors center** (809-635-1722; www.27charcos.com) and restaurant are near the entrance.

To get to the falls, go south from Imbert on the highway for 3.3km (and cross two bridges) until you see a sign on your left with pictures of a waterfall. From there it's about 1km down to the visitors center. Alternatively, take a Javilla Tours *guagua* from Puerto Plata and ask to get off at the entrance.The big Texaco station at Imbert serves as a crossroad for the entire area. There is a frequent *guagua* service to Santiago (RD$80, one hour) and Puerto Plata (RD$40, 30 minutes).

The main trunk roads in Puerto Plata are serviced by *guaguas* following lettered routes, which cost RD$20. Lines C and F will be of most interest to you: they run from as far west as Cofresí, through town and past Playa Dorada to the east. Line C runs direct; line F makes lots of twists and turns as it barrels through town.

PLAYA DORADA & COSTA DORADA

These two adjacent pretty beaches a few miles east of Puerto Plata string together a handful of all-inclusive resorts and one five-star hotel. Both developments are marked by large archways – Playa Dorada is the much larger one and the first you come to on the highway from the airport. A prolonged downturn in Puerto Plata's mass-market tourism has led to the mothballing of many properties, reminders of developers' outsized ambitions and subpar products, and of the national government's prioritizing of resort projects in the southeast. However, signs point to a small-scale revitalization that might see a contraction in the number of rooms with a renewed focus on quality.

Names and parent companies have changed over the years; however, a few worth considering, in addition to those reviewed below, are the Gran Ventana Beach Resort, Be Live Grand Marien and Celuisma Playa Dorada. Most offer day and night passes (US$45 to US$60), which entitle you to unlimited access to their facilities and a buffet lunch or dinner. The Playa Dorada minimall has a handful of infrequently visited shops selling cheap souvenirs and package tours, a cinema (closed due to remodeling on our visit), two banks with ATMs and a Budget car-rental agency.

Activities

Playa Dorada Golf Club GOLF
(809-320-4262; www.playadoradagolf.com; 7am-7pm) This well-regarded 6218m, par-72 Robert Trent Jones course is the centerpiece of the Playa Dorada complex. The greens fee for nine holes is US$50, for 18 holes, US$75; caddies (US$8/15 for nine/18 holes) are obligatory, golf carts (US$15/25 for nine/18 holes) are not.

Sleeping & Eating

Suncamp APARTMENTS $
(809-320-1441; www.suncampdr.com; Calle Principal; campsite US$10, r US$20;) Surrounded by lush jungle and set on a river near the village of Muñoz, 3km inland from Playa Dorada, thoroughly rustic Suncamp looks like a typical Dominican compound – concrete floors, corrugated-iron roof and makeshift furnishings. A stay here can be worthwhile if your standards of comfort are low.

There's a variety of rooms, some have private bathroom (basically, a curtained-off toilet) and their own kitchen, though appliances are aged. Bring a flashlight and mosquito repellent. Diane, the Canadian owner, is friendly and welcoming and can help you plan trips in the region; airport transfers (US$30). Popular with young volunteers as well as retirees looking for an inexpensive way to while away the days.

Barcelo Puerto Plata RESORT **$$**
(809-320-5084; www.barcelo.com; Playa Dorada; r from US$75;) Good value, though pretty much a by-the-numbers all-inclusive, Barcelo has managed to remain vital at least in part because of its discounted internet deals enjoyed by a mix of Dominican families and guests from abroad, both young and old. The tile-floored, attractive rooms have comfortable beds and maintenance is prompt with repairs.

Granted, the pool areas aren't the elaborate fantasias of some resorts, but the beachfront lives up to most people's Caribbean expectations. Like most of its kind, check-in and check-out can be slow and there's a hefty charge for wi-fi.

★ **Casa Colonial Beach & Spa** LUXURY HOTEL **$$$**
(809-320-3232; www.casacolonialhotel.com; Playa Dorada; r US$450-1450;) This extraordinary hotel is one of the finest in the country. It offers 50 indulgent suites, each with marble floors, sparkling fixtures, canopied beds, ample balconies, a cedar-lined closet, and plush bathrobes and slippers. The grounds are set in a sprawling mansion and boast a tropical garden with orchids growing at seemingly every turn.

A fantastic bar and an infinity pool with four Jacuzzis are located on the roof, providing spectacular views of the ocean. A high-end spa and two elegant restaurants are also on site. It's important to note that rates are not all-inclusive.

Blue Bay Hotel & Resort RESORT **$$$**
(809-320-3000; www.bluebayresorts.com; Playa Dorada; per person all-incl RD$3200;) One of the few adults-only resorts on the north coast, Spanish-owned Blue Bay styles itself as a boutique option for singles and couples looking for a holiday evocative of a Miami Beach hotel. The front lobby area is all flowing drapery, super-high ceiling and blue pastel accents, though the try-hard minimalism room design is slightly undermined by the lower-quality furniture.

It's more compact and less sprawling than other Playa Dorada options and the spa and food, especially the stand-alone Asian fusion Jade Garden (non-guests can eat here; mains RD$650), are a step up from its competitors.

Iberostar Costa Dorada RESORT **$$$**
(809-320-1000; www.iberostar.com; Costa Dorada; all-incl s/d US$135/165;) One of the better-value all-inclusives in the region, Iberostar receives its fair share of repeat customers. There is a certain Disneyland cheesiness about the place – you'll be greeted at reception by a porter wearing a pith helmet, for instance – but the grounds are enormous and well kept, the pool is immense, and the food better than average.

Getting There & Around

The Playa Dorada taxi association charges many times the price you'd pay if you hailed a taxi on the street. Their taxis can be found at any of the hotel entrances and also in front of Playa Dorada Plaza. A ride to the airport will cost you US$33, to Sosúa US$35, to Cabarete US$40, and within the hotel complex US$10; to Puerto Plata US$7.

Or you can walk to hotel complex's entrance on the highway and hail down a *guagua* to Puerto Plata (RD$20).

COSTAMBAR

Less a traveler's destination than an expat hideaway, Costambar is worth a visit for its beautiful, palm-shaded white-sand beach with shallow water and patches of coral reef. Several informal seafood restaurants, including the especially recommended **El Farolita** (meal RD$300) at the western end, line the beach; these are great places to while away a few hours (lounge chairs for rent). All of Costambar's services – including **Yenny's Market** (Calle Principal; 8am-9:30pm), a medium-sized grocery (no ATM), an internet cafe and a small fast-food eatery (no ATM) – are in the small village just past the gated entrance.

This is a private community that consists primarily of time-share units and vacation homes, some run down, some half-built and many occupied for six months of the year by North Americans on the run from winter. Condo associations might rent by the week and occasionally by the night in low season. A local monthly newsletter (www.costambarmonthly.com) can keep you up to date.

A *motoconcho* from Puerto Plata will cost you RD$100, and a taxi US$17. If you're already in Costambar, try the local **taxi association** (☎809-970-7318). *Guagua* lines C and F from Puerto Plata pass the front gate (every 15 minutes from 6am to 6pm), although the village is a good kilometer from the highway, and the beach another kilometer past that.

TUBAGUA PLANTATION ECO LODGE

To take a break from the north coast sun and sand, head inland on Rte 25 to Tubagua Plantation Eco-Village (p170) for a scenic trip that takes you through the Cordillera Septentrional all the way to Santiago.

PLAYA COFRESÍ

Five kilometers west of Puerto Plata lies the quiet, condo-dwelling hamlet of Cofresí. At one end is **Ocean World** (☎809-291-1000; www.oceanworld.net; adult/child US$55/40; ⏰9am-6pm), a Dominican version of Sea World with dolphins, sharks, sea lions and manta rays, an aviary and more that will certainly keep the kiddies entertained. You can also swim with the dolphins (per person US$155) or the sharks (US$60). For a trippy Las Vegas–style show, a sort of 'around the world in 120 costumes', there's **Bravissimo** ($45, $75 including dinner) in the Ocean World marina complex. The garishly clad, hard-working dancers perform high-energy tributes to Lady Gaga, Elvis Presley and a number of Latin pop stars. To make it a double-header evening, head several floors up to the **Lighthouse Lounge & Disco**, one of the best places for dancing in the area, especially on Saturday nights. The complex's **Posiedon restaurant** has a recommended all-you-can-eat Sunday brunch (US$35) that includes prime rib and lobster.

At the other end of Cofresí sprawls **Lifestyle Holidays Vacation Resort** (☎809-586-1227; www.lhvcresorts.com; all-incl r per person US$150; ❄@≋), an enormous complex with an array of compounds with a variety of levels of membership-like benefits, though regardless of your class, from elite to hoi polloi, all share a beautiful half-moon bay and white-sand beach. Sandwiched between Ocean World and Lifestyle is a tiny community of expats and condo dwellers, and a couple of restaurants. **Chris & Mady's** (mains RD$350; ⏰8am-11pm; 📶) has a wide-ranging menu with reasonable prices and a Sunday barbecue popular with locals and expats alike. The menu at **Los Charos** (mains RD$200; ⏰11am-late; 📶) is full of Mexican fare, and German-run **Le Papillon** (☎809-970-7640; mains RD$550; ⏰6-11pm Tue-Sun), up a small hill 100m east of Cofresí, is a fine-dining option with specials like leg of rabbit, smoked yellowtail and vegetable curry.

Three large resorts, all under the Riu banner, line the pretty Bahia Maimon around 6km west of the access road to Cofresí. Construction was underway next door on a large docking facility to handle Carnival Cruise Line ships (possibly Royal Caribbean as well).

Getting There & Away

Take *guagua* C or F (RD$12) from Puerto Plata. Going back to town take only the C – the F does lots of twists and turns in the city and takes twice as long to get you to the center. It's a steep downhill walk of about 700m to the main beach area. There's *guagua* service until about 7pm. If you're driving, simply follow the main highway west.

There's also a taxi stand (US$25 to Puerto Plata and US$50 to the airport) located just outside Lifestyle Holidays.

SOSÚA

POP 49,600

Sosúa by day and Sosúa by night are two different creatures. When the sun is out, the beach and calm bay are ideal for swimming and attract a broad swath of Dominicans, foreigners and families alike. When evening comes, it's no longer a PG destination. The inescapable fact, despite the mayor's efforts otherwise, is that Sosúa is known for sex tourism. Bars fill up with Dominican and Haitian sex workers, and men, single and in groups, can expect to be accosted and propositioned. Nevertheless, there are a number of hotels and good restaurants. And despite its more confronting qualities, Sosúa is the base for the area's scuba-diving operations and conveniently located for exploring the north coast. The town's seemingly curious status as the cheese and dairy capital of the DR was established by around 350 families of Jewish refugees who fled Germany and other parts of Europe in 1940. Since few were farmers,

Sosúa

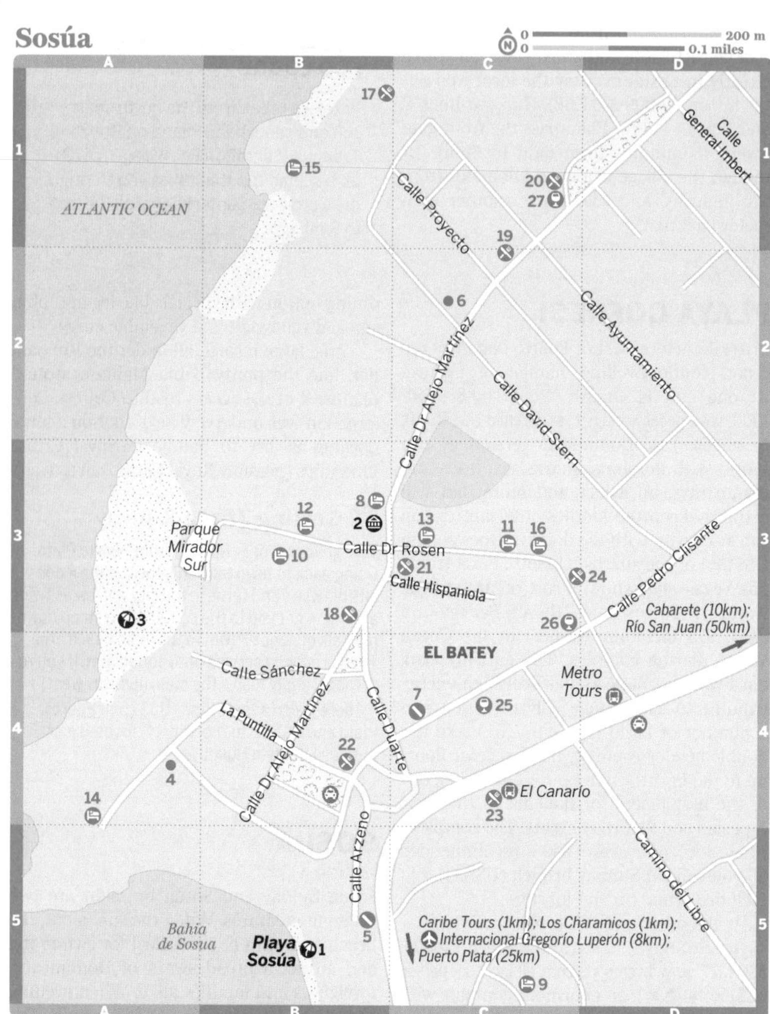

most left after just a couple of years, but not before building many fine homes.

Sights

Museo de la Comunidad Judía de Sosúa MUSEUM

(Jewish Community Museum of Sosúa; 809-571-2633; Calle Dr Alejo Martínez; admission RD$150; 9am-1pm & 2-4pm Mon-Fri) This museum, near Calle Dr Rosen, has exhibits (Spanish and English text) describing the Jewish presence in the DR. At the multinational Evian conference in 1938 the DR was the only country to officially accept Jewish refugees fleeing Nazi repression in Germany. If the gate is locked during opening hours, ring the number listed above – someone should arrive in less than five minutes to let you in.

Beaches

★Playa Sosúa BEACH

Playa Sosúa is the main beach, and practically a city within a city. Located on a crescent-shaped bay with calm, turquoise waters, this narrowing (due to erosion) stretch of sand is backed by palm trees and a seemingly endless row of souvenir vendors, restaurants, bars and even manicurists. The crowds of

Sosúa

Dominican families and long-term visitors staying in local hotels and condos make this beach a great place for people-watching. Snorkel gear is available for rent (two hours RD$400, includes life jacket, bottle of Coca-Cola for you and bread for the fish).

Playa Alicia BEACH

An ordinary and wide patch of brownish-yellow sand (no shade) lapped by calm waters, Playa Alicia has steadily grown and been 'replenished' since its creation nearly a decade ago. Whether this has been done in an environmentally sound manner is disputed. Steps leading down to the beach can be found at the end of Calle Dr Rosen in **Parque Mirador Sur**, a small paved plaza with benches and a cafe kiosk.

Activities

Diving & Snorkeling

Sosúa is generally considered the diving capital of the north coast. In addition to the dozen or so dive sites within boating range of Sosúa Bay, dive shops also organize excursions as far afield as Río San Juan (through mangroves and freshwater Dudu Cave) and Cayo Arena. There's a good variety of fish plus hard and soft corals (several projects to restore depleted coral are in the works), drop-offs and sponges.

Among the popular dive spots nearby are Airport Wall, featuring a wall and tunnels in 12m to 35m of water; Zíngara Wreck, an upright 45m ship sunk in 1993 as an artificial reef in around 35m of water; and Coral Gardens and Coral Wall, both offering coral formations in depths ranging from 14m to 53m.

Prices are generally US$90 for two dives with gear, around US$10 less if you have your own equipment, and slightly more for dives further afield. Booking a dive package brings the price down considerably – with a 10-dive package, the per-dive price can be as low as US$35 if you have your own gear. All of Sosúa's shops offer certification courses. Snorkeling trips are available at all shops, and cost US$30 to US$45 per person, depending on the length and number of stops; equipment is always included.

One big difference about the shops is that the predominant language among the staff is German, though English and Spanish are spoken by all.

Northern Coast Diving DIVING

(809-571-1028; www.northerncoastdiving.com; Calle Pedro Clisante 8) This well-respected dive shop is one of the best, and the most willing to create customized excursions to little-visited dive sites.

Dive Center Merlin DIVING

(809-571-4309; www.divecenter-merlin.com; Playa Sosúa) At the end of the road to Playa Sosúa.

Zip-Lining

Monkey Jungle OUTDOORS

(829-649-4555; www.monkeyjungledr.com; zip-line adults/children US $50/30; 9am-5pm) Follow the access road to El Choco a further

BEST DIVES ON THE NORTH COAST

Three Rocks Good for beginners; three giant coral heads; 17m.

Airport Wall Sharp drop-off with small cave; 21m.

Garden Fan coral and tube sponges to 24m.

Pyramids Gulleys, cliffs and swim-throughs; 18m.

9km for Monkey Jungle, a working organic farm with a sanctuary for rescued squirrel and capuchin monkeys and a thrilling 4400ft zip line. All proceeds go to the on-site medical and dental clinic which provides free care to the surrounding communities. In what might seem like a disconcerting clash to some, a handgun firing range shares the property.

Courses

Casa Goethe LANGUAGE COURSE
(☎809-571-3185; www.edase.com; La Puntilla 2) This German-run outfit has private and group Spanish classes in the mornings, and the center can organize activities like scuba diving or salsa-dancing classes in the afternoon. Long-term housing arranged either at the center itself or in area hotels.

Holiday Spanish School LANGUAGE COURSE
(☎809-571-1847; www.holiday-spanish-school.com; Calle Pedro Clisante 141) Spanish classes, for beginners and advanced students alike, are offered at Hotel El Colibrí, just east of the town center. Most are given in two-hour increments, divided equally between grammar and vocabulary and conversation. Prices vary according to the length of the course and the number of students.

Tours

There are a lot of cheesy package tours on offer at numerous agencies along the north coast. Many involve spending the majority of your day on a gaudily painted 'safari' bus getting to and from your destination. Be wary of any tour purporting to show you 'Dominican culture' – the 'local school' you'll visit will be more a Potemkin village than an authentic place of learning.

Tours that are most worth doing include rafting in Jarabacoa (four hours each way, US$60 to US$80), Cayo Arena for snorkeling (three hours each way, US$55 to US$65), whale-watching in Samaná (from mid-January to mid-March, four hours each way, US$120 to US$140), and anything involving a boat – catamaran tours (US$55 to US$90) and deep-sea fishing (US$50 to US$100) are hard to fake, and are generally good value. Try checking in with **Mel Tours** (☎809-571-2057; www.mel-tour.com; Calle David Stern) and **Sosua Game Fishing** (☎829-810-8799; www.sosuagamefishing.com).

Sleeping

Hotel El Rancho HOTEL $
(☎809-571-4070; www.hotelelranchososua.com; Calle Dr Rosen 36; r from US$40; ❄ 📶) The rather pleasant leafy pool and garden area is the centerpiece of this small centrally located hotel only a block from Playa Alicia. A three-story modern concrete building decorated with vaguely Mexican murals and topped with a *palapa*-style roof for show, El Rancho has clean, well-kept rooms.

Hotel Casa Valeria HOTEL $$
(☎809-571-3565; www.hotelcasavaleria.com; Calle Dr Rosen 28; s/d incl breakfast US$55/65; ❄ 📶 🏊) All nine rooms at this cozy hotel are slightly different, whether in size, furnishings or decor. Three units have kitchens (with gas burners), the others are hotel-like rooms with comfortable beds, attractive furnishings and a pink colour scheme. Rooms are set around a leafy courtyard with a kidney-shaped pool in the middle; all have cable TV, fans and ceramic-tiled bathrooms.

Hotel Casa Cayena Club HOTEL $$
(☎809-571-2651; www.hotelcasacayena.com; Calle Dr Rosen 25; s/d US$65/85; ❄ 📶 🏊) This well-managed hotel contains 24 rooms on two floors, connected by broad breezy corridors. All rooms have red-tile floors, clean modern bathrooms with hot water, cable TV and security boxes. There's a nice pool area, and Playa Alicia is just down the street. A small outdoor restaurant serves breakfast.

New Garden Hotel HOTEL $$
(☎809-571-1557; www.hotelnewgarden.com; Calle Dr Rosen 32; s/d/tr incl breakfast RD$2800/3450/4090; ❄ 📶 🏊) The fact that the front desk sells condoms tells you something about this hotel's clientele. Your reaction no doubt will color whether the New Garden is worth considering. Rooms, especially those in the newer building, are what you

might find at any good-quality chain motel in North America. A bar area and pool are in front. Rents scooters for US$20 per day.

★ **Casa Veintiuno** BOUTIQUE HOTEL **$$$**
(☎829-342-8089; www.casaveintiuno.com; Calle Piano 1; r incl breakfast US$175-200;) This whitewashed modernist home on a hill just outside town has been transformed into a comfortable and intimate B&B, both a quiet refuge and a base for exploring the area. The Belgian owners Saskia and Mark – and their two dogs – provide personable and attentive service, even shuttling every guest into town for a private tour. Many guests, however, choose to spend much of their time lounging around the courtyard pool area and upstairs lounge, which has a telescope, treadmill, Wii game system and a 'library' of DVDs, books and boardgames. Lunch and dinner – the quality of the food is some of the best in town – are served Wednesdays through Sundays. Nonguests can eat here, but reservations are required.

Terra Linda Hotel Spa & Resort HOTEL **$$$**
(☎809-571-2220; www.terralindaresort.com; Calle Dr Rosen 22; s/d US$90/130;) Three stories of well-kept and comfortable rooms with small flatscreen TVs surround Terra Linda's large inner courtyard, which has an Olympic-sized pool – it feels like an oasis from the noisy street. Look for the entrance below street level, concealed behind the Scotch 'n' Sirloin restaurant.

Piergiorgio Palace Hotel HOTEL **$$$**
(☎809-571-2626; www.piergiorgiopalace.com; La Puntilla; r incl breakfast US$95;) Understandably popular with wedding planners, the PierGiorgio is built on a rocky cliff overlooking the ocean, ornately constructed with a white gingerbread facade and a grand red-carpeted staircase that spirals to the top floor. The room furnishings are aging and don't match the magnificent sea views – ask for a room on the 3rd floor. The cliffside restaurant (mains RD$600) is an undeniably romantic spot.

Sosúa by the Sea RESORT **$$$**
(☎809-571-3222; www.sosuabythesea.com; cnr Calles Bruno Philips & David Stern; s/d incl breakfast US$85/140;) Set on a coral spit on the aptly named Playa Chiquita, this hotel's rooms are minimally furnished in an attractive way. Unfortunately, however, the pool area out back could use some attention, even just a tree or two to break up the concrete. All rooms do have mini refrigerators and an all-inclusive service (all meals) is available for a US$20 surcharge.

Casa Marina Beach Resort RESORT **$$$**
(☎809-571-3690; www.amhsamarina.com; Calle Dr Alejo Martínez; all-incl s/d US$150/200;) A large complex with three pools, five restaurants, almost 400 rooms arranged in three-story buildings and direct access to Playa Alicia, though it's no great shake of a beach. The rooms are classic all-inclusive: clean and comfortable but not memorable in any way, with cable TV and a balcony, and most looking onto the pool.

Eating

A handful of restaurants are within a block of Parque Central and most hotels have their own. Pedro Clisante is lined with informal bars and restaurants, as is the path along Playa Sosúa – head to the flag-strewn Scandinavian Bar, to the left of the central stairs down to the beach, for good BBQ ribs. **Playero Supermarket** (☎809-571-1821; ⏲8am-10pm) on the main highway has a good selection of local produce and imported delicacies.

★ **Michael Snack Bar** SEAFOOD **$$**
(☎829-861-4621; Calle Julio Arzeno; mains RD$330; ⏲10am-9pm) Perched on a cliff at the very southern end of Playa Sosúa, this simple eatery combines million-dollar views with freshly prepared crab, fish and lobster. Diners are mostly locals, but it's welcoming to newcomers and definitely worth seeking out. Accessed only by following the road (through the 'neighborhood' of Los Charamicos) down from the highway.

Scotch & Sirloin/ Pizza Uno/El Batey Grill STEAKHOUSE, PIZZA, DOMINICAN **$$**
(Calle Dr Rosen; mains RD$375; ⏲7am-11pm;) Three restaurants – with three separate menus – are housed in this attractive open-air pavilion above the Terra Linda Hotel. Scotch & Sirloin specializes in burgers, steaks and baby back ribs (RD$600); Pizza Uno in wood-fired brick-oven pizza; and El Batey Grill in an extensive menu of Dominican dishes.

Infiniti Blu MEDITERRANEAN, MIDDLE EASTERN **$$**
(☎809-571-2717; Calle Dr Alejo Martinez; mains RD$350; ⏲7:30am-11pm;) Housed in a corner of the luxury condo development of

the same name is this contemporary white-tablecloth restaurant. Equally recommended for its extensive breakfast menu, especially its fresh croissants, as it is for its lunch and dinnertime menu featuring kebabs, falafel and kibbeh. The exceedingly cute cafe attached serves fanciful pastries and cakes – children will love the mini-furnishings.

Bologna ITALIAN **$$**
(☎809-571-1434; Calle Dr Alejo Martínez 33; mains RD$300-600; ⏰8am-11:30pm; 📶) Locals and expats rave about the quality of the pizza and pasta, not to mention the oreo cheesecake, at this family-friendly place just north of the town center. The vibe, encouraged by regulars, is of a small-city neighborhood joint with a diner feel. Delivers.

Bailey's INTERNATIONAL **$$**
(☎809-571-3085; Calle Dr Alejo Martínez; mains RD$250-600; ⏰7:30am-11:45pm) A favorite among expats, this Austrian-owned restaurant offers specialities such as chilli burgers and enormous schnitzel sandwiches. The decor includes lots of rattan furniture and potted plants, as well as a welcome continually spraying mist of water to keep things cool.

Marua Mai DOMINICAN **$$**
(☎809-571-3682; cnr Calles Pedro Clisante & Arzeno; mains RD$450; ⏰7:30am-11pm) This Dominican/German-owned restaurant has been a solid midrange choice – with great burgers, seafood and lobster by the kilo – for several decades now. There's a pleasant bar for a quiet drink before or after. Good breakfasts, too.

Rocky's Rock & Blues Bar Hotel DOMINICAN, AMERICAN **$$**
(Calle Dr Rosen 24; mains RD$250; ⏰7am-late; 📶) The sign outside says 'World Famous Ribs,' but that's just the beginning – the breakfasts, served until 3pm, are great value, the steaks are Dominican beef (not imported), and the beers are some of the cheapest in town. Pizza is served after 5pm and the music is pure rock and blues.

★ **Baia Lounge** SEAFOOD **$$$**
(Ocean Club, Calle Bruno Philips; tasting menu RD$2000; ⏰6-11pm Tue-Fri, noon-midnight Sat & Sun) This beachfront space is part of the Ocean Club, an ultramodern condo development still under construction at the time of our visit. The Chilean chef designs an ever-changing tasting menu involving freshly caught seafood and wine pairings for every course.

La Finca INTERNATIONAL **$$$**
(☎809-571-3925; cnr Calles Dr Rosen & Dr Alejo Martínez; mains from RD$600; ⏰5-11pm; 📶) This longtime Sosúa culinary landmark with a colonial-era design scheme takes its cuisine seriously, both in its presentation and price. Steak and seafood are the rock stars here – there's chateaubriand, surf and turf, and a mixed seafood platter for two (US$50). It has an amazing cocktail list, and the menu is in five languages, including Russian.

Drinking & Nightlife

Sosúa's nightlife – the epicenter is along Calle Pedro Clisante – is packed with bars and clubs, many catering to prostitutes and their customers. A mayoral initiative to enclose every open-air place with walls and windows to make prostitution less visible has yet to take effect. Restaurants, wherever they are in town, are often a more relaxed place for a drink.

Infiniti Blu BAR
(Calle B Philips; ⏰noon-11pm; 📶) Sandwiched between the Infinit Blu's restaurant and cafe is this smart and fashionable sliver of a bar. It's a good place for watching sports, especially as every drink is under RD$200.

El Flow Latin Bar BAR
(cnr Calles Pedro Clisante & Dr Rosen; ⏰10am-3am) Dominicans come here for merengue, *bachata* and the occasional reggaeton, as well as the cheap beer. Especially crowded on Friday from 4pm.

Britannia Pub BAR
(☎809-571-1959; Calle Pedro Clisante 13; ⏰8am-11pm) Popular with expats, this is a pleasant spot for a quiet drink. There's a good book exchange at the back, and the cheap bar food, like burgers and wings, isn't bad.

Information

Banco Popular (cnr Calles Dr Alejo Martínez & Sánchez; ⏰9am-4:30pm Mon-Fri, to 1pm Sat)

Banco Progreso (Calle Pedro Clisante; ⏰9am-4:30pm Mon-Fri, to 1pm Sat)

Caribe Internet (☎809-915-2688; Calle Duarte 5; per hr RD$70; ⏰9am-9pm Mon-Sat, 10:30am-5pm Sun)

Centro Medico Cabarete (CMC) (☎809-571-4696; www.centromedicocabarete.com; ⏰24hr) Despite its name, this private hospital is on the main highway only 1km east of Sosúa.

Run by an Argentinian doctor – an actual brain surgeon – and his American wife, this is where expats recommend going for serious medical issues.

Family Laundry (☎809-324-7922; cnr Calles Dr Rosen & Dr Alejo Martínez; per kilo RD$55)

Farmacia KH3 (☎809-571-2350; Calle Pedro Clisante; ⊙8am-9pm Mon-Sat, 9am-6pm Sun)

Getting There & Away

AIR

Sosúa is much closer to the **Aeropuerto Internacional Gregorío Luperón** (POP; ☎809-586-0107; www.puerto-plata-airport.com) than Puerto Plata, although it's commonly referred to as 'Puerto Plata airport.' A taxi from the airport to Sosúa is US$25. You can also walk 500m from the terminal to the highway and flag down a passing *guagua* (RD$15, 10 minutes).

BUS

Metro Tours (☎809-571-1324; cnr Av Luperón & Calle Dr Rosen) has its depot on the highway in the middle of town. It runs services to Santiago (RD$200, two hours) and onward to Santo Domingo (RD$380, five hours, 8:20am, 10:20am, 1:20pm, 3:20pm and 5:50pm; also 2:20pm and 4:20pm Sundays). **Caribe Tours** (☎809-571-3808) has a depot on the highway at the edge of Los Charamicos neighborhood, 1km southwest of the city center. It offers a service from Sosúa to Santo Domingo (RD$320, hourly from 5:20am to 6:20pm). Grab the same bus for Puerto Plata (RD$35, 20 minutes), Santiago (RD$170) and La Vega (RD$200). Bring warm socks, a sweatshirt (the air-con is on high) and earplugs (the sound from pirated DVDs is on full blast).

El Canarío (☎809-291-5594) is a Puerto Plata–based bus that leaves daily to Samaná (RD$250, three hours) at 7am from the main *parada* (bus stop). Be sure to call the day before to reserve your seat.

GUAGUA

For eastbound destinations along the coast, go to the highway and flag down any passing *guagua*. They pass every 15 minutes or so, with services to Puerto Plata (RD$35, 30 minutes), Cabarete (RD$25, 20 minutes) and Río San Juan (RD$75, 1½ hours).

Getting Around

You can walk just about everywhere in Sosúa, except to the hotels east of the center, which are better reached by *motoconcho* or taxi. The former are easy to find around town, while shared and private taxis for intercity travel along the coast can be located at a **taxi stand** (☎809-571-3093) on the corner of Calles Morris Ling and Arzeno. A trip to Cabarete should run around RD$500.

To rent a car, make your way to the airport (8km away).

CABARETE

POP 14,600

This one-time fishing and farming hamlet is now the adventure-sports capital of the country, booming with condos and new development. You'll find a sophisticated, grown-up beach town, with top-notch hotels, and a beach dining experience second to none (not to mention the best winds and waves on the island). Cabarete is an ideal spot to base yourself for exploring the area – you're within two hours' drive of the best that the coast has to offer, and if you want to go surfing, or windsurfing, or kitesurfing, heck, you don't even need to leave town. You'll hear a babble of five or six languages as you walk Cabarete's single street, where the majority of the hotels, restaurants and shops are located.

Sights & Activities

The surfing high season is the kitesurfing low season. While there are winds year round, the best months for the latter are July, August and the beginning of September. February can be a good month, and though December is crowded, the winds aren't the most consistent.

Whether you spend your day lounging on the beach or pursuing a more athletic endeavor, it's worth considering a therapeutic visit to **N Day Spa** (☎809-905-6510; www.cabaretespa.com; Plaza el Patio, Calle Principal; massage US$65; ⊙9am-6pm Mon-Sat) for a relaxing massage.

Parque Nacional El Choco

Part of the park, the caves of Cabarete are walking distance from town. Here you can take a two-hour **tour** (US$15; ⊙9am-3:30pm) of a number of privately managed caves and the surrounding forest. Bring a swimsuit – the crystal-stalactite caves 25m below the surface offer two opportunities to swim in small clear pools, provided the guide can still see you with his flashlight.

Kitesurfing

Cabarete is one of the top places in the world for kitesurfing, which long ago eclipsed windsurfing as the town's sport *du jour*. Kite

Cabarete

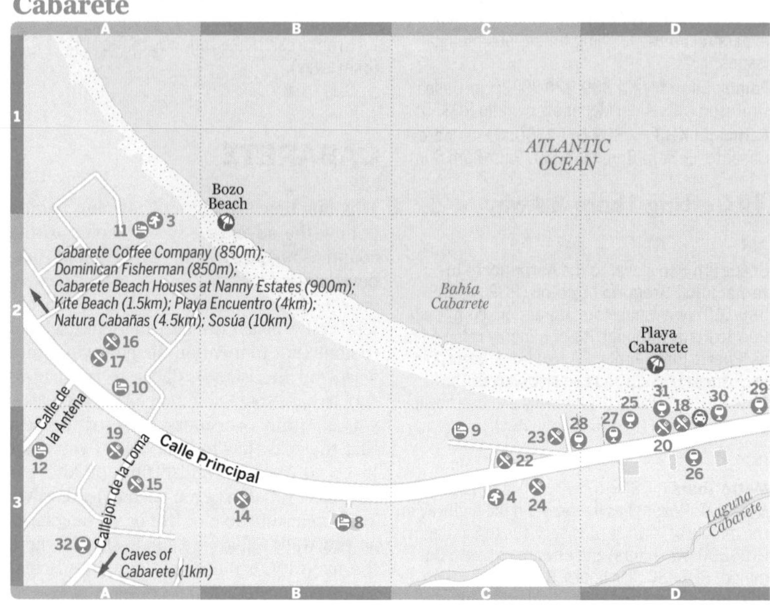

Cabarete

Activities, Courses & Tours

- Ali's Surf Camp .... (see 5)
- 1 Cabarete Language Institute F3
- 2 Carib Wind Center E2
- Dive Cabarete .... (see 8)
- Iguana Mama .... (see 29)
- 3 Laurel Eastman Kiteboarding A2
- 4 N Day Spa C3
- Northern Coast Diving .... (see 29)
- Swell Surf .... (see 12)
- Vela Windsurf Center .... (see 18)

Sleeping

- 5 Ali's Surf Camp F3
- 6 El Magnifico F2
- 7 Hotel Alegría F2
- 8 Hotel Kaoba B3
- 9 Hotel Villa Taína C3
- 10 L'Agence A2
- 11 Millennium Luxury Beach Resort & Spa A2
- 12 Swell Surf Camp A3
- 13 Velero Beach Resort F2

Eating

- 14 Belgium Bakery B3
- 15 Bliss A3
- 16 Burger Joint A2
- 17 Gordito's Fresh Mex A2
- 18 La Casita de don Alfredo D3
- 19 La Parilla de Luis A3
- 20 Mojito Bar D3
- 21 Otra Cosa F2
- 22 Panadería Repostería Dick C3
- 23 Pomodoro C3
- 24 Restaurant Chino C3

Drinking & Nightlife

- 25 Bambú D3
- 26 Blue Bar D3
- 27 Casanova D3
- 28 Lax C3
- 29 Lazy Dog D2
- 30 Ojo D3
- 31 Onno's D3
- 32 Vodoo Lounge A3
- Voy Voy .... (see 18)

Shopping

- 33 Janet's Supermarket F2

Beach, 2km west of town, has ideal conditions for the sport, which entails strapping yourself to a modified surfboard and a huge inflatable wind foil, then skimming and soaring across the water. Bozo Beach at the west end of the city beach is also a good spot and typically less crowded. A number of kitesurfing schools offer multiday courses for those

who want to learn – just to go out by yourself you'll need at least three to four days of instruction (two to three hours' instruction per day). Lessons generally don't begin until after 1pm when winds pick up, though if the wind is too strong, say about 20 knots, they may be canceled. The learning curve for the sport is quite steep – you'll need several weeks to get good enough to really enjoy yourself.

Expect to pay US$200 to US$280 for four hours of beginner lessons, or anywhere from US$300 to US$500 for a three- to four-day course (around eight hours total). Small groups are charged less per person; however, because newbies pick things up at different speeds, this can be frustrating for some. Schools and instructors vary considerably, so spend time finding one where you'll feel comfortable. Kitesurfing is a potentially dangerous sport, and it is extremely important that you feel free to ask questions and voice fears or concerns, and that you receive patient, ego-free answers in return. The **International Kiteboarding Organization** (www.ikointl.com) has a feature listing student ratings for schools and instructors.

About half of the schools are located on Kite Beach. You can check conditions on www.windalert.com or www.windguru.com. Most shops rent complete gear if you already know the ropes (around US$40 per hour or US$75 per day in low season).

Laurel Eastman Kiteboarding KITESURFING
(☎809-571-0564; www.laureleastman.com; Cabarete) Run by one of the world's top kiteboarders, this is a friendly, safety-conscious operation located on the beach at the high-end Millennium Resort. High-quality equipment and lessons offered in five languages. Nifty-looking bags made by local tailors from old, donated kites are sold in the shop – profits go to Kiters 4 Communities (www.kiters4communities.org), an organization building a school in a nearby Haitian community.

Kite Club KITESURFING
(☎809-571-9748; www.kiteclubcabarete.com; Kite Beach) This well-run club is at the top of Kite Beach, and has a fantastic atmosphere for hanging out and relaxing between sessions. The tiny kitchen delivers delicious fresh ahi tuna salads and sandwiches.

Kitexcite KITESURFING
(☎829-962-4556; www.kitexcite.com; Kite Beach) This German-owned school (Dominican instructors), one of the first in Cabarete, uses radio helmets and optional offshore sessions to maximize instruction.

Dare2Fly KITESURFING
(☎809-571-0805; www.dare2fly.com; Kite Beach) Owned by Vela Windsurf Center, Dare2Fly, which has European instructors, is located at Agualina Kite Resort.

Surfing

Waves of up to 4m, among the best waves for surfing on the entire island (p38), break over reefs 4km west of Cabarete on Playa Encuentro. The waves break both right and left and are known by names such as Coco Pipe, Bobo's Point, La Derecha, La Izquierda and most ominously, Destroyer. Several outfits in town and on Playa Encuentro rent surfboards and offer instruction. Surfboard rental for a day is around US$25 to US$30; a three-hour course costs US$45 to US$50 per person, and a five-day surf camp costs US$200 to US$225 per person. All the surf schools have small offices on Playa Encuentro.

Newbies should keep in mind that surfing is generally an early morning sport and most people stop in the early afternoon before the wind picks up (some will head out again around 5pm).

WHERE TO SHACK UP

Cabarete's beaches are its main attractions, and not just for sun and sand. They're each home to a different water sport, and are great places to watch beginner and advanced athletes alike.

Playa Cabarete Main beach in front of town, the best place for watching windsurfing, though the very best windsurfers are well offshore at the reef line. Look for them performing huge high-speed jumps and even end-over-end flips.

Bozo Beach On the western downwind side of Playa Cabarete, and so named because of all the beginner windsurfers and kiteboarders who don't yet know how to tack upwind and so wash up on Bozo's shore. There are more kiteboarders at Bozo than at Playa Cabarete, and the surf here is better for boogie boarding.

Kite Beach Two kilometers west of town, Kite Beach is a sight to behold on windy days, when scores of kiters of all skill levels negotiate huge sails and 30m lines amid the waves and traffic. On those days there's no swimming here, as you're liable to get run over.

Playa Encuentro Four kilometers west of town, this is the place to go for surfing, though top windsurfers and kiteboarders sometimes come here to take advantage of the larger waves. The beach itself is a long, narrow stretch of sand backed by lush tropical vegetation and palm groves as it curves east toward Cabarete; strong tides and rocky shallows make swimming difficult. To find the beach, look for the fading yellow archway and sign that says 'Coconut Palms Resort.' Definitely not safe to walk around here at night.

Bobo Surf's Up School SURFING
(☎809-882-5197; www.bobosurfsup.com; Playa Ecuentro)

Take Off SURFING
(☎809-963-7873; www.321takeoff.com; Playa Ecuentro) The German owner also organizes the Master of the Ocean competition.

Pau Hana Surf Center SURFING
(☎809-975-3494; Playa Encuentro) One of the first schools on the beach, Pau Hana has a good reputation and primarily employs local kids.

Cabarete Buena Onda SURFING
(☎829-877-0768; www.cabaretebuenaonda.com; Playa Encuentro)

Swell Surf SURFING
(www.swellsurfcamp.com; Cabarete)

Ali's Surf Camp SURFING
(☎809-571-0733; alissurfcamp.com; Cabarete)

Windsurfing

Cabarete's 'discovery' by French Canadians in the late 1980s as one of the best places for windsurfing in the Caribbean – strong, steady winds, relatively shallow water and a rockless shore – was what put the village firmly on the international tourists' radar. Once high profile, the sport's popularity has been waning. Board and sail rentals average US$30 to US$35 per hour, US$60 to US$65 per day or US$280 to US$300 per week. Renters are usually required to purchase damage insurance for an additional US$50 per week. Private lessons cost around US$50 for an hour, US$200 for a four-session course, with discounts for groups.

Vela Windsurf Center WATER SPORTS
(☎809-571-0805; velacabarete.com; Cabarete) Vela Windsurf Center, on the main beach, uses excellent gear and works in conjunction with kitesurfing school Dare2Fly. It also rents sea kayaks (per hour US$10 to US$15).

Sailing

Carib Wind Center SAILING
(☎809-571-0640; www.caribwindcabarete.com; Calle Principal, Cabarete) With more than 20 years' experience, the Israeli-owned Carib Wind Center is for those who prefer an actual boat attached to your sail. It rents Lasers and provides instruction.

Wakeboarding

Kitesurfers swear that this is a great way to develop your board skills, and on windless days you'll find more than a few from around the world at La Boca, 7km east of town at the mouth of the Río Yásica. It's an ideal spot with 2km of straight, flat river water to practice your latest tricks. There were no fully functioning wakeboarding operations open when we were in town; it's worth asking around at other companies listed here for more information.

Diving

Northern Coast Diving DIVING
(☎809-571-1028; www.northerncoastdiving.com; Cabarete) Well-respected Sosúa-based dive shop with a rep in Iguana Mama on Calle Principal. Organizes excursions from Río San Juan in the east to Monte Cristi in the west.

Dive Cabarete DIVING
(☎809-915-9135; www.divecabarete.com; Plaza Hotel Kaoba, Calle Principal) The only PADI dive center in the town of Cabarete.

Mountain Biking

Max 'Maximo' Martinez GUIDED TOUR
(☎809-882-5634; maxofthemt@gmail.com; full day incl rental per person US$75) If strapping a GPS and a machete to your bike and going out bush is your idea of a good time, hook up with Max 'Maximo' Martinez, a passionate and experienced mountain-bike guide. Maximo can tailor trips to any length and stamina level.

Stand-Up Paddleboarding

Increasing in popularity is this somewhat meditative, less athletic method of boarding. All-around ocean sport athlete, trainer and colorful storyteller, John Holzall (methodlodge@gmail.com) will take you on a paddle around the lagoon near Kite Beach. Laurel Eastman Kiteboarding (p145) rents boards for US$20 per hour; only mornings when the ocean is calm.

Horseback Riding

Rancho Luisa TOUR
(☎809-986-1984) A young French-Canadian guy runs this ranch out near Sabaneta de Yasica. A 2½-hour ride ($45 including transport to/from Cabarete) takes you through beautiful mountain scenery and past waterfalls and rural villages.

Rancho Mirabal TOUR
(☎809-912-5214) The fully equipped Rancho Mirabal riding stables are situated right on Playa Encuentro. A one-hour ride on the beach is US$25, two hours US$40 and a longer half-day ride in the mountains is US$75 including food.

Rancho Montana TOUR
(☎809-739-0733; www.ranchomontana.com) Located near Sabaneta de Yasica, this operation conducts trips into the mountains around Gaspar Hernandez, to the east of Cabarete.

Courses

Cabarete Language Institute LANGUAGE SCHOOL
(☎809-713-5002; www.cabaretelanguage.com; Pro-Cab Calle B, Cabarete) Conversational Spanish lessons for all levels. Expect to pay around RD$900 per hour. It's two doors down from Ali's Surf Camp.

Tours

★**Iguana Mama** OUTDOOR ADVENTURES
(☎809-571-0908, cell 809-654-2325; www.iguanamama.com; Calle Principal, Cabarete) This very professional and family-run adventure-sports tour operator on the north coast is in a class of its own. Its specialities are mountain biking (from easy to insanely difficult, US$65) and canyoning. Trips to Damajagua (US$85) go to the 27th waterfall, and Iguana Mama pioneered a canyoning tour to Ciguapa Falls, which only this operator offers. The highest jump, which you can avoid by rapeling, is over 10m. There's also a variety of hiking trips, including a half-day walk (US$35) into Parque Nacional El Choco, and a full-day trip to Mount Isabel de Torres (US$80), just outside Puerto Plata. Its Pico Duarte trek is handy if you want transportation to and from Cabarete (per person US$450). Iguana Mama can also arrange a number of other half-day and full-day canyoning trips in the area (US$90 to US$125). Action and adventure junkies should ask about the one-week 'Mama Knows Best' tour – seven days of nonstop adrenaline.

Kayak River Adventures OUTDOOR ADVENTURES
(☎829-305-6883; www.kayakriveradventures.com) Helmut, the German man who runs this highly recommended operation, is enthusiastic and professional and will tailor canyoning, kayaking and stand-up paddleboarding trips to your needs (including late morning start times).

Cabarete Coffee Company TOUR
(☎809-571-0919; www.cabaretecoffeecompany.com; Calle Principal, Cabarete; ⏰Tue-Thu) Small groups (up to 10 people) can take half-day cacao tours (US$75 per person), essentially 'cultural' tours where you lunch in a local's home and hike to a small village in the foothills of the Cordillera Septentrional. They're great for kids, photographers and kitesurfers, since you're back in town by 2pm when the winds pick up. Tours of

a coffee plantation around Jarabacoa are by reservation with groups of six or more (US$125 per person). Run by Patricia Suriel of the Mariposa Foundation (p234).

Dominican Fisherman FISHING
(☎809-571-0919; www.dominicanfisherman.com; Calle Principal, Cabarete Coffee Company) This particular 'Dominican Fisherman' takes small groups out deep-sea fishing (in a self-described 'rustic' boat; four hours, US$105 per person) or on the Rio Yásica (three hours, US$45 per person) and nearby reef (four hours, US$95 per person). You can arrange to have your catch cleaned and cooked.

Festivals & Events

Master of the Ocean SPORTS
(www.masteroftheocean.com; last week Feb) A triathlon of water sports – surfing, windsurfing and kitesurfing. From the beach you can watch some spectacular performances.

Dominican Jazz Festival MUSIC
(www.drjazzfestival.com; 2-3 Nov) Also held in Puerto Plata (Oct 31) and Sosúa (Nov 1), this long-running festival attracts top musical talent from around the country and abroad. Most of the visiting musicians run workshops for kids; in 2013, Bernie Williams, former Yankee turned guitarist, taught both baseball and jazz.

Sleeping

In low season you can pick up great deals on long-term rentals, but in high season – when condo owners return – hotel rooms can be hard to find. **L'Agence** (☎809-571-0999; www.agencerd.com), located in Ocean Dream Plaza, can help you find a condo rental. Or one place you can contact directly is **El Magnifico** (☎809-571-0868; www.hotelmagnifico.com; Calle del Cementerio; r from US$110, apt for 4 from US$240;), a compound of buildings on the beach at La Punta near Janet's Supermarket at the eastern end of town. Others worth looking into are **Sea Lane Beachfront Condo Rentals** (☎809-885-4080, in Miami 305-600-0849) or **Cabarete Beach Houses at Nanny Estates** (☎809-571-0744; www.cabaretebeachhouses.com; Cabarete).

New developments are emerging at either end of town and on the inland side of Calle Principal. The one by-the-numbers all-inclusive establishment is Viva Wyndham Tangerine, which is a few hundred meters west of town.

In Town

★**Ali's Surf Camp** BACKPACKER $
(☎809-571-0733; www.alissurfcamp.com; s US$29-44, d US$33-66, apt US$75-120;) On the edge of a lagoon a five-minute walk inland, this lushly landscaped property has small, colorful and rustic backpacker-style cabins; larger, modern rooms with kitchenettes in a two-story Victorian-style building; and, best of all, two colonial-style all-wood rooms with louvered windows in a 'tower' above the kitchen and dining area.

During the high season, Ali's has a fun, social scene with great barbecue dinners, so nonguests should consider heading here for a meal. A nice pool and surfing and kitesurfing packages are offered – in fact, it's ideal for those looking for a laid-back base from which you can learn how to surf or kitesurf.

Hotel Alegría HOTEL, APARTMENTS $
(☎809-571-0455; www.hotel-alegria.com; Callejón 2; r from US$30, studio/apt US$60/110;) Hidden down one of Cabarete's few side streets, the Alegría may not have beach access, but from the wooden deck that towers from the top of the hotel you have an unrivalled view out over the ocean. There's a small gym with treadmill and weights, and the studios and apartment each have kitchens, but more importantly the owner and staff are friendly, informative and professional.

Hotel Kaoba HOTEL, APARTMENTS $
(☎809-571-0300; www.kaoba.com; r/bungalows/apt from US$45/32/70;) Occupying a large piece of property at the western end of town, Kaoba is sandwiched between the Calle Principal and the Laguna Cabarete. Service is impersonal and inattentive and some of the bungalows carry a whiff of mildew or air freshener meant to mask the smell. Those complaints aside, there's a wide range of accommodations and a pleasant enough pool.

Hostel Laguna Park HOSTEL $
(☎829-804-6640; www.facebook.com/HostelCabarete; Calle Castillo 1, Pro Cab; dm US$12, private room US$35;) Converted by its gregarious Italian owner into a cavernous hostel, the facade of this large brick building, a rather anomalous sight, resembles a suburbanite's version of a castle replete with a turret. It's a conventional-looking space inside with concrete floors, spare and second-hand

furnishings, a common room with a pool table and a mix of dorm and private rooms.

Wall murals add a dash of color, there's a large pool out back and a bar operates during busy winter months. Breakfast and dinner will run you an extra US$13 more per night; surfing and kitesurfing packages offered. The hostel is located 950m from the ProCab development gate and a *motoconcho* to town/Kite Beach/Playa Encuentro costs RD$35/50/125.

★Swell Surf Camp SURF HOTEL **$$**
(☎809-571-0672; www.swellsurfcamp.com; week-long incl breakfast and 4 dinners dm/s/d US$425/635/1000;) Designed with the discerning surfer in mind, Swell is far from a crash pad. The spare clean lines, plush bedding, modern photographs and funky furniture say 'boutique', but the pool, ping-pong and foosball tables and social vibe suggest otherwise. A huge wood communal table is the center of the hanging-out action.

Water, coffee, tea and bananas are always on hand and a self-serve bar means drinks are available 24 hours. Week-long packages are available for those who want to learn how to kitesurf or surf – internationally qualified instructors are on staff. Provides shuttle service to Playa Encuentro and other spots. Airport transfers included in rates.

Velero Beach Resort HOTEL **$$$**
(☎809-571-9727; www.velerobeach.com; La Punta 1; r from US$175;) Distinguished by boutique-style rooms and its location down a small lane at the relatively traffic-free eastern end of town, Velero is an excellent choice. True to its four-star rating in service, professionalism and property maintenance, the Velero's only downside is it's on a small spit of a beach, but the pool and lounge area more than make up for this.

Millennium Luxury Beach Resort & Spa BOUTIQUE HOTEL **$$$**
(☎809-571-0407; www.cabartemillennium.com; r US$125, apt from US$350;) Ultra-modern, quintessential Miami Beach (now in vogue in Cabarete), the Millennium is a swanky beachfront property with a cool, if somewhat chilly, ambience. The spacious rooms are furnished in a minimalist style and the infinity pool is especially nice. Some kinks and management issues, however, were still being worked out when we visited.

Hotel Villa Taína HOTEL **$$$**
(☎809-571-0722; www.villataina.com; r/apt incl breakfast from US$115/160;) This appealing boutiquey hotel at the western end of town has 55 tastefully decorated rooms, each with balcony or terrace, air-con, comfortable beds and modern bathroom. It has a small, clean pool and a nice beach area fringed by palm trees. Suites and deluxe suites are also available.

West of Town

Extreme Hotels HOTEL **$**
(☎809-571-0330; www.extremehotels.com; Kite Beach; r US$50;) Trapeze, kickboxing, physical therapy camp, a half pipe for skateboarders, certainly not your standard hotel offerings. Then again, this ecologically minded, solar-powered and self-described 'upscale hostel' is meant for those seeking an unconventional beach holiday. No TVs and no air-con in the spacious and simply furnished fan-cooled rooms. Mojito Bar, a popular restaurant, has a location here.

Families and groups should consider the huge three-bedroom, three-bathroom penthouse that sleeps 10. All of the produce (even hard-to-find kale!) is either grown on the property (using aquaponics) or on an organic farm in Los Brazos near Sabaneta de Yasica. Attached and affiliated with the hotel is the kitesurfing school Go Kite Cabarete.

Kite Beach Inn HOTEL **$**
(☎809-490-5517; www.kitebeachinn.com; r with fan/aircon US$40/45;) Budget-minded kitesurfers should consider this place (a work in progress at the time of our visit), opened in 2013 by a couple from Chicago. Clean and simply furnished rooms with new flatscreen TVs are in a building set just off the road. While the inner courtyard and small pool are ordinary, the beachfront deck is to be prized. There are close to a dozen units, which are more like one-bedroom apartments with kitchenettes and sea-facing balconies. Cash and Paypal only.

★Hooked Cabarete BUNGALOWS **$$**
(☎809-935-9221; www.hookedcabarete.com; Playa Encuentro; s/d/tr US$48/64/75;) If a beachfront location isn't a priority, then this small property down a dirt road 200m or so from Playa Encuentro is a nice place to ensconce yourself – especially if you're a surfer. A handful of modern bungalow-style studio apartments with kitchenettes and attractive

wooden porches surround a quiet garden courtyard and small pool.

The new owners, a Swiss-American couple, have if anything improved upon the original. It also rents scooters, so you can get into town easily.

Agualina Kite Resort HOTEL **$$**
(809-571-0787; www.agualina.com; Kite Beach; r US$80;) Opened in 2004, this is the most comfortable lodging on Kite Beach. Studios and apartments have stylish, well-equipped kitchens – stainless-steel refrigerators are an especially nice touch – and large modern bathrooms with glass showers and gleaming fixtures. There's free wi-fi throughout the building.

Kite Beach Hotel HOTEL **$$**
(809-571-0878; www.kitebeachhotel.com; Kite Beach; s/d incl breakfast US$80/95;) This oceanfront hotel boasts well-appointed rooms with gleaming tile floors, good-sized bathrooms and satellite TV. All suites and apartments have balconies that afford at least partial ocean views. The laid-back pool area makes a great place to watch the action in the sky and on the water. An extensive breakfast buffet is also included in the rate.

★ **Natura Cabañas** RESORT **$$$**
(809-571-1507; www.naturacabana.com; s/d incl breakfast US$153/212; @) Owned and designed by a Chilean husband-wife team, this collection of marvelously designed thatched-roof bungalows about halfway between Cabarete and Sosúa is the epitome of rustic chic. Everything is constructed from natural materials – mahogany, bamboo and stone – and a gravel path leads to a secluded beach. Two open-air restaurants serve exquisitely created dishes (US$15 to US$30).

Eating

Dining out on Cabarete's beach is the quintessential Caribbean experience – paper lanterns hanging from palm trees, a gentle ocean breeze and excellent food (even if it does cost the same as you'd pay back home). After your meal, dig your toes into the sand and kick back with a cocktail. Many of the bars on the beach serve good food as well; anywhere from a quarter to a half close up shop for all or part of October.

Expats head to midrange restaurants (such as Burger Joint, Yamazato and Gordito's) in Ocean Dream Plaza, just west of the center of town. Or there are several eateries, from cheap kiosks to upscale fine dining, down the village's Callejon de la Loma.

On busy nights, opposite Onno's and next to Blue Bar on Calle Principal, the 'pork sandwich man' sets up shop; a whole leg of barbecue pork costs RD$70.

The biggest and best market is **Janet's Supermarket** (809-571-0404; Calle Principal) at the east end of town.

★ **Mojito Bar** SALADS, SANDWICHES **$**
(mains RD$170; 11:15am-8pm, closed Tue;) One of the few reasonably priced beachfront places, Mojitos has an excellent selection of natural juices, healthy salads and sandwiches (some vegan and vegetarian). It's a sliver of a space near the middle of the beach. Happy hour is from 4pm to 7pm (two mojitos RD$170). There's another location at Extreme Hotels on Kite Beach.

Panadería Repostería Dick BAKERY **$**
(809-571-0612; Calle Principal; set breakfasts RD$150; 7am-3pm Thu-Tue) A morning destination for its large set breakfasts with juice and strong coffee. The bakery does whole-wheat bread and tasty Danish pastries.

Cabarete Coffee Company CAFE **$**
(809-571-0919; www.cabaretecoffee.com; Calle Principal; mains RD$150; 7am-3pm;) A tiny spot with all-day breakfast menu (waffles, omelettes and even bagels), healthy paninis, fresh smoothies and, as you'd expect, excellent coffee – organic and locally sourced ingredients. Owned and operated by Patricia Suriel of the Mariposa Foundation. Open end of April to beginning of May.

Restaurant Chino CHINESE **$**
(Calle Principal; mains RD$150; 11am-10pm) Despite zero frills and all-concrete decor, this greasy spoon is popular with expats and Dominicans for its cheap Cantonese dishes; the egg rolls are more like egg logs.

★ **Belgium Bakery** BAKERY, SANDWICHES **$$**
(Plaza Popular Cabarete, Calle Principal; mains RD$260; 7am-7pm;) Hands down *the* place for breakfast in Cabarete: strong coffee, delicious bread and pastries and large omelets. Though it fronts a parking lot and not the beach, the outdoor patio seating is an ideal spot to while away several hours. Burgers, paninis and salads are served throughout the day.

La Parilla de Luis BARBECUE $$
(Callejon de la Loma; mains RD$220; closed Thu) Ignore the noise and fumes from idling *motoconchos* and pull up a plastic chair to enjoy delicious plates of barbecue chicken and yucca.

Pomodoro ITALIAN $$
(809-571-0085; mains RD$380; 3-11pm Mon-Fri, from 11:30am Sat & Sun;) Run by Lorenzo, an Italian jazz fiend (and the organizer of the Jazz Festival), Pomodoro serves the best crispy-crust pizza on the beach. It uses only quality toppings – including pungent, imported Italian cheese – and there's live jazz on Thursday nights (8pm to 10pm). Delivers.

Gordito's Fresh Mex MEXICAN $$
(www.gorditosfreshmex.com; Ocean Dream Plaza, Calle Principal; mains RD$375; 11:30am-8:30pm, closed Sun;) California transplants have opened this immediately popular Dominican version of Chipotle. However, that fast-food chain certainly doesn't do a chicken yucatan (honey buttermilk marinated chicken with corn sauce, *queso fondito*, avocado and *pico de gallo*) or for that matter fish tacos and empanadas. Locally sourced ingredients here and at the next door full-service, slightly more formal Gorditos Cantina (dinner Tuesday to Saturday): try the chef's four-course tasting menu (RD$650) or any dish with delicious mole.

Burger Joint BURGERS $$
(Ocean Dream Plaza, Calle Principal; mains RD$275; 11:30am-9pm, closed Sun) This small, newly opened casual spot does only one thing, but it does it extremely well. Choose from a half-dozen varieties of fish (sea bass), chicken or beef burgers; all come with fries and salad. Eat in or takeout.

OUT-OF-TOWN EATS

If you should ever grow tired of the beachside scene in Cabarete, the following restaurants are wonderfully unique options. Even if it weren't for the excellent food, they would be worthy destinations simply for the chance to get out into the countryside.

Castle Club (809-357-8334; www.castleclubonline.com; Los Brazos; per person excl drinks US$35; vary) Set in the mountains around a half-hour drive (taxi is US$25 one-way) from Cabarete is this rambling, eccentric home – a castle of sorts, though one perpetually a work in progress. The charming and entertaining owners grow much of their own food on the property, and will prepare one of the more memorable meals you'll have in the DR. Expect dishes like coconut sea bass, exquisite salads and cold lemon soufflé. The schedule can be erratic – book at least two days in advance. It can cater for groups from six to 100. From Cabarete, head east on the highway to Sabaneta and turn right onto the road to Moca. Around 12km later you pass a bridge in the town of Los Brazos, where you should look for a sign to your left as you climb the hill.

Blue Moon Hotel & Restaurant (809-757-0614; www.bluemoonretreat.net; Los Brazos; mains RD$600; dinner with reservations) Just 200m before Castle Club, this bungalow-style hotel and restaurant hosts family-sized Indian dinners (minimum six people, reserve in advance). Food is quality South Asian fare, including two different veggie dishes, a main course such as tandoori or curried chicken or fish, rice, salad, coffee, tea and dessert. It feels like a slightly gimmicky experience: you sit on the floor and eat with your hands. The bungalows (US$50 to US$60 including breakfast per bungalow) are cool and comfortable, with inventive Indian-style decor.

Wilson's (mains RD$200) This is a little BBQ shack on the Yasica River in Islabon, around 8km southeast of town on the way to Sabaneta de Yasica. The eponymous Wilson, who speaks perfect English, serves up wood-fired fish, chicken and lobster.

Restaurante Chez Arsenio (809-571-9948; restaurantechezarsenio@hotmail.com; Hideaway Beach Resort; mains RD$500; 11am-10pm Mon-Fri, from 9am Sat & Sun) Occupying a spectacular stretch of the western end of Playa Encuentro, Hideaway Beach Resort's (primarily condo rentals) restaurant serves up a wide variety of Dominican, Italian and especially recommended seafood dishes. Choose either the open-air poolside dining room or a table on the perfectly manicured lawn under a towering palm tree. Look for a sign marking the access road off the highway on the way to Sosúa.

Kite Club Cafe CAFE $$
(Kite Beach; mains RD$250; 10am-late) Attached to the Kite Club kitesurfing school, this casual New Yorker–owned beachfront spot is one of the best places to eat on Kite Beach. Regulars rave about the smoothies, dorado burgers and mango salsa. It serves sandwiches, wraps and salads as well; the grill closes at 5:30pm.

★ **Otra Cosa** FRENCH $$$
(809-571-0607; otracosa_lapunta@hotmail.com; La Punta; mains RD$600; 6:30-11pm;) Located at a secluded spot with marvelous sea breezes at dusk, this French-Caribbean restaurant guarantees an incredible dining experience. You can listen to the surf and watch the moon rise over the water while sipping wine and feasting on dishes that are expertly prepared and *très délicieux*, such as seared tuna in ginger flambéed in rum (RD$650).

An *amuse-bouche* of eggplant caviar and a shot of *mamajuana*, both complimentary, serve as bookends to the meal. Reservations recommended and cash only.

Bliss MEDITERRANEAN $$$
(809-571-9721; Callejon de la Loma; mains RD$750; 6pm-midnight, closed Wed) It may not be on the beach, but sitting around the small, crystal-blue pool with a top-shelf cocktail in your hand, you can be forgiven for not caring. By all accounts, the new Italian owners have not only maintained the kitchen's high standards but introduced homemade pastas as well – the seafood risotto and linguini with lobster can be especially recommended.

La Casita de don Alfredo SEAFOOD $$$
(mains RD$650; 11am-11pm, closed Sun;) Also known as Casita de Papi's, this French-owned beachfront restaurant does a great garlic shrimp paella dish as well as lobster and grilled fish.

Drinking & Entertainment

Cabarete nightlife is centered on the bars and restaurants that spill out onto the beach – it's a fun and vibrant scene. Most are open to around 3am. 'Subtle' prostitution exists at some nightspots, but most importantly keep an eye on your valuables and do not walk on the beach at night east of Villa Taina, essentially the stretch between Cabarete Beach and Punta Goleta.

Onno's NIGHTCLUB
(9am-late) This edgy, Dutch-owned restaurant and nightclub is a European and hipster hangout and serves good-value food on the beach. At night a DJ spins a decent set.

Lax BAR, NIGHTCLUB
(www.lax-cabarete.com; 9am-1am) This mellow bar and restaurant serves food until 10:30pm, when the DJ starts to spin. In many ways it's the social headquarters of Cabarete.

Lazy Dog BAR
(8am-late) Winnipeg Jets fans? Anyone? Diehards of the Canadian city's NHL franchise can rejoice since Lazy Dog's owner, a Winnipeg native himself, shows every televised game at his place on the far eastern end of Cabarete's beach. Spanglish, a local cover band, plays every Wednesday and Friday from 4pm. Two of the very large menu's highlights are the calamari and spicy shrimp.

Casanova BAR
(809-571-0806; 9am-late) You'll think you're on a beach in southern Thailand. Casanova is lavishly decorated with Buddha statues and other Asian-inspired trinkets – the usual suspects like surf and turf make an appearance, as do salads and pizza (mains RD$350).

Bambú BAR, DISCO
(6pm-late) Loud house music and reggaeton and the crowd spills out onto the beach.

Ojo BAR
(10pm-late Thu-Sat) On the beach directly behind the offices for Iguana Mama, this bar/club has salsa dancing on Thursday and Friday nights.

Voy Voy CAFE, BAR
(6pm-late) Vela Windsurf Center by day, bar by night, this small, hip cafe also serves sandwiches and snacks. Monday karaoke is a mandatory part of Cabarete beach life. Closed much of September and October.

Vodoo Lounge BAR
(Callejon de la Loma; 5pm-late) A nice open-air loungey spot with DJs Friday and Saturday nights (doesn't get properly started until 11pm), open mic night on Wednesdays and live jazz every other Sunday night. Tapas are on the menu.

Blue Bar BAR
(Calle Principal) Before hitting the beach bars on Friday and Saturday nights (around

10pm), young expats and Dominicans alike spill out of this bare bones (yes, blue-walled) hole-in-the-wall. A plastic-cup of rum and coke (mostly rum) costs RD$50.

Information

@Internet (Calle Principal; 8am-11pm) Half hour/hour internet access is RD$30/60.

Active Cabarete (www.activecabarete.com) A website with a range of information, including activities and events, weather, and 'special stuff.'

Banco Popular (Calle Principal; 9am-4:30pm Mon-Fri, to 1pm Sat)

Family Lavandería (Calle Principal; per kg RD$50; 8am-6pm Mon-Sat) Eastern end of town, opposite Janet's Supermarket.

Fujifilm Digital (809-571-9536; Calle Principal; per hr RD$60) Fast internet connection and headphones.

Politur (Tourist Police; 809-571-0713; Calle Principal) At the eastern entrance to town.

Scotiabank (Calle Principal; 9am-4:30pm Mon-Fri, to 1pm Sat)

Servi-Med (809-571-0964; Calle Principal; 24hr) English, German and Spanish are spoken, and travel medical insurance and credit cards accepted.

Getting There & Around

BUS

None of the main bus companies offer service to Cabarete (or for that matter further east to Samaná) – the closest depots are in Sosúa. They zip through town without stopping on their way to Nagua before turning south to Santo Domingo.

A large, white bus with aircon on its way from Puerto Plata to Samaná stops at the Texaco station just east of town every day at 1:30pm. From Cabarete, the three-hour trip costs RD$250.

CAR

If you want to rent a car, the best place to do so is at the Puerto Plata airport when you arrive. If you're already in town, you can take a *guagua* (30 minutes) to the airport road (just past Sosúa), walk 500m to the terminal and shop around at the numerous car-rental agencies there.

It's around a 2½-hour drive in your own vehicle from Cabarete to Samaná.

GUAGUA

Heaps of *guaguas* ply this coastal road, including east to Sabaneta (RD$25) and Río San Juan (RD$80, one hour) and west to Sosúa (RD$20, 20 minutes) and Puerto Plata (RD$50, 45 minutes). Hail them anywhere along Cabarete's main drag. A *guagua* to Santo Domingo is RD$280, but you're better off catching a bus in Sosúa.

ROUTE 21

The quickest route from Cabarete to Santo Domingo is to take Rte 21, a 'shortcut' through the mountains that heads inland from the coastal highway near Sabaneta de Yasica. It passes through beautiful mountain scenery and small villages before hitting Moca and then empties into Hwy 1 at La Vega. Depending on your driving skill and weather conditions, the trip can be made in around three hours.

MOTOCONCHO

Transportation in town is dominated by *motoconchos*, who will attempt to charge you two to three times the price you'd pay for a similar ride in Puerto Plata. Don't be surprised if you can't haggle them down. A ride out to Kite Beach should cost RD$50 and Playa Encuentro RD$100.

SCOOTER

A popular option is to rent a scooter or a motorcycle. Expect to pay around US$20 per day, less if you rent for a week or more. There are lots of rental shops along the main drag, and some hotels rent two-wheeled transportation too. Be aware that helmets are pretty much nonexistent in this country, so if that's important to you consider bringing your own.

TAXI

The motorcycle-shy can call a **taxi** (809-571-0767; www.taxisosuacabarete.com), which will cost RD$250 to Encuentro, US$35 to Aeropuerto Internacional Gregorío Luperón 18km west, and US$35 to Puerto Plata. For the Santiago airport it's around US$100. There's also a taxi stand in the middle of town.

RÍO SAN JUAN

POP 9000

Only an hour east of Cabarete, this sleepy town is distinctive because of its location on a mangrove lagoon and its business-owning French expat community. Several of the north coast's best beaches are within easy driving distance, and diving and snorkeling are nearby. The small **Campo Tours** (809-589-2550; Calle Duarte 17) agency sells predigested package tours, including a glass-bottomed laguna boat tour (US$20) and a three-hour deep-sea fishing trip (US$70).

Laguna Gri-Gri, which shares the same ecosystem as Los Haitises south of Península de Samaná, at the northern end of Calle

Duarte, was once Río San Juan's claim to fame. Unfortunately, overuse and pollution mean the lagoon is no longer pristine and swimming is not recommended. It's still picturesque and a dozen or more boatmen offer hour-long tours (US$35 for up to seven people) through tangled mangrove channels, including interesting rock formations. Look for a small shack next to the public bathrooms down by the Laguna – you'll find it easier to join a group on weekends, when Dominicans come to take this trip.

Other than the small town beach on the bay, which is good for swimming, **Playa Caletón** is the closest beach. It's a small, peaceful bay (weekends can be crowded and loud with car radios pumping out merengue) with tawny sand, almond trees and towering palms only 1km east of town. Food stands are near the entrance. Take a *guagua* (RD$15) or a *motoconcho* (RD$35) to the turn-off, from which it's a 200m walk down a rocky access road past a goat farm to the beach.

Activities

Diving & Snorkeling

Río San Juan has a great variety of nearby dive sites, including **Seven Hills**, a collection of huge coral heads descending from 6m to 50m, and **Crab Canyon**, a series of natural arches and swim-throughs. Twenty minutes east of Río San Juan is **Dudu Cave**, one of the best freshwater cavern dives in the Caribbean, where the visibility is almost 50m. Most dive shops require an Advanced Diver certificate or at least 20 logged dives to do these trips. There's no dive center in Río San Juan; your best bet is to organize something in Sosúa, where you'll pay roughly US$100 to US$120 per person for a full day of diving (minimum three people).

Golf

Playa Grande Golf Course GOLF
(☎809-582-0860; www.playagrande.com; Carretera a Nagua; 9/18 holes US$80/140; ⏲7am-4:30pm) This par-72 course, built on a verdant cliff before Playa Grande, is part of a perpetually stalled and ambitious private development – the latest involves Aman resorts and a renovation of the course. Be sure to call ahead.

Sleeping

Bahía Blanca HOTEL $
(☎809-589-2563; bahia.blanca.dr@claro.net.do; Calle Gaston F Deligne; r RD$1500; 📶) Perched on a rocky spit over turquoise-blue waters and marking the eastern end of the town

PLAYAS GRANDE & PRECIOSA

Just 8km east of Río San Juan is **Playa Grande**, one of the most beautiful beaches in the DR. The long, broad, tawny beach has aquamarine water on one side and a thick fringe of palm trees on the other, with stark white cliffs jutting out into the ocean in the distance.

Facilities at the eastern end of the beach include a little 'village' of pastel-colored clapboard shacks selling freshly caught seafood like lobsters, prawns and grilled snapper served with rice and plantains, and pina coladas made with real pineapple and coconut juice. Plastic tables and chairs are usually available so you can chow down on the beach in comfort. Facilities also include souvenirs, and bathrooms with outdoor showers. These amenities and the newly paved access road have diminished the previously remote and wild feel of the area. Vendors rent beach chairs (per day RD$150), umbrellas (per day RD$175), snorkel equipment (full day RD$500), body boards (per hour RD$150) and surfboards (per hour RD$500). If seeking solitude, walk west along the beach, away from the entrance.

Only 25m down a path leaving from just in front of Playa Grande's bathrooms is another spectacular stretch of sand called **Playa Preciosa**. Pounded by serious waves, few attempt to play in the surf. Those who do – typically surfers at dawn – do so for the thrill. Some of the narrow beach is covered during high tide.

A word about safety: these beaches have heavy surf and a deceptively strong undertow. Riptides – powerful currents flowing out to sea – form occasionally, and people have drowned here. Be conservative when swimming, and children and less-experienced swimmers should probably not go in at all unless the surf is low. If caught in a riptide, swim parallel to the shore until out of the current and then swim in.

If you take a *guagua* from town, drivers will let you off just before the security gate marking the entrance to the beaches. You can also hire a *motoconcho* (RD$75) or a taxi (RD$300) to take you directly there.

beach, the long-running Bahía Blanca has undeniably beautiful ocean views. Rooms are decidedly basic – clean, tile-floored and with private bathroom – but show their age. All but two have at least partial ocean views, and wide balconies on each of the three floors provide plenty of opportunities to enjoy the beauty.

Villa le Cap B&B $$
(809-669-2324, 809-855-5733; villalecap-rsj@hotmail.com; Calle 27 de Febrero 1; r incl breakfast from US$80;) Overlooking the western end of the town's beach, this contemporary French-owned villa is a stylish refuge especially good for families and small groups. The whitewashed home has a half-dozen rooms, an airy lounge and living room area and small roof deck with lounge chairs.

Eating & Drinking

La Casona DOMINICAN $
(809-589-2597; Calle Duarte 6; mains RD$200; hr vary) This friendly restaurant serves extra-good empanadas.

La Orquidea FRENCH, DOMINICAN $$
(Calle FR Sánchez; mains RD$300-550; 7am-11pm) Directly in front of the lagoon, this serves standard French/Dominican fare.

Estrella Bar & Restaurant DOMINICAN, FRENCH $$
(Calle Duarte; mains RD$300-600; 6am-11pm;) A few blocks up from the lagoon, Estrella complement the standard French/Dominican menu with especially good seafood specials.

Cheo's Café DOMINICAN $$
(Calle Billini 6; mains RD$250; hr vary) Informal Cheo's does familiar beef, chicken and pasta dishes.

Information

Banco Progreso (809-589-2393; Calle Duarte 38; 9am-4:30pm Mon-Fri, to 1pm Sat) Just off the main coastal highway.

Politur (tourist police; 809-754-3241) Located on the highway, 300m west of Calle Duarte.

Tourist Office (cnr Calles FR Sánchez & Lorenzo Adames) You may find a few maps and brochures on hand.

Getting There & Around

It's only about a 1½-hour drive from here to Samaná.

NAGUA

Nagua is a hot, dusty town 54km southeast of Río San Juan whose interest to tourists is strictly as a transportation hub. It is the main transfer point for *guaguas* heading south or in either direction along the coastal highway. The inland road to San Francisco de Macorís, Moca and Santiago begins here as well. **Caribe Tours** (809-584-4505; cnr 27 de Febrero & Mercedes Bello) has almost a dozen buses running to Santo Domingo (RD$320, 3½ hours) every half-hour to hour from 7:30am to 5pm and four buses to Samaná (RD$75, 7am, 9:30am, 1:30pm and 4pm).

BUS

Caribe Tours (809-589-2644), just west of Calle Duarte on the coastal highway just outside town, provides bus service between Río San Juan and Santo Domingo (RD$330, 4½ hours) and stops along the way at Nagua (RD$65, 45 minutes) and San Francisco de Macorís (RD$75, 2½ hours). Buses depart at 6:30am, 7:30am, 9:30am, 2pm and 3:30pm.

WESTBOUND GUAGUA

These come and go from the northwest corner of Calle Duarte and the coastal highway, known around town as *la parada* (the stop). Departures occur nearly every 15 minutes from 6am to 5pm to Cabarete (RD$80, 1½ hours), Sosúa (RD$90, 1½ hours) and Puerto Plata (RD$100, two hours).

EASTBOUND GUAGUA

These line up on the northeast corner of Calle Duarte and the coastal highway and leave every 10 minutes from 6:30am to 6pm for Playa Caletón (RD$17, five minutes), Playa Grande (RD$34, 15 minutes) and Nagua (RD$76, 1¼ hours). From Nagua you can catch *guaguas* to Samaná.

TAXI

There's a **taxi stand** (809-589-2501) on Calle Duarte between Calles Luperón and Dr Virgilio García. Sample fares: Playa Caletón RD$100, Playa Grande RD$400, Cabarete RD$1800, Aeropuerto Puerto Plata RD$2500 and Las Terrenas on the Península de Samaná RD$3000.

CABRERA

East of Playa Grande is Cabrera, a sleepy town of stone houses with colorful shutters, flower boxes and well-kept gardens, as well as lavish vacation homes owned by

Dominicans and expats. Because electricity and hence nighttime lights are scarce, stargazing is excellent.

Nearby **Playa Diamante** is a small, fairly ordinary-looking beach with shallow water good for children; **Playa El Breton**, within Parque Nacional Cabo Francis, has excellent snorkeling; most noteworthy of all, **Playa Entrada** is one of the longest, most picture-postcard-worthy beaches in the country. Privacy is easy to come by. A couple of informal shacks sell seafood and drinks (these might be abandoned on weekdays).

Nearby **Laguna Dudu**, a unique site for divers, is a waterfilled limestone cave that runs all the way to the ocean! Non-divers can access the landscaped picnic area (RD$100) for cliff jumping and rope swinging.

The area has been colonized by a collection of spectacular, private, high-end, fully staffed villas for rent, part of a development called Orchid Bay Estates; these include Balinese-inspired **Sunrise Villas** (☎866-998-4552; www.sunrise-villa.com; villas from US$1350), Mediterranean-style Villa Castellamonte and the 35,000-sq-ft ultramodern Casa Kimball (all have eight bedrooms). Otherwise travelers can head to **Hotel La Catalina** (☎809-589-7700; www.lacatalina.com; r incl breakfast US$100;), perched on a lush hill several kilometers inland and west of town. It offers charming and airy rooms with fresh white linens and wicker furniture, as well as spectacular views from the restaurant and pool area. Free shuttles take guests to and from Playa Grande.

WEST OF PUERTO PLATA

The coastal area west of Puerto Plata remains largely undeveloped, and sees few foreign visitors. Inland villages are surrounded by sugarcane fields and cattle country, and roadside eateries advertise *chivo picante* (or *chivo liniero*), the oregano-flavored goat meat the province is famous for. Punta Rusia, a fairly remote seashore village, and the nearby offshore island Cayo Arena are worth considering as a destination. History buffs can visit Parque Nacional La Isabela, where Columbus founded the second settlement in the New World. Boaters will already know of Luperón – famous as a 'hurricane hole' – but landlubbers have little reason to visit. If you're on your way to Haiti, Monte Cristi is worth a stop and it's possible to visit the outlying islands. The twice-weekly Haitian market at Dajabón may be of interest, if only to see how strikingly different are the lives of the two peoples who share this island.

Luperón

POP 9300

Luperón is famous as a 'hurricane hole' – a safe haven from rough seas for boaters (treasure hunters suspect several Spanish galleons foundered and sunk just before reaching safety here). There are two fairly run-down marinas and on average anywhere from 40 to 70 craft in the harbor. Unless you're a boater, though, the town has little appeal. Deeply rutted and dusty streets are quiet during the day and in near total darkness at night. However, nearby **Playa Grande** is a beautiful long strip of palm-backed white sand with wavy blue waters. The shabby all-inclusive resort fronting the beach has closed (mercifully for guests but an unfortunate blow to Luperon's economy); however, the property's buildings remain, abandoned and dilapidated. The easiest access is down a dirt and gravel road running beside the former resort. A *motoconcho* ride from town is about RD$75.

With enough time and patience, it's possible to arrange a boat trip at **Marina Puerto Blanco**. There are no official tours, but if you put the word out that you're interested someone is bound to turn up sooner or later. Prices vary widely depending on the captain, but expect to pay US$40 to US$60 for a half-day trip, or US$70 to US$120 for a full day.

The road from Imbert enters Luperón from the south. Staying to your left, the highway becomes Calle Duarte and eventually intersects with Calle 27 de Febrero, Luperón's main east–west drag. This intersection is the commercial center of town. The marina is 1km west of there and Parque Nacional La Isabela beyond that.

Sleeping & Eating

Estancia Principe Aparthotel APARTMENT $$
(☎809-298-5491; www.estanciaprincipe.com; Calle Principal 4; apt RD$1200;) Located at the southern entrance to town, this utilitarian brick building is probably the most comfortable and secure accommodation in Luperón. The apartments, which include fully stocked kitchens and living rooms with

wicker furniture, are certainly more space than the average overnighter needs. Cable TV and aircon work according to the town's power supply.

Letty's DOMINICAN, INTERNATIONAL **$$**
(Calle Duarte; mains RD$275) Open-air concrete pavilion (no fans). Standard fare.

Restaurant de la France DOMINICAN, INTERNATIONAL **$$**
(Calle Duarte; mains RD$275) Standard menu served in fanless, open-air concrete pavilion.

Information

Luperon's sole ATM, a Banreservas on Calle Duarte across the street from Politur, is notorious for being frequently out of cash or not functioning. **Thornless Path** (www.thornlesspath.com) is Caribbean cruiser and Luperón resident Bruce Van Sant's website tribute to the town.

Getting There & Away

Guaguas to Imbert (RD$50, 30 minutes, every 15 minutes 5am to 6:30pm) leave from a stop on Calle Duarte at 16 de Agosto, four blocks south of Calle 27 de Febrero. From Imbert you can pick up *guaguas* headed south to Santiago or north to Puerto Plata.

A taxi from Puerto Plata should cost around RD$3800. From Luperón to Punta Rusia costs around RD$2000.

Parque Nacional La Isabela

This historically significant **national park** (admission RD$100; 8am-5pm) near the town of El Castillo marks Columbus' second settlement on Hispaniola. When he arrived at the first settlement at Cap-Haïtien in Haiti on his second voyage to the New World, he found it destroyed, so he shifted 110km east and set up a new camp here; the foundations of several oceanfront buildings are all that remain. A small, fairly lackluster museum visited frequently by groups of Dominican primary-school students marks the occasion. Exhibits in Spanish include sociopolitical explanations of the Taíno communities Columbus encountered, some old coins, rings, arrowheads and a small-scale replica of Columbus' house. Across the road from the park is the **Templo de las Américas**, a loose and much larger replica of La Isabela's original church built as part of the settlement's 500th anniversary celebrations.

Near the park is **Playa Isabela**, a broad outward-curving beach with coarse sand and calm water. There are a couple of small beach restaurants and usually at least one knick-knack stand that rents snorkeling gear (RD$150). When swimming or wading, be alert for sea urchins lurking in the rock patches in the shallows.

Rancho del Sol (809-696-0325; s/d incl breakfast with fan RD$700/1400, with air-con RD$1200/1900;), a rambling, idiosyncratic hotel near the entrance to the national park, might be open again in the near future.

Getting There & Away

A taxi from Luperón, 11km to the east, will set you back US$60 return (if the driver waits) and a *motoconcho* around RD$250 one way.

It's possible, but somewhat harder, to get to La Isabela from the main highway between Santiago and Monte Cristi. Turn off at Cruce de Guayacanes and head north 25km to Villa Isabella, passing through Los Hidalgos on the way. The signs can be confusing, so ask for 'El Castillo' – the town where the park is located – as you go. The park is 7km from Villa Isabella.

Punta Rusia

POP 500

With an improved access road, this beachfront village feels only a little less remote than in the past. However, most people who venture out this way are from Puerto Plata area all-inclusives on day trips to **Cayo Arena** (aka 'Paradise Island'), a picturesque sandbar around 9km northwest of Punta Rusia. The corals around the atoll are pristine and the snorkeling good; however, the throngs in the water can detract from the experience. **El Paraíso Tour** (809-320-7606; www.cayoparaisord.com; incl drinks & lunch $50) speedboats shuttle groups to the Cayo Arena sandbar for several hours before returning via **Estero Hondo**, the mangrove lagoon just to the west (you might spot a manatee; a project to set up observation posts was in the works when we visited).

If you want to avoid the crowds, contact **Martinez** (829-262-0073), a local fisherman (Spanish only) for a more customized and rewarding experience. He provides snorkeling equipment and an interesting return route from Cayo Arena through the mangroves. The more people, the lower the per person cost, but prices are in the RD$1500 ballpark.

On weekends, hundreds of people, primarily Dominicans from Santiago, occupy **Playa Ensenada**, a narrow strip of sand with calm, shallow water 3km east of Punta Rusia. Don't expect quiet or privacy, but with coastal mountains within view to the northwest, water like a bathtub and a seafood meal from one of the nearly two-dozen shacks (lobster RD$300; open till 6pm) lining the beach behind a row of palm trees and picnic tables, it's easily worth a long afternoon visit.

Sleeping & Eating

★Casita Mariposa CABINS $
(Casa Libre; ☎809-693-5010, 809-834-5992; s/d incl breakfast RD$1000/1200) A German-French couple runs Casita Mariposa, a handful of colorfully painted rustic cabins wonderfully situated on a bluff overlooking the ocean just east of town. Though the grounds are nearly concealed and overrun by a tangle of flowering trees, you can settle into one of the three cabins' front-porch hammocks or a dining-area perch for mesmerizing unobstructed views.

This is a place to unwind and disconnect – no locks and no wi-fi. A stairway leads down to what is, for all intents and purposes, a private white-sand beach. Dinner can be prepared upon request and ocean kayaks are available for guests' use. Marco can arrange for transport from Isabela (RD$250 per person). Call to reserve a room in advance, lest you risk coming all this distance only to be turned away.

Villa Rosa B&B $$
(☎809-801-8160; s/d incl breakfast US$48/52;) The cafe and lounge area of this intimate, seven-room French-owned place is on the village's sandy beachfront. Set back from the road are a tiny plunge pool/Jacuzzi and a small thatch-roofed building with tastefully furnished rooms with rainwater shower heads and cable TV. Pasta and seafood are served up for meals upon request, and kayaks are available for rent.

Getting There & Away

A recently paved road connects Punta Rusia to Villa Isabella 25km to the east, and even further to Luperón. The other route is from Villa Elisa, 20km west of Laguna Salada on Hwy 1. From there, the road north is a passable patchwork of dirt, rocks and pavement – take it slow in a compact vehicle.

Monte Cristi

POP 25,000

A dusty frontier town originally founded by the Spanish crown in 1750, Monte Cristi's allure, if it can be said to have one, lies in its end-of-the-road feel. Most travelers are passing through on their way to or from Haiti. Its formerly prosperous incarnation as the base of the Grenada Fruit Company can be seen in the wide streets and dilapidated Victorian homes in the immediate vicinity of the Parque Central. Some have been restored enough to appreciate their one-time glory. Residents continue to make their living fishing and tending livestock, just as they've done for generations. Another source of revenue is salt harvested from evaporation ponds north of town and sold in the US by Morton Salt.

Monte Cristi celebrates what is considered the most brutal Carnival in the country – participants carry bullwhips and crack each other as they walk through the streets.

Sights & Activities

El Morro MOUNTAIN
Part of the 1100-sq-km **Parque Nacional Monte Cristi** (admission free; 8am-5pm) FREE that surrounds Monte Cristi on all sides, El Morro (The Hill) sits 5km northeast of town – follow Av San Fernando north to the beach and continue to your right until the road dead-ends. Opposite the ranger station, 585 wooden stairs lead to the top (239m). If you manage to safely scramble over the rotting planks and loose gravel, you'll be rewarded with excellent views. It's about an hour return.

Parque Central PARK
Notable solely for the 50m clock tower designed by French engineer Alexandre Gustave Eiffel. Imported from France in 1895, the tower deteriorated until 1997 when the Leon Jimenez family, of Aurora cigar and Presidente beer fortune, financed its restoration.

Beaches

Tucked behind the hill in the national park and backed by a towering precipice, **Playa Detras del Morro** is the prettiest beach in the area. There's a stretch of tan sand with some rocks thrown into the mix. Just past the ranger station where the road dead-ends is a short dirt path down to the beach. **Playa Juan de Boloños** is an unremarkable narrow strip of sand 1km north of town. Only if you have time and a 4WD, **Playa Popa** is a little strip of sand 16km from town down a rough road – it's difficult to find, so ask directions. It's not especially beautiful but is little-visited.

Tours

Most of the hotels in town or the tour operator **Sorayo & Santos** (☎809-691-6343; www.ssmontecristitours.com), located next to the Politur office across from the marina down by Playa Juan de Boloños, organize snorkeling tours, trips to the isolated beach at Isla Cabra (RD$2000), and boat trips to Los Cayos de los Siete Hermanos (RD$12,000), a collection of seven uninhabited islands inside the national park (usually up to eight people). Your best bet is to come on weekends in the high season (November to March) or expect high prices and the possibility of not finding an available boatperson.

The corals here make excellent diving, but then there are equally good corals more easily accessible elsewhere. Fortune-hunting wreck divers work this coastline, but the many wooden galleons that sank here have long since rotted away, leaving very little for recreational divers to see.

Sleeping

Hotel Los Jardines BUNGALOWS **$**
(☎809-853-0040; hoteljardines@gmail.com; Playa Costa Verde; r with fan/air-con RD$1700/2000;) The perfectly manicured grounds punctuated with a towering palm tree or two feel like a sanctuary from the dusty streets. The five basic rooms are something of a letdown but each has a porch with chairs. Head north out of town toward El Morro and turn left onto the waterfront dirt road.

Chic Hotel HOTEL **$**
(☎809-579-2316; Benito Monción 44; r with fan/air-con RD$650/1100;) The front-desk person is dressed sharply and the entranceway is marked by columns, and yet this hotel is a far cry from chic. However, the 50 or so rooms are kept clean and you can pop out for a bite to eat at its restaurant and ice-cream store with streetside seating.

Many of the rooms are windowless and street noise can be a problem in front. Check out the mango tree the hotel was built around – you'll pass the trunk in the hallway.

Cayo Arena APARTMENTS **$$**
(☎809-579-3145; www.cayoarena.com; Playa Costa Verde; ste RD$3500;) A two-story modern building with a handful of two-bedroom suites with full kitchens, living rooms and balconies, especially recommended for families or small groups. A small pool and restaurant are on site. Head north out of town toward El Morro and turn left onto the waterfront dirt road.

★**El Morro Eco Adventure Hotel** BUNGALOWS **$$$**
(☎849-886-1605; www.elmorro.com.do; Calle El Morro; r incl breakfast US$115;) Fairly remote, though only a short walk from the base of El Morro, this collection of high-end boutique bungalows, easily the choicest accommodation from Monte Cristi to Puerto Plata, is worth the journey. Contemporary design touches like flatscreen TVs and large, black-and-white photos of Monte Cristi are seamlessly integrated into the property's natural design aesthetic. Dinner is served in a nautically themed dining area and the pool area is a fantastic place to lounge the day away.

Eating & Drinking

A result of the fact that goats feed on oregano plants, the *chivo* here is renowned for its spiciness. Ask to try different varieties: *ripiado* (pulled goat), *horneado* (partly blackened, firm on the inside) and *picante* (traditional stew). **Lilo Supermercado** (Calle Alvarez), one block south of Duarte, is the place to stock up on supplies.

★**Restaurant Cocomar** SEAFOOD, DOMINICAN **$$**
(☎809-579-7354; mains RD$250-800; ⏲8am-10pm) Look for this restaurant with oceanfront outdoor seating just before the green monstrosity of the Hotel Montechico. Buoys and fishing nets hang from the indoor dining room ceiling, befitting its maritime theme and seafood-focused menu.

Lilo Cafe & Restaurant DOMINICAN **$$**
(Calle Juan de la Cruz Alvarez 27; mains RD$275; ⏲7am-midnight;) Businesspeople and office workers popularize this sleek, contemporary place across the street from the grocery of the same name. The menu is fairly typical with grilled fish, chicken and meat dishes as well as crab, lambi and four types of *mofongo*. Shaded outdoor patio seating is available.

Super Fria Nina BEER GARDEN
(cnr Calle Duarte & Colón) A large beer garden that gets packed almost every evening, but especially on weekends.

Terraza Fedora BEER GARDEN
(Calle San Fernando) A popular beer garden, particularly on weekends. Five blocks north of Calle Duarte.

Information

Everything you'll need is on or within a block or two of Calle Duarte, including a pharmacy and BanReservas with ATM on Duarte, next to the post office. The modest **Hospital Padre Fantino** (809-579-2401; Av 27 de Febrero; 24hr) is two blocks north of Calle Duarte.

Getting There & Away

Hwy 1 enters Monte Cristi from the east, where it turns into Calle Duarte and becomes the main east–west road through town. Av Mella becomes Hwy 45 to Dajabón, which is now fully paved.

Caribe Tours (809-579-2129; cnr Mella & Carmargo) has a depot a block north of Calle Duarte. Buses to Santo Domingo (RD$350, 4½ hours) leave at 7:30am, 8:30am, 10am, 1:45pm, 3pm and 4pm, with a stop in Santiago (RD$190, 2¼ hours).

The Expreso Liniero *guagua* terminal is on Calle Duarte near the eastern entrance to town; it goes to Dajabón (RD$50, 40 minutes, every 20 minutes from 7:30am to 10pm). For Puerto Plata, take any Santiago-bound *guagua* and get off at the junction in Navarrete (RD$190, 1½ hours, every 20 minutes) to change to another *guagua* (RD$140, one hour, every 20 minutes).

Dajabón

POP 25,200

Most foreigners here are on their way to or from Haiti. Every Monday and Friday is the **Haitian market** (7am-7pm). When the border bridge opens, Haitians pour across to buy fruit and vegetables from the DR and sell just about everything else, as well as contraband (including donations from international organizations, which are sold here wholesale and then shipped elsewhere in the country). Crowds push and shove wheelbarrows, motorcycles burrow through the throng and crates of goods are piled high on women's heads. With your hands pressed flat at your sides you might be able to wedge yourself further into the covered market.

Two acceptable, though equally problematic options for the night are the four-story **Super Hotel Brisol** (809-579-8703; Calle Padre Santa Anna 18; s/d with fan RD$600/800, with air-con RD$900/1300;), only a few blocks from the border, and the **Hotel Raydan** (809-579-7366; raydan38@hotmail.com; Av Pablo Reyes 16; r with fan/air-con RD$400/700;), which has a small patio and restaurant closer to transportation terminals in the center of town. Expect dim lighting, erratically functioning TV, air-con, wi-fi and hot water pressure at both. Ask to see several rooms before choosing. One of the few eating options with electricity at night is the modern, cafeteria-style **D House Restaurant** (mains RD$250; 7am-11pm;), whose wraps and sandwiches qualify as fine dining in Dajabón. Vendors sell grilled corn and hot dogs in the main park.

Several major banks with ATMs are located around a circle at the northern entrance to town.

Getting There & Away

Reaching the border is simple; coming from Monte Cristi on Hwy 45, as most people do, you'll come to a huge arch (the formal entrance to town) and a short distance afterward the Parque Central on the east side of the street. Just past the park is Calle Presidente Henriquez; turn right (west) and the border is six blocks ahead. If you're arriving by Caribe Tours bus, the bus station is on Calle Presidente Henriquez. Just walk west from the bus station five blocks to get to the border (open 9am to 5pm, except Monday and Friday market days 8am to 4pm).

Caribe Tours (809-579-8554; cnr Calles Carrasco & Henríquez) buses to Santo Domingo (RD$350, five hours), with stops in Monte Cristi and Santiago (RD$190, 2½ hours), leave at 6:45am, 7:45am, 9:30am, 1pm, 2:15pm and 3:15pm.

Expreso Liniero (809-579-8949) *guaguas* go to Monte Cristi (RD$50, 40 minutes) and Santiago (RD$190, 2½ hours). The terminal is just beyond the arch at the entrance to town on the east side of the road.

Central Highlands

Includes ➡

Best Places to Eat

- Aroma de la Montana (p176)
- Il Pasticcio (p167)
- Camp David (p165)

Best Places to Stay

- Rancho Baiguate (p175)
- Tubagua Plantation Eco-Village (p170)
- Alto Cerro (p180)
- Camp David (p165)

Why Go?

Even diehard beach fanatics will eventually overdose on sun and sand. When you do, the cool mountainous playground of the central highlands is the place to come; where else can you sit at dusk, huddled in a sweater, watching the mist descend into the valley as the sun sets behind the mountains? Popular retreats, roaring rivers, soaring peaks and the only white-water rafting in the Caribbean beckon. Below, on the plains in the Valle del Cibao, is where merengue spontaneously erupted onto the musical landscape, and where you'll find some of the best Carnival celebrations in the country. Economic life in the central highlands revolves around Santiago, the DR's second-largest city and the capital of a vast tobacco- and sugarcane-growing region.

When to Go

- **February to March** Some of the most raucous Carnival celebrations in all the DR are in Santiago and La Vega.
- **January to March & June to August** It tends to be dry during these times in the area around Santiago. Rains can be torrential in May and again September to November.
- **Year-round** Temperatures in mountain towns such as Jarabacoa and Constanza are cooler year-round and can fall below freezing at night.

Getting There & Around

Santiago's Aeropuerto Internacionál del Cibao (p168) offers frequent international air service to major destinations. There's a good selection of car-rental agencies at the airport.

Santiago sits on the main trunk highway that runs north from Santo Domingo to Puerto Plata, with bus services to all points of the compass. First-class buses service all major destinations, except for Constanza – you'll need to hop on a *guagua* (local bus). As always, renting a car, preferably an SUV, will give you more freedom to explore the countryside.

SANTIAGO

POP 691,000

One of the oldest settlements in Spain's New World empire, Santiago is the country's second-largest city, spilling over its original border, the Río Yaque del Norte. This sprawling city churns out rum and cigars, feeding off the large-scale tobacco and sugarcane plantations that make up much of the topography of the surrounding valley floor. The Cordillera Central to the west and Cordillera Septentrional to the north hem in the city, which is bifurcated by Highway Duarte, the country's primary north–south thoroughfare.

Overlooked by most travelers, Santiago is a good place to familiarize yourself with the ordinary Dominican's way of life. Typical of

Central Highlands Highlights

1. **White-water rafting** (p172) on the Caribbean's only raftable river, the turbulent Río Yaque del Norte near Jarabacoa
2. Watching the sunset as the mist descends into the valley in high-altitude **Constanza** (p179)
3. Lingering at the top of **Pico Duarte** (p177), taking in the views of the Atlantic and the Caribbean
4. Dancing merengue till the wee hours at one of the bars surrounding the Monument in **Santiago** (p167)
5. Partying with the locals in **La Vega** (p169) in February, when it throws the country's biggest Carnival celebrations
6. Visiting the **Centro León** (p163) in Santiago, an exceptional museum with more than a century's worth of works by the very best Dominican artists

poor barrios throughout the country, Santiago's are a maze of haphazardly constructed homes made with corrugated iron roofs. Meanwhile, just east of downtown is the neighborhood of Cerros de Gurabo – surely one of the wealthiest in the DR – where the roads are lined with enormous mansions concealed behind high walls. But all strata of society cheer for the hometown baseball team and come together around the Monument, the city's raucous nightlife center.

History

Santiago was founded in 1495 by Christopher Columbus' elder brother, Bartholomew. But the earthquake of 1562 caused so much damage to the city that it was rebuilt on its present site beside the Río Yaque del Norte. It was attacked and destroyed several times by invading French troops, as part of long-simmering tension between Spain and France over control of the island. Santiago also suffered terribly during the DR's civil war in 1912.

The years immediately following the civil war were some of the city's best. WWI caused worldwide shortages of raw tropical materials, so prices soared for products such as sugar, tobacco, cocoa and coffee – all of which were being grown around Santiago. From 1914 through the end of the war and into the 1920s, Santiago's economy boomed. Lovely homes and impressive stores, electric lighting and paved streets appeared throughout town. In May 1922, Highway Duarte opened, linking Santiago with Bonao, La Vega and Santo Domingo to the south.

Sights & Activities

The center of town is Parque Duarte, a usually crowded, leafy park with a gazebo, the cathedral to its south and Palacio Consistorial to its west.

★Centro León — MUSEUM

(☎809-582-2315; www.centroleon.org.do; Av 27 de Febrero 146, Villa Progreso; adult/child RD$100/70, Tue free; ⏲10am-7pm Tue-Sun, closed Mon) This large, modern museum built by the tobacco wealth of the León Jimenez family is a world-class institution with an impressive collection of paintings that trace the evolution of Dominican art in the 20th century. There are three exhibition rooms in the main building: one focuses on the island's biodiversity, Taíno history and cultural diversity; the upstairs room displays a permanent collection of Dominican art and photography; and the third houses temporary art exhibits. There's an aviary out back.

An excellent gift shop sells books on Dominican history, art, culture and food, and there's an appealing cafeteria serving up sandwiches and drinks. During the evenings, the center offers an ever-changing schedule of art appreciation classes, art house cinema and, sometimes, live musical events.

The Centro León is a few kilometers east of downtown. A taxi there will cost around RD$100, or pick up a Ruta A *concho* (private car that follows a set route; RD$12) along Calle del Sol – not all Ruta A *conchos* go as far as the Centro León, though, so be sure to ask.

Monumento a los Héroes de la Restauración de la República — MONUMENT

(Av Monumental; ⏲9am-6pm Tue-Sun) On a hill at the east end of the downtown area is Santiago's most visible and recognizable sight, the Monument to the Heroes of the Restoration of the Republic. This eight-story boxy behemoth was originally built by Trujillo to celebrate Trujillo, but was rededicated after his assassination to honor the Dominican soldiers that fought the final war of independence against Spain. Large bronze statues of the celebrated generals gaze down upon Santiago from the steps.

The site boasts life-sized museum exhibits of Dominican history, and is often visited by large groups of uniformed primary-schoolers (the spire is closed due to safety concerns). Joggers cross train on the steps around dusk.

Estadio Cibao — STADIUM

(☎809-575-1810; Av Imbert) **Santiago's Águilas** (www.aguilas.com.do) baseball team is one of six in the country and the most successful in the league's history. Watching local fans root for the home side is almost as fun as the games themselves, held two to three times a week in winter. The 18,000 seat stadium is northwest of the city center and tickets start at RD$150; it's wise to book in advance. To get there, take a taxi or hop on any Ruta A *concho* westbound on Calle del Sol.

Fortaleza San Luis — MUSEUM

(cnr Calle Boy Scouts & San Luis; ⏲9am-5pm) Built in the late 17th century, the Fortaleza San Luis operated as a military stronghold until the 1970s, when it was converted into a prison. Today it houses a small museum, with an emphasis on Dominican military

Santiago

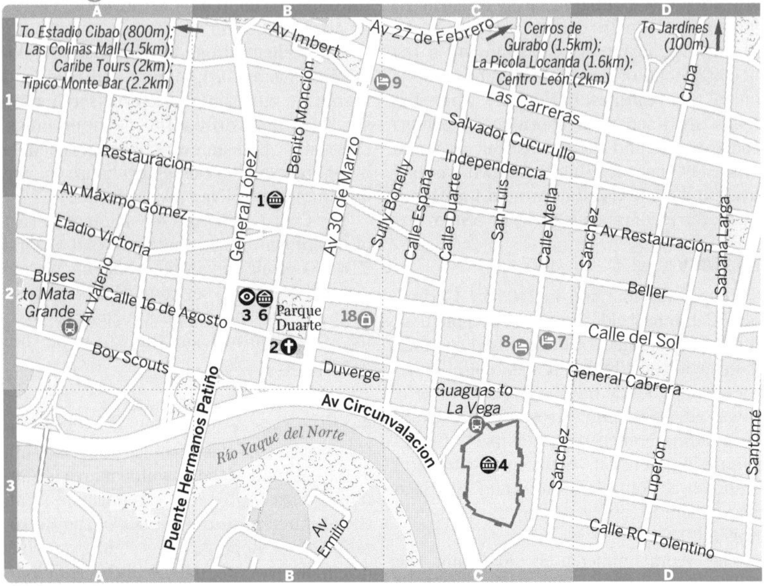

history, including ancient rusty weapons and a collection of 20th-century tanks and artillery.

Catedral de Santiago Apóstol CHURCH
(cnr Calles 16 de Agosto & Benito Monción; 7-9am Mon-Sat, to 8pm Sun) Santiago's cathedral, opposite the south side of Parque Duarte, was built between 1868 and 1895 and is a combination of Gothic and neoclassical styles. The cathedral contains the marble tomb of the late-19th-century dictator Ulises Heureaux, an elaborately carved mahogany altar and impressive stained-glass windows by contemporary Dominican artist Dincón Mora.

Palacio Consistorial MUSEUM
(Parque Duarte; 9am-noon & 2-5pm Mon-Sat) FREE On the west side of Parque Duarte you'll find the former town hall and a small museum devoted to the city's colorful history. If you're here during Carnival, don't miss the huge and stunning display of masks and *fichas* (posters), part of a yearly competition that draws entries from the top artists and mask-makers from across the country.

Casa del Arte ART GALLERY
(809-471-7839; Benito Monción 46; 9am-7pm Mon-Sat) FREE This small gallery displays Dominican painting, photography and sculpture. Some nights of the week a film club meets to screen arthouse and good-quality Hollywood flicks (free admission). There's sometimes live music (from RD$100) and, on Saturdays, live theater (RD$100).

Tours

Camping Tours ADVENTURE TOURS
(809-583-3121; www.campingtours.net; Calle Two 2, Villa Olga) Offers the cheapest trek to Pico Duarte. Expect Spanish-speaking guides and groups of 20 to 25 people. Prices per person are US$220 on foot and US$255/290 with a shared/private mule.

Sleeping

Hotel Colonial BUDGET HOTEL $
(809-247-3122; colonialdeluxe@yahoo.com; Salvador Cucurullo 113-115; r with fan RD$655, s/d with air-con RD$1000/1300;) If price is an object, the Colonial is an acceptable hotel in the center. But staying beyond a night or two can't be recommended. Hallways reminiscent of a military barracks lead to no-frills rooms, some lit by single light bulbs; all have small TVs with cable and some have fridges.

The rooms in the hotel's ambitiously named **Colonial Deluxe** building next door are of a similar quality and there a few other budget flophouses on the same block.

Santiago

Sights

1	Casa del Arte	B2
2	Catedral de Santiago Apóstol	B2
3	Centro de la Cultura de Santiago	B2
4	Fortaleza San Luis	C3
5	Monumento a los Héroes de la Restauración de la República	E2
6	Palacio Consistorial	B2

Sleeping

7	Aloha Sol Hotel	C2
8	Hodelpa Centro Plaza	C2
9	Hotel Colonial	C1

Eating

10	El Tablon Latino	E3
	La Brasa	(see 14)
11	Marisco Centro	E2
12	Noah Restaurant & Lounge	E2

Drinking & Nightlife

13	Ahi-Bar	E2
14	Barajanda Bar	E2
15	Kukara Macara Country Bar & Restaurant	E2
16	Puerta del Sol	F3

Entertainment

17	Hotel Matum	F2

Shopping

18	Calle del Sol Indoor Market	B2
	Outdoor Market	(see 18)

★ Camp David HOTEL $$
(☎809-276-6400; www.campdavidranch.com; Carretera Luperón Km 71/2; s/d incl breakfast RD$2500/3000; P ❄ 📶) On a mountain ridge about 30 minutes northeast of Santiago at 923m, Camp David offers sweeping vistas over the city and valley below. The recently upgraded, extremely large rooms, now with high-end boutique-style features like marble sinks and porcelain tile floors, still come with private balconies.

Ask for room 2203 for fantastic city views and room 2205 for comparable mountain ones. The property was founded by an admirer of Trujillo which explains why the former dictator's 1956 Cadillac is displayed in the lobby. As it's set several kilometers off the main road, you'll need a car to get here (or helicopter – it has its own heliport), or take a taxi (RD$500).

The white-tablecloth **restaurant** is easily the most romantic spot around. Service is worthy of a resort called Camp David; beef is the specialty here – go for the filete generalissimo, 8oz of Angus beef (mains RD$550 to RD$1300).

Hotel Platino HOTEL $$
(☎809-724-7576; www.hotelplatinord.com; Av Estrella Sadhalá; s/d incl breafkast from RD$1900/2400; P ❄ 📶) Set at the back of a small strip mall, a short drive from town, this is an excellent-value midrange option. While standard rooms, especially the small basement rooms, with a good dose of natural light are scarce, the beds are comfortable and rooms have a small desk, TV and minifridge; executive floor rooms have plasma TVs and attractive wood floors. A large gazebo marks the entrance.

To get your bearings on a map, Platino is across the street from an entrance to Pontifica Universidad Catolica Madre y Maestra (PUCMM).

Hodelpa Centro Plaza HOTEL $$
(☎809-581-7000; www.hodelpa.com; cnr Mella 54 & Del Sol; r incl breakfast US$100; P ❄ 📶) The fact that this business-class hotel, part of the Hodelpa chain, is located only a block from the primary commercial artery in the heart of the city means that lower floors suffer from street noise. Expect courteous,

professional service but fairly plain rooms, some dimly lit. There's a restaurant, tapas bar, lounge and small casino attached.

Aloha Sol Hotel HOTEL **$$**
(809-583-0090; www.alohasol.com; Calle del Sol 50; s/d incl breakfast from RD$2100/3000;) This centrally located hotel is a good deal if you don't mind the mildly stale quality of the furnishings, both in the rooms and the common areas. Be sure to ask for a room with window exposure and check out several before committing – the lighting situation varies. Breakfast buffet is better than average and for what it's worth, there's a casino attached.

Bora Bora Apart Hotel LOVE HOTEL **$$**
(www.borabora.com.do; Autopista Duarte Km 51/2; from RD$2700;) Granted, a garishly designed couples hotel (aka, *cabaña turisticos* or more colloquially 'no tell hotels') along the highway that charges by the hour is not for everyone. But if arriving on a late flight this might be a practical choice for the adventurous. Food is available as well.

Several of the suites, such as the 'Oriental' and 'African' rooms, not to mention the disco room that has a stripper pole in the middle, are quite gaudy.

Hodelpa Gran Almirante HOTEL **$$$**
(809-580-1992; www.hodelpa.com; Av Estrella Sadhalá; r/ste US$205/285;) The obvious choice for business travelers on an expense account, Gran Almirante's sundeck, spa and gym also entices tourists looking for extra comfort. The rooms are top-notch, there's a variety of restaurants and bars and an on-site casino. It's several kilometers from downtown but the surrounding neighborhood has a handful of good restaurants within walking distance.

Eating

Quality eating options in the downtown area are few and far between. There's a handful of Dominican and international fast-food joints on and around Calle del Sol and hole-in-the-wall *comedors* in the surrounding blocks. Virtually all the bars and lounges around the western and southern side of the Monument serve good food as well – **La Brasa** (Calle Beller; mains RD$200; 10am-3am) is a friendly and informal open-air parrilla and **Kukara Macara Country Bar & Restaurant** (809-241-3143; www.kukaramacara.net; Av Francia 7; mains RD$475; 10am-2am), a sprawling, kitschy western themed place, fun for a meal or drink. A woman selling empanadas sets up her cart on the south side in the early evening.

Francepan (Av 27 de Febrero; 9am-10pm Mon-Fri, from 8am Sat & Sun) and **La Campagna** (Av Juan Pablo Duarte; mains RD$300; 8am-midnight Sun-Thu, to 1am Fri & Sat;) are similar restaurants in the Jardínes neighborhood east of downtown. Both are relatively upscale cafes with outdoor patio seating areas and large menus, with everything from healthy smoothies (RD$110) and salads (RD$200) to burgers (RD$180) and heavy soups (RD$300).

El Carrito de Marchena DOMINICAN **$**
(Av Estrella Sadhalá; mains from RD$150; 24hr;) This open-air pavilion, only 25m before the Hotel Platino and a few kilometers from the Monument, is where groups of friends roll up after a night of dancing and boozing. A few large-screen TVs tuned to sports and

STRAIGHT TO THE STOAGIE SOURCE

Many of the world's top cigar brands are made in and around Santiago – Aurora, Montecristo, Arturo Fuente, to name a few. Many of those name brands contract the work to local, Dominican cigar-makers, who then offer the 'label-less' cigar to locals and travelers at half the price. It's critical when buying cigars to test whether they've been made well and stored properly. Pick up the cigar: it should have a springy tightness, indicating solid construction. If it's too soft or too hard, it won't draw well. It shouldn't crackle under your fingers either; that means it's too dry, and will smoke like kindling.

Many of the factories are located northeast of Santiago at the foot of the Cordillera Septentrional in the village of Tamboril (27 de Febrero turns into Carretera Tamboril). The easiest to visit is **La Aurora Parque Industrial** (809-734-2563; Tamboril; 8am-noon & 2pm-3:30pm), 'affiliated' with the Centro León which used to have a small Aurora workshop. All of the producers, including **Fabrica Anilo de Oro** (809-580-5808; Tamboril) and **Tabacalera Jacagua** (809-580-6600; Tamboril), offer free tours (most open Monday through Friday) and reservations are preferred.

DON'T MISS

CARNIVAL!

Held in February, Carnival is big all over the country, but especially so in Santiago and La Vega. The latter hosts the largest and most organized celebrations in the country, and Santiago is famous for its artistic and fantastical *caretas* (masks) and hosts an annual international *careta* competition in the lead-up to the big event. Rival neighborhoods in Santiago, La Joya and Los Pepines, make up the bulk of the parade with onlookers watching from overpasses, apartment buildings, even the tops of lamp posts. In La Vega, townspeople belong to one of numerous groups, which range from 10 to 200 members. Regardless of the city, it's the costumes – colorful, baggy outfits with capes and diabolical masks – that are the highlight. Watch your backside though – participants swing *vejigas* (inflated cow bladders) and hit each other – and onlookers – on the behind.

If you decide to come to either city for Carnival, be sure to make reservations – rooms fill up fast this time of the year.

an extensive menu, which includes tacos (RD$100), burritos (RD$250) and *mofongo* (fried plantains mashed together and mixed with a variety of meats or other fillings; RD$240).

★ **Il Pasticcio** ITALIAN **$$**
(☎809-582-6061; www.ilpasticciord.com; Calle 3 & Av Del Llano, Cerros de Gurabo; mains RD$375; ⊙noon-3.30pm & 7-11pm Tue-Sun) Long on character and style, Paolo the Italian owner has been welcoming Santiago's powerful and bohemian since 1995. Curiously decorated with a range of objets d'art, the restaurant is a reflection of his personality, and the menu of fresh pasta, meat and seafood is truly satisfying. We enjoyed the salmon carpaccio.

Marisco Centro SEAFOOD **$$**
(☎809-971-9710; cnr Calle del Sol & Av Francia; mains RD$425; ⊙9am-midnight, to 2am Fri & Sat) This long-running restaurant serves grilled fish and seafood in an elegant indoor dining room, breezy outdoor garden or more ordinary, brightly lit back room. Sushi specials Wednesday nights, live music Fridays, but especially worth planning for is seafood brunch Sunday (adult/child RD$600/300).

El Tablon Latino SOUTH AMERICAN **$$**
(Calle del Sol 12; mains RD$400; ⊙11am-1am) The casually cool ultra-contemporary design echoes the menu of inventive pan-Latino fare – or you can go with more simple but above average burgers and filets. Located on a lively stretch of pavement on the south side of the Monument.

La Picola Locanda ITALIAN **$$**
(☎809-724-8831; cnr Valverde & Av Metropolitana; mains RD$220-400; ⊙10am-1am) More than a dozen varieties of pizza and pasta are on the menu at this modern, postage-stamp sized restaurant in the Jardines neighborhood. A surprising bonus if you want to mix things up, you can also order sushi (rolls RD$185) and other Japanese fare from the even smaller attached Sushi Ya.

Noah Restaurant & Lounge DOMINICAN **$$**
(☎809-971-0550; www.noahrestaurant.com; Calle del Sol 4; mains RD$600; ⊙11am-midnight Mon-Thu, to 3am Fri & Sat) Possibly downtown's and the Monument's most upscale restaurant, stylish Noah does pasta, fish and meat dishes, plus more than a dozen varieties of pizza and sushi rolls.

Drinking & Entertainment

Clustered around the Monument are a dozen or so bars, restaurants and late-night eateries (especially on Calle Beller), making this Santiago's best place for general revelry – try Barajanda Bar on Av Francia for live music nightly. Most also serve more than passable food. Vendors sell beer from coolers and locals blast music from their car stereos till dawn. While not especially dangerous, the center can be dodgy in the wee hours so it's best to take a taxi home. Monday to Wednesday nights are generally subdued.

Hotel Almirante and **Hotel Matum** (☎809-581-3107; www.hotelmatum.com; Av Las Carreras 1) have dance clubs of their own and the **Soho Rooftop Lounge** (☎829-579-8423; 5th fl, Plaza Bella Terra, Av Pablo Duarte) has live jazz Monday nights.

Puerta del Sol LOUNGE
(cnr Calle del Sol & Calle 6; ⊙4pm-late; wi-fi) A cross between a VIP airport lounge, sports bar and stylish Miami nightclub, this sleek establishment stretches along the southern

side of the Monument. Large-screen plasma TVs cover the back wall, while the other sides are open to the street. In addition to drinks, there's an eclectic and large menu of Dominican and international fare (mains are RD$375).

Confusingly, the sign for its telecom provider, Wind, is more prominent than the restaurant's.

Ahi-Bar BAR

(809-581-6779; cnr Calle RC Tolentino & Av Restauración; 4pm-late) The best of a string of bars on Calle RC Tolentino, Ahi's modern open-air patio is set above street level. Most people come to drink, but in case you miss dinner, the food is pretty good. There's live outdoor jazz on Mondays and a sister **dance club** (karaoke Thursday nights) across the street that attracts the young and stylish.

Tipico Monte Bar DANCE CLUB

(809-575-0300; Av 27 de Febrero 18; admission varies; 5pm-late, closed Tue) A diverse mix of locals, dom-yors (Dominicans living in New York City) and even a celebrity baseball player or two come here for serious merengue music and dancing. Set amid a series of auto-repair shops in the Las Colinas neighborhood north of the center, you'll want to take a cab there and back (RD$100 one way).

Shopping

Calle del Sol, the primary commercial artery in the downtown area, is lined with mostly unremarkable clothing shops, banks, hair salons and small department stores. There is, however, a two-story **indoor market** (btwn Calle España & Av 30 de Marzo) worth visiting if you're looking for souvenirs such as cigars, *mamajuana* (a mixture of herbs, dried bark, rum, wine and honey) and rum. Directly behind this building, on several small side streets, is a chaotic covered outdoor market, with stall after stall of secondhand clothes, shoes and other items.

Santiago has several shopping malls, including upscale **Plaza Bella Terra** (Av Duarte; 8am-11pm) and the older **Plaza Internacional** (Av Duarte; 8am-11pm, movie theaters 7pm-late Mon-Fri, 4pm-late Sat & Sun) near one another east of the Monument, and **Las Colinas Mall** (Av 27 de Febrero; 8am-11pm, movie theaters 7pm-late Mon-Fri, 4pm-late Sat & Sun) anchored by the aptly named Supermercado Jumbo. All have food courts and movie theaters showing mostly contemporary Hollywood fare for around RD$150.

Information

The **BanReservas** (Calle del Sol 66) and **Scotiabank** (cnr Calle del Sol & 30 de Marzo) on Calle del Sol have ATMs.

Centro de Internet Yudith (809-581-4882; Calle 16 de Agosto near Mella; per hr RD$35; 8:30am-8:30pm Mon-Fri, to 5pm Sat)

Farmacia Jorge (809-582-2887; cnr Calle España & Av Gómez)

Hospital Metropolitano de Santiago (809-947-2222; www.homshospital.com; Autopista Duarte Km 2.8; 24hr)

Getting There & Away

AIR

Santiago's **Aeropuerto Internacionál del Cibao** (809-233-8000; www.aeropuertocibao.com.do), around 12km south of downtown, is serviced by the following airlines:

Taxis are your only option to and from town – US$15 to $20 one way.

Aerolineas Mas (in Santo Domingo 809-682-9399; www.aerolineasmas.com) Flights to Punta Cana and Port-au-Prince, Haiti.

Air Turks and Caicos (809-233-8262; www.airturksandcaicos.com)

American Airlines (809-200-5151; www.aa.com) Direct flights to Miami.

American Eagle (809-583-0055; www.aa.com) For San Juan, Puerto Rico and Puerto Prince, Haiti.

Copa Airlines (809-200-2772; www.copaair.com) For Panama City, Panama.

Delta (809-200-9191; www.delta.com) Daily flights to JFK.

Jet Blue (809-200-9898; www.jetblue.com) Daily flights to JFK and San Juan, Puerto Rico.

Spirit Airlines (809-587-9326; www.spirit.com) Early morning to Fort Lauderdale, Florida – possibly the cheapest flight between the DR and US.

BUS

Caribe Tours (809-241-1414) has two terminals in Santiago (all buses, except the one for Haiti – from Las Colinas station only – stop at both stations): in Las Colinas on Av 27 de Febrero about 3km north of the center, and more conveniently in the Jardínes neighborhood at Maimon and 27 de Febrero, just steps from the competing **Metro** (809-587-3837). All three terminals are on or near the Ruta A *concho* line, or take a taxi. Destinations include the following:

DESTINATION	FARE (RD$)	DURATION	FREQUENCY
Cap-Haïtien, Haiti	1060	4hr	noon daily
Dajabón	200	2½hr	take Monte Cristi bus
La Vega	80	45min	take Santo Domingo bus
Monte Cristi	190	1¾hr	6 times daily, 8:45am-6:15pm
Puerto Plata	120	1¼hr	hourly, 8:15am-9:15pm
Santo Domingo	280	2½hr	26 times daily, 6am-8:15pm
Sosúa	160	2hr	take Puerto Plata bus

CAR

The airport has a good selection of reliable international car rental companies, including **Avis** (☎809-233-8154; www.avis.com), **Europcar** (☎809-233-8150; www.europcar.com) and **Hertz** (☎809-233-8555; www.hertz.com), all open from 7am to 11pm. Have RD$25 on hand for the toll to leave the parking lot. Close to a dozen local companies line the access road between the terminal and highway – most arrange pick-up from the airport.

Getting Around

Regular radio taxis ply the streets looking for passengers – the in-town fare when we were there was around RD$100.

Conchos are private cars that follow set routes around town and charge RD$12 to RD$20 (up to six passengers per vehicle). After dark, however, the unlicensed *piratas* take over, and you should exercise caution before hopping into some random person's car.

SAN JOSÉ DE LAS MATAS

POP 38,600 / ELEV 518M

This small mountain town 45km southwest of Santiago is a jumping-off point for two major hiking trails in the Parque Nacional Armando Bermúdez. It's a pleasant enough town, with nice mountain views, several rivers and *balenarios* (swimming holes) to swim in – a place to linger the day before or after a long hike. If you do happen to be out here, follow the trail that starts behind the post office on Calle 30 de Marzo. It leads to a cliff-top park with great views of the surrounding mountains. It's about an hour return.

By far the best accommodation in town is a former Trujillo retreat called **Hotel La Mansión** (☎809-571-6868; www.hotellamansionsajoma.com; s/d RD$1700/2300;), an enormous complex with spacious, contemporary rooms with panoramic views, a pool area, bar and **restaurant** (mains RD$300; 9am-11pm); when it hosts live music events it comes alive. The rustic **Ventana Rio Lindo** (☎809-214-4430; www.ventanariolindohotel.com; s/d RD$500/1000;) with very basic, concrete rooms is at the end of a rough road perched over the Inoa river around 9km west of town; simple food (RD$150) is available.

Guaguas for Santiago (RD$100, one hour, from 6am to 7pm) leave from opposite the Texaco station at the town entrance. Buses leave roughly every 15 minutes in the mornings, but you may have to wait an hour or more in the middle of the day. By car it's only 45 minutes from Santiago.

LA VEGA

POP 248,000

Pressed hard up against the highway halfway between Santo Domingo and Santiago, La Vega is known primarily as a transportation hub and the site of the country's most boisterous Carnival celebrations. And while in most respects it's a lackluster town – dusty and noisy during the day – La Vega's origin story is an interesting one. In the 1490s, Christopher Columbus himself ordered a fort built in the area to store gold mined nearby. Over the next 50 years, the first mint in the New World was established, the nation's first commercial sugar crop was harvested, and the first royally sanctioned brothel in the western hemisphere opened its doors for business in La Vega. But this prosperity came to an abrupt end in 1562, when an earthquake leveled the city. The damage was so severe that the city was moved several kilometers to its present site on the banks of the Río Camú. You can visit what remains of the old city near the town of Santo Cerro.

OFF THE BEATEN TRACK

TOUR THROUGH THE MOUNTAINS TO THE NORTHERN COAST

Ideal for the eco-conscious traveler, this rustic mountaintop retreat is about as far from an all-inclusive as you can get. Set high on a ridge with breathtaking views of the valley below, **Tubagua Plantation Eco-Village** (809-696-6932; www.tubagua.com; r incl breakfast from US$25;) is the vision of longtime DR resident and community and conservation minded Canadian consul Tim Hall. By his own description, accommodations here are 'Robinson Crusoe style' which shouldn't discourage anyone. There are several wooden cabins with palapa roofs and basic bedding with mosquito nets – simple but comfortable – and a shared bathroom, closed on three sides, is open on the fourth with an empty hanging picture frame highlighting the panoramic scene. The most upscale of the bunch, with a Balinese-style feel and its own outdoor shower, is perfect for honeymooners. Grab a coffee and a book and you won't want to leave the open-air lounge and dining area.

Don't try driving here at night – 20km from Puerto Plata (taxi US$30) and around 40km from Santiago – since the road is rough and there are no lights.

Tim, an enthusiastic advocate of low-impact sustainable tourism, can arrange day, overnight and week-long itineraries for travel anywhere in the country. From Tubagua, a half-day hike to the pools of **Charcos los Militares** is especially recommended. In addition, for several years now Tim has been central in helping to develop a 30km sightseeing route through the mountains, between Montellano in the north (12km east of Puerto Plata) and La Cumbre in the south, called **Ruta Panoramica** (www.rutapanoramica.com).

The 'highway', rough in patches, winds up and over the **Cordillera Septentrional**, climbing to 2200ft at La Cumbre – a nearby monument marks the spot where bodies of political dissidents the Mirabal sisters were left by Trujillo assassins. The mountain slopes in the area are pockmarked with **amber mines** (blue, the most valuable variety, is found here), essentially small shovel and pickaxe-dug holes with plastic tarps strung up as makeshift shelters. It's a fairly desperate and unpredictable undertaking. Carmen, the wife of a miner, will prepare lunch and coffee in their modest home, and she and her sons will answer questions about the life of an amber miner.

A small coffee growing region is also nearby, around the pretty little town of **Pedro Garcia**, about 10km north of La Cumbre. In **Pedro Garcia** itself, you can buy coffee (RD$300 for 1lb bag) and locally produced trinkets at **Artesania La Factoria** (Calle JP Duarte 125), a shop attached to the area's sole coffee processing plant (there were once six). After a berry borer beetle epidemic wiped out most of the beans in 2000, the mountainsides were cleared and converted into cattle ranches. The impact has been felt economically and environmentally, leading to the exodus of many villagers – the population is a quarter of what it was in 1970. There's a fledgling effort to obtain a reforestation grant, develop organic single origin coffee production and promote ecotourism. In the meantime, you can ask staff at Tubagua to arrange a roasting and tasting demonstration in a small hilltop shelter with beautiful views of the countryside.

Sights & Activities

Santo Cerro CHURCH

Legend has it that Columbus placed a cross he received as a bon-voyage gift from Queen Isabella atop this hill, which commands fantastic sweeping views of the Valle del Cibao. During a battle between Spaniards and Taínos, the latter tried to burn the cross but it wouldn't catch fire. The Virgen de las Mercedes appeared on one of its arms and the Taínos are said to have fled in terror.

Today the cross is gone – supposedly in private hands – but you can still see the Santo Hoyo (Holy Hole) in which the cross was allegedly planted. The hole is inside the **Iglesia Las Mercedes**, covered with a small wire grill and tended by nuns and Jesuit priests. The beige-and-white church, with its red-tile roof, is a major pilgrimage site, drawing thousands of believers every September 24 for its patron-saint day. Be sure to look for a fenced-off tree near the steps leading to the church – it is said to have been planted in 1495.

Santo Cerro is northeast of La Vega, several kilometers east of Highway Duarte, up a steep winding road. It's somewhat confusing to find your way leaving the city, so ask for directions.

La Vega Vieja HISTORICAL SITE
(admission RD$100; ⏲8am-5pm) What's left of the original site of the city are the ruins of the fort Columbus ordered built and a church. After the great earthquake of 1562, most of what remained of the structures was taken to the latter-day La Vega, where it was used in construction. With some imagination and the help of a guide (Spanish speaking only), it's possible to begin to grasp the historical implications of what you're seeing.

A small museum in the back of the site contains both Taíno and Spanish tools, weapons and ceramics. The cost of admission and guide seems open to negotiation and depends on the number in your party.

To get here, continue around 4km past the turn-off for Santo Cerro and look for an old and battered sign on the left-hand side of the road.

Catedral de la Concepción CHURCH
(cnr Av Guzman & Adolfo; ⏲varies) La Vega's infamous cathedral is a fascinating eyesore that looks like a cross between a medieval fortress and a coal plant. It is an odd mixture of Gothic and neoindustrial styles, though the large, contemporary interior is easier on the eyes. The cathedral faces the main plaza, where families and young people gather in the evenings and weekends.

Sleeping & Eating

Unless you're in La Vega for Carnival, there is no real reason to stay overnight. **Hotel Rey** (☎809-573-9797; Calle Restauración 3; r from RD$1500, restaurant mains RD$200; P❄📶), a comfortable and convenient choice that caters to business travelers is close to the highway and a half dozen or so blocks from the cathedral.

Food stands serving fried chicken and *pastelitos* (flaky fried dough stuffed with meat, cheese or veggies) can be found in front of the cathedral. One of the few full-on restaurants in the heart of town is **Macao Grill** (Calle Don Antonio Guzman 82; mains RD$150-300; ⏲11am-9pm; 📶), on the eastern side of the cathedral plaza. Beside the usual Dominican fare, it does excellent deep dish-style pizza and good burgers and burritos. Otherwise, there are several large open-air *comedors* and Dominican fast-food restaurants scattered along the highway.

Getting There & Away

La Vega is a regular stop on the well-traveled Santo Domingo–Santiago route. **Caribe Tours** (☎809-573-2488; Av Rivera) has its terminal on the main highway, 1.5km from the center of La Vega. The main street, Av Antonio Guzman runs north–south and intersects Highway Duarte on the north side of town.

DESTINATION	FARE (RD$)	DURATION	FREQUENCY
Jarabacoa	100	1hr	buses from Santo Domingo pass by at 7am, 10am, 1:30pm & 4:30pm
Puerto Plata	250	2hr	take the Sosúa bus
Santiago	100	40min	take the Sosúa bus
Santo Domingo	270	1½hr	every 30-60 min, 6:30am-7:45pm
Sosúa	280	2½hr	hourly, 7:30am-8:30pm

Another option for the trip to Santiago is to catch a *guagua* (RD$85, 50 minutes) leaving from a terminal on the main road into town. Alternatively, *guaguas* and pickups for Jarabacoa (RD$65) leave when full from a stop called Quinto Patio (about 1km from the center, RD$70 in a taxi) from 7am to 6pm.

To Constanza, there are two direct second-class buses (RD$150, two to three hours) leaving from the *mercado público* (public market) at about 8am and 2pm, though departure times can vary.

JARABACOA

POP 40,550 / ELEV 488M

Nestled in the low foothills of the Cordillera Central, Jarabacoa maintains an under-the-radar allure as the antithesis to the clichéd Caribbean vacation. Nighttime temperatures call for light sweaters, a roiling river winds past forested slopes that climb into the clouds, and local adventurers share their exploits over a beer in the handful of bars or nightclubs near the town's Parque Central. The fact that thousands of well-to-do Dominicans from Santo Domingo and Santiago have built summer homes here is a

Jarabacoa

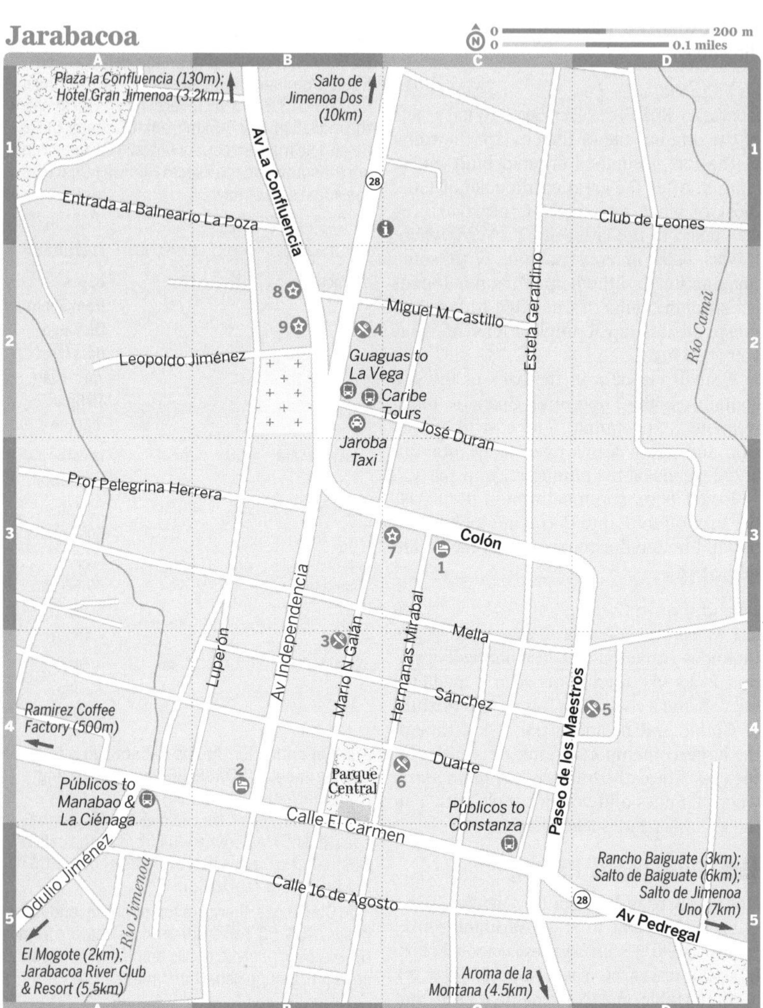

Jarabacoa

Sleeping

1 Hostal Jarabacoa C3
2 Hotel Brisas del Yaque II B4

Eating

3 Mercado Modelo B4
4 Panadería & El Rancho B2
5 Pizza & Pepperoni D4
6 Restaurant Del Parque Galería C4

Entertainment

7 Entre Amigos C3
8 Liquor Bar & Grill B2
9 Venue Bar & Lounge B2

testament to Jarabacoa's laid-back charm as the 'City of Eternal Spring'. With a number of good hotels outside town, this is the place to base yourself if you want to raft, hike, bike, horseback ride, go canyoning or simply explore rural life. On weekends, locals head to the Balenario la Confluencia, where the Rio Yaque and Rio Jimenoa meet 4km north of town, to swim and picnic.

Activities

White-Water Rafting

Promising and delivering thrills, chills and, for the unlucky, spills, a rafting trip down the Río Yaque del Norte is an exhilarating ride. A typical rafting excursion begins with breakfast, followed by a truck ride upriver to the put-in. You'll be given a life vest, a helmet and a wetsuit, plus instructions on paddling and safety. You're usually only asked to paddle part of the time; in the rapids to keep the boat on its proper line, and occasionally in the flat water areas to stay on pace. You'll stop for a small snack about two-thirds of the way downriver, and then return to Jarabacoa for lunch.

The rapids are rated 2 and 3 (including sections nicknamed 'Mike Tyson' and 'the Cemetery') and part of the fun is the real risk of your raft turning over and dumping you into a rock-infested, surging river. A cameraman leapfrogs ahead of the group along the riverbank so you can watch (and purchase) the instant replay afterwards over a beer.

The Río Yaque del Norte has level 4, 5 and 6 rapids much further up in the mountains. No official tours go that far, but some intrepid guides raft it for fun on their own time. Ask around at Rancho Baiguate (p175) – if you don't mind paying a premium, you might be able to organize something.

A lot of people come from the north coast to raft and then head straight back. This involves at least four hours each way on a bus. Consider spending a couple of nights in Jarabacoa – you'll enjoy your trip much more if you do.

Canyoning

For those whose adrenaline fix isn't satiated by white-water rafting, a few hours rappelling, jumping, sliding, zip-lining and swimming down a mountain river will have you feeling like a Navy Seal or Hollywood stunt person. Rancho Baiguate's standard canyoning trip (US$50, all gear provided) ends with a rappel down Salto Baiguate.

Waterfalls

The falls are easy to visit if you've got your own transportation. If not, a *motoconcho* tour to all three will set you back around RD$1000, and a taxi US$80 to US$100.

Salto de Jimenoa Uno WATERFALL

(admission RD$100) So picturesque are these waterfalls near Jarabacoa that an opening scene of the movie *Jurassic Park* was filmed here. It's definitely the prettiest – a 60m waterfall pouring from a gaping hole in an otherwise solid rock cliff. There's a sandy beach and nice swimming hole, but the water is icy cold and potentially dangerous; if you do swim, stay far away from the swirling currents.

The trailhead to the waterfall is 7km from the Shell station in Jarabacoa along the road to Constanza. Look for the small shed housing the 'office' for this community project – admission comes with a bottle of water. The steep path down is slippery after rain and sweat-inducing all other times (expect each way to take between 20 minutes and half an hour).

Salto de Jimenoa Dos WATERFALL

(admission RD$50) Generally just referred to as Salto Jimenoa, come here for the views only since access to bathing pools at the foot of this 40m cascade is fenced off. From the parking area, it's a 500m walk over a series of suspension bridges and trails flanked by densely forested canyon walls. The turn-off to the falls is 4km northwest of Jarabacoa on the road to Highway Duarte.

Coming from town, you'll reach a major fork in the road with a large bank of signs; the falls are to the right. From there, a paved road leads 6km past a golf course to the parking lot.

Salto de Baiguate WATERFALL

FREE In a lush canyon, Baiguate is not as visually impressive as the others, but it's the most accessible for swimming. A lovely 300m trail cut out of the canyon wall leads from the parking lot to the salto – canyoning trips end here with a rappel down the falls.

To get there, take Calle El Carmen east out of Jarabacoa for 3km until you see a sign for the waterfalls on the right-hand side of the road. From there, a badly rutted dirt road, which at one point is crossed by a shallow creek, leads 3km to a parking lot.

Hiking

In addition to the trek to Pico Duarte, there are a number of shorter half-day and full-day walks you can take in the area.

You can get a taste of the ecology of **Parque Nacional Armando Bermúdez** with a one-day hike to **Los Tablones** (seven hours; about 10km). The trail is not especially well-marked and it's highly recommended to go with a local guide. Rancho Baiguate can arrange the trip (US$150 per person including meal, minimum two people), which involves a four-hour walk up and another four hours back down, or you can make your way to the park yourself, pay the entrance fee of RD$200 and negotiate with guides. It's a 10-minute drive southwest of La Cienaga on a very rough road to the Los Tablones trailhead.

A challenging steep hike is to **El Mogote**, a peak (1573m) west of town; to get to the trailhead 5km away, hop in a taxi (one way RD$200). You'll encounter a Salesian monastery where the monks have taken a vow of silence. From here it's a stiff five-hour hike to the summit – only to be attempted by the very aerobically fit. Start early, wear boots if you have them, and bring plenty of water. It's a slippery walk (or slide) down from the top (at least the first half).

La Jagua (around four hours; about 6km), a shorter walk in the area, can also be arranged by Rancho Baiguate (US$40 per person including meal).

Paragliding

If launching yourself off a cliff sounds like fun then you've come to the right place. Make a point of looking up Antonio Rosario Aquino, otherwise known as **Tony** (809-848-3479; www.paraglidingtonydominicanrepublic.com; tandem flights RD$2500), a native of Jarabacoa, one of the most experienced pilots on the island. After the initial take-off, it really only requires an ability to sit in a comfortable contraption. See if you can hold your lunch after a series of high-speed 360-degree whirls. Remember to bring your camera – it's an opportunity for fantastic panoramic photos.

Tours

Jarabacoa's biggest and best tour operator dominates the stage. A few smaller outfits come and go, but for safety and reliability we recommend Rancho Baiguate (p177). While its main clientele are Dominican groups from the capital and foreign guests from the all-inclusive resorts near Puerto Plata, independent travelers are more than welcome to join any of the trips, usually by calling a day or two in advance (except for Pico Duarte, which should be arranged with more notice). Overnight guests can pop in to the office in the afternoon and see what adventures are on for the following day.

Activities have the following prices (all include breakfast and lunch): **rafting** (US $50), **canyoning** at Salto Baiguate (US$50), **mountain biking** (US$25 to US$50 depending on trail). Rancho Baiguate also offers **horseback/jeep** tours to the waterfalls (US$16 to US$21 with lunch, US$9 to US$11 without lunch). Its Pico Duarte trips range in price depending on the number of people and the side trips you take; a group of four people for three days with no side trips costs US$380 per person.

A popular excursion, often done by groups on a whistle-stop tour of the area, but also easily arranged by independent travelers with a little notice, is a visit to nearby organic coffee farms where you can learn about the labor-intensive art of turning beans into your daily caffeine fix.

Ramirez Coffee Factory COFFEE PLANT
(809-574-2618; www.ramirezcoffee.com; Altos del Yaque; 8am-1:30pm & 2-4pm) The 8000-sq-km family-run farm is near Manabao, but the processing factory itself, which you can tour, is just outside the center of Jarabacoa (cross the bridge over the river). You can sample a cup of its Monte Alto brand in a little cafe-cum-shop in the parking lot.

Sleeping

In Town

Hotel Brisas del Yaque II HOTEL $
(809-574-2100; hotelbrisasdelyaque@hotmail.com; Av Independencia 13; r from RD$1500; P) The low-slung Yaque II has large, comfortable and modern rooms and front-desk staff able to answer travel-related questions. The twin rooms are distinctive in having two bathrooms, one for each guest. Ask for a 'mountain-facing' room, if only to avoid street noise. It's nearby sister hotel, the Brisas del Yaque was closed due to extensive renovations when we visited.

Hostal Jarabacoa HOTEL $
(809-574-4108; Calle Hermanas Mirabal; r with fan/air-con RD$900/1300; P) A good-value option if staying in town is a priority. There's no real lobby or public spaces to speak of, only clean rooms with small bathrooms and TVs lining a long hallway. Even though it feels like a hospital, the owners are friendly and welcoming.

Out of Town

Soon after we visited, a charming and tranquil retreat called **Villa Celeste Estate** (201-381-1875; www.villaceleste.com; Calle Los Pinos; r incl breakfast US$100-150;) opened on Rte 28, only 12km from La Vega.

★**Rancho Baiguate** RESORT $$
(☎809-574-6890; www.ranchobaiguate.com; Carretera a Constanza; all-incl s US$77-107, d US$126-163, tr US$170-220, q US$252; P 📶 🏊) A wonderful base to explore the mountains, Baiguate is a rustic resort set in an enormous 72-sq-km leafy compound. Ask for a room in the low-slung building along the river – large, comfortable, tile-floored rooms have private patios with wicker chairs. There's a pool on the other side of the river that runs through the complex, a beach volleyball court, table tennis and pool tables, and good bird life for those who just want to sit still and chill.

Large groups of students pack the place on weekends and holidays but midweek in the low season you might have it all to yourself. An on-site veggie garden supplies the competent Dominican cook, and a worm farm and a gray-water treatment plant reduce the resort's impact on the environment. The friendly staff speak English; the best adventure tour company in the area is here. The hosts can pick you up from town.

Hotel Gran Jimenoa HOTEL $$
(☎809-574-6304; www.granjimenoahotel.com; Av La Confluencia; s/d/tr incl breakfast from RD$1375/1870/2400; P ❄ @ 📶 🏊) Set several kilometers north of town directly on the roaring Río Jimenoa, this is the Cordillera Central's most upscale hotel. It's neither on the beach nor an all-inclusive hotel, but you could easily spend a week here without leaving the extensive grounds, which include a footbridge to a bar on the far bank of the river.

Tables at the hotel's fine restaurant are on a deck along the edge of the river; dishes (mains RD$550) cover the standard Dominican, Italian and French, as well as guinea hen and rabbit in wine sauce.

Jarabacoa River Club & Resort HOTEL $$
(☎809-574-2456; www.jarabacoariverclub.com; s/d incl breakfast RD$2150/3100; P ❄ @ 🏊) This rambling multilevel fun-for-all-ages complex sits on both sides of the roaring Río Yaque del Norte, around 26km south of town on the way to Manabao. White-water rafting trips put-in the river north of here; you can hang out at the riverside restaurant or cafe, or at one of the pools and see them pass below. The low-slung two-story building has spacious, modern rooms but it's the views that are special.

SONIDO DEL YAQUE

A steep walk down several hundred steps brings you to **Sonido del Yaque** (Cabanas Cazuelas de Dona Esperanza; ☎809-846-7275; per person RD$500), a community tourism project initiated by the women of the village of Los Calabazos, around halfway between Jarabacoa and Manabao. It's a handful of wood and concrete cabins set amid lush jungle above the roaring Yaque del Norte river, each with bunk beds and a porch. There's electricity, cold-water showers and mosquito nets. Meals can be made with advanced notice and served in an unfinished two-story wooden structure. It's not signposted, so coming from Jarabacoa look for a tiny shop at the right hand side of the road.

Eating

All of the accommodation options listed have their own restaurants, especially important for those located out of town. Plaza La Confluencia, a small, newly opened (and when we visited, not yet fully occupied) two-story shopping mall (free wi-fi access), has several places to eat including Helados Bon (ice cream) and Carrito de Moshe (burritos, wraps and burgers) kiosks and a Pala Pizza franchise. Several modern supermarkets are in the center of town and the small **Mercado Modelo** (Av Mario N Galán; ⏰9am-5pm Mon-Sat) sells fresh fruit, vegetables and other foodstuffs.

Panadería & El Rancho CAFE, INTERNATIONAL $$
(Av Independencia & Duarte; mains RD$200-400; ⏰7am-10pm; 📶) This space across from the Esso gas station at the northern part of town includes a cafe serving simple sandwiches and excellent espresso and a slightly more upscale restaurant and bar. The latter, decorated with colorful artwork, has a varied menu with fish and pasta dishes and recommended *cazuela de mariscos* (soupy stew made with a variety of seafood; RD$400).

Owned by the folks at Rancho Baiguate who have attached a little kiosk (8am to 8pm) where you can go for tourist related information.

Restaurant Del Parque Galería DOMINICAN $$
(☎809-574-6749; Calle Hermanas Mirabal; mains RD$200-800; ⏰11:30am-10:30pm; 📶) This

long-running restaurant is built directly around a tree and miniature children's playground overlooking Parque Central. The large menu includes Dominican specialties such as *conejo criollo* (rabbit prepared Creole-style, RD$440) and the *cabrito al vino* (goat in wine sauce, RD$380) as well as international favorites.

Pizza & Pepperoni PIZZA $$
(☎809-574-4348; Paseo de los Maestros; pizza RD$200-300; ⏰11am-11pm; 📶) The straightforward name isn't entirely accurate: excellent pepperoni pizzas are on the menu, along with more than a dozen other varieties, but so are calzones, burgers, pasta, grilled meat and fish dishes. It has a modern outdoor dining area with TVs tuned to sports. Delivers.

★ **Aroma de la Montana** INTERNATIONAL $$$
(☎829-452-6879; www.jamacadedios.com; mains RD$600-1500; ⏰10am-10pm Mon-Thu, to 11pm Fri & Sat; 📶) The fact that the top floor of this sophisticated mountaintop restaurant rotates 360 degrees (weekends only) is almost besides the point. Sweeping, practically aerial views of the entirety of the Jarabacoa countryside are available anytime from the balcony seating. Lunchtime has a family atmosphere but there's a distinctly romantic candlelit vibe on weekend nights (reservations highly recommended), at least on the rotating top floor. The menu includes ribeye steaks, chicken, salmon and a recommended, for meat lovers, parrilla for two.

The road to the restaurant, part of a large property development called Jamaca de Dios, winds its way up between the Pinar Quemado and Palo Blanco mountains south of town. In its original incarnation, an informal spot serving free hotdogs and hamburgers, it was meant to encourage potential vacation home buyers to stop and take in the fresh air and views. Have some form of ID on hand for the guards at the development's entryway security gate. Motorcycles, because of noise, aren't allowed on weekends.

Drinking & Nightlife

Social life in Jarabacoa revolves around Parque Central: the church and restaurants are all here. At night, the numerous *colmados* pump loud merengue and beery customers onto the sidewalk, where the party really gets going.

Two other nightspots next to one another, across from the Esso petrol station at the northern end of town, are **Venue Bar & Lounge** (Av La Confluencia) and **Liquor Bar & Grill** (Av La Confluencia); the latter has outdoor seating on the 2nd-floor balcony.

Entre Amigos DANCE CLUB
(☎809-574-7979; Colón 182; ⏰9pm-late Fri-Sun) This thumping bar is the best party in town – expect merengue, salsa and reggaeton, and elbow-to-elbow service at the bar. There's often karaoke early in the evening, ending at 11pm.

Information

Banco Popular (Av La Confluencia) In Plaza La Confluencia.

BanReservas (cnr Calles Sanchez & Marío N Galán)

Centro de Copiado y Papelería (☎809-574-2902; cnr Duarte & Av Independencia; per hr RD$35)

Clínica Dr Terrero (☎809-574-4597; Av Independencia 2A)

Cluster Turistico de Jarabacoa (☎809-574-6699; www.jarabacoar.com; Av Independencia; ⏰8am-noon & 2-5pm) Small shop with a few locally produced ceramic pieces for sale and information on activities and tours (Spanish only); also excellent map of the town and surrounding area for sale (RD$150).

Farmacia Miguelito (☎809-574-2755; Calle Marío N Galán 70)

Politur (☎809-754-3216; cnr Calles José Duran & Marío N Galán) Tourist police, behind the Caribe Tours terminal.

Scotiabank (cnr Av Independencia & Colón)

Getting There & Away

TO SANTO DOMINGO

Caribe Tours (☎809-574-4796; José Duran, near Av Independencia) offers the only 1st-class bus service to Jarabacoa. Four daily departures to Santo Domingo (RD$280, 2½ hours, at 7am, 10am, 1:30pm and 4:30pm) include a stop in La Vega (RD$80, 45 minutes).

TO LA VEGA

A **guagua terminal** (cnr Av Independencia & José Duran) provides frequent service to La Vega (RD$85, 30 minutes, every 10 to 30 minutes from 7am to 6pm). If you prefer to hire a cab, the ride costs between RD$1000 to RD$1500.

TO CONSTANZA

Públicos leave from diagonally opposite the Shell petrol station (cnr Deligne and Calle El Carmen) at around 9am and 1pm daily (RD$60, 40 minutes). The asphalt road has made this scenic drive a breeze as far as your car's shock absorbers are concerned; dozens of switchbacks however will test your driving skills. Once you hit El Río, the remaining 19km passes through a lush valley.

TO LA CIÉNAGA

Públicos (RD$85, 1½ hours) leave roughly every two hours from Calle Odulio Jiménez near Calle 16 de Agosto. The road is 42km long, of which the first 33km are mostly paved. Returning can be a challenge, especially if returning from an afternoon hike. Hail down any truck heading toward Jarabacoa: chances are the driver will let you hop aboard.

Getting Around

To get to outlying hotels and sights you can easily flag down a *motoconcho* during the day. If you prefer a cab, try **Jaroba Taxi** (809-574-4640) next to the Caribe Tours terminal or hail one at the corner of José Duran and Av Independencia.

There are several car-rental agencies in Jarabacoa, but we recommend that you bring a car with you if you need one.

PARQUES NACIONALES BERMÚDEZ & RAMÍREZ

In 1956 the Dominican government established Parque Nacional Armando Bermúdez with the hope of preventing the kind of deforestation occurring in Haiti. The park encompasses 766 sq km of partially tree-flanked mountains and pristine valleys. Two years later, an adjoining area of 764 sq km to the south was designated Parque Nacional José del Carmen Ramírez. Between them, the parks contain three of the highest peaks in the Caribbean, and the headwaters of 12 major rivers, including the Río Yaque del Norte, the country's only white-water, and most important, river.

Activities

Climbing Pico Duarte

Pico Duarte (3087m) was first climbed in 1944, as part of a celebration commemorating the 100th anniversary of Dominican independence. During the late 1980s, the government began cutting trails in the parks and erecting cabins, hoping to increase tourism to the country by increasing the accessibility of its peaks. These days, about 3000 people a year ascend Pico Duarte.

For all the effort involved, odds are you might not even be able to appreciate the views because the peak is so often shrouded in mist and fog. Up to around 2000m, you travel through rainforest, passing foliage thick with ferns and some good bird life. You quickly pass above this limit, however, and spend most of the trip amdist burnt-out *pino caribeño* – a monoculture plantation that looks suspiciously like Monterey pine (the stuff loggers like because of its spindly, knot-free branches). Numerous forest fires have left the landscape barren, and the only animals you're likely to see are marauding bands of cawing crows and possibly a wild boar or two. Although amid the bleakness you may see the occasional colorful epiphyte.

There are **ranger stations** (park admission RD$200; 8am-5pm) near the start of the major trails into the parks. As a safety precaution, everyone entering the park, even for a short hike, must be accompanied by a guide.

WHAT TO BRING

Cold- and wet-weather clothing are musts for anyone intending to spend a night in either park. While the average temperature ranges between 12°C and 20°C most of the year, lows of -5°C are not uncommon, especially in December and January. Rainstorms can happen at any time during the year. While the soil is sandy and drains well, you'll still want sturdy boots and a raincoat. It's best to also pack your gear (including flashlight, sun screen and bug repellent) in dry bags and carry an extra one for the sleeping bag and mattress you're provided on Pico Duarte trips. If on an organized tour, ask in advance if these are supplied. A good stock of energy bars are also recommended so you can refuel on the go.

Tours & Guides

The easiest way to the summit is to take an organized tour. Prices vary widely and depend on how many people are going and for how long. Expect to pay roughly US$100 to US$200 per person per day. Best to book as far in advance as possible.

➡ **Rancho Baiguate** (809-574-6890; www.ranchobaiguate.com; Carretera a Constanza) is the best overall choice for non-Spanish speakers, as it is based in Jarabacoa, and also offers a detour through Valle del

Parques Nacionales Bermúdez & Ramírez

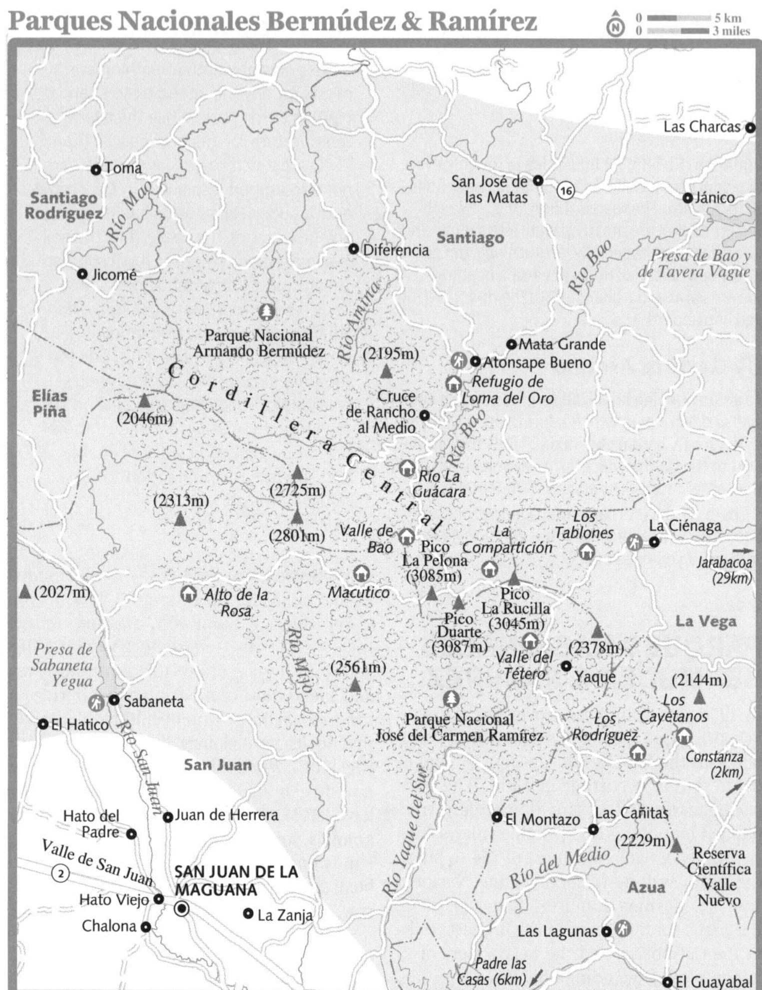

Tétero. It's three days/two nights 'Pico Express' trip is around US$380 per person.

➡ Iguana Mama (p147) in Cabarete is good if you want transportation to and from the north coast. Only four officially listed dates a year but likely can arrange customized group trips.

➡ Camping Tours (p164) in Santiago is the cheapest, as it caters primarily to Dominicans, but the guides speak only Spanish. This is your only option if you want to walk Mata Grande to Pico Duarte and exit at La Ciénega.

Self-Organized Tours

Your other option – assuming you speak good Spanish and you're not in a hurry – is to go to La Cienaga in person and organize mules, food and a guide on your own. Keep in mind however that no matter what time of day you show up you won't be ready to leave until the following morning. Travelers with their own camping gear can spend the night in a tent at the park entrance. Mules and muleteers go for around RD$700 per day each, and the lead guide around RD$1000 per day (minimum one guide for every five hikers). Be aware also that if you walk out a different entrance to where you came in, you'll have to pay several days' extra wages for your guides to get back to the starting point (where they live). Guides can organize basic provisions for you. There is a small spring of drinking water halfway up the trail from La Ciénega, but you're well advised to pack your own water (water-cooler-sized bottles, which the mules carry).

Attempting to climb Pico Duarte without mules is neither possible nor desirable – you can't enter the park without a guide, and a guide won't go without mules. And walking with a full pack in the heat would likely drain whatever enjoyment you might get from the walk. Mules are also essential in case someone gets injured.

Routes to the Top

There are two popular routes up Pico Duarte. The shortest and easiest (and by far the most used) is from **La Ciénaga** via Jarabacoa. It is 23km in each direction and involves approximately 2275m of vertical ascent en route to the peak. It's strongly recommended to do this route in three days – one long, slog of a day to arrive at the La Compartición campground (2450m), one easy day to hike up and enjoy the views (if you're an early riser, the sunrise) and one long day back out again. The trip can be done in two days by getting up at 4am for a dawn summit, but afterward it's a grueling, hot slog down the mountain. Consider also adding a fourth day to do the side trip to the **Valle del Tétero**, a beautiful valley at the base of the mountain.

The second most popular route is from **Mata Grande**. It's 45km to the summit and involves approximately 3800m of vertical ascent, including going over La Pelona, a peak only slightly lower than Pico Duarte itself. You'll spend the first night at the Río La Guácara campground and the second at the Valle de Bao campground. You can walk this route in five days (return), but it's far more interesting to walk out via the Valle del Tétero and La Ciénega (also five days). Camping Tours offers the hike from Mata Grande, which tends to begin from the town of San José de las Matas.

It is also possible to reach the peak from **Sabaneta** (via San Juan de la Maguana), **Las Lagunas** (via Padre las Casas) and Constanza. These routes are little traveled, significantly more difficult, and not offered by any tour companies – you'll need to organize a guide and mules yourself.

Sleeping

There are approximately 14 campgrounds in the parks, each with a first-come-first-served cabin that hikers can use free of charge. Each cabin can hold 20 or more people and consists of wooden floors, walls and ceiling, but no beds, cots, mats or lockers of any kind and latrines are outside. If you have a tent, consider bringing it along.

Most of the cabins also have a stand-alone 'kitchen': an open-sided structure with two or three concrete wood-burning stoves. Fallen dead wood is usually abundant near the campgrounds – be sure you or your guide bring matches and some paper to get the fire started.

CONSTANZA

POP 34,700 / ELEV 1097M

There's a saying here in the mountains: 'God is everywhere, but he lives in Constanza.' Set in a fertile valley and walled in by towering mountains, you can see why – it's a breathtaking spot. Dusk, especially, is awesome – as the sun sets behind the peaks, a thick mist sinks down into the valley floor. This is the capital of industrialized agriculture and hence pesticide use – 80% of fruits and vegetables (mainly potatoes, strawberries, apples, lettuce and garlic) and 75% of flowers are grown on farms around here. There isn't a whole lot to do (hardcore mountain bikers might disagree), though Dominicans from the lowland cities journey here for weekend getaways, drawn by the cooler climate and feeling of remoteness. Drivers beware, because of the scarcity of functioning streetlights, potholes, nonsignposted one-way streets and plethora of vehicles of varying road worthiness sharing narrow streets, it can be unnerving driving around town at night.

Also calling Constanza home are a couple of hundred Japanese farmers who arrived during the 1950s at Trujillo's invitation. In return for providing superior farmland at dirt-cheap prices to 50 Japanese families, Trujillo hoped the Japanese would convert the fertile valley into a thriving agricultural center, which they did.

Sights & Activities

On weekends, Constanza's Parque Central comes alive with locals drinking at the end of the day – a sociable place to hang out for an hour or two. **Softball games** are held almost every night at 7pm at the field a few blocks west of here. The main sights are all quite distant and require a 4WD. Most hotels in the area can organize ad hoc tours in their own vehicles, or call **Safari Constanza** (☎809-539-3839; www.safariconstanza.com).

Aguas Blancas WATERFALL

This breathtaking waterfall, reputedly the largest in the Greater Antilles, is a scenic but rough 16km drive from Constanza (you need a 4WD). The falls – actually one cascade in three different sections – crash some 135m down a sheer cliff into a pool of clear blue and extremely cold water. Because you don't get a full view until close up after a walk through a tight canopy of jungle, the approach feels especially dramatic.

Turn north at the Isla gas station and continue past Colonia Japonésa. If you haven't got your own vehicle, many hotels can take you there for around RD$2500 (up to five people). The way through the mountains passes by a couple of extremely poor communities of Haitian and Dominican farm workers.

Reservo Científica Valle Nuevo NATURE RESERVE

Also known as Parque Nacional Juan Pérez Rancier, this remote park begins around 17km southeast of Constanza. **Las Pirámides**, a monument marking the geographic center of DR, is 46km away. The area records the coldest temperatures in the country, sometimes reaching -8°C during the night and, at 2438m, is the highest plain in the Caribbean. In theory, you can drive all the way to San José de Ocoa, around 90km to the south (though you might need a military vehicle).

Reservo Cientifica Ebano Verde NATURE RESERVE

Look for the entrance to this 23-sq-km reserve on the road from Santiago. If time is limited, there's an easy 2km-long nature trail through tropical forest where you might spot Dominican magnolias, the Green Ebony tree and bird life like red-tailed hawks. A more difficult 6km path leads to a pool you can swim in at the base of a small waterfall.

Piedras Letradas CAVE ART

Meaning 'Inscribed Stone,' Piedras Letradas is a shallow cave containing scores of Taíno petroglyphs and pictograms, mostly depicting animals and simplistic human-like figures. The site is a good 30km northwest of Constanza via the town of La Culeta. The road to La Culeta is paved, but it deteriorates quickly after that – you'll need a 4WD.

Festivals & Events

Every September – the date varies – Constanza goes nuts during **Fiestas Patronales**, a nine-day-long party that is nominally in honor of the Virgen de las Mercedes, the town's patron saint. There are live music events, beer tents in the park, and the whole shebang culminates in the crowning of the new *reina* – a Miss Constanza pageant, of sorts.

Sleeping

Constanza fills up on weekends and holidays and empties during the week. The center of town is noisy, with the constant din of motorcycles and scooters.

Hotel Vistas del Valle HOTEL $

(☎829-689-9808; socratesgp@hotmail.com; Calle Antonio Maria Garcia; s/d with fan RD$450/700; P) Granted, the competition is less than fierce, but this well-maintained family-owned hotel on the western side of town offers comfortable accommodations. The second-floor rooms even have views outside their front doors.

★ **Alto Cerro** HOTEL $$

(☎809-539-6192; www.altocerro.com; Calle Guarocuya 461; s/d/tr incl breakfast RD$1800/2100/2500, villas for 2/5/7 people RD$2800/5200/7800, camping per person RD$350; P ❄ 📶) Easily the best accommodation in Constanza, this large, family-owned complex is 2km east of town off the road toward Hwy Duarte (look for the turn-off just past the airport on your left). More than a dozen buildings line a hillside perched partway up a high bluff. The rooms themselves are unremarkable, but they have balconies with terrific views of the whole valley, and the large suites and two-story villas are equipped with kitchens.

The hotel's **restaurant** (mains RD$340), probably Constanza's best, has breathtaking views from the second-floor balcony and well-dressed waitstaff serving Dominican and European-style dishes. There's a small store with basics for a simple meal as well. Behind the main building is a well-maintained campground, popular with Dominican families and big groups. A full-service spa was still in the works at the time of research.

Eating

Across from Isla petrol station is **Super El Económico** (Luperón; ⏲7:45am-noon & 1:45-8pm Mon-Sat, 9am-noon Sun), a medium-sized grocery, and the **Mercado Municipal** (cnr Gratereaux & 14 de Julio; ⏲7am-6pm Mon-Sat, to noon Sun) has locally grown produce.

Restaurant Aguas Blancas DOMINICAN $$
(Espinosa 54; mains RD$200-450; ⏲9am-10pm; 📶) The cozy (chilly at night so bring a sweater) log-cabin-like dining room qualifies as fine dining in Constanza. Along with usual Dominican fare are a few simple pasta dishes and the specialty, *guinea guisada.*

Lorenzo's Restaurant DOMINICAN $$
(☎809-539-2008; Luperón 83; mains RD$250; ⏲11am-10pm) You'll find solid Dominican fare and heaping portions at this restaurant on the western edge of town. Crowded at lunchtime, especially on Sundays when few other restaurants are open, Lorenzo's doles out sandwiches, pasta, pizza, fish and hearty *sancocho* (RD$150) – a stew of meat, sausage, plantain and potato.

Dilenia DOMINICAN $$
(Calle Fernando Deligne; mains RD$320-420; ⏲11am-8pm Mon-Thu, to 10pm Fri & Sat, to 5pm Sun) Tucked down a residential side street at the entrance to town, Dilenia has a small all-wood dining room and an even smaller Spanish/English menu with dishes like shrimp in garlic sauce, guinea in wine and good 'ol chicken fingers.

Information

Banco Léon (Luperón 19)

BanReservas (Abreu 48)

Constanza Information Center (☎809-539-1022; www.constanza.com.do) In the airport parking lot. English and Spanish spoken.

Copy Centro (Calle Sanchez 9; per hr RD$30; ⏲8am-10pm Mon-Fri, to 5pm Sat)

Farmacia San José (☎809-539-2516; Miguel Abreu 87) At the northeast corner of the park.

Hospital Pedro Antonio Cespede (☎809-539-3288, 809-538-2420; Calle Antonio Isacc; ⏲24hr) Fully equipped emergency room. On your right as you come into town, just past the airport.

Politur (☎809-539-3020) Tourist police – opposite the airport, 2km east of town.

Getting There & Away

GUAGUA

Transporte La Cobra (☎809-539-2119) services Santiago (RD$300, two hours) and Santo Domingo (RD$300, 2½ hours). Other *guaguas* travel to Jarabacoa (RD$150, 40 minutes). *Guaguas* also regularly service El Albanico (RD$160, 40 minutes), where you can change for a *guagua* to Santo Domingo and La Vega.

CAR

The roadway between Jarabacoa and Constanza, once jaw-rattlingly bad, has been completely paved. Compact cars can make the trip in around 45 minutes to an hour depending on how many slow moving trucks are navigating the switchbacks. If coming from Hwy Duarte, the turn-off at El Albanico is 89km north of Santo Domingo, and from there it's 51km on a well-paved, twisty mountain road that passes through lush scenery and a handful of small villages. Keep in mind however that you'll need a SUV to venture anywhere outside of town.

EAST OF SANTIAGO

San Francisco de Macorís

POP 188,000

San Francisco de Macorís is a bustling, relatively prosperous city surrounded by cocoa and rice fields in the heart of the Valle del Cibao. There are a number of colonial buildings, a large, pretty plaza, as well as the stadium for the Gigantes (Giants), one of the DR's six professional baseball teams.

The best reason to venture out this way is a day trip to **Loma Quita Espuela**. Another is to tour a chocolate farm. Currently, the DR is the number-one producer of organic cacao worldwide. **Sendero del Cacao** (☎809-547-2166; www.cacaotour.com; La Paja; tour without transportation US$45) offers two-hour tours (Spanish, English and French) of a working plantation, including explanations and demonstrations of the entire process; the tours end with a large lunch. With your own vehicle, it's only a 10-minute drive from Parque Duarte.

Hotel Las Caobas (Mahogany Hotel; ☎809-290-5858; las_caoba_hotel@gmail.com; cnr Calle Carrón & Av San Diego; s/d RD$2700/3000; P❄📶🏊) only seems true to its name in the lobby and restaurant's furniture and paneling; otherwise, the property looks decidedly non-arboreal. The hotel's rooms are

RESERVA CIENTÍFICA LOMA QUITA ESPUELA

The 'Mountain of the Missing Spur' – a reference to the dense underbrush that ripped boot spurs from cowboys – is a remote and lovely national park, containing the largest rainforest on the island. It is full of endemic species that are on the point of extinction. The NGO **Fundación Loma Quita Espuela** (☎809-588-4156; www.flqe.org.do; Urbanización Almánzar, cnr Calle Luis Carrón & Av del Jaya; ⏰8am-noon & 2-5pm) is actively involved in developing sustainable ways for local farmers to use this natural resource.

The foundation offers a hike to the top of Loma Quita Espuela (942m, RD$500 for up to five people, plus RD$100 per person park entrance fee), where an observation tower commands excellent views over the Valle del Cibao. A guide is mandatory (Spanish only).

There's also a shorter walk that tours several cocoa plantations, where you can buy *bola de cacao* – crude chocolate balls that are used to make hot chocolate. The tour ends at a local *balenario* (swimming hole), where you can take a dip; there are several Taíno caves nearby, too.

Simple accommodations are available at **Rancho Don Lulú** (☎809-863-8929; www.ranchodonlulu.com; r RD$350) just 1km from the Loma Quita Espuela trailhead. There's eight rooms in a rustic cabin a couple of hundred meters from the owners' home, where you eat (meals RD$150).

The entrance to Loma Quita Espuela is 15km (30 minutes) northeast of San Francisco de Macorís on a rough road that gets progressively worse; don't try it without a good 4WD.

up to the standards of local business travelers, the pleasant cafe and restaurant is open all day, and a large pool and lounge area is out the back. It's also conveniently located just a few hundred meters from the offices of Fundación Loma Quita Espuela.

On the southern side of Parque Duarte is **Buffalo Steak House** (☎809-290-3444; Calle San Francisco 63; mains RD$280; ⏰noon-11pm Sun-Thu, to 1am Fri & Sat), a western-themed restaurant with a relatively upscale open-air dining area and excellent burgers, seafood and, of course, steaks.

The turn-off from Hwy Duarte is about 15km (10 minutes) south of La Vega. It's possible but more difficult (and on much worse roads) to come south from the coast via Nagua. **Caribe Tours** (☎809-588-2221; cnr Calle Castillo & Hernández) runs more than a dozen buses daily to Santo Domingo (RD$260, 6am to 6:30pm).

Moca & Around

The country town of Moca has prospered in recent decades as a result of its production of coffee, cocoa and tobacco. The tallest building in town is also its only tourist attraction, the **Iglesia Corazón de Jesus** (admission free; ⏰varies) FREE, with a panel of beautiful stained glass imported from Turin, Italy.

During the 18th century, Moca was one of the Spanish colony's chief cattle centers. In 1805, an invading army took Moca, killed virtually the entire population and burned the town to the ground. Moca struggled back, and in the 1840s began to raise tobacco as a commercial crop; now, some of the world's finest cigars contain tobacco grown on the hillsides around the town.

East of Moca and around 4km east of the town of Salcedo is the **Museo de Hermanas Mirabel** (☎809-587-7075; admission RD$20; ⏰9am-5pm Mon-Fri, to 5:45pm Sat & Sun). The home of the Mirabel sisters, Patria, Minerva and María, assassinated by agents of Trujillo because of their opposition to his regime, has been turned into a time-capsule museum. Everything in the rooms – from bedrooms to kitchen to study – is presented as if they had just left; even the garments they were wearing when they were killed are displayed. Price of admission includes a guided tour (Spanish only).

There's not much point coming out this way if you haven't got your own car.

The Southwest & Península de Pedernales

Includes ➡

Best Places to Eat

- Rancho Tipico (p194)
- Brisas del Caribe (p192)
- Casa Bonita (p195)
- Rincón Mexicano (p188)
- Restaurante Luz (p195)

Best Places to Stay

- Casa Bonita (p195)
- Hotel Casablanca (p195)
- Piratas del Caribe (p195)
- Salinas Hotel (p185)
- Ecoturismo Comunitario Cachóte (p193)

Why Go?

Talk about criminally undervisited. Few travelers make it to the southwest: it's remote, and its little-known highlights take some effort to uncover – but that's exactly the reason to visit. You can explore the cloud forests of the mountains with their soundtrack of twittering birdsong, or the cactus-studded desert that stretches all the way to the Haitian border. Then there's the stunning coastline of the Península de Pedernales, which offers miles of pristine, empty sands and clear turquoise sea. When you reach the Bahía de Las Águilas, a 10km deserted stretch of postcard-perfect beach, you'll feel as though you've hit the traveler's jackpot.

When to Go

- **March and April** Laguna Oviedo's biodiversity is in full evidence now, so this is the best time for nature lovers to see birds and wildlife that migrate here.
- **December to February** With sunny skies and seemingly endless fiestas on every corner, this is the busiest time for the DR as a whole. North American and European holidays are in swing now.
- **June** Caffeine fiends will want to visit the Polo Organic Coffee Festival, held in the first week of the month.

The Southwest & Península de Pedernales Highlights

1. Taking the boat ride to **Bahía de Las Águilas** (p194), the most remote and beautiful beach in the country
2. Spotting flamingos and turtles on a boat tour to super-salty **Laguna Oviedo** (p196)
3. Staying in a remote cabin in the cool, tranquil cloud forest of **Cachóte** (p193) and seeing a different side to the Caribbean
4. Rubbing elbows with iguanas on **Isla Cabritos** (p199)
5. Cooling off in the idyllic freshwater pool at **Los Patos** (p193) near Paraíso
6. Renting some wheels and driving along the eastern shoreline of the **Península de Pedernales** (p190), one of the most beautiful unknown coastal routes in the Americas
7. Sourcing your own semiprecious stone at the **Larimar Mine** (p196)
8. Wandering the spectacle that is the **Haitian Market** (p189) in Comendador del Rey

Getting There & Around

Although there's one nominally international airport just outside of Barahona, no commercial airlines flew there at time of research, so your only way to get here is by bus or car. Caribe Tours has regular service to Barahona and San Juan de la Maguana, but after that only *guaguas* (small buses) transit the rest of the region. Because of union agreements, *guaguas* plying the coastal highway do not stop at every town along the way, even though they pass right through them. Be careful to get on the right bus, or else you'll be let off outside of town and you'll have to walk or catch another ride in.

WEST OF SANTO DOMINGO

Heading west from the city takes you not only in the opposite direction to the eastern beach resorts but also to a different DR – one whose landscape isn't defined by tourism but scenes of ordinary, everyday life. From Santo Domingo, Hwy 2 cuts inland to the provincial capital of San Cristobal and from there it continues south to the city of Baní. Hwy 41, north to San José de Ocoa, takes you into the foothills of the Cordillera Central.

Baní

POP 92,153

Notable mainly as a convenient stopping point for those driving between Santo Domingo and Barahona, Baní also marks the turn-off for the beach and sand dunes of Las Salinas, 25km to the southwest.

Sights

Monumento Natural Dunas de las Calderas NATURE RESERVE

(admission RD$50, guide per groups of 10 RD$300; 8am-5pm Mon-Fri, to 6pm Sat & Sun) This protected reserve, part of the Península de las Salinas, is 20 sq km of gray-brown sand mounds, some as high as 12m. A guided tour offers views of the dunes and beaches beyond and is well worth a look if you want to see a unique landscape in the Caribbean. The brown sandy beach nearby gets crowded on weekends, and is particularly popular with windsurfers. Weekdays, it's all yours.

To get to Las Salinas, take Av Máximo Gómez 400m west of Parque Duarte and turn left at the Isla gas station onto Av Fernando Deligne; this eventually bears right onto a single paved road that passes through several small 'towns,' at least one of which has an ATM. There's a naval station at the end of the road; continue past the guard's pillbox and turn left. Follow this road into town. The entrance to the dunes is 1.5km east of Salinas Hotel & Restaurant, a great place to bed down if you come.

Sleeping & Eating

Hotel Caribani HOTEL $$

(809-522-3871; hotelcaribani@gmail.com; cnr Calles Sánchez 12 & San Tomé; s/d RD$1500/1800;) Conveniently located only one block from the northwestern edge of Parque Duarte. Each basic room has a cable TV, air-con, a faux floral arrangement and a standard safe box in the bathroom.

WORTH A TRIP

SALINAS HOTEL & RESTAURANT

You'll feel like you need a passport to visit this lovely hotel (809-866-8141; www.hotelsalinas.net; Puerto Hermosa 7; d RD$3500, d all-incl RD$6000;), located at the near-literal end of the road on the peninsula, 20km southwest of Baní, amid semi-arid dunes and desert, striking mountains and a postcard-blue bay – it looks more like the American southwest than the DR. All the rooms in this surprising four-story hotel with thatched roof have stunning views of the mountains across the bay, as does the restaurant – easily the best place to eat in town, with lobster (RD$700), fresh fish (RD$395) and chicken (RD$325). It's all decked out very shabby-chic with rustic furnishings and kitschy paraphernalia and antiques. The extra large top-floor suites go for the same price, so it pays to ask for them specifically. Sailboats are docked at the attached marina and the hotel has its own yacht, on which guests get a free ride on Sunday sails. Otherwise, it's most easily reached by car, but there are *guaguas* to Baní (RD$55, 40 minutes) that pass the hotel four times a day (9:40am, noon, 1:15pm and 3pm). In Baní, they depart from the Asomicaba terminal at the southern end of Av Fernando Deligne.

CAR RENTAL

If you're thinking of renting a car, two thoughts: there are no rental car agencies of any kind in the southwest, so rent your vehicle in Santo Domingo; and two, a 4WD is probably unnecessary. Save Cachote, all of the southwest's main attractions are reachable in an economy rental.

Pala Pizza ITALIAN **$$**
(cnr Calles Duarte & Sánchez; mains RD$116-278, pizzas RD$254-631; ⏲10am-midnight; 📶) Yes, it's a chain, but this is Baní and locals swear it's better than anything else nearby. Think of it as a Dominican Pizza Hut: there's perfectly decent pizza, and also tacos, calzones, pasta, burgers and decent brownies with ice cream.

Information

Banco León (cnr Hwy Sánchez & Calle Mella)

BanReservas (cnr Calle Sánchez & Señora de Regla) One block east of the park; another is half a block east of the *guagua* stop for Barahona.

Centro Médico Regional (☎809-346-4400; cnr Presidente Billini & Restauración; ⏲24hr) A recommended hospital four blocks east of Parque Duarte.

Farmacia Santa Ana (cnr Calles Presidente Billini & Mella; ⏲8am-11pm Mon-Sat, to 10pm Sun) On the southeast corner of the park.

Getting There & Away

Asomiba express *guaguas* to Santo Domingo (RD$100, 1¼ hours, every 15 minutes from 4am to 8pm) leaving from a terminal half a block west of the main park.

Passengers wait for *guaguas* to Barahona (RD$200, two hours) at the corner of a small orange food stall called Cafeteria La Paradita about 650m west of the park on Av Máximo Gómez. They pass roughly hourly from 8am to 7:30pm – they're coming from Santo Domingo and don't have a fixed schedule for Baní. They don't linger long, so be alert.

Ázua

Ázua is the first and largest town you'll encounter as you approach the southwest from the east, but unless you are incapacitated, sleeping here would be a quirky choice. For those on a trajectory to or from the Haitian border at Comendador/Elías Piña, Ázua might be a transit hub for buses to the interior west. Otherwise, Baní is a much more pleasant place to spend the night.

Asodema express *guaguas* to Santo Domingo (RD$180, two hours, on the hour from 6am to 5pm) and regular *guaguas* (RD$180, 2½ hours, every 10 minutes from 4:20am to 7pm) leave from a terminal on Calle Duarte, on the corner opposite the park. For San Juan (RD$130, 1¾ hours, every 20 minutes from 5am to 6pm) and the path to the Haitian border, *guaguas* depart from the small Asodumas terminal on Calle Bartolomé Peréz near Parque 19 de Marzo, three blocks from Parque Central. *Guaguas* to Barahona (RD$100) also pass by here every 20 minutes from 6am to 4pm – it's infinitely better to pick up a *guagua* for Barahona at points east of here.

Caribe Tours (☎809-521-5088; www.caribetours.com.do; cnr Calle Nuestra Señora de Fatimas & Francisco Sone) buses running between Santo Domingo and Barahona stop in Ázua, arriving and departing from a small office three blocks northeast of Parque Central. If you're already in Ázua and headed to Santo Domingo, buses depart at 7:15am, 7:30am, 10:45am, 11:15am, 2:45pm and 6:15pm (RD$190, two hours).

INLAND

Three highways lead west to the Haitian border. Fifteen kilometers west of Ázua the highway branches west to San Juan de la Maguana and the border at Elías Piña, and south to Barahona. At Barahona the road splits again – the interior road runs past Lago Enriquillo to the busy Jimaní border post, and the southern road hugs the coast before dead-ending at Pedernales and the residential border crossing to Haiti.

San Juan de la Maguana

POP 78,313

Monument-heavy San Juan de la Maguana is a pleasant place to kill a night in transit. Haitians are increasingly moving in as Dominicans move away, bringing a Vodou influence to the city's Dominican Catholic culture. It's known as La Ciudad de los Brujos, the City of Shamans – most shamans live in the hills outside the city however, and are definitely not tourist attractions.

OFF THE BEATEN TRACK

RAFAEL TRUJILLO'S SAN CRISTOBAL

Most visitors heading west from the capital pass through San Cristobal, the home town of dictator Rafael Trujillo. Trujillo erected all sorts of monuments to himself here and built extravagant buildings, but today it is a traffic-clogged provincial capital just 30km from Santo Domingo that few folk stop in. Little evidence of Trujillo's brutal and authoritarian regime remain, but San Cristobal's strangest sight remains open for visits – the **Castillo del Cerro** (809-983-7692; admission free; 8:30am-4:30pm) FREE. Currently used as the National Penitentiary School, the castle was built on Trujillo's orders for himself and his family in 1947 (at a cost of US$3 million) but he reportedly hated the finished product and never spent a single night there. The name means 'Castle on the Hill,' which is pretty accurate – it overlooks the city – but the concrete-and-glass structure looks more like an office building than a castle. Inside, however, huge dining rooms, ballrooms and bedrooms have fantastic ceilings and wall decorations painted in gaudy colors. The bathrooms – of which there must be 20 – have tile mosaics in reds, blues and gold leaf. There are six floors in all, and you can spend a half-hour or more just wandering through the once-abandoned structure. There is also a small museum detailing some of Trujillo's atrocities, including a few original instruments of torture and murder, a replica electric chair and – huh? – loads of exquisite bed frames.

Any taxi driver or *motoconchista* (motorcycle taxi driver) can take you there – it probably makes sense to ask the driver to come back in 30 to 60 minutes to pick you up. If you've got a vehicle, from Parque Independencia take Calle María Trinidad Sánchez west for 700m. Take a left onto Calle Luperón and follow it up the hill 500m until you reach a fork in the road. There, veer right and head up the hill another 700m to the entrance gates. Visitors must adhere to the dress code of shirts and closed-toe shoes.

Also interesting is the informal **Museo Jamas El Olvido Será tu Recuerdo** (809-474-8767; Calle Gral Leger 134; adult/child RD$200/100) in the home of local resident José Miguel Ventura Medina, known to some as 'El Hippi.' The museum's name translates literally to 'Forgetfulness will never be your remembrance,' or simply 'You will never be forgotten.' The 'you' in this case is none other than Generalísimo Trujillo, who, along with John F Kennedy, was Ventura's favorite world leader. Most will not agree with Ventura's assessment of Trujillo as a 'good dictator,' but the extensive collection of photos and other memorabilia – plus a slew of random antiques – is worth poking around. If Ventura is not home, give him a call (809-474-8767). When we came through, he was converting two *very* rustic rooms into a B&B (r RD$300), so you can now sleep amid the history if you so fancy. It's located on Calle General Leger, 6½ blocks north and one block east of Parque Colón – look for a small white car perched on the rooftop.

Buses for San Cristobal leave Santo Domingo from Parque Enriquillo (RD$50, one hour). In San Cristobal, *guaguas* for the capital (RD$75, 45 minutes, every 20 minutes from 6:45am to 7pm) leave from a stop at the southeast edge of the park. *Guaguas* to Baní (RD$85, 45 minutes, every 25 minutes from 7am to 7:30pm) leave from beside Isla gas station on Carretera Sánchez (Calle Padre Borbón), 600m west of Parque Colón. For towns further west, you have to go out to the Isla gas station, 4.3km north of Parque Colón on the main highway, and flag down a passing bus: to Ázua (RD$150, 1½ hours) and Barahona (RD$225, 3½ hours), for example.

Sights

El Corral de los Indios HISTORICAL SITE

Despite being referred to as 'the Stonehenge of the Dominican Republic,' this pre-Colombian site – one of the few in the Antilles – doesn't quite live up to the hype. The site is composed of a large circular clearing, with a 1.5m-long gray stone with a face carved on one end. Research here is thin, but it's said to have originally contained two rows of block stones forming two concentric circles around the center. One theory is that it was formerly a ceremonial place for the Caonabo and Anacaona Indians as well as an astronomical instrument. Today, the only thing surrounding the center is a football and baseball field. It's located 5km north of Calle Independencia.

DON'T MISS

RESERVA ANTROPOLÓGICA CUEVAS DEL POMIER

There are 55 limestone **caves** (☎829-680-4423; admission RD$100, guide RD$500; ⏲8am-4pm) in the area just 10km north of central San Cristobal, five of which are open to the public, with Cave 1 carrying the mother lode, some 590 prehistoric paintings. The caves contain thousands of drawings and carvings that constitute the most extensive example of prehistoric art yet discovered in the Caribbean, including works by Igneri and Caribs as well as the Taínos. The faded drawings, painted with a mix of charcoal and the fat from manatees, depict birds, fish and other animals, as well as figures that may be deities. Relatively little is known about Hispaniola's earliest inhabitants, though the paintings here, believed to be as much as 2000 years old, provide some tantalizing clues. Sir Robert Schomburgk, who left his name and that of his companions on the wall, first discovered the principal cave in 1851.

It's a challenge to get to the caves on your own, even with the slew of signs. The easiest way there is to take a taxi or *motoconcho*, which should cost between RD$300 to RD$500 roundtrip including wait time. If you're driving, follow Calle General Cabral north from Parque Colón to Calle Máximo Gomez, head one block east to Av Constitución and follow it north to La Toma, a small community across the highway from San Cristobal, where there is an easy-to-spot sign just over the bridge. From there, it's 400m until a right turn on Carratera de Medina (there's no official sign but a faded, hard-to-see 'Francis Gas' signs mentions the caves). Follow this road 2.6km to a prominent T-intersection, where you turn left (it's unsigned but look for the 'Club Gallistico El Pomier' cockfighting ring) and proceed up the hill another 2.6km. Just past the DoCALsa factory entrance, turn right at the sign (it will seem as though you are turning into a mining quarry, which you are). Stay straight another 600m, veering left at the fork, until you come upon a small field with a small green house on your left – this is the entrance. Ask as you go, as the turn-offs are easy to miss. Be alert for giant dump trucks coming down the road from the mine – there are a number of blind curves.

The RD$500 guide is obligatory – and they don't speak English. But you can ask for a handy English translation pamphlet for your tour, which can last anywhere from 30 minutes to a full day, depending on your interest.

Sleeping & Eating

Hotels in San Juan are generally full of Dominican business travelers, and for this reason are often good value.

Hotel Nuevo Tamarindo HOTEL **$**
(☎809-557-7002; hoteltamarindosjm@hotmail.com; Calle Dr Cabral 26; s/d/tr with air-con RD$900/1400/1700, without air-con RD$600/1000; ❄📶) Clean and simple rooms, international cable TV, a fast wi-fi signal and a small but charming courtyard hang area all feature in this perfect location right across the street from Caribe Tours.

Hotel Maguana HOTEL **$$**
(☎809-557-2244; hotelmaguana@hotmail.com; Av Independencia 72; s/d/tr/ste incl breakfast on weekends RD$1450/1600/2450/2800; ❄📶) Built at dictator Trujillo's request in 1947, the Maguana's imposing facade and interior courtyard suggest a grandeur that has now faded, but that doesn't mean it's not interesting. All the rooms have hot water and TV, although some lack windows and singles are cramped.

There's a great (but noisy) alfresco bar in the parking lot and a quieter interior bar. If you can afford it, ask for the Trujillo suite, where his highness used to lay his head. Breakfast is weekends only.

★ **Rincón Mexicano** MEXICAN **$**
(cnr Calle 27 de Febrero & Capotillo; mains RD$75-575; ⏲6pm-midnight) Owned by a real live *Mexicana* (who does the cooking) and her Dominican husband, this airy, immeasurably pleasant restaurant pumps out authentic Mexican tacos (RD$85) as well as enchiladas, fajitas and the like. Chase it all back with the excellent margaritas and toast to your good fortune that a place this good exists in San Juan.

La Galeria del Espía DOMINCAN **$**
(Calle Independencia 5; mains RD$170-520; ⏲11am-4pm & 6:30pm-1am; 📶) Don't let the tinted facade just opposite Parque Central deter you, this is a friendly, mega-popular

spot for simple and quick Dominican food. The plate of the day goes for RD$195 and there's the usual otherwise: Beef or chicken served with rice, beans and salad.

Hotel y Supermercado El Detallista GROCERIES $
(☎809-557-1200; cnr Calle Trinitaria & Puello) For groceries, Hotel y Supermercado El Detallista is one-stop shopping: the best grocery store, an ATM, and a Western Union branch.

Information

Banco León (☎809-557-6094; cnr Calle Independencia & Mariano Rodríguez)

BanReservas (☎809-557-2230; cnr Calle Independencia & 27 de Febrero)

Centro Médico San Juan (☎809-557-5345; Calle Trinitaria 55) Your best bet for private medical attention.

Farmacia Iguamed (cnr Calle Trinitaria & Dr Cabral; ⏰8am-10pm Mon-Sat, 9am-1pm Sun) Centro Médico San Juan's affiliated pharmacy.

InposDom (www.inposdom.gob.do; Calle Mella btwn Calles 16 de Agosto & Capotillo; ⏰8am-4pm Mon-Fri, to noon Sat)

Policia Nacional (National Police; ☎809-557-2380; cnr Calle Independencia & Dr Cabral; ⏰24hr) Located one block west of the large white arch at the east entrance of town.

Getting There & Around

When the highway hits the town, it splits into two one-way streets – the westbound street is Calle Independencia, and the eastbound is Calle 16 de Agosto. A large white arch modeled on the Arc de Triomphe in Paris stands dramatically at the eastern entrance of the city. At the western end of town is San Juan's large plaza, with a pretty cream-colored church on one side and a school of fine arts on the other.

Caribe Tours (☎809-557-4520; www.caribetours.com.do) has a terminal 75m west of Hotel Maguana next to Pollo Rey. Buses to Santo Domingo (RD$270, three hours) depart at 6:30am, 10:15am, 1:45pm and 5:30pm.

Guaguas for Santo Domingo (RD$250, 3½ hours, every 25 minutes from 3am to 6:30pm) leave from the Tenguerengue terminal three blocks east of the arch, just west of the Shell gas station. There are three express buses (RD$250, 6:30am, 9:30am and 3pm), which make the trip a half-hour faster because they don't make a food stop along the way.

If you are going to Barahona, you can take any of the four Caribe Tours buses to Ázua (RD$130, one hour) or catch a Asodumas *guagua* from their small terminal on Calle Eusebio Puello half a block south of the Tenguerengue terminal (RD$130, 1½ hours, every 20 minutes from 5am to 6:30pm); and catch a Barahona-bound bus there. Alternatively, take a Santo Domingo *guagua* and get off at Cruce del Quince (RD$130, one hour), the main highway intersection 15km west of Ázua, and catch a southbound *guagua* from there.

For Comendador/Elías Piña, *guaguas* (RD$120, 1½ hours) depart every 25 minutes from 7am to 7pm from the *guagua* stop at the far western end of town, past the Mesopotamia bridge. You can walk with a pack, but probably not with luggage. Head out of town west on Calle Caonabo, four blocks north of Calle Independencia. Additionally, make absolutely sure your bus is going all the way to Elías Piña: if there aren't enough passengers, they may dump you halfway (at Las Matas) and you'll have to wait for another bus to come through (or pay a premium for a taxi). A taxi direct to the border for up to four passengers costs RD$1500.

Taxis and *motoconchos* may be found near Parque Central; or phone **Taxis del Valle** (☎809-557-6200).

Comendador del Rey (Elías Piña)

POP 19,344

Comendador del Rey, or Comendador for short, is the official name of the border town west of San Juan. However, almost everyone who doesn't live there calls it Elías Piña, which is the name of the state, and you'll have more luck using that name anywhere but in town. Comendador is best known for the Haitian market held there every Monday and Friday, when hundreds of Haitians arrive on donkeys and on foot to sell their wares.

Comendador also has a major military base and a police headquarters, and security (aimed at preventing illegal Haitian immigration) is tight. Even foreign travelers may find themselves detained and questioned if not carrying their passport.

Sights

Haitian Market MARKET
(⏰6am-4pm) The Haitian market is impossible to miss; just stay on the main road through town until you run into it. Vendors lay their goods out on the ground, shaded by large plastic tarps suspended from every available tree, road sign and telephone pole. Cooking utensils, clothing, shoes, fruits and vegetables are the primary items, sold for discounts as much as 50%.

BUYING LARIMAR

There are a few small artisan shops selling handmade larimar jewelry along the coastal road. This rare stone, unique to the Dominican Republic is a great memento to remind you of the remarkable color of the sea along this coast. Stones range in price from RD$300 to RD$6000 depending on the size of the raw piece. The best spot is **Gift Shop Noelia** (829-816-2433; 9am-7pm) along the beachside road that goes through Bahoruco and La Ciénega next door to Restaurant Luz and run by the same family. Once you enter Bahoruco on the main highway, you'll pass the baseball 'diamond,' cross a bridge and there will be an unsigned road that goes to your left along the beach. Follow that road to the beach for a half-mile and you'll see Restaurant Luz on your left, Noelia on your right.

There's not much in the way of handicrafts, since few tourists attend the market, but just wandering around and taking in the scene is worthwhile. Of most interest to tourists might just be a bottle of Barbancourt Haitian rum (and who knows, maybe you'll see a colander you like).

Sleeping

If you get stuck here there's one serviceable hotel-cum-hardware store.

Casa Teo Hotel y Ferretería HOTEL **$**
(809-881-6701; cnr Calles Santa Teresa & Las Mercedes; s/d/tr with fan RD$300/500/1000;) Every border town should have one of these places – for all your holiday hardware needs! It faces the park and is predictably prison cell-like, with barren walls and rather gruff service.

Information

For emergencies, contact the **Policía Nacional** (809-527-0290; cnr Calles 27 de Febrero & Las Mercedes; 24hr). BanReservas has a 24-hour ATM at its branch office located at a traffic circle near the market on the west end of town. There is a public hospital at the eastern entrance of the town, near the military base, but really, you are better off moving on to San Juan unless you're at death's door.

Getting There & Away

The highway splits into two one-way streets when it enters town. The westbound street is Calle Santa Teresa and the eastbound is Calle 27 de Febrero. Almost everything you need is on or near those two streets. The park is at the eastern end of town, between Calles Las Carreras and Las Mercedes. There's a large traffic circle at the western end of town, at which point the roads merge again and lead to the Haiti–DR border, about 2km away.

The main *guagua* terminal is on Av 27 de Febrero, at the eastern end of the main park. Buses leave from here for Santo Domingo (RD$400, four hours) every 30 minutes from 7am to 7:45pm). If you're just going to San Juan (RD$125 one hour), take one of the *guaguas* parked just outside the terminal, as the Santo Domingo bus doesn't officially stop in San Juan. For Barahona, take a Santo Domingo bus to Cruce del Quince (the main highway intersection 15km west of Ázua; RD$200, 1½ hours) and then catch a southbound bus from there. Or use Caribe Tours.

If you are exiting/entering here, look for uniformed **CESFRONT** (www.cesfront.mil.do) border patrol officers, who can point you towards Dominican customs.

PENÍNSULA DE PEDERNALES

The Península de Pedernales contains some of the most outstanding attractions of the Dominican Republic: Bahía de Las Águilas, Laguna Oviedo and Parque Nacional Jaragua; Cachóte; and world-class birdwatching in the Parque Nacional Sierra de Bahoruco. Despite all this, tourism in this part of the country is surprisingly low.

The peninsula was originally a separate island, but tectonic movement pushed it north and upward into Hispaniola, closing the sea channel that once ran from Port-au-Prince to Barahona, and creating many of the unique geographical features you'll see today.

The southwest is the best place on the island to go birdwatching, as you can see nearly all the endemic species here. At last count, there are roughly 310 known birds in the DR and 32 endemic birds on the island.

Half of these birds are migratory, making winter the best time to spot them.

Tours

★Ecotour Barahona ECOTOURS
(☎809-856-2260; www.ecotourbarahona.com; apt 306, Carretera Enriquillo 8, Paraíso) This professional French-owned tour company has been pioneering tourism in the southwest since 2004. It offers good day trips to Bahía de Las Águilas, Isla Cabritos, Laguna Oviedo and Cachóte, among others. It also offers a handful of day hikes in the hills around Paraíso, and can organize one-day and multiday horseback-riding tours. Most day trips cost US$119 for two people and go down in price as groups get larger and include an excellent three-course picnic lunch.

Tody Tours BIRDWATCHING
(☎809-686-0882; www.todytours.com; Santo Domingo) The only birdwatching-specific tour company based in the DR. The expatriate American owner has more than 15 years' experience as a guide and charges US$200 per day plus expenses; all transportation, food and accommodations are organized for you. Minimum bookings of one week are preferred.

Barahona

POP 62,054

Barahona is an unavoidable eyesore on an otherwise dramatically beautiful coast, full of industrial smokestacks and of little interest to travelers. A growing number of quality, good-value accommodations sit along the coastal road between here and Paraíso, making it somewhat unavoidable when exploring the region. It's home to the only ATM until Pedernales, so you'll need to come here to get cash; and it's also a necessary transfer point if you're traveling by bus.

History

By Dominican standards, Barahona is a young city, founded in 1802 by Haitian general L'Ouverture as a port to compete with Santo Domingo. For over a century, residents mostly made their living taking what they could from the Caribbean Sea, but today fishing accounts for only a small part of Barahona's economy. The dictator Rafael Trujillo changed everything when he ordered many square kilometers of desert north of town converted into sugarcane fields for his family's financial benefit. More than three decades after his assassination, the thousands of hectares of sugarcane continue to be tended, only now they are locally owned and benefit the community.

Sleeping

Unless you're after dirt-cheap budget accommodations, there's no reason to stay in the city itself. A far more enticing plan is to stay in the numerous hotels that string themselves along the coast south of Barahona on the road to Paraíso and use Barahona for services only.

★Hotel Loro Tuerto GUESTHOUSE $
(☎809-524-6600; www.lorotuerto.com; Av Del Monte 33; s/d/tr RD$1300/1500/1700; ❄ wifi) This charming nine-room guesthouse on noisy Av Del Monte has far more character than any of its competitors. Frida Kahlo reproductions dot the walls and simple rooms empty out into a peaceful courtyard with hammocks. There's a cafe in the front (mains RD$200 to RD$300) that does breakfast, too.

Hotel Las Magnolias HOTEL $
(magnolia.cdm@hotmail.com; Calle Aracoana 13; s/d/tr 1100/1200/1900; ❄ wifi) This small 15-room hotel wins a star for its hands-on, friendly owner, who makes sure the place runs smoothly. Rooms are simple, and bathrooms need a bit of renovating, but it's a comfortable spot with slightly more personality than average. Free coffee, too.

Hotel Cacique HOTEL $
(☎809-524-4620; Calle Peña Gómez 2; s with fan RD$400, s/d/tr with air-con RD$850/1350/1250; ❄ @ wifi) A good-value option, especially if you opt for a room without AC. Our AC room was better than the aged common interiors suggested, with a renovated bathroom, cable TV, hot water and nicely tiled floor.

There's a simple restaurant, (wickedly sweet) free coffee, wi-fi in the lobby and a small but pretty internal patio. Although

> **LAST CALL FOR CASH**
>
> Stock up on cash in Barahona – there are no more ATMs for more than 100km. But if you have to return from the south for cash, you don't have to come all the way into town. There is a BanReservas at the Isla gas station at the southern entrance to town.

there is a little too much local foot traffic from family and friends for our tastes, the night stayed surprisingly quiet. There's no parking but a night security guard keeps an eye on the cars parked in front of the hotel.

Eating & Drinking

Barahona has a few decent restaurants, but you won't stretch your tastebud limits here. Most of the drinking takes place in bars and restaurants along the waterfront on Av Enriquillo, centered around dueling open-air watering holes **Junior's** (cnr Nuestra Senora del Rosario & Av Enriquillo; mains RD$200-800; ⏲10am-midnight Sun-Thu, to 2am Fri & Sat) and **La Pompa** (cnr Nuestra Senora del Rosario & Av Enriquillo; ⏲10am-midnight).

Restaurant Pizzería D'Lina DOMINICAN **$**
(Av 30 de Mayo 11; mains RD$125-400; ⏲7am-midnight) This is your requisite Dominican cheapie which caters to a loyal clientele who come for simple home-cooked food. It's certainly not friendly, but cheap sandwiches (RD$70 to RD$175), decent pizza and various meat, chicken and seafood dishes – try the *lambi* (conch) *a la vinaigrette* – are served on a pleasant and breezy palapa-topped patio.

Brisas del Caribe SEAFOOD **$$**
(Carretera Batey Central; mains RD$275-750; ⏲8am-11pm) The kitchen here dishes out fresh seafood as the seasons dictate (though the seasons sometimes affect consistency as well). The perfectly sized seafood soup appetizer (RD$150) has more seafood than broth; and the fish medallions *al ajillo* (RD$350) are tasty as well, though not medallions.

Supermercado H y M SUPERMARKET **$**
(cnr Peña Gómez & Padre Billini; ⏲8am-8:30pm Mon-Sat, to 1pm Sun) Stock up on rations for travels further south at Supermercado H y M.

Information

Banco Popular (☎809-524-2102; cnr Calles Jaime Mota & Padre Billini) 24-hour ATM at Parque Central.

> **PLANNING**
>
> Fifteen kilometers south of Paraíso (and 54km south of Barahona) is the typical Dominican town of Enriquillo, notable for having the last few hotels and gas station until Pedernales, some 82km away.

BanReservas (☎809-524-4006; cnr Calles Peña Gómez & Padre Billini) Two blocks around the corner from Banco Popular. Has a 24-hour ATM.

Centro de Información Turística (☎809-471-1618; www.gobarahona.com; ⏲9am-2pm Mon-Fri, 9pm-noon Sat) This small information kiosk is sponsored by the member-driven Cluster Ecoturístico de la Provincia de Barahona, but it's friendly and happy to help with whatever. It's located at the far northern outskirts of town, making in mostly inaccessible for those without a car. You can pick up a decent Pedernales map, too.

Centro Médico Regional Magnolia (☎809-524-2460; cnr Calle Peña Gómez & Fransisco Vásquez; ⏲24hr) The best private clinic.

Farmacia Dotel (cnr Av Del Monte & Duverge; ⏲8am-9pm Mon-Sat, to 3pm Sun) Well-stocked pharmacy.

InposDom (www.inposdom.gob.do; Parque Central; ⏲8am-4pm Mon-Fri)

Politur (Carretera Batey Central) Along the waterfront, 550m north of Av Del Monte.

Getting There & Away

The highway enters town from the west; after a large traffic circle with a prominent square arch, it becomes Av Luís E Del Monte and Barahona's main drag.

AIR

Aeropuerto Internacional María Móntez is located 10km north of town. There were no commercial flights at time of research.

BUS

There is frequent *guagua* service to all points of the compass during daylight hours. You can also pick up south-bound *guaguas* at a stop on the highway at the southern end of town. *Guaguas* generally leave every 15 to 30 minutes during daylight hours.

There is a frequent express service to Santo Domingo (RD$250, 2½ hours, hourly from 6am to 7pm) leaving from the Sinchomiba terminal on Av Casandra Damirón near the northwestern entrance to town. Regular service (RD$225, three hours, every 15 minutes from 6am to 7pm) also departs from here.

For Paraíso (RD$120, 30 minutes, every 20 minutes between 7am and 6:30pm) *guaguas* depart from the corner of Calle 30 de Mayo and Av Del Monte. For Pedernales (RD$250, three hours, 8am to 2pm), *guaguas* depart on Calle Peña Gómez next to Supermercado H y M.

Guaguas heading west to the Haitian border at Jimaní call at Calle María Móntez just north of Calle Colón (RD$200, two hours, every 40 minutes from 7am to 6pm). It's also possible but difficult to visit Isla Cabritos via *guagua* – take any bus to Neiba (RD$120, 1¼ hours, every 20 minutes from 6am to 6pm) from the corner of Calle

TOUCH THE SKY – CACHÓTE'S CLOUD FOREST

About 25km (1½ hours' drive) west of Paraíso on an impressively bad road – you ford the same river half a dozen times – sit the remote cabins of Cachóte. At 1400m you're in the heart of Caribbean cloud forest, where a low mist hangs heavy over the trees. It's here that seven rivers spring from the ground to supply the coastal towns below.

In order to protect the water supply, coffee-growing was ended in the 1990s, and today, with the help of Peace Corps volunteers, cabins have been constructed and short trails built in the regenerating forest.

The cabins themselves are rustic but comfortable, and each has one large queen-size bed and a triple-decker dormitory-style bunk. Prices start from RD$1400 per person per night with lunch for one to two people and get cheaper the larger the group. More expensive all-inclusive packages are also available. You can camp for RD$300 per person per night for up to five people if you have your own tent (but you must pay for cooking services – RD$1000 – even if you brought your own food). Transportation is not included in the price. Hiring a 4WD and driver can run upwards of RD$6000 for up to 10 people, but it's more economical (and less comfortable!) to catch the local transport for folks living in the mountains (RD$400 per person) in La Cienega or Barahona.

Contact **Ecoturismo Comunitario Cachóte** (☎829-863-8833; soepa.paraiso@yahoo.com) at least two weeks in advance to book or Ecotour Barahona (p191), which runs a day-trip to Cachóte (US$119), stopping at the small communities along the way; and can arrange overnight stays.

Hikes in the area offer great birdwatching (45 types of endemic birds have been identified here, including the Dominican parrot, Cotorra Hispaniola) and visits to a traditional Dominican mountain village. Guides can point out plants in the area used in medicine and even local Haitian Voodoo.

Padre Billini and Av Del Monte and transfer for a La Descubierta-bound bus (RD$100, one hour, every 20 minutes between 6:10am to 6pm).

For San Juan de la Maguana, take any non-*expreso* Santo Domingo–bound *guagua* and get off at the Cruce del Quince (15km west of Ázua; RD$100), and wait at the junction for a westbound bus to San Juan (RD$130, one hour).

Caribe Tours (☎809-524-4852; cnr Peña Gómez & Calle Apolinar Perdomo) has 1st-class service to Ázua (RD$155, one hour) and Santo Domingo (RD$260, 3½ hours) departing at 6:15am, 9:45am, 1:30pm and 5:15pm.

Getting Around

Barahona is somewhat spread out, though the area around the center is navigable by foot. For points further afield, taxis and *motoconchos* can be found beside the Parque Central and along Av Del Monte, or call the local **taxi association** (☎809-524-4003). It's unwise to take *motoconchos* along the coastal road after dark.

South of Barahona

Sights & Activities

Paraíso BEACH

About 35km south of Barahona is the aptly named town of Paraíso (population 13,500), with a spectacular beach and mesmerizing ocean – who knew there could be so many shades of blue? Paraíso is a good budget alternative to Barahona, and is walking distance (or *motoconcho* distance) to the *balneario* (swimming hole) at Los Patos. If you're driving, be sure to check out the *mirador* (lookout) just north of town – the views of the beach and ocean are jaw-dropping.

★**Los Patos** BEACH, SWIMMING

If humans coveted polished-stone beaches rather than those of floury sands, the small hamlet of Los Patos would be Eden. **Playa Los Patos**, a pretty white-stone beach, and its adjacent *balneario*, are idyllic traveler finds. The water here flows clear and cool out of the mountainside, forming a shallow lagoon before running into the ocean. Small shacks serve good, reasonably priced food and cold cerveza, making this an easy place to kill a day. On weekends it's crowded with Dominican families, but is much less busy midweek.

Seaside Villages

The adjoining seaside villages of **Bahoruco** and **La Ciénaga** are 17km south of Barahona, and are typical of the small communities

DON'T MISS

BAHÍA DE LAS ÁGUILAS

Bahía de Las Águilas is the kind of beach that fantasies are made of. This pristine utopia is located in the extremely remote southwestern corner of the DR, but those who do make it are rewarded with 10km of nearly deserted beach, forming a gentle arc between two prominent capes.

To get there, take the paved (and signed) road to Cabo Rojo, about 12km east of Pedernales. You'll reach the port of Cabo Rojo after 6km. Continue following the signs to Bahía de Las Águilas (the road turns nasty after Cabo Rojo but it's manageable – slowly – in a normal car) to a tiny fishing community called Las Cuevas 6km after that. Note the namesake cave in the middle of the settlement – fishing folk used to live inside it. There are two ways to get to Las Águilas from here. One is to have a really good 4WD (and a driver with significant off-road experience) and attempt to drive there on a steep, pockmarked track through the coastal cactus forest. The far more spectacular alternative is to go by boat. Sailing past these gorgeous cliffs, with cacti clinging to the craggy edges and sea-diving pelicans nearby, might just be the perfect introduction to this beautiful beach.

The gorgeously located restaurant **Rancho Tipico** (809-753-8058; cuevasdelasaguilas@hotmail.com; Las Cuevas; mains RD$250-850; 10am-6pm) in Las Cuevas offers tours. Prices are as follows: for groups of one to five, RD$200 per boat; six to eight, RD$350 per person; nine to 10, RD$325 per person; 11 to 15, RD$275 per person; 16 to 20, RD$275 per person and so on. The owner also rents snorkeling kits for RD$300. It also serves excellent food, specializing in seafood and fantastic *mofongos* (try the *pulpo*) and sits on the edge of aquatic perfection, vying with El Cabito in Las Galeras for the most stunning setting in all of the DR.

You can also negotiate with guides/boatsmen that gather around the national park ranger station just off the parking lot in Las Cuevas and milling about the small pier a few meters past Rancho Tipico. Snorkeling gear is included in their prices, but they don't always have it, so bring your own if you can. If you arrive here solo, the best option is to form a group with others to share the boat ride – easier at weekends when it's busy.

With all choices, you'll also need to pay the national park entrance fee (RD$100).

Ecotour Barahona (p191) runs a day trip here (US$119). It organizes all the logistics, picks you up and drops you off at your hotel, supplies lunch, and can show you where the best corals are to go snorkeling.

There's a very small shelter with bathrooms on the beach, and a small lookout tower, but otherwise no facilities. Camping is permitted.

along the east coast of the Península de Pedernales, with friendly local residents and a gravelly beach used more for mooring boats than bathing.

Especially in La Ciénaga, after dark almost any night of the week you're likely to find small, no-name colmados (small bars) and discos pumping merengue music out to the stars, and people drinking and dancing outdoors. If you decide to join them you'll likely be the only gringo in the place.

Sleeping & Eating

Given the overall sense of isolation in this part of the country, it makes sense that most of the hotels along the Barahona–Paraíso coastal highway also have their own restaurants, which are generally excellent and open to nonguests.

Hotelito Oasi Italiana HOTEL $
(829-926-9796; www.lospatos.it; Carretera Km 37, Los Patos, Calle José Carrasco; d RD$1200) Set on a rise a few hundred meters from the beach, this Italian-owned hotel offers spacious but sometimes stuffy rooms, though the real star of the show here is the food at the guest-only restaurant. No gastro-gimmicks here, just simple pizza and pasta well-prepared by the chef-owner from Verona.

Hotel Comedor Kalibe HOTEL, RESTAURANT $
(809-243-1192; Calle Arzobispo Meriño 16, Paraíso; s/d with fan RD$1300/1500, with air-con RD$1600/1800) This small budget hotel in the center of Paraíso is two blocks from the beach. Well-kept rooms include cable TV. The simple but decent restaurant (mains RD$310 to RD$450) serves plenty of seafood dishes.

There's a pleasant courtyard and TV room poolside and hospitality here is without a doubt more appreciative and welcoming; and the rooms are top notch.

Hotel Casablanca B&B $$
(☎809-471-1230; www.hotelcasablanca.com.do; Carretera Barahona-Paraíso Km 10; s/d/tr incl breakfast US$45/60/85; 📶) This Swiss-owned B&B offers this coast's most personalized experience in this price range. Six simple but comfortable rooms are situated in a well-tended garden and have a fan and either a king-size bed or a queen and twin. Fifty meters away a beautiful curving cliff provides a dramatic view of the Caribbean.

Stairs lead to a narrow beach that's mostly rocky but has some nice sandy spots. The included breakfast is one of the best you'll have in the entire country. Ditto for dinner – even if you aren't staying here, consider phoning ahead in the morning to reserve a spot – the owner is one of the peninsula's best cooks! Anything she does with *lambi* (conch) or octopus will knock you out.

Playazul RESORT $$
(☎809-454-5375; www.playazulbarahona.com; Carretera Barahona-Paraíso Km 7; s/d/tr incl breakfast RD$1800/2500/3500; ❄📶🏊) This French-run, 20-room miniresort offers good value in its tastefully decorated rooms, most of which face the pool and sea and offer a bit of privacy on their palapa-roofed patios. It's built on a bluff with great ocean views, and you'll be dodging free-roaming peacocks along the concrete slabs leading down to a pretty (though rocky) private beach. Breakfast is served in the French-influenced restaurant (mains RD$200 to RD$520), which is also popular with nonguests.

★**Casa Bonita** HOTEL $$$
(☎809-476-5059; www.casabonitadr.com; Carretera Barahona-Paraíso Km 17; r incl breakfast Dominicans/foreigners from US$217/280; ❄@📶🏊) 🌿 Formerly the vacation retreat of a wealthy Dominican family – and now run by siblings as a discerning boutique hotel – Casa Bonita is set on a hill with stunning Caribbean and mountain views in all directions. It is easily the most remarkable hotel in the southwest.

Rooms aren't lavish but are modestly stylish, all with views, and are just a short walk to the stunning infinity pool, Jacuzzi and hammock-strung gardens. The restaurant is steeped in sustainability, with everything plated coming from its own organic vegetable garden or sourced locally. Specialties include a remarkable baked artisanal cheese (RD$450) from Polo. You won't soon forget the Tanama spa, built into the forest, where you can be massaged on a bed *in the river*. A 10-platform canopy tour and mountain biking trails have also been added, giving the hotel an adventure edge. It's refined, personal and close to perfect.

Piratas del Caribe HOTEL $$$
(☎809-243-1140; www.hotelpiratasdelcaribe.com; Calle Arzobispo Nouel 1; s/d incl breakfast US$139/179; ❄📶🏊) Entering through the gates of this new little boutique oasis in the heart of Paraíso feels like an epiphany. You'll be greeted with just five rooms, all with large private patios, four of which offer second-floor sea views and are idyllic for taking breakfast on. It's Spanish-French owned and Spanish-German managed, so there's a European air about the place.

Restaurante Luz SEAFOOD, DOMINICAN $
(mains RD$200-450; ⌚8:30am-10:30pm) On the coastal road in the adjoining villages of Bahoruco and La Ciénaga, this good option has a tidy second-floor dining room overlooking the shore, and a nice ocean breeze. It's old-school Dominican, serving mainly grilled fish and *lambi*.

ℹ Information

Paraíso is one of the few reliable places for internet between Barahona and Pedernales, though wi-fi is still slow. Try **Papelaria Cheche** (Calle José Castillo; per hr RD$40; ⌚8am-noon & 2-10pm) on Calle José Castillo, a small

DON'T MISS

POLO MAGNÉTICO

Twelve kilometers west of Barahona is the town of Cabral and the turn-off south for nearby Polo. About 11km south of the turn-off you'll encounter a famous mirage. Put your car in neutral, let go of the brake and watch your car get 'pulled' uphill. The effect is best between the towns of El Lechoso and La Cueva, and works on a smaller scale, too – get out of the car and put a water bottle on the road. It, too, will show a mysterious desire to climb uphill. The effect is known as 'gravity hill,' an optical illusion caused by slope's shape and its relation to the surrounding landscape.

transport container with a few computers. For medical emergencies, there's the **Clínica Amor el Prójimo** (☎809-243-1208; Calle Arzobispo Noel), also in Paraíso; or head to Enriquillo.

Getting There & Away

The Barahona *guagua* stop in Paraíso is on the highway at Calle Enriquillo, 1km uphill from the beach. From here you can get buses north to Barahona (RD$250, 40 minutes, every 20 minutes). Southbound *guaguas* to Enriquillo (RD$50, 20 minutes), Laguna Oviedo (RD$100, one hour) and Pedernales (RD$200, 1½ hours) pass by roughly every 20 minutes between 6:30am and 6pm. You can also flag southbound *guaguas* down where the main highway intersects with the town's main road south of the village.

Santo Domingo–bound express buses from Pedernales pass through here around 4:30am and 3:30pm (RD$350, four hours). If you want a guaranteed seat on either, you'll need to put your name on a list at the office of **Transportes Cuchi** (☎809-243-1270; Calle Arzobispo Noel 41, Paraíso) in town. The morning bus will pick you up at your hotel, the afternoon ride loads at the office.

Larimar Mine

All larimar in the DR – and, indeed, the world – comes from this one mine. Discovered in 1974 by Miguel Méndez, the name comes from Larissa (Méndez's daughter) plus *mar* (sea). Its scientific name is blue pectolite.

The mining operations are done not by a large mining concern but by a small collective of individual miners. You can visit the mines and even go down some of the mine shafts. A small group of basic shacks sells cut-rate larimar jewelry at the mine, and a few no-name eateries sell food and drink to the miners.

To get there, look for the turn-off in the small hamlet of El Arroyo, 13km south of Barahona (3km north of Bahoruco). There's no sign, but there is a European Commission sign referring to the mine. It's an hour's drive on a rough road (4WD absolutely required). Ecotour Barahona (p191) offers a tour here (US$119). Alternatively, take a *guagua* to the turn-off early in the morning; you may be able to hitchhike in with one of the miners. As in any other part of the world, hitching is never entirely safe however, and we therefore don't recommend it. Travelers who hitch should understand that they are taking a small but potentially serious risk.

Parque Nacional Jaragua

The largest protected area in the country, **Parque Nacional Jaragua** (admission RD$100; ⌚8am-5pm) is 1400 sq km. The park includes vast ranges of thorn forest and subtropical dry forest and an extensive marine area that spans most of the southern coastline, including Laguna Oviedo, Bahía de Las Águilas and the islands of Isla Beata and Alto Velo.

Laguna Oviedo

This hypersalinic lake, separated from the ocean by a thin 800m-wide strip of sand, is a popular birdwatching destination, and home to a small colony of flamingos, which swells in population during winter. You're also likely to spot ibis, storks and spoonbills, especially in late spring and early summer. The enormous, one-ton *tinjlare* turtle comes here from April to August to lay and hatch its eggs, but can usually be seen only very late at night.

You can take a boat tour from the well-organized **visitors center** (☎829-808-8234; ⌚6am-6pm). A three-hour tour costs RD$3500 per boat (up to five people), including a Spanish-speaking guide. There's also the national park entrance fee (RD$100). The tour includes a brief visit to a small Taíno cave, plus a short walk across the dividing strip to the ocean and the beach there, a beautiful yellow strand marred by an unbelievable quantity of plastic flotsam and jetsam – broken buckets, empty bleach bottles and the occasional light bulb. Wear shoes. If you're especially interested in turtles, arrange a tour with **Francisco Saldaña Cuevas** (☎829-808-8924).

There are two viewing platforms – one at the shore behind the visitors center, another on the biggest of the 24 or so islands in the lake, where you'll also find lots of big iguanas. The lake is so salty that in the dry season you'll see crystallized salt mixed with the sand on the islands.

Ecotour Barahona (p191) offers a day-trip here (US$119).

There's a well-marked entrance to the park and lagoon off the coastal highway about 3km north of the town of Oviedo. Oviedo and Pedernales buses can drop you at the park entrance. The last bus back to Barahona passes by around 4pm. If you get stuck, the new and dead-simple **Hotel Begó**

(☎829-808-8924; Carretera Pedernales; r RD$500-1000; ❄), just a bit up the highway from the visitors center, offers four basic rooms and lagoon views from its second-floor terrace.

Isla Beata & Alto Velo

These are end-of-the-world spots, difficult to access but seductive because of their remoteness. They are challenging for independent travelers to visit, and can be enjoyed more fully by taking a tour.

Isla Beata, once home to a prison for political dissidents under the dictatorship of Trujillo in the 1950s, remains under joint management of the military and the Parque Nacional Jaragua. The small fishing village of **Trudille** sits directly on **Playa Blanca**, a 40km-long white-sand beach full of iguanas. The prison was destroyed after Trujillo's assassination but you can still visit the ruins.

Alto Velo is a smaller, uninhabited island 1½ hours further south of Isla Beata. It's the southernmost point in the DR. Windswept and covered in bird droppings (from the swarms of seagulls that live there), there's a lighthouse at the highest point of the island (250m). It's a two-hour return walk (about 2.5km each way) with amazing views. There's no beach, though.

The best way to visit the islands is to take a tour with Ecotour Barahona (p191), which offers a day-trip to Isla Beata (US$140 per person, minimum six), with the option of adding a night in Las Cuevas; and trips to Alto Velo on a private basis.

Pedernales

POP 14,590

The coastal highway dead-ends in Pedernales. Haiti is reachable through a residential street and border post about 1.5km from central Pedernales. Otherwise, this end-of-the-road town is principally of interest to those wanting to linger at Bahía de Las Águilas or in the national parks nearby; and those wanting to take in the well-organized Haitian market on Mondays and Fridays. Although it's rarely used by foreigners, this is by far the least chaotic and easiest border to cross between the countries.

The most pleasant place to stay is the wonderful **Hostal Doña Chava** (☎809-524-0332; www.donachava.com; Calle P N Hugson 5; d/tr with fan RD$900/1000, s/d/tr/qd with air-con RD$900/1100/1300/1500; ❄@📶) 🍃, which offers simple rooms with tidy bathrooms and cable TV and wonderful common areas: there's a jungly courtyard (bring insect repellent) and sustainable touches all over, including organic coffee; and breakfast (RD$160 to RD$180) is available. Be aware that management is very fussy about early check-ins (before 4pm), even if a room is ready.

The best spot to eat in town is the seafood-centric **King Crab** (Calle Dominguez 2; mains RD$200-550; ⏲8am-11pm). There's no printed menu but usually you'll find crab, whole red snapper (*chillo*; per lb RD$550) and lobster (RD$500).

BanReservas (Calle Duarte) has two ATMs, the second is free-standing on Av Libertad on the road into town.

Sinchomipe *guaguas* leave for Santo Domingo (RD$400, six hours) six times per day: 5am, 6am, 8am, 10:30am, 11:30am, 1:30pm and 3pm from the corner of Calle 27 de Febrero and Calle Santo Domingo. *Guaguas* go back and forth between Pedernales and Barahona (RD$250, two hours, hourly from 8am to 3pm) from the same spot.

A quick *motoconcho* ride (RD$50) along Calle 27 de Febrero leads to the Haitian border and the small village of Anse-à-Pitres, 1.5km from the intersection near BanReservas. The **Dirección General de Migración** (www.migracion.gov.do) is in the small trailer on your left just before the border. Knock on the door.

Parque Nacional Sierra de Bahoruco

This **national park** (admission RD$100; ⏲8am-5pm) directly west of Barahona covers 800 sq km of mostly mountainous terrain and is notable for the rich variety of vegetation that thrives in its many different climates, from lowland desert to cloud forest. Valleys are home to vast areas of broad-leafed plants, which give way to healthy pine forests at higher elevations. In the mountains the average temperature is 18°C, and annual rainfall is between 1000mm and 2500mm. Together with Parque Nacional Jaragua and Lago Enriquillo, Parque Nacional Sierra de Bahoruco forms the Jaragua-Bahoruca-Enriquillo Biosphere Reserve, the first Unesco Biosphere Reserve in the country.

Within the national park there are 166 orchid species, representing 52% of the country's total. Around 32% of those species are endemic to the park. Flitting about among the park's pine, cherry and mahogany trees are over 75 species of bird, including the white-necked crow and 28 others of the 32 endemic species found on Hispaniola. The high mountain habitat is home to the la Selle's thrush, white-winged warbler, Hispaniolan spindalis, emerald hummingbird, Hispaniolan trogons, narrow-billed todies, western chat-tanager and Hispaniolan parrots. At lower elevations, you'll see white-necked crows, flat-billed vireos and the elusive bay-breasted cuckoo.

Tody Tours (p191) runs a birdwatching camp near Puerto Escondido on the border of the park and a remote birdwatching camp within the Biosphere Reserve called **Villa Barrancoli** (809-686-0882; www.todytours.com; cabins per person US$10, food per day per person US$3). When the camp is not otherwise in use independent travelers are welcome – be sure to email ahead for reservations several days in advance. You'll want a good 4WD, and some experience of driving one. To get there from Barahona, head to the town of Duvergé along the southern side of Lago Enriquillo. In town, look for the mural of the cuckoo and the parrot on the left hand side a few blocks past the gas station. Turn left here and drive ahead for about half an hour to Puerto Escondido. You'll see the park office on your right as you enter. Continue to a T intersection, then turn left, following the sign to Rabo de Gato. Turn right and cross the canal. At the next fork turn right again and follow the signs to Rabo de Gato until you come to the campsite.

Hoyo de Pelempito

Part of Parque Nacional Sierra de Bahoruco, the 'hole' at Pelempito is actually a deep gorge formed when the Península de Pedernales jammed itself up into Hispaniola umpteen million years ago. The tourist office, perched on the edge of a cliff at 1450m, offers breathtaking views, north and east, of completely untouched national park. The cliff itself is a 600m drop.

The tourist office has information (in Spanish) on the various flora and fauna in the area, and a number of short nature walks have small signs identifying the various plants. Serious birdwatchers scoff that this is a poor birdwatching location, but for the casual tourist the views make it worth the drive.

Pelempito sits on the south side of the Sierra de Bahoruco. The turn-off is about 12km east of Pedernales. Shortly after the turn-off to Bahía de Las Águilas, you'll cross a small bridge. Immediately after, you turn left on a dirt road that swings around to the paved road north to Hoyo de Pelempito (it actually ends up being same road that leads to Bahía de Las Águilas but you'll take the opposite direction). Around 14km later, you'll come to a **ranger station** (admission RD$100; 9am-4:30pm). From here, the paved highway-like road continues for 6km, turning into a rutted dirt track for the last 7km. Rains frequently destroy this part of the road, so you'll need a 4WD or a very high vehicle.

WORTH A TRIP

THE POLO ORGANIC COFFEE FESTIVAL

Started in 2004, the **Festival de Café Orgánico de Polo** (Festicafé; 809-682-3386; www.festicafe.org) is held on the first weekend in June in the small town of Polo, nestled on the south slopes of the Sierra de Bahoruco. From Friday to Sunday local coffee-growers celebrate the end of the coffee-harvesting season. There's live merengue and *bachata* (Dominican music) in the evenings, and during the day stands sell coffee and typical southwestern arts and crafts. There's a 'coffee parade,' and lots of (decaffeinated) games for the kids. The organizers also lead hiking trips to remote coffee plantations in the mountains.

There's no real hotel in town, but during the festival the organizers can put you up in a spare room in someone's house – be sure to call several weeks ahead, as rooms fill up fast. Even if the festival's not on, various shops around town sell the coffee packaged to go – it's excellent if you take your caffeine seriously and worth the side trip if you have wheels.

From Barahona, drive 12km west to Cabral and look for the marked southbound turn-off in the middle of town (there's a flashing traffic light). From there it's about a 20km (30-minute) drive to Polo.

NORTH OF PEDERNALES

Lago Enriquillo & Isla Cabritos

Parque Nacional Lago Enriquillo & Isla Cabritos (☎809-880-0871; admission Dominican/foreigner RD$30/50; ⏰8am-6pm) comprises an enormous saltwater lake 40m below sea level with the 12km-long desert island Isla Cabritos in the center. Lago Enriquillo is the remains of an ancient channel that once united the Bahía de Neiba to the southeast (near Barahona) with Port-au-Prince to the west. The accumulation of sediments deposited by the Río Yaque del Sur at the river's mouth on the Bahía de Neyba, combined with an upward thrust of a continental plate, gradually isolated the lake. Today it is basically a 200-sq-km inland sea with no outlet.

The highlights are the lake's creatures, including an estimated 200 American crocodiles, some of which can be seen at the edge of the lake. From December to April you'll also see flamingos and egrets.

The island, which varies in elevation from 40m to 4m below sea level, is a virtual desert, supporting a variety of cacti and other desert flora. In summer, temperatures of 50°C have been recorded – go early. It is home to Ricord iguanas and rhinoceros iguanas, some more than 20 years old and considerably bigger than most house cats. The island also has lots of scorpions, so wear covered shoes if possible.

There is a tourist office here, with information on the history and geology of the island. From March to June you'll see a blooming of cactus flowers, and June sees a small swarm of butterflies.

The park entrance is about 3km east of La Descubierta. The local **guide association** (☎809-880-0871) offers boat tours of the park for RD$3500 for up to 10 people – expect a sore, wet bum (and salt stains). Be sure to call ahead – if a tour group has the boat reserved, you might be out of luck. Additionally, these guys don't seem to hang around – you must call them in advance. The boat will take you to the mouth of the Río de la Descubierta – where the most crocodiles and flamingos are visible – and Isla Cabritos. The tour usually lasts two hours and the last boat departs at noon. Bring a hat and plenty of water.

A short distance east of the park entrance, look for **Las Caritas** (The Masks). On the north side of the highway, bright yellow handrails lead up to a small rock formation with what are believed to be pre-Taíno petroglyphs. A short but somewhat tricky climb up the hillside – you'll need shoes or decent sandals – affords a close look at the pictures and a fine view of the lake. Very little is known about the meaning of the figures. Note that much of the rock here is actually petrified coral, remnants of the time the entire area was under the sea.

Ecotour Barahona (p191) offers a popular day trip to Isla Cabritos (US$139), including lunch at the swimming hole at La Descubierta and a visit to Las Caritas and the Haitian market at Jimaní, though this border area often floods, canceling the market.

Sleeping & Eating

About 3km west of the park entrance lies the small town of La Descubierta, which is popular for its large swimming hole right in the middle of town. There are food shacks in town, near the park and swimming hole.

Hotel Iguana GUESTHOUSE **$**
(☎809-958-7636; Calle Padre Billini 3; r per person without/with full board RD$400/1000) There's not much reason to spend the night here, but if you get stuck, Hotel Iguana, on the main road west of the park, will do in a pinch. Rooms are small and simple, but also clean and quiet, with private bathrooms and better-than-expected beds. Call ahead to arrange excellent home-cooked meals.

Getting There & Away

You're better off driving yourself if you're coming this far north of Pedernales, but you can also grab a *guagua* from Barahona to Neyba. Tell the driver to stop at the ranger station, where you can then change for any westbound *guagua*.

Jimaní

POP 10,034

This dusty border town is on the most direct route from Santo Domingo to Port-au-Prince, and is therefore the busiest of the four official border crossings. Dominicans from as far away as Santo Domingo come here for the daily market. There are also a few *tiendas* selling Haitian beer (Prestige) and rum (Rhum Barbancourt), both arguably better than their Dominican counterparts. The market is just past the Dominican border post in no-man's-land. This area – including immigration posts and other border control facilities – are seriously prone to flooding from the alarmingly expanding shoreline of Etang Saumâtre, Lago Enriquillo's twin lake on the Haitian side (also known as Lake Azuéi), whose southeast end sits just 1km from the border post under normal conditions.

Sleeping & Eating

Hotel Taíno Frontera HOTEL $
(☎809-248-3208; www.hoteltainofrontera.blogspot.com; Calle 19 de Marzo 4; s/d incl breakfast 1200/1400; ❄📶) This hotel is run by the friendly and helpful Pascale, a Haitian who's fluent in English, Spanish, French and Creole, along with her Dominican husband. Rooms are decked out with nice furniture and big, modern bathrooms, and the breezy restaurant specializes in goat (mains RD$75 to RD$300). It's a straight 2.5km shot from the border next to the new road to La Descubierta – just the kind of place you'd like to lay your head before or after crossing a crazy border.

Information

BanReservas has a 24-hour ATM and is at the west end of Calle 19 de Marzo, the main road from Neyba just before it leaves town for the Haitian border. A Banco Popular ATM is right across the street from **Farmacia Melenciano** (⏲8am-10pm), on the uphill road to/from Duvergé. If you run into any trouble, head to **Policía Nacional** (☎809-248-3043; Calle 19 de Marzo).

Getting There & Away

Jimaní is served by *guaguas* from Santo Domingo, passing La Descubierta, Neyba and Baní along the way; and from Barahona via Duvergé and the south side of Lago Enriquillo. Both bus stops are on the sloping road that enters town from the Duvergé side. Coming to/from La Descubierta, a new road has been built in order to circumvent the rising waters of Lago Enriquillo.

For Santo Domingo, Asodumichocoji has a proper terminal near the bottom of the hill (RD$450, five hours, every 40 minutes from 7am to 5pm). For La Descubierta, it's RD$50 and takes 30 minutes. *Guaguas* to Barahona (RD$200, 2½ hours, every 40 minutes from 4am to 3pm) leave from a shady corner about 200m up the hill, across from a small supermarket. Caribe Tours has a direct service from Santo Domingo to Port-au-Prince, with a stop in Jimaní.

Understand Dominican Republic

Dominican Republic Today

Young and old alike groan equally about endemic corruption and lack of opportunities, and with a past filled by strong-man dictators and corrupt politicians, the average Dominican has learned to live through hardships, and approaches the present with a healthy skepticism. Despite this, there's a general equanimity, or at the very least an ability to appreciate the good things in life: family, togetherness, music and laughter.

Best on Film

La Hija Natural (Love Child) A teenager's anguished attempt to find and get to know her estranged father. Dominican entry for Best Foreign Film at 2011 Academy Awards.

Sugar Story of a Dominican baseball prospect's journey to minor leagues in middle America.

Ladrones a Domicilio (Robbers of the House) A political satire and slapstick comedy involving a robbery and kidnapping, and corruption in everyday life.

Best in Print

Dead Man in Paradise Canadian journalist JB Mackinnon, the nephew of a priest murdered during the Trujillo regime, tries to piece together the unsolved crime.

Fiesta del Chivo (Feast of the Goat) Peruvian novelist Mario Vargas Llosa's imaginative telling of dictator Rafael Trujillo's final days.

The Brief Wondrous Life of Oscar Wao Junot Díaz's inventive story of a self-professed Dominican nerd in New Jersey and the tragic history of his family in the DR.

The Farming of Bones Edwidge Danticat's novel movingly recreates the events around the 1937 massacre of Haitians in the DR.

The Mood

Most Dominicans would consider themselves religious and, while a deeply Catholic country, few attend Mass regularly. Evangelical Protestant Christianity attracts adherents with dramatic faith healings, fiery sermons and exorcisms. An underlying mix of popular legends, folk superstitions, syncretic African rituals and Vodou spiritualism, in part introduced by Haitian immigrants and their descendants, are alive and well, though less visible.

Reformists took heart in Leonel Fernández' decision not to pursue constitutional changes that would have allowed him to run for a fourth presidential term in 2012. Instead, Danilo Medina, an economist from the PLD *(Partido Liberación Dominicana)* and former chief-of-staff for Fernández, narrowly won with 51% of the vote over former president Mejia, the leader of the PRD *(Partido Revolucinario Dominicana)*, the main opposition party. In the immediate aftermath, Mejia accused the PLD of vote-rigging. Since then, Medina has been credited with a more populist tone than his predecessor, in part because of 'listening tours' he's taken through rural regions.

The Other Half

Many Dominicans still refer angrily to the Haitian occupation of their country over 160 years ago. Haitians are typically blamed for overburdened schools, insufficient healthcare and rising crime rates, especially guns, drugs and prostitution, and for taking Dominican jobs. Haitians continue migrating to the Dominican Republic (DR) in large numbers to work on the vast sugar plantations or in construction, risking violence, discrimination, poor living conditions and lack of legal protections; most workers on sugarcane plantations only have work during the *zafra*, the four- to six-month harvest period. One of the most reflexively-held prejudices across all strata of society is the assumption that the lighter the skin the higher the class and vice versa.

In September 2013, the Dominican Constitutional Court ruled that 'people born in the Dominican Republic to undocumented parents' weren't automatically afforded citizenship themselves. The decision, which applies to anyone born after 1929, was widely and strongly condemned by human rights activists, foreign governments and influential Dominican writers, artists and intellectuals as a racist ruling that targets Dominicans of Haitian descent. According to critics, it would officially strip vital rights from tens to hundreds of thousands of people who are fully integrated into Dominican society, many for generations. The government argues that it is finally putting in place a system to regularize the status of immigrants.

Haiti, after the US, is the second largest export market for Dominican goods (this doesn't include an estimated several hundred million dollars of contraband). Trade disputes, however, are commonplace, including accusations that the DR ships lesser and unsafe goods to Haiti and that Haitian products are glaringly absent from Dominican stores. In response, the Haitian government began building a wall 8km from the border crossing at Elías Piña, it claims in order to collect taxes on imported Dominican goods. Nationalists from both sides have talked of building a wall that lines the entire 300km (190 miles) border.

The Economy

Many Dominicans lack electricity, while the remainder experience regular blackouts. Women, who make up less than one-third of the DR's paid workforce, are poorly represented in government and politics, and abortion, under all circumstances, is illegal. Recently, the economy has been growing at a hearty 4.5% clip and Ikea stores and luxury car dealerships point to the growing purchasing power of a small segment of society. However, nearly 40% of Dominicans live below the poverty line, the monthly take home pay for minimum wage jobs is only US$140 per month and, according to the gross domestic product per capita, the DR is the fourth poorest country in the Caribbean. When thousands of public hospital workers went on a three-day walkout in September 2013 demanding higher wages, the average monthly salary was between US$600 and US$1000 for doctors and US$500 for nurses.

The DR earns more tourism dollars than any other country in Latin America except Mexico and Brazil. The service industry, primarily tourism but the free-trade zone areas as well, is the largest employer and earner in the DR. Around 500,000 people work in the organic cocoa industry – the DR is the largest exporter in the world. Another revenue source is remittances from Dominicans living abroad – more than one million people collectively send over US$1 billion to the DR yearly. Families are large and children are expected to help care for elders, but with so many young Dominicans leaving for the US, this creates a unique domestic stress, albeit offset somewhat by the remittances sent home.

POPULATION: **10,219,630**

AREA: **48,670 SQ KM**

GDP PER CAPITA: **US$9,800 (2012 EST)**

UNEMPLOYMENT: **14.3% (2012 EST)**

POP BELOW POVERTY LINE: **34.4% (2010 EST)**

if the Dominican Republic were 100 people

73 would be mixed race
16 would be white
11 would be black

belief systems

(% of population)

5

Roman Catholic

other

population per sq km

DOMINICAN REPUBLIC

USA

UK

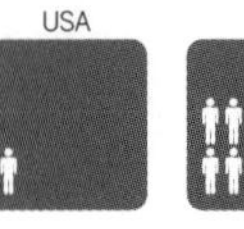

≈ 30 people

History

Since 1492, when Columbus landed on the island of Hispaniola, the Dominican Republic (DR) has seen wave after wave of foreign interlopers. The destruction of the native population led to periods of intermittent neglect and conflicts between the French and Spanish colonial systems. Shaping its identity as much as anything, is its relationship with Haiti, its onetime invader and neighbor sharing the island. Decades of dictatorial and general misrule left scars, both physical and psychological, though Dominicans are proud of their Spanish heritage and recent years have seen relative stability and a resurgence of nationalist pride.

A Brief History of the Caribbean: From the Arawak and Carib to the Present by Jan Rogozinski does an excellent job of placing Hispaniola into the larger currents of Caribbean history.

The Taínos

Hispaniola had been inhabited for three millennia before Christopher Columbus sailed into view, colonized by a successive wave of island-hopping incomers from South America. Most notable were the Arawaks, and then the Taínos ('the friendly people'), who prospered on the island for around 700 years until the clash of civilizations with Europe brought their ultimate downfall. The Taínos were both farmers and seafarers, living in chiefdoms called *caciques*, with a total population of around 500,000 at the time of Columbus' arrival. Each chiefdom comprised several districts with villages of 1000 to 2000 people.

Comparatively little of Taíno culture has survived to the modern age. Pottery and stone tools form the most common artifacts, along with jewelry of bone, shell and gold that was panned from rivers. Clothing was made of cotton or pounded bark fibers. While Taíno artifacts are relatively few, the crops they bequeathed to the world were revolutionary, from tobacco to yams, cassava and pineapples. Hispaniola's inhabitants, however, were barely to survive their first encounter with Europe.

The Columbus Brothers

In 1492 Christopher Columbus sailed from Spain with 90 men in the *Pinta,* the *Niña* and the *Santa María,* bound for Asia. He sailed west rather than east, expecting to circumnavigate the globe, instead discover-

TIMELINE

4000 BC

Earliest evidence of human colonization of Hispaniola. Stone-flaked tools found at archaeological digs are thought to have been brought by hunter-gatherers migrating from the Yucatan peninsula in Mexico.

1200 BC

Ancestral Arawaks arrive in Hispaniola, via the Lesser Antilles. Dubbed 'the Saladoid culture,' they live in settled agricultural communities, and are best known for their sophisticated pottery.

AD 500–1000

A third wave of migration arrives in Hispaniola, with the rich seafaring culture of the Taínos. The population expands rapidly, and is divided into a series of interdependent but competing chiefdoms.

ing the New World for the Old. After stops at the small Bahamian island of Guanahaní and present-day Cuba (which Columbus initially mistook for Japan), a mountainous landscape appeared before the explorers. Columbus named it 'La Isla Española' or 'the Spanish Island,' which was later corrupted to 'Hispaniola.' He made landfall at Môle St-Nicholas in modern Haiti on December 7, and days later ran the *Santa María* onto a reef. Here on Christmas Day he established Villa La Navidad, the first settlement of any kind made by Europeans in the New World.

Columbus was greeted with great warmth by the Taínos, who impressed him further with their gifts of gold jewelry. Capturing a handful of Taínos to impress his royal patrons, he sailed back to Spain to be showered with glory. He returned within a year, leading 17 ships of soldiers and colonists.

La Navidad had been razed by the Taínos in reprisal for the kidnappings by the settlers, so Columbus sailed east and established La Isabela, named for Spain's queen, on the north coast of the DR; the first church in the Americas was erected here. However, La Isabela was plagued with disease, and within five years the capital of the new colony was moved to Santo Domingo, where it has remained.

Columbus' early administration was a disaster and appointing his brother Bartholomé proved no better. Their haphazard rule soon had the colonists up in arms, and a replacement sent from Spain returned the brothers home in chains. The colony would now be run with military harshness.

The Taínos were the ones to bear the brunt of this. They were already stricken by European illnesses that sent their numbers crashing, but on top of this Spain introduced *encomienda,* forced labor requiring the natives to dig up quotas of gold. The Spanish broke up Taíno villages, killed their chiefs and put the entire population to work. Within three decades of their first meeting with Europeans, the Taínos were reduced to a shadow of their previous numbers.

'I cannot believe that any man has ever met a people so good-hearted and generous, so gentle that they did their utmost to give us everything they had' – Christopher Columbus on meeting the Taínos.

Pre-Colonial Sites

- *Cueva de las Maravillas, La Romana*
- *Reserva Antropológica Cuevas del Pomier, San Cristobal*
- *Parque Nacional de Este, near Bayahibe*
- *Piedra Letrada, Constanza*
- *El Corral de los Indios, near San Juan de la Maguana*

European Competition & Colonization

As Taíno civilization collapsed, so did the gold mines, and no amount of imported African slaves could make up the shortfall. Spain dropped Hispaniola as quickly as it had found it, turning its attention instead to the immense riches coming from its new possessions in Mexico and Peru. Santo Domingo was reduced to a trading post for gold and silver convoys, but couldn't even hold onto that position with the opening of new trade routes via Cuba. After the English admiral Sir Francis Drake sacked Santo Domingo in 1586, it was effectively abandoned for the next 50 years, further signaling the decline of Spanish Hispaniola.

1492

Christopher Columbus makes landfall on Hispaniola on Christmas Day and founds the settlement of La Navidad (Nativity) near modern-day Cap-Haïtien in Haiti, before returning to Spain with Taíno captives.

1496

Nueva Isabela founded by the Spanish. Rebuilt as Santo Domingo after a 1502 hurricane, it quickly receives a royal charter, making it the oldest European city in the New World.

1500

A Santo Domingo governor captures Christopher Columbus and returns him to Spain in shackles; Queen Isabella orders him released soon after.

1503

Queen Anacaona of the Taíno kingdom of Xaragua in central Hispaniola is arrested by the Spanish governor and publicly executed, effectively marking the end of Taíno independence on the island.

For the next three centuries, Europe was riven by war. Imperial Spain slipped into a slow decline, and the English and French took advantage, competing not just in the Old World but in North America and the Caribbean. Hispaniola was considered a great prize. The colony was stagnating under Spanish rule. Both the English and French encouraged piracy against the Spanish, even licensing the pirates as 'privateers,' and the rugged coast and mountainous interior of Hispaniola made it an ideal base for operations. Although a few captains became notorious raiders, most divided their time between hunting the wild cattle and pigs that thrived on the island and plundering for booty. The lack of any governmental control also made the island a haven for runaway slaves.

Colonial Sites

- *Zona Colonial, Santo Domingo*
- *Castillo de San Felipe, Puerto Plata*
- *La Vega Vieja, La Vega*
- *Parque Nacional La Isabela, North Coast*
- *Casa Ponce de Leon, near San Rafael del Yuma*

For security, the Spanish convoys sailed en masse once a year, a system that effectively cut Hispaniola off from trade with the mother country – not only were visiting ships few and far between, but the colonists were banned from trading with non-Spaniards. The colony shrank to the area around Santo Domingo, leaving the rest of the island open for the taking.

The English attempted to come in through the front door in 1655, but their army of 13,000 soldiers was repelled at the gates of Santo Domingo. Years of neglect meant the 125,000-person Spanish colony missed out on the sugar rush for now (Spanish investors had preferred to put their money into booming Cuba), relying primarily on cattle ranching for its lifeblood. Slave imports had never been high, as they simply couldn't be afforded, and slaves made up less than 1% of the population.

French tobacco farmers grabbed more and more territory until France had formed a de facto colony (which would become Haiti). The Spanish could do nothing, especially as France was beating them on the battlefields of Europe. At the close of the 17th century, France had managed to grab the western two-thirds of Hispaniola, christening them the colony of Saint-Domingue. It was the richest colony in the world due to sugar and slavery (around half the world's sugar and coffee came from the colony and the produce of 8000 plantations was providing 40% of France's foreign trade).

PIRATES OF THE CARIBBEAN

The purported remains – mostly pieces of cannons, anchors and wood – of the *Quedagh Merchant,* which belonged to the Scottish privateer Captain William Kidd, were found in the waters off Isla Catalina, near the shores of the Casa de Campo resort. The ship was scuttled and set on fire after Kidd returned to England to face charges of piracy. Despite the fact that he was often acting under the authority of the English navy, he was convicted of piracy and hanged in London in 1699.

1510

King Ferdinand of Spain issues first royal charter to import slaves to Hispaniola. Demand booms, to supplement rapidly crashing Taíno workforce.

1519–1533

A Taíno *cacique* named Enriquillo leads a rebellion against the Spanish in the Bahoruco mountains near the present-day DR–Haiti border.

ALFREDO MAIQUEZ / GETTY IMAGES ©

➡ Museo Alcázar de Colón (p49)

1586

Following the outbreak of war between England and Spain, Sir Francis Drake leads a devastating naval raid against Santo Domingo, leaving the city virtually razed.

Separation Anxiety

While France and Spain's power in Europe waxed and waned, so, too, did their imperialist ambitions. Conflict within the colonies became an avenue for waging proxy wars against their rivals, so when the enslaved African population of western Hispaniola's Saint-Domingue rose up in bloody revolt, Spain supported the revolution. However, once the French agreed to abolish slavery, the former slaves turned their attention to liberating the entire island – the Spanish colony had about 60,000 slaves of its own. Lacking the appetite, will and ability to forcefully oppose the uprising, Spain and France haggled over the details, one of which involved the injunction that Spanish colonists abdicate their lands in exchange for ones in Cuba.

In 1801, frustrated by the slow pace of negotiations, François Dominique Toussaint Louverture, a former slave and leader of the rebel forces, marched into Santo Domingo and, without French authority, declared that the abolition of slavery would be enforced throughout the island. At odds with French leaders, especially Napoleon Bonaparte who now viewed him as a loose cannon, he was betrayed to the invading forces, who sent him in chains to France, where he died of neglect in a dungeon in April 1803.

Jean-Jacques Dessalines, who had been one of Toussaint's chief lieutenants, crowned himself emperor of the Republic of Haiti (an old Taíno name for the island) with the clearly stated ambition of uniting Hispaniola under one flag. Free, educated mulattoes were spurned, laborers were forced back onto the plantations to rebuild the economy, the remaining whites were massacred and the Spanish colony was invaded by General Henri Christophe whose forces participated in mass killings of civilians in Santiago and Moca. Dessalines' rule was brutal and the reaction inevitable – in 1806, he was killed in an ambush outside Port-au-Prince.

For the Spanish colonists in Santo Domingo, this new imperialist threat compelled them to ask Spain to reincorporate them into the empire. But through neglect and mismanagement Spain completely bungled its administration of Santo Domingo and on November 30, 1821, the colony declared its independence once again. Colonial leaders intended to join the Republic of Gran Colombia (a country that included present-day Ecuador, Colombia, Panama and Venezuela) but never got the chance – Haiti invaded and finally achieved its goal of a united Hispaniola.

Dominicans chafed under Haitian rule for the next 22 years, and to this day both countries regard the other with disdain and suspicion. Resistance grew until February 27, 1844 – a day celebrated as Dominican Independence Day – when a separatist movement headed by Juan Pablo Duarte captured Santo Domingo in a bloodless coup. The Puerto del Conde in Santo

Alan Cambeira's *Azucar! The Story of Sugar* is a fascinating novel that portrays the human toll of sugar production in the DR, with much of the information, descriptions and events based on real events.

Christopher Columbus, Hernán Cortés, Francisco Pizarro, Juan Ponce de León and Vasco Nuñez de Balboa all spent time in what is now the DR.

1605
Spain sends the army to relocate most of its colonists to Santo Domingo city by force, to prevent contraband trade with foreign merchants, effectively abandoning claims to western Hispaniola.

1655
An English military expedition is dispatched by Oliver Cromwell to conquer Santo Domingo. Although beaten back, the navy saves face by managing to grab Jamaica as a permanent Caribbean foothold.

1697
The Treaty of Ryswick settles the nine-year pan-European War of the Grand Alliance. As a result, Hispaniola's borders are settled, dividing the island into Spanish Santa Domingo and French St-Domingue.

1821–22
Colonists of Santo Domingo, known as Spanish Haiti, declare independence from Spain in November 1821, only to be invaded by Haiti nine weeks later and incorporated into a united Hispaniola.

Domingo marks the spot where Duarte entered the city. Despite the reversal of fortunes of the two countries in the 20th century, many Dominicans still view Haiti as an aggressive nation with territorial ambitions.

Fearing another invasion and still feeling threatened by Haiti in 1861, the Dominican Republic once again submitted to Spanish rule. But ordinary Dominicans did not support the move and, after four years of armed resistance, succeeded in expelling Spanish troops in what is known as the War of Restoration. (Restauración is a common street name throughout the DR, and there are a number of monuments to the war, including a prominent one in Santiago.) On March 3, 1865, the Queen of Spain signed a decree annulling the annexation and withdrew her soldiers from the island.

The *trinitaria*, a bougainvillea that blooms purple, red and magenta, also refers to Juan Pablo Duarte, Francisco de Rosario Sánchez and Ramón Mella, the three fathers of the republic, and to the secret cells of three that were organized in 1838 to struggle for independence from Haiti.

Power from the North

With no strong central government, the newly independent Dominican Republic was a fractured nation, divided up among several dozen caudillos (military leaders) and their militias. From 1865 until 1879 there were more than 50 military uprisings or coups and 21 changes in government. In 1869, after Buenaventura Báez, the leader of a coalition of plantation owners, mahogany exporters and a significant portion of residents of Santo Domingo, was installed as president, he attempted to sell the country to the US for US$150,000. Even though the treaty was signed by Báez and US president Ulysses S Grant, the agreement was defeated in the US Senate.

The US was to involve itself once again in Dominican affairs, this time at the invitation of General Ulises Heureaux, who stabilized the musical chairs of political and military leadership from 1882 until his assassination in 1899. The general, known as Lilí, borrowed heavily from American and European banks to finance the army, infrastructure and sugar industry. But after a sharp drop-off in world sugar prices, Lilí essentially mortgaged the country to the US-owned and -operated San Domingo Improvement Company just before his death. Because the Dominican government was bankrupt, the US government intervened in 1905 by taking control of the customs houses and guaranteeing repayment of all loans, stopping just short of ratifying President Theodore Roosevelt's plan to establish a protectorate over the DR.

Between 1844 and 1916, the Dominican Republic had 40 different governments.

Despite some economic growth, after the assassination of another president in 1911, Dominican politics mostly remained chaotic, corrupt and bloody. In 1916, under the dual pretext of quelling yet another coup as well as guarding the waters from German aggression during WWI, President Woodrow Wilson sent US marines to the DR – they remained for the next eight years. (Similarly, Wilson sent the marines into Haiti in 1915, claiming, ironically, that unrest there made it vulnerable to a

1844

Coalition of Santo Domingo intellectuals and rebel Haitian soldiers spark a largely bloodless coup and the Dominican Republic declares its independence from Haiti, after 22 years of occupation.

1849

Buenaventura Baez begins the first of five terms – between 1849 and 1878 – as president of the DR. One of his first acts was an attempt to have his country annexed by the USA.

1865

Two years after the initial uprising in Santiago, triggered by the Spanish authority's continual erosion of Dominican rights, the DR gains independence by defeating Spanish troops in the War of Restoration.

1880–1884

A handful of modern sugar mills begin operating in San Pedro de Macorís, the start of the Dominican sugar industry.

German invasion – the occupation lasted 20 years.) Though deeply imperialistic, the US occupation did succeed in stabilizing Dominican politics and the economy. Once the DR's strategic value to the US had dropped, and a new strain of isolationism had entered American discourse, the occupation ended and the troops were sent home.

BIG SUGAR

After the island's gold reserves were quickly exhausted and the native population decimated, Spanish colonists harvested the first sugar crop in 1506. While the tropical climate and topography rendered it an ideal physical environment, labor was in short supply. Slaves imported from Africa rebelled and fled to the western part of the island – soon after, Spain discovered sugar was being sold to France and Holland and so decided to burn all they could.

It wasn't for another several hundred years, when in the mid-19th century prosperous Cuban plantation owners began to seek out new territory, that sugar took root once again in the DR. Cuba's failed 10-year war of independence only accelerated the migration, and only when slavery was abolished in other Spanish colonies like Cuba and Puerto Rico in the 1870s could the DR begin to compete in terms of production costs.

The first steam-powered sugar mill *(ingenio)* was opened in 1879 near San Pedro de Macoris on the southeast coast. This commercial port town was soon booming, with more than a half-dozen modern plants in operation by 1920. San Pedro, which would later become synonymous with baseball, became a relatively elegant and cosmopolitan town known for its poets as well as sugar wealth. When the European sugar industry was destroyed by WWI, Caribbean suppliers stepped into the void. Sugar became the DR's leading export and the US its leading buyer.

But Dominicans, able to survive with their own small plots of land, were largely uninterested in the backbreaking, low-paying work. Companies started turning to workers from the British-speaking Caribbean islands, who were more eager for seasonal labor and disinclined to push for better pay or improved working conditions. These migrant workers from the eastern Caribbean came to be called *cocolos* and where they lived *bateyes*. A backlash was inevitable – in 1919 a law was passed banning non-Caucasians from immigrating to the DR. Though thousands of *cocolos* and their families remained around San Pedro working for the mills, Haitians began to replace them during the harvest, in part because it was easier for the companies to 'repatriate' them when the work was over.

When the bottom dropped out of the price of sugar on the world market in the 1930s, around the same time Trujillo came to power, the financial well-being of the industry in the DR was inextricably tied to quotas obtained through negotiations with the US. Just as he did in other sectors of the economy, Trujillo consolidated control and ownership in his family and coterie and was able to influence many members of the US Congress into supporting his regime through continued trade in sugar.

1904–1905

US Marines are sent to Santo Domingo to assist the Dominican government fighting rebels; customs collections are turned over to the US.

1916–24

After years of civil wars, the US occupies the Dominican Republic under the pretense of securing debt payments owed by the defaulting Dominican government.

➡ Catedral Primada de América (p49)

The Rise of the Caudillo

Like the calm before the storm, the years from 1924 to 1930 were in many ways positive, led by a progressive president, Horacio Vásquez, whose administration built major roads and schools and initiated irrigation and sanitation programs. Vásquez extended his four-year term to six, a constitutionally questionable move that was nevertheless approved by the Congress. When a revolution was proclaimed in Santiago, Rafael Leónidas Trujillo, chief of the former Dominican National Police (renamed the National Army in 1928), ordered his troops to remain in their barracks, effectively forcing Vásquez and his vice president from office. After a sham election in which he was the sole candidate, Trujillo assumed the presidency. Within weeks he organized a terrorist band, La 42, which roamed the country, killing everyone who posed any threat to him. An egomaniac of the first degree, he changed the names of various cities – Santo Domingo became Ciudad Trujillo, for example – and lavished support on San Cristobal, the small city west of the capital where he was born; a never-used palace Trujillo had built there can still be visited.

Central Romana Corporation, which accounts for 74% of the DR's total sugar production, is owned by the Fanjuls who also own Casa de Campo resort.

Trujillo ruled the Dominican Republic with an iron fist from 1930 to 1961, lavishing over 21% of the national budget on the ever-expanding Guardia Nacional and creating a handful of intelligence agencies dedicated to suppressing any dissent. The torture and murder of political prisoners was a daily event in Trujillo's DR. Two of the more infamous incidents were the kidnapping and murder of a Spanish professor teaching in New York City, who had criticized his regime, and plotting to assassinate the Venezuelan president Rómulo Betancourt. Trujillo, in spite of being part black, was deeply racist and xenophobic; he sought to 'whiten' the Dominican population by increasing European immigration and placing quotas on the number of Haitians allowed in the country.

Life in Santo Domingo during the Trujillo regime was regimented: begging was allowed only on Saturdays, laborers were awakened with a siren at 7am, while office workers were given an extra hour to sleep in; their siren was at 8am.

During these years, Trujillo used his government to amass a personal fortune by establishing monopolies that he and his wife controlled. By 1934 he was the richest man on the island. Today there are many Dominicans who remember Trujillo's rule with a certain amount of fondness and nostalgia, in part because Trujillo did develop the economy. Factories were opened, a number of grandiose infrastructure and public works projects were carried out, bridges and highways were built, and peasants were given state land to cultivate.

Border Bloodbath

The zenith of the Haiti xenophobia was Trujillo's massacre of tens of thousands of Haitians in 1937. After hearing reports that Haitian peasants were crossing into the Dominican Republic, perhaps to steal cattle, Trujillo ordered all Haitians along the border to be tracked down and

1924–30

The country is led by a progressive president, Horacio Vásquez, whose administration builds major roads and schools and initiates irrigation and sanitation programs.

1930

After six years of relatively stable government, Rafael Trujillo, the chief of the Dominican National Police, declares himself president after an election in which he was the sole candidate.

1934

Trujillo uses his government to amass a personal fortune by establishing monopolies that he and his wife control. By 1934 he is the richest man on the island.

1937

In the culmination of his xenophobia, paranoia, racism and tyranny, dictator Rafael Trujillo orders the extermination of Haitians along the border; tens of thousands are killed in a matter of days.

executed. Dominican soldiers used a simple test to separate Haitians from Dominicans – they would hold up a string of parsley (*perejil* in Spanish) and ask everyone they encountered to name it. French- and Creole-speaking Haitians could not properly trill the 'r' and were summarily murdered. Beginning on October 3 and lasting for several days, at least 15,000 – and some researchers claim as many as 35,000 – Haitians were hacked to death with machetes, their bodies dumped into the ocean.

Trujillo never openly admitted a massacre had taken place, but in 1938, under international pressure, he and Haitian president Sténio Vicente agreed the Dominican Republic would pay a total of US$750,000 as reparation for Haitians who had been killed (US$50 per person). The Dominican Republic made an initial payment of US$250,000 but it's unclear if it ever paid the rest.

Trujillo's titles include Benefactor of the Fatherland, Founder and Supreme Chief of the Partido Dominicana, Restorer of Financial Independence, First Journalist of the Republic and Doctor Honoris Causa in the Economic Political Sciences.

False Starts

When Trujillo was assassinated by a group of Dominican dissidents on May 30, 1961, some hoped that the country would turn a corner. The promise of change, however, was short-lived. President Joaquín Balaguer officially assumed the office. He renamed the capital Santo Domingo. After a groundswell of unrest and at the insistence of the USA, a seven-member Council of State, which included two of the men who'd taken part in Trujillo's deadly ambush, was established to guide the country until elections were held in December 1962. The first free elections in many years in the DR was won by the scholar-poet Juan Bosch Gaviño.

Nine months later, after introducing liberal policies including the redistribution of land, the creation of a new constitution and guaranteeing civil and individual rights, Bosch was deposed by yet another military coup in September 1963. Wealthy landowners, to whom democracy was a threat, and a group of military leaders led by Generals Elías Wessin y Wessin and Antonio Imbert Barreras installed Donald Reid Cabral, a prominent businessman, as president. Bosch fled into exile but his supporters, calling themselves the Constitutionalists, took to the streets and seized the National Palace. Santo Domingo saw the stirrings of a civil war; the military launched tank assaults and bombing runs against civilian protesters.

Trujillo's nicknames included Hot Balls, the Goat, the Chief and the Butcher.

The fighting continued until the USA intervened yet again. This time the Johnson administration, after losing Cuba, feared a left-wing or communist takeover of the Dominican Republic, despite the fact that Bosch wasn't a communist and papers later revealed US intelligence had identified only 54 individuals who were part of the movement fighting the military junta. The official reason was that the US could no longer guarantee the safety of its nationals and so over 500 marines landed in Santo

1956

Ozzie Virgil (Ozvaldo Virgil) becomes the first Dominican to play in the baseball major leagues as an infielder for the New York Giants.

1961

Despite the support he has received over the years from the US as a staunch anticommunist ally, Rafael Trujillo is assassinated by a group of CIA-trained Dominican dissidents.

1962–63

In the first democratic election in nearly 40 years, Juan Bosch, leader of the left-leaning Dominican Revolutionary Party, is elected president and later removed in a coup orchestrated by a three-person junta.

1965

Lyndon Johnson ultimately sends 42,000 US Army personnel and Marines to invade the DR, ostensibly to prevent a civil war. The troops remain until October 1966.

Domingo on April 27, 1965. A week later, and only 40 years since the previous occupation, 14,000 American military personnel were stationed in the Dominican Republic.

Caudillo Redux

After losing power to revolutionaries led by Fidel Castro, Cuban dictator Fulgencio Batista fled to Trujillo City.

Elections were held in July 1966. Balaguer defeated Bosch. Many voters had feared a Bosch victory would lead to civil war. Bosch would go on to contest elections in 1978, 1982, 1986, 1990 and 1994, always losing. Balaguer, meanwhile, would outlast every Latin American ruler except Fidel Castro. Not the typical authoritarian dictator, Balaguer was a poet and a writer – in one book he argues against interracial marriage – who lived in the servant's quarters of his female-dominated home.

Taking a page from Trujillo's playbook, Balaguer curtailed opposition through bribes and intimidation and went on to win reelection in 1970 and 1974. Despite economic growth, in part fueled by investment and aid from the USA, who saw Balaguer as a staunch anticommunist ally, Balaguer lost the 1978 election to a wealthy cattle rancher named Silvestre Antonio Guzmán. The transfer of power wouldn't come easily, however; Balaguer ordered troops to destroy ballot boxes and declared himself the victor, standing down only after US president Jimmy Carter refused to recognize his victory.

In honor of the Mirabal sisters (Minerva, Paria and Maria Teresa), activists who were murdered by Trujillo's agents, the UN declared November 25, the day of their death, International Day for the Elimination of Violence Against Women.

As a result of plunging sugar prices and rising oil costs, the Dominican economy came to a standstill under Guzmán's administration; he committed suicide shortly before leaving office in 1982. His successor, Salvador Jorge Blanco, adhered to a fiscal austerity plan under pressure from the International Monetary Fund, measures that were far from popular with many ordinary Dominicans. (Blanco, who passed away in 2011, is the only president in the DR to have been prosecuted for corruption.) But old dictators don't go easily and Balaguer, 80 years old and blind with glaucoma, returned to power in the 1986 election.

For the next eight years Balaguer set about reversing every economic reform of the Blanco program; the result was five-fold devaluing of the Dominican peso and soaring annual inflation rates. With little chance of prospering at home, almost 900,000 Dominicans, or 12% of the country's population, had moved to New York by 1990. After Balaguer won the 1990 and 1994 elections (amid accusations of electoral fraud), the military grew weary of his rule and he agreed to cut his last term short, hold elections and, most importantly, not be a candidate. But it wouldn't be his last campaign – he would run once more at the age of 92, winning 23% of the vote in the 2000 presidential election. Thousands would mourn his death two years later, despite the fact that he prolonged the Trujillo-style dictatorship for decades. His most lasting legacy may be the Faro a Colón, an enormously expensive monument to

1966

Trujillo's former vice-president, Dr Joaquín Balaguer, is elected president.

➡ Punta Cana (p96) became popular with tourists in the '70s

February 1973

A state of emergency is declared by Balaguer after a small guerilla invasion fails; Bosch goes into hiding after Balaguer implicates him in insurgency.

the discovery of the Americas that drained Santo Domingo of electricity whenever the lighthouse was turned on.

Moving Away From the Past

The Dominican people signaled their desire for change in electing Leonel Fernández, a 42-year-old lawyer who grew up in New York City, as president in 1996; he edged out three-time candidate José Francisco Peña Gómez in a runoff. Still, the speed of his initial moves shocked the nation. Fernández forcibly retired two dozen generals, encouraged his defense minister to submit to questioning by the civilian attorney general and fired the defense minister for insubordination – all in a single week. In the four years of his first presidential term, he presided over strong economic growth and privatization, and lowered inflation and high rates of unemployment and illiteracy – accusations of endemic corruption, however, remained pervasive.

Hipólito Mejía, a former tobacco farmer, succeeded Fernández in 2000 and immediately cut spending and increased fuel prices – not exactly the platform he ran on. The faltering US economy and September 11 attacks ate into Dominican exports, as well as cash remittances and foreign tourism. Corruption scandals involving the civil service, unchecked spending, electricity shortages and several bank failures, which cost the government in the form of huge bailouts for depositors, all spelled doom for Mejía's reelection chances.

More of the Same

Familiar faces reappear again and again in Dominican politics and Fernández returned to the national stage by handily defeating Mejía in the 2004 presidential elections. In 2005, to the consternation of many, the Dominican Supreme Court ruled that the children of visitors 'in transit' were not afforded citizenship. This ruling defined illegal immigrants, which virtually all Haitian workers are, as 'in transit', meaning that even those Haitians who were born in the DR and lived their entire lives there were denied citizenship. And on the border, by the end of 2007 there were 200 UN soldiers, mostly from other Caribbean countries, helping to buttress the DR army's attempts to stop the flow of drugs and arms across the Haitian border. In early 2008 tensions flared again along the border over accusations of cattle rustling and reprisals, and Dominican chickens being turned away because of fears over avian flu.

In May 2008, with the US and world economies faltering and continued conflict with Haiti, Fernández was reelected to another presidential term. He avoided a runoff despite mounting questions about the logic of spending US$700 million on Santo Domingo's subway system, rising

The Dictator Next Door: The Good Neighbor Policy and the Trujillo Regime in the Dominican Republic, 1930-1945, by Eric Paul Roorda, details the compromises the US government made with Trujillo's regime and its complicity in its survival.

The Dominican Republic: A National History, by Frank Moya Pons, is the most comprehensive book on the country's colorful history.

Why the Cocks Fight, by Michele Wucker, examines Dominican-Haitian relations through the metaphor of cockfighting.

1982

Distraught over revelations of financial corruption and improprieties, incumbent President Silvestre Antonio Guzman commits suicide, with just over a month left in term.

1986

After an eight-year hiatus, Joaquín Balaguer, 80 years old and blind, is elected to his fifth term as president despite his previous administration's corruption and dismal human rights record.

1996

After massive election fraud and widespread national and international pressure, Balaguer agrees to step down after two years and Leonel Fernández is elected president.

2003–04

A growing financial crisis sparks widespread public unrest and protests, including a general strike in which several people are killed and scores injured by police.

gas prices, the fact that the DR still had one of the highest rates of income inequality in Latin America and the government's less-than-stellar response to the devastation wrought by Tropical Storm Noel in late October 2007. Over 66,000 people were displaced from their homes by the storm and around 100 communities were completely isolated, some for over two weeks, because of damaged roads and bridges. There were massive layoffs in the agricultural industry after crop production took a major hit.

Though considered competent and by some even forward-thinking, it's still common to hear people talk about Fernández unenthusiastically as the typical politician beholden to special interests. The more cynical observers claim that the Fernández administration was allied with corrupt business and government officials that perpetuated a patronage system different from Trujillo's rule in name only.

The Last Playboy: The High Life of Porfirio Rubirosa, by Shawn Levy, tells the life story of the DR's most famous womanizer and Trujillo intimate.

Aftershocks

In the aftermath of the devastating earthquake that struck Haiti in January 2010, the Dominican government provided medical and humanitarian assistance, and much of the aid from other countries was shipped overland through the DR. However, the thaw in relations only lasted so long. Haiti's cholera epidemic that erupted the following year led to the temporary closure of some border crossings, which ignited more conflict: several Haitians were killed and scores injured in protests. A rising number of incidents at the end of 2010 and beginning of 2011 left dozens of Haitians dead and hundreds injured in clashes in poor barrios around the country. Some Dominicans, claiming they were trying to evict illegal Haitians, say they were justified by the threat of cholera and crime. In the beginning of February 2011, the Dominican government initiated a widespread crackdown, deporting 'illegal' Haitians back over the border.

2008	2010	2011	May 2012
In May Leonel Fernández convincingly wins reelection to his third presidential term; a 2002 constitutional amendment allows him to again run for office.	Haiti's cholera epidemic, following the devasting earthquake, spreads into the DR, reigniting border conflicts.	La Romana's Los Toros del Este sweep the Estrellas of San Pedro in five games to win only their second DR winter baseball pennant.	Danilo Medina wins the presidential elections (after Fernandez decided not to pursue constitutional changes that would have allowed him to run for a fourth term).

Music & Dance

Life in the Dominican Republic seems to move to a constant, infectious rhythm, and music has always been an important part of the country's heritage. Despite, or perhaps in part because of, the country's tumultuous history of bitter divisions, revolutions and dictatorial rule, the DR has made significant contributions to the musical world, giving rise to some of Latin music's most popular and influential styles.

Merengue

Merengue is the national dance music of the Dominican Republic. From the minute you arrive until the minute you leave, merengue will be coming at you full volume: in restaurants, public buses, taxis, at the beach or simply walking down the street. Rhythmically driven and heavy on the downbeat, merengue follows a common 2-4 or 4-4 beat pattern and Domnicans dance with passion and flair. But what sets merengue apart from other musical forms is the presence of traditional signature instruments and how they work within the two- or four-beat structure. Merengue is typically played with a two-headed drum called a tambora, a guitar, an accordion-like instrument known as a melodeon, and a güira – a metal instrument that looks a little like a cheese grater and is scraped using a metal or plastic rod.

Since 1986 merengue and bachata superstar Juan Luís Guerra has won almost every major music award possible, including two Grammys, 15 Latin Grammys and three Premios Soberanos, the DR's highest musical award.

If you hit a dance club and take a shine to the music, you may want to pick up some CDs before leaving the country. A few of the most popular musicians include Johnny Ventura, Coco Band, Wilfredo Vargas, Milly y Los Vecinos, Fernando Villalona, Joseito Mateo, Rubby Perez, Miriam Cruz, Milly Quezada and, perhaps the biggest name of all, Santo Domingo–born Juan Luis Guerra. Rita Indiana y los Misterios, led by the eponymously named vocalist and an accomplished writer, have created an 'experimental' merengue sound, blending alternative rock and pop with traditional forms.

Even if you don't dance – something Dominicans will find peculiar – you'll be impressed by the skill and artfulness of the way even amateurs move their feet and hips in perfect time to the music. The *merengue típico*, or traditional folk genre, is a fast two-step dance characterized by the close proximity of the dancers. The most prevalent of the folk styles, called *perico ripiao*, originated in the northern valley region of Cibao and is still commonly played today.

From its humble rural beginnings, merengue evolved into a more modernized orchestral 'big band' style, largely due to its elevated status as a national symbol embraced by Trujillo in the 1930s. In typical Trujillo fashion, he ordered many merengues to be composed in his honor. While the earlier traditional forms established the complexities of the rhythm and the development of the dance, it was the orchestral style, called *orquesta merengue* or *merengue de salon*, that drove merengue's rise to prominence by the 1980s, becoming a worthy competitor of salsa. By the 1990s, contemporary merengue had incorporated electronic drum beats and synthesizers, and this new sound was heard blaring out of cars, stereos and nightclubs from Puerto Rico to New York City.

Top Music Festivals

- *Carnaval – end of February, all over the country*
- *Dominican Republic Jazz Festival – end of October and beginning of November in Puerto Plata, Sosúa and Cabarete*
- *Santo Domingo Merengue Festival – last week in July/first week in August*
- *Puerto Plata Merengue Festival – end of September*

For most Dominicans, talk of merengue's origins – and Dominican merengue didn't emerge as its own distinct genre until the mid-19th century – are wrapped up in notions of national and racial identity. Earlier versions existed in Cuba and Haiti, but Dominicans are often disinclined to admit African and Haitian influences on their culture. Many theories point to European-derived ballroom-dance styles. According to one popular myth, merengue originated in 1844, the year that the Dominican Republic was founded, to poke fun at a Dominican soldier who had abandoned his post during the Battle of Talanquera in the War of Independence. The Dominicans won the battle and, while celebrating the victory at night, soldiers mocked the cowardly deserter in song and dance. Eurocentric critics emphasize merengue's European elements; Afrocentric scholars may emphasize its African and Haitian elements; and those who celebrate racial amalgamation point to its synergistic nature.

BOOKS

Bachata: A Social History of Dominican Popular Music, by Deborah Pacini Hernandez, and *Merengue: Dominican Music and Dominican Identity,* by Paul Austerlitz, are academic examinations of the DR's two most important musical contributions and obsessions.

Bachata

Whereas merengue might be viewed as an urban sound, *bachata* is definitely the nation's 'country' music, of love and broken hearts in the hinterlands. Born in the poorest of Dominican neighborhoods, *bachata* emerged in the mid 20th century, after Trujillo's death, as a slow, romantic style played on the Spanish guitar. The term initially referred to informal, sometimes rowdy backyard parties in rural areas, finally emerging in Santo Domingo shanties.

The term *'bachata'* was meant as a slight by the urban elite, a reference to the music's supposed lack of sophistication. Often called 'songs of bitterness,' *bachata* tunes were no different to most romantic ballad forms, such as the Cuban bolero, but were perceived as low class, and didn't have the same political or social support as merengue. In fact, *bachata* was not even regarded as a style per se until the 1960s – and even then it was not widely known outside the Dominican Republic.

But widespread interest and acceptance grew largely because of the efforts of musician and composer Juan Luis Guerra, who introduced international audiences to this rich and sentimental form. Already credited with developing a more modern and socially conscious merengue, Guerra nearly single-handedly brought *bachata* out of obscurity, paving the way for many Dominican artists to come.

While merengue continues to be the more popular style, *bachata* has risen in popularity, particularly in New York City's Dominican community. Among the big names are Raulín Rodríguez, Antony Santos, Joe Veras, Luis Vargas, Quico Rodríguez, Frank Reyes and Leo Valdez. *Bachata Roja* is a compilation of classic *bachata* from the early 1960s to late 1980s; the pre-electric era when the music was entirely guitar based and drew on a variety of musical traditions, including Mexican *ranchera,* Puerto Rican *jíbaro,* Cuban bolero, guaracha and *son.* The record includes legendary musicians such as Edilio Paredes and Augusto Santos.

THE GÜIRA

The *güira* is a popular musical instrument used to infuse a song with a rhythmical rasping sound. It was originally adopted by Hispaniola's indigenous people – the Taínos – who employed dried, hollowed-out-gourds and a forked stick to produce music for their *areítos* (ceremonial songs). Today the *güira* has been modernized – but not by much. Instead of using vegetables, the modern *güira* is made of latten brass; it typically looks like a cylindrical cheese grater that is scraped with a long metal pick. The rasping sound is essentially the same – the modern-day instrument just lasts a little longer. The next time you hear a merengue or a *bachata* song, listen for this centuries-old sound.

COCOLOS

Cocolos (English-speaking immigrants from the Eastern Caribbean who primarily settled in the region around San Pedro de Macorís) have their own distinctive musical and dance culture. A good time to experience this hybrid of African and Caribbean rhythms is February 27, the national holiday celebrating Dominican independence from Haiti.

Salsa

Salsa, like *bachata*, is heard throughout the Caribbean, and is very popular in the DR. Before they called it salsa, many musicians in New York City had already explored the possibilities of blending Cuban rhythms with jazz. In the 1950s, the Latin big-band era found favor with dancers and listeners alike, and in the mid-1960s, Dominican flutist, composer and producer Johnny Pacheco founded the Fania label, which was exclusively dedicated to recording 'tropical Latin' music.

In 1818 the Spanish colonial governor ordered nighttime dancing in the street without a permit to be illegal.

With Cuba cut off from the United States politically as well as culturally, it was no longer appropriate to use the term 'Afro-Cuban'. The word 'salsa' (literally 'sauce') emerged as a clever marketing tool, reflecting not only the music but the entire atmosphere, and was the perfect appellation for a genre of music resulting from a mixture of styles: Cuban-based rhythms played by Puerto Ricans, Dominicans, Africans and African Americans.

By the 1970s salsa was hot, not only in the US, but also in South America and Central America. Even European, Japanese and African audiences were treated to this new sound. In the 1980s, salsa evolved into a bland version of itself – the so-called '*salsa romántica*' genre – and during this time Dominican merengue served up some worthy competition. Since the 1990s, however, salsa rebounded and spread throughout the globe, living on in new generations of musicians and dancers alike.

The following individuals and groups enjoy particularly favorable reputations in the DR: Tito Puente, Tito Rojas, Jerry Rivera, Tito Gómez, Grupo Niche, Gilberto Santa Rosa, Mimi Ibara, Marc Anthony and Leonardo Paniagua.

Hit Songs

Joseito Mateo – 'El Negrito de Batey' (merengue)

Luis Vargas – 'Volvia el Dolor' (merengue)

Antony Santos – 'Voy pa'lla' (bachata)

La Fabrica – 'En Cuatro Gomas' (reggaeton)

Don Miguelo – 'Que tu Quieres' (reggateon)

Reggaeton & Rap

Reggaeton, a mix of American-style hip-hop and Latin rhythms, has exploded onto the Dominican scene. Reggaeton has a distinctly urban flavor, and its fast-paced danceable beats, street-life narratives and catchy choruses make it the party music of choice for many young Dominicans. In terms of origins, Panama claims it was the first country to bring Spanish-influenced reggae to the underground scene in the late 1970s. But it was Puerto Rico that gave the music a whole new beat and name in the 1980s and '90s.

Since that time, reggaeton has become increasingly popular throughout the DR, and Dominican artists have made their own stamp on the genre. Like hip-hop in the US, reggaeton has evolved from a musical genre to an entire culture, with its own brand of fashion and commerce. Artists to look out for include the well-known reggaeton duo Wisin & Yandel, Pavel Nuñez, an established star whose music is a mix between folk and Latin, and Kat DeLuna, a pop singer whose music is a hodgepodge of styles and rhythms.

Rap Dominicano, a relatively new musical sub-genre, is pounded out of the Dominican barrios, and has taken its place alongside reggaeton as the most popular forms of music among Dominican youth. Although rap is an imported genre and the sounds blasting from the speakers don't resemble the typical sounds of the DR, Dominican rap artists have managed to weave the sounds of *bachata* and merengue into their tracks, rapping about an urban upbringing that is uniquely their own. A few artists to look out for are El Lapiz Conciente, Vakero, Joa, Toxic Crow, Punto Rojo and R1.

Baseball: A Dominican Passion

Not just the USA's game, *beísbol* is an integral part of the Dominican social and cultural landscape. So much so that Dominican ballplayers that have made good in the US are without doubt the most popular and revered figures in the country. Over 400 Dominicans have played in the major leagues (in 2013, nearly 100 out of a total of 856 players were Dominican-born), including stars like David Ortiz, Albert Pujols, Robinson Cano, Sammy Sosa and Juan Marichal, the only Dominican to be inducted into the Hall of Fame.

Getting to First Base

The origin of baseball in the DR is intertwined with the beginnings of the sugar industry, first in Cuba and later in the DR. Around the same time that American business ambitions were directed toward the Caribbean, particularly Cuba, baseball was being established in the states. When Cuban plantation owners fled their country during a failed war of independence in 1868, they brought with them their passion for the game, which they learned from the Americans (where and when the game was originally established is open for dispute).

Workers from the English-speaking Caribbean who were brought to the DR to work in the cane fields were already skilled cricket players, bringing a familiarity with the general concepts of batting, pitching and fielding. With few leisure activities available, plant owners encouraged baseball rather than cricket and organized competitive teams into a 'sugar league.' Cubans, Americans and Dominicans in Santo Domingo, La Vega and near Santiago also formed their own teams.

But it was the US embargo of Cuba that began in 1962 (as well as free agency that began in the 1970s) that really accelerated the recruitment of Dominican players, since fewer Cubans were willing to defect – a requirement imposed by the government. Major-league scouts turned to other Caribbean countries, including the DR, to pick up the slack and Dominicans, unlike Puerto Ricans who are American citizens, were not subject to draft rules at the time.

The movie *Sugar* tells the story of a young Dominican baseball prospect drafted to play in the US minor leagues, and the loneliness and dislocation he and other players experience.

Santiago's baseball team was originally named 'Sandino' in honor of Augusto César Sandino, the Nicaraguan guerrilla leader who resisted the US invasion forces. After Trujillo came to power he forced the team to change its name to Aguilas Cibeanas.

Drafting Dilemmas

For a young prospect in the Dominican Republic the financial incentives of just being drafted, let alone actually playing a single game, in the major leagues are considerable. The average bonus (US$100,000) alone can provide a down payment on a home and provide for family members. However, the odds are overwhelmingly against success – only 3% of those signed make it to the majors – and when a young teenager pins their hopes on baseball (players are eligible for recruitment at 16), education usually falls by the wayside.

A series of high-profile issues have arisen, complicating the often incestuous relationship between Dominican baseball and the major leagues. Nearly every team has an academy here – a mix of university

BASEBALL TEAMS

- **Tigres de Licey** (Santo Domingo)
- **Leones del Escogido** (Santo Domingo)
- **Aguilas Cibeanas** (Santiago)
- **Estrellas Orientales** (San Pedro de Macorís)
- **Los Toros del Este** (La Romana)
- **Gigantes del Cibao** (San Francisco de Macorís)

dormitory, work camp and health club. Problems include steroid use, which isn't technically illegal in the DR, fake birth certificates intentionally misstating a player's age (younger to overstate potential and older to allow recruitment) and the increasingly questionable role that unregulated *buscones* play in the whole system. Taken from the Spanish verb '*buscar*,' to look for, *buscones* are more than merely scouts. They train, feed, house and educate promising players, grooming them to be signed by the majors in the hopes of one day gaining a large percentage of whatever signing bonus their prospects earn.

According to critics, the legacy of this homegrown corruption helps explains why more than 50% of players caught violating the major league's drug policy since 2007 are Dominicans (the most high profile case of course involves the Yankees' Alex Rodriguez who is of Dominican descent).

One in six of the 471 Dominicans who played at least one game in the major leagues up to 2008 (the most recent, reliable count) came from San Pedro de Macorís.

Take Me Out to 'El Partido de Beísbol'

The Dominican professional baseball league's season runs from October to January, and is known as the Liga de Invierno (Winter League; the winner of the DR league competes in the Caribbean World Series against other Latin-American countries). The country has six professional teams. Because the US and Dominican seasons don't overlap, many Dominican players in the US major leagues and quite a few non-Dominicans play in the winter league in the DR as well.

Needless to say, the quality of play is high (the DR went undefeated in winning the World Baseball Classic in 2013), but even if you're not a fan of the sport, it's worth checking out a game or two. It's always a fun afternoon or evening. Fans are decked out in their respective team's colors waving pennants and flags, as rabidly partisan as the Yankees–Red Sox rivalry, and dancers in hot pants perform to loud merengue beats on top of the dugouts between innings. Games usually don't start on time and the stands aren't filled until several innings have passed. The best place to take in a game is Estadio Quisqueya (p70) in Santo Domingo. For tickets, head to the stadium with time to spare before the start of play (as early as possible for big games).

From June to August there is also a Liga del Verano (Summer League) if you're in the DR outside of regular season. Various major-league franchises – the San Francisco Giants, the Toronto Blue Jays, the Arizona Diamondbacks and the New York Yankees, to name a few – maintain farm teams in the DR, and summer-league play is a semiformal tournament between these teams. Games are held at smaller stadiums around town.

The Eastern Stars: How Baseball Changed the Dominican Town of San Pedro de Macorís, by Mark Kurlansky, is a comprehensive history of baseball in the DR, with a focus on San Pedro de Macorís, known as the 'city of shortstops'.

Art & Architecture

The legacy of Hispaniola's diversity of peoples, from the original Taíno inhabitants to European settlers and Haitian emigres, has translated into a mix of artistic voices and styles. Walking down city streets lined with some of the finest examples of Spanish colonial architecture in the New World, you'll hear a soundtrack of merengue beats. Many writers are preoccupied with politics, history and questions of national identity and a through line in the visual arts has been a romanticization of the Dominican rural life.

Literature

The Dominican Republic's literary history dates to the Spanish colonial period (1492–1795). It was then that Bartolomé de Las Casas, a Spanish friar, recorded the early history of the Caribbean and pleaded for fair treatment of the Taínos in his famous *Historia de las Indias* (History of the Indies). In the same era, Gabriel Téllez, a priest who helped to reorganize the convent of Our Lady of Mercy in Santo Domingo, wrote his impressive *Historia general de la Orden de la Mercéd* (General History of the Order of Mercy).

During the Haitian occupation of Santo Domingo (1822–44), a French literary style became prominent, and many Dominican writers who emigrated to other Spanish-speaking countries made names for themselves there. With the first proclamation of independence in 1844, Félix María del Monte created the country's principal poetic form – a short, patriotic poem based on local events of the day.

POETS

San Pedro de Macorís is known for its poets: Gastón Fernando Deligne, Pedro Mir and René del Risco Bermúdez, among others, were either born here or drew their inspiration living in this city.

Dominican poetry flourished in the late 19th century, primarily through the three figures of Salome Ureña, Joaquín Pérez and Gastón Fernando Deligne. Pérez's collection, *Fantasías Indíginas* (Indian Fantasies), imagines encounters between Spanish conquistadores and the native Taíno. Pedro Mir established himself while living in exile in Cuba during the Trujillo regime and was later named Poet Laureate in 1984.

During the late 19th and early 20th centuries, three literary movements occurred in the DR: *indigenismo, criollismo* and *postumismo. Indigenismo* exposed the brutalities the Taínos experienced at the hands of the Spaniards. *Criollismo* focused on the local people and their customs. And *postumismo* dealt with the repression that Rafael Trujillo's iron-fisted leadership brought. Some writers, such as Manuel and Lupo Fernández Rueda, used clever metaphors to protest against the regime. Juan Bosch Gaviño, writing from exile, penned numerous stories that openly attacked Trujillo. Bosch, who held the presidency for only seven months in 1963, is one of the more influential literary figures in the DR, both as an essayist tackling social problems and as a novelist and short-story writer.

Only a few Dominican novels have been translated into English. Viriato Sención's *They Forged the Signature of God,* winner of the DR's 1993 National Fiction award (after realizing that the book was critical of both Trujillo and himself, Balaguer rescinded the prize) and the country's all-time best seller, follows three seminary students suffering oppression at the hands of both the state and the church. Though slightly preachy, it

AN UNLIKELY MAN OF LETTERS

Joaquín Balaguer, president of the DR from 1960 to 1962, 1966 to 1978, and from 1986 to 1996, was a writer as well as a strongman ruler. He published over 50 works, from poetry and biographies to criticism and a novel. Maybe his most infamous work was his autobiography *Memorias de un Cortesano de la Era de Trujillo* (Memoirs of a Courtesan in the Era of Trujillo). In it he includes a blank page, which refers to the murder of outspoken Dominican journalist Orlando Martinez Howley in 1975. Balaguer apparently intended the page to be a memorial to Howley and assigned someone to reveal the details of the assassination – Balaguer denied he gave the orders – after his death. He died in 2002 and no one has come forward.

provides another perspective on the Trujillo regime besides the exceptional *Fiesta del Chivo* (Feast of the Goat) by the Peruvian novelist Mario Vargas Llosa.

Ten years after publishing the short-story collection *Drown*, Junot Díaz received critical acclaim for his 2007 novel *The Brief Wondrous Life of Oscar Wao*, a stylistically inventive story of a self-professed Dominican nerd in New Jersey and the tragic history of his family in the DR. Less well known, but perhaps a more devastating picture of the Dominican diaspora's rejection of the conventional American Dream, is Maritza Pérez's *Geographies of Home*. For Spanish readers, other recommended young Dominican authors are Pedro Antonio Valdés *(Bachata del angel caído, Carnaval de Sodoma)*, Rita Indiana Hernández *(La estrategia de Chochueca, Papi)* and Aurora Arias *(Inyi's Paradise, Fin del mundo, Emoticons)*.

In the Time of the Butterflies is an award-winning novel by Julia Álvarez, about three sisters slain for their part in a plot to overthrow Trujillo. Also by Álvarez is *How the García Girls Lost Their Accents,* describing an emigrant Dominican family in New York. Other well-known contemporary Dominican writers include José Goudy Pratt, Jeannette Miller and Ivan García Guerra. A recommended Spanish language website focused on past and contemporary Dominican writers is www.escritoresdominicanos.com.

Those colorful and bright canvases of simple rural scenes lined up on virtually every street corner and piece of pavement where tourists are expected are actually reproductions of iconic Haitian paintings; these are often churned out with house paint.

Painting

The Dominican art scene today is quite healthy, thanks in no small part to dictator Rafael Trujillo. Although his 31 years of authoritarian rule in many ways negated the essence of creative freedom, Trujillo had a warm place in his heart for painting, and in 1942 he established the Escuela Nacional de Bellas Artes (National School of Fine Arts). Fine Dominican artwork predates the school, but it really wasn't until the institution's doors opened that Dominican art underwent definitive development.

If the artwork looks distinctly Spanish, it's because the influence is undeniable. During the Spanish Civil War (1936–39), many artists fled Franco's fascist regime to start new lives in the Dominican Republic. Influential artists include Manolo Pascual, José Gausachs, José Vela-Zanetti, Eugenio Fernández Granell and José Fernández Corredor.

In the late 1960s in Santiago, Grupo Friordano, as well as other small groups of socially engaged artists, began politically conscious and ideological aesthetic movements. Painters like Daniel Henriquez, Orlando Menicucci and Yori Morjel considered their work as engaged critiques of society; Morjel painted traditional rural scenes and helped develop a distinctly Dominican vernacular style.

If you visit any of the art galleries in Santo Domingo or Santiago, keep an eye out for Cándido Bidó's bright, colorful paintings of scenes from his native Cibao valley (Bidó passed away in 2011); Adriana Billini

Best Art Museums

Centro León, Santiago

Museo de Arte Moderno, Santo Domingo

Museo Bellapart, Santo Domingo

Gautreau, who is famous for portraits that are rich in expressionist touches; the cubist forms of Jaime Colson, emphasizing the social crises of his day; Luis Desangles, considered the forerunner of folklore in Dominican painting; Mariano Eckert, representing the realism of everyday life; Juan Bautista Gómez, whose paintings depict the sensuality of the landscape; Guillo Pérez, whose works of oxen, carts and canefields convey a poetic vision of life at the sugar mill; Ivan Tovar's surrealist Dali-esque works; the traditional realist paintings of Ada Balcacer; Mariam Balcacer, a photographer who lives in Italy; the steel sculptures of Johnny Bonnelleg Ricart; and, finally, the enigmatic and dream-like paintings of Dionisio Blanco.

The Eduardo León Jimenes Art Contest in Santiago began in 1964 and is the longest-running privately sponsored art competition in Latin America.

Also well represented is what's known as 'primitive art' – Dominican and Haitian paintings that convey rural Caribbean life with simple and colorful figures and landscapes. These paintings are created by amateur painters – some would say skilled craftsmen – who reproduce the same painting hundreds of times. They are sold everywhere there are tourists; you're sure to get an eyeful regardless of the length of your trip.

A good resource on Dominican art is the authoritative *Enciclopedia de las Artes Plásticas Dominicanas* (Encyclopedia of Dominican Visual Arts) by Cándido Gerón. Illustrations and Spanish text are followed by English translations; look for copies at used bookstores in the Santo Domingo's Zona Colonial.

Architecture

The quality and variety of architecture found in the Dominican Republic has no equal in the Caribbean. Santo Domingo's Zona Colonial, a well-preserved grid of Spanish colonial buildings, is a showcase of landmarks. An imposing fortress – the oldest still intact in the Americas – stands adjacent to mansions and Dominican and Franciscan convents. The Americas' oldest functioning cathedral, the Catedral Primada de América, whose construction began in 1514, stands in the center. You'll see plenty of the Baroque, Romanesque, Gothic and Renaissance styles which were popular in Europe during the colonial times.

Buildings Not to Miss

- *Museo Alcázar de Colón, Santo Domingo*
- *Catedral Primada de América, Santo Domingo*
- *Basilica de Nuestra Señora de la Altagracia, Higuey*
- *Catedral de la Concepción, La Vega*

Elsewhere in Santo Domingo and Santiago you can see examples of Cuban Victorian, Caribbean gingerbread and art deco. The buildings in Puerto Plata vary between the vernacular Antillean and the pure Victorian; sometimes English, sometimes North American. Sugar magnates in San Pedro de Macorís built late-Victorian style homes with concrete (it was the first city in the DR to use reinforced concrete in construction). And rural clapboard homes – Monte Cristi in the far northwest has these in spades – have a charm all their own: small, square, single-story and more colorful than a handful of jelly beans, you'll find yourself slowing down to take a longer look.

More contemporary and postmodern architecture is best seen in homes commissioned by wealthy Dominicans, in upscale neighborhoods in Santo Domingo and Santiago. Elsewhere, including Jarabacoa in the central highlands, along the southeastern coastline around Punta Cana, and around Puerto Plata on the north coast, are enclaves of vacation homes; these communities are worth a look for creative and high-concept design.

Easily the best book on architecture in the country is *Arquitectura Dominicana: 1492–2008*, edited by Gustavo Luis More (available at bookstores in Santo Domingo and the Museo Centro León in Santiago). Another excellent resource is *Interiors*, a book of photographs by Polibio Diaz, which shows glimpses into the homes of ordinary Dominicans with respect and care.

Dominican Landscapes

If wealth was measured by landscape, the DR would be among the richest countries in the Americas. Sharing the island of Hispaniola, the second-largest island in the Caribbean (after Cuba), it's a dynamic country of high mountains, fertile valleys and watered plains, and an amazing diversity of ecosystems. The rich landscape is matched by an equally rich biodiversity with over 5600 species of plants and close to 500 vertebrate species on the island, many of these endemic.

The Land

The island's geography owes more to the Central American mainland than its mostly flat neighboring islands. The one thing that Hispaniola has in spades is an abundance of mountains. Primary among mountain ranges is the Cordillera Central that runs from Santo Domingo into Haiti, where it becomes the Massif du Nord, fully encompassing a third of the island's landmass. The Cordillera Central is home to Pico Duarte, the Caribbean's highest mountain (at 3087m), which is so big it causes a rain shadow that makes much of southwest DR very arid. Other ranges include the Cordillera Septentrional, rising dramatically from the coast near Cabarete, and the Cordillera Orientale, along the southern shoreline of Bahía de Samaná. Between the ranges lie a series of lush and fertile valleys. Coffee, rice, bananas and tobacco thrive here, as well as in the plains around Santo Domingo. In comparison, sections of southwest DR are semi-desert.

One of the coldest parts of the country is Reservo Científica Valle Nuevo, southeast of Constanza on the way to San Jose de Ocoa, with temperatures as low as -8°C and vegetation similar to the European Alps.

The unique landscape of Hispaniola is due to the 90-million-year-old movements of the earth's crust. As it slowly ground past North America, the Caribbean Plate cracked and crumpled to form the islands stretching from Cuba to Puerto Rico. The plate is still moving at 1cm to 2cm per year, and continues to elevate Hispaniola.

Wildlife

The problems of colonizing an island are clear, with plants heavily reliant on seeds and roots arriving on floating rafts of vegetation, often with animal hitchhikers. Reptiles make the best long-distance voyagers and over 140 species are found on the island, compared to around 60 amphibians and 20 land mammals (only two of which survived the arrival of Europeans).

Published in 2013, *Ruta Barrancolí: A Bird Finding Guide to the Dominican Republic*, by Steven Latta and Kate Wallace has 33 maps and descriptions of 44 sites.

Birds

More than 300 species of bird have been recorded in the DR, including more than two dozen found nowhere else in the world. Species include the white-tailed tropicbird, magnificent frigatebird, roseate spoonbill and greater flamingo, plus unique endemic species such as the Hispaniolan lizard-cuckoo, ashy-faced owl and Hispaniolan emerald hummingbird.

Travelers are most likely to encounter birds on beaches and coastal waterways – specifically herons, egrets, ibis, rails, pelicans and gulls. Some of the best spots for twitchers in the DR are Parque Nacional

Jaragua (p196), Parque Nacional Los Haitises (p106), Parque Nacional Monte Cristi (p158) and Laguna Limón. More-determined travelers taking the time to wander into some of the rich wildlife areas in the DR's interior can expect to encounter a tremendous variety of forest birds.

Favorites among birdwatchers include the odd palmchat, DR's national bird, which builds large apartment-like nests where each pair sleeps in its own chamber.

Bats are the only nonendangered, protected species on the island. They eat as many as 2000 mosquitoes a night, helping to reduce the transmission of dengue and other mosquito-borne diseases.

Land Mammals

The arrival of Europeans, who introduced many disruptive species of their own, proved disastrous for Hispaniola's land mammals. Rats, cats, pigs and mongooses all tore through the local wildlife with severe consequences.

Just two native mammal species remain, clinging to survival in scattered pockets throughout Haiti and the DR. These are the hutia, a tree-climbing rodent, and the solenodon, an insectivore resembling a giant shrew. The solenodon is particularly threatened, and both species are nocturnal, making sightings extremely difficult.

Marine Mammals

The DR is world famous for its marine mammals, with manatees and humpback whales the star attractions. Travelers, however, are more likely to see dolphins unless they arrive in the right season or make a special trip to the right habitat. Several thousand humpback whales migrate south from frigid arctic waters to breed and calve in the tropical waters of the DR each winter (with their numbers peaking in January and February). The Bahía de Samaná is one of the foremost places in the world for boat-based whale-watching, and the Banco de Plata (Silver Banks) is one of only two places in the world where you can swim and snorkel (under supervision, on week-long live-aboard trips) with these truly magnificent creatures.

Most of the humpbacks visiting the DR spend the winter gorging on krill in the feeding grounds of the Gulf of Maine, off the US coast. They don't eat during their entire Caribbean stay.

Manatees feed on the seagrass meadows surrounding Hispaniola, hence their alternative name of 'sea cow'. Weighing up to 590kg and reaching 3.7m in length, manatees are shy, docile creatures; Parque Nacional Estero Hondo (near Punta Rusia) and Parque Nacional Monte Cristi (p158) are two of the better places to try to spot them.

Fish & Marine Life

The shallow coastal waters and coral reefs that surround the DR are home to a tremendous variety of sea life. So many species of tropical fish, crustaceans, sponges and corals can be found here that it takes a specialized field guide to begin to sort them out. Where they remain relatively intact and unfished – such as at Sosúa and Monte Cristi – they are stupendously beautiful. Some of the more colorful Caribbean reef fish include fluorescent fairy basslet, queen angelfish, rock beauty and blue tang, but each visitor will quickly find their own favorite. The warm waters are also home to four species of sea turtle: green, leatherback,

HURRICANE ALLEY

Caribbean hurricanes are born 3000km away off the west coast of Africa, where pockets of low pressure draw high winds toward them and the Earth's rotation molds them into their familiar counterclockwise swirl. The strongest and rarest of hurricanes, Category 5, typically build up in July and August and pack winds that exceed 250km/h. Hispaniola has often been hit hard by hurricanes. If you're near the coast when one is approaching, head inland, preferably to a large city where there are modern buildings and emergency services. Large resorts in the DR have sturdy hurricane shelters and evacuation procedures. Stay away from the beach, rivers, lakes and anywhere mudslides are a risk. Avoid standing near windows, as flying debris and sudden pressure changes can shatter the glass. The **National Hurricane Center** (www.nhc.noaa.gov) is the place to head for current information.

NATIONAL PARKS OF THE DOMINICAN REPUBLIC

The DR, home to some of the largest and most diverse parks in all the Caribbean, has set aside over 10% of its land as *parques nacionales* (national parks) and *reservas científicas* (scientific reserves) and is doing a reasonably good job of protecting these important local resources in the face of external pressures.

- **Parque Nacional Armando Bermúdez** This 766-sq-km park (p177) in the humid Cordillera Central is blanketed in pine trees, tree ferns and palm trees.
- **Parque Nacional del Este** In the southeastern part of the country, this park (p88) consists of dry and subtropical humid forest, with caves featuring Taíno petroglyphs, as well as the sandy beaches of Isla Saona. Look out for manatees and dolphins off the coast.
- **Parque Nacional Isla Cabritos** In the southwest, this park (p199) is a 24-sq-km island surrounded by the saltwater Lago Enriquillo. It is a refuge for crocodiles, iguanas, scorpions, flamingos, crows and cacti.
- **Parque Nacional Jaragua** At 1400 sq km, this is the largest park (p196) in the DR. It is made up of an arid thorn forest, an extensive marine area and the islands of Beata and Alto Velo. The park is rich in birdlife, particularly sea and shore birds, and its beaches are nesting grounds for hawksbill turtles.
- **Parque Nacional José del Carmen Ramírez** This 764-sq-km park (p177) is home to the Caribbean's tallest peak – Pico Duarte – and the headwaters of three of the DR's most important rivers: Yaque del Sur, San Juan and Mijo. Although there is occasional frost, the park is considered a subtropical humid mountain forest.
- **Parque Nacional La Isabela** On the north coast, this park (p157) was established in the 1990s to protect the ruins of the second European settlement in the New World. An on-site museum contains many objects that were used by the earliest European settlers.
- **Parque Nacional Los Haitises** On the Bahía de Samaná, this park's (p106) lush hills jut out of the ocean and are fringed with mangroves, tawny beaches and several Taíno caves. Bamboo, ferns and bromeliads thrive, along with the Hispaniolan parakeet.
- **Parque Nacional Monte Cristi** This 530-sq-km park (p158) in the extreme northwest contains a subtropical dry forest, coastal lagoons and seven islets. It is home to many seabirds. American crocodiles also inhabit the park's lagoons.
- **Parque Nacional Sierra de Bahoruco** In the southwest, this 800-sq-km park (p197) stretches from desert lowlands to 2000m-high tracts of pine. Along with the broad range of plant life (orchids abound), it's rich in birds, including the endemic white-necked crow.
- **Parque Nacional Submarino La Caleta** Only 22km from Santo Domingo, this 10-sq-km park (p39) is one of the country's most visited. Containing several healthy coral reefs and two shipwrecks, it is one of the top diving spots in the country.

hawksbill and loggerhead. You may have occasional encounters with these turtles while snorkeling, but from May to October they can be viewed in places such as Parque Nacional Jaragua (p196), coming ashore at night to lay their eggs on sandy beaches.

Reptiles & Amphibians

Reptiles were Hispaniola's most successful vertebrate colonists. You can expect to see lots of lizards (geckos in particular), but also keep your eye out for snakes, turtles and even the American crocodile (or caiman), found in sizable numbers in the brackish cross-border Lago Enriquillo – on the Haiti side it's Lac Azueï. There is also a Hispaniolan boa, its numbers reduced by mongoose predation. At opposite ends of the spectrum are the Jaragua lizard, which is the world's smallest terrestrial vertebrate (adults measure only 2.8cm), and the massive 10kg rhinoceros iguana. Frogs are the most numerous amphibians.

Want to put a name to that frog or gecko? Consult *Amphibians and Reptiles of the West Indies*, by Robert Henderson and Albert Schwartz.

Plants

Hispaniola presents a bewildering assortment of plants. In every season there is something flowering, fruiting or filling the air with exotic fragrances, and it makes the place truly magical. Nearly a third of the 5600-odd species are endemic, spread across more than 20 discrete vegetation zones, ranging from desert to subtropical forest to mangrove swamp.

Of these vegetation zones, by far the most prevalent is the subtropical forest, which blankets the slopes of many of the DR's valleys and is found throughout the Península de Samaná. This is a majestic landscape, dominated by royal palms with large curving fronds, and native mahogany trees.

True tropical rainforest is rare, both because areas receiving enough rainfall are scarce and because the grand trees of this forest type have been extensively logged. Green-leaved throughout the year, these dense humid forests support a wealth of tree ferns, orchids, bromeliads and epiphytes. Examples can still be found in the Vega Real.

Above 1830m, the habitat gives way to mountain forests characterized by pines and palms, as well as ferns, bromeliads, heliconias and orchids. Although threatened by coffee plantations and ranching, large tracts still exist in Parques Nacionales Armando Bermúdez and José del Carmen Ramírez.

Thorn and cacti forests abound in the southwest corner of the DR. Parque Nacional Jaragua (p196), the country's largest protected area, consists largely of thorn forest, cacti and agaves, and receives less than 700mm of rain a year.

Mangrove swamps are a characteristic feature along the coast around the DR's Bahía de Samaná and pockets along the northern coastline. They're hugely important wildlife habitats, serving as nurseries for many marine species and nesting grounds for water birds, as well as buffering the coast against the erosive power of storms and tides.

Waterfalls Not to be Missed

- *Salto de Jimenoa Uno, Jarabacoa*
- *Cascada El Limón, Las Terrenas*
- *Damajagua, south of Puerto Plata*
- *Aguas Blancas, Constanza*
- *Cascadas Ciguapa, south of Gaspar Hernández*

Environmental Issues

The DR has a rapidly growing population and millions of tourists a year, all of whom put severe pressure on the land. Water use, damage to marine ecosystems and, most of all, deforestation, present acute environmental challenges. Despite the government's continual efforts in setting aside pristine land, and at times banning commercial logging, parks and reserves remain chronically underfunded, and illegal logging and agricultural encroachment remain a problem, especially in the central highlands. It's estimated that the DR has lost 60% of its forests in the last 80 years (only 5% of Haiti's remain).

One of the more puzzling and serious issues concerns the rising waters of Lago Enriquillo which is twice as large as it was a decade ago. Tens of thousands of acres previously occupied by yucca, banana and cattle farms are now eerily submerged and the government is attempting to move an entire town threatened by flooding. The Ministry of the Environment, to the outrage of many residents and environmentalists, began clearing the Loma Charco Azul Biological Reserve (part of the Jaragua-Barahuco-Enrquillo Biosphere) in 2013 in order to replace lost agricultural acreage. Not only is the reserve home to many endemic species of flora and fauna (including Ricord's iguana and the Hispaniolan solenodon), but farmers also argue the arid land isn't a suitable trade-off for what was lost.

An overview of Caribbean coral reefs can be found in the eye-opening *A Guide to the Coral Reefs of the Caribbean*, by Mark Spalding.

Coastal resorts and villages continue to have a tremendous impact on the very seas that provide their livelihood. Pollution, runoff and other consequences of massive developments have destroyed many of the island's foremost reefs. Overfishing and the inadvertent destruction caused by careless humans transform reefs into gray shadows of their former selves.

Vertebrate species particularly endangered on Hispaniola include the Caribbean manatee, Caribbean monk seal, Atlantic spotted dolphin, American crocodile, rhinoceros iguana, Hispaniolan ground iguana, sea turtles, three species of freshwater turtle and dozens of bird species.

Survival Guide

Directory A–Z

Accommodations

Compared to other destinations in the Caribbean, lodging in the Dominican Republic is relatively affordable. That said, there is a limited number of options for independent travelers wishing to make decisions on the fly and for whom cost is a concern.

In some places, such as Santo Domingo, you can stay in restored colonial-era buildings with loads of character with comfortable accommodations (Santo Domingo's Sofitel Nicolas de Ovando is the choicest example) for less money than you would spend for a night at a bland international-chain-style hotel (Holiday Inn, Marriott and Sheraton, amongst others have a presence). And a good number of all-inclusives, especially outside the holidays and the high season, can be remarkably good deals considering what you get.

From US$200 and up (the ceiling is high for the most exclusive resorts), there's a big jump in terms of the quality of furnishings, food and service, and in the Dominican Republic, maybe more than elsewhere, you truly get what you pay for.

Pay budget room rates and you won't necessarily feel like you're on vacation, especially in the cities, but there are some exceptions. The DR has few proper hostels, and little backpacker culture of the sort found in the rest of Latin America, Europe and elsewhere. The walled compounds generically called '*cabañas turisticas*', with names suggestive of intercourse or romantic love, on the outskirts of most large towns are short-time hotels for couples seeking privacy.

Following are some guidelines to keep in mind:

- Assume that low-season rates are 20% to 50% less than high-season rates.
- Rooms booked a minimum of three days in advance on the internet are far cheaper (especially so at the all-inclusive resorts) than if you book via phone or, worst-case scenario, simply show up without a reservation.
- Be sure the rate you are quoted already includes the 23% room tax. We've experienced sticker shock when paying the bill after making reservations and booking online.
- The Dominican government doles out stars, from one to six (very few have received a six), though the qualifications for the rankings probably wouldn't match North American or European standards.
- Hotels geared towards business travelers, especially in Santo Domingo and Santiago, offer weekend discounts.
- Reservations are recommended for independent hotels in the high season.

SLEEPING PRICE RANGES

The following price ranges refer to a double room with bathroom in high season (December to March and July to August).

We've listed prices in the currency they are most commonly quoted on the ground – either RD$ or US$. Unless otherwise indicated the room tax of 23% is included in the price. We indicate when breakfast is included, which is often.

$ Less than RD$2100 (US$50)

$$ RD$2100-4200 (US$50-100)

$$$ More than RD$4200 (US$100)

SORTING THROUGH ALL THE ALL-INCLUSIVES

Consider the following questions if you're trying to choose an all-inclusive resort:

- **Location** What part of the country is the resort in? What sights are nearby?
- **The fine print** Other than the buffet, are all restaurants included? All alcoholic beverages? Motorized water sports?
- **Ocean front** Is the resort on the beach, across the street, a bus ride away?
- **Children** Is this a kid-friendly resort? Is there a kids' club? Babysitting service?
- **Entertainment** Are there nightly performances or live-music venues? How about a disco?
- **Busy?** Your mood and experience can be affected, depending on your tastes, if it's too crowded or too empty.

All-Inclusive Resorts

Easily the most popular form of lodging in the DR is the all-inclusive resort. Much of the prime beachfront property throughout the country is occupied by all-inclusives. By far the largest concentrations are in the Bávaro/Punta Cana area in the east, followed by Playa Dorada in the north; Boca Chica and Juan Dolio, both within easy driving distance of Santo Domingo, have small concentrations as well.

If you're looking for a hassle-free vacation, it's easy to understand the appeal of the all-inclusive. The majority offer at least one all-you-can-eat buffet and several stand-alone restaurants (these sometimes require reservations once you've arrived and sometimes cost extra) and food is usually available virtually around the clock.

Drinks (coffee, juice, soda, beer, wine, mixed drinks) are also unlimited and served up almost 24/7 from restaurants, beach and pool bars, cafes, discos etc. Most are located on the beach and have lounge chairs and towels, as well as several pools.

A variety of tours are on offer daily, including snorkeling, diving, trips to parks and sights in the surrounding area, city tours and horseback riding. If there isn't a golf course on the property, no doubt the concierge can arrange a tee time.

Several companies dominate the resort landscape in the Dominican Republic. Names such as Melia, Barcelo and Wyndham are plastered on signs everywhere from Puerto Plata to Bávaro. Often there will be several Melias, Barcelos or Wyndhams in the same area, ranging widely in terms of quality and costs – it can get confusing. While choosing the best resort for you or your family requires some homework, it's well worth the effort. Too often people's vacations are ruined by unrealistic expectations fostered by out-of-focus photos and inaccurate information found online; mediocre food is the most common complaint.

And if it's your first time visiting the Dominican Republic, it's difficult to have a sense of the geography of the area you're considering. For example, the Bávaro/Punta Cana region is quite large, and while some resorts are within walking distance of one another and local restaurants and shops, others are isolated and without a rental vehicle you might end up feeling stranded.

In reviews in this book, all-inclusive options will include a mention of 'all-incl' in the practicalities details where costs are shown.

Camping

Other than the basic free cabins en route to Pico Duarte, there are only a handful of formal campgrounds. You might have some luck in rural mountain areas or along deserted beaches – inland, you should ask the owner of the plot of land you are on before pitching a tent, and on the beach always – this can't be stressed enough – ask the Politur (tourist police) or local police if it is allowed and safe.

Rental Accommodations

If you'll be in the Dominican Republic for long – even a couple of weeks – renting an apartment, condo or villa can be a convenient and cost-effective way to enjoy the country. Many homes and condos are in private,

BOOK YOUR STAY ONLINE

For more accommodations reviews by Lonely Planet authors, check out http://lonelyplanet.com/hotels/. You'll find independent reviews, as well as recommendations on the best places to stay. Best of all, you can book online.

secure developments, have reduced week- and month-long rates and often many bedrooms, making them ideal for large groups (personal chefs are sometimes an option); alternatively, look for 'apartahotels,' which have studio, one-bedroom and two-bedroom apartments, usually with fully equipped kitchens. Some hotels have a small number of units with kitchens – such cases are indicated in the listings.

Vacation Rentals by Owner (www.vrbo.com) Directly contact owners at this online rental marketplace with a wide range of accommodation listings in the DR.

Children

All-inclusive resorts can be a convenient and affordable way for families to travel, as they provide easy answers to the most vexing of travel questions: when is dinner? Where are we going to eat? What are we going to do? Can I have another Coke?

For independent-minded families the DR is no better or worse than most countries – its small size means no long bus or plane rides, and the beaches and outdoor activities are fun for everyone. At the same time, navigating the cities can be challenging for parents and exhausting for children. For excellent general advice on traveling with children, check out Lonely Planet's *Travel with Children*.

Practicalities

All-inclusive resorts have the best child-specific facilities and services, from high chairs in the restaurants to child care and children's programming. That said, not all resorts cater to families with young children (some even have adults only policies). Independent travelers will have a harder time finding facilities designed for children.

Child safety seats are not common, even in private cars, and are almost unheard of in taxis or buses. If you bring your own car seat – and it's one that can adapt to a number of different cars – you may be able to use it at least some of the time.

Breastfeeding babies in public is not totally taboo, but nor is it common. It is definitely not done in restaurants, as in the US and some other countries. Nursing mothers are recommended to find a private park bench and use a shawl or other covering. Major grocery stores sell many of the same brands of baby food and diapers (nappies) as in the US.

Climate

Santiago

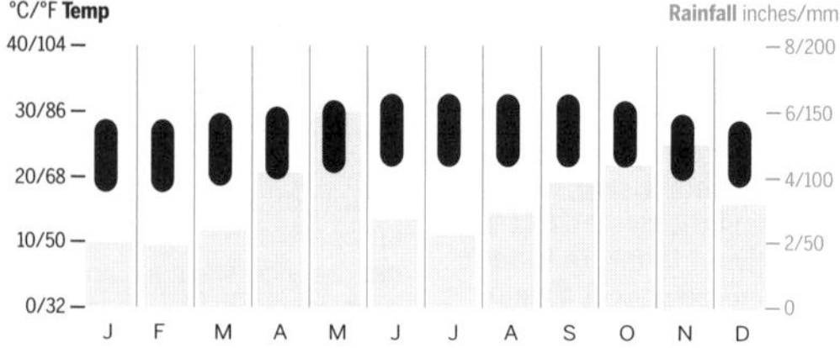

Santo Domingo

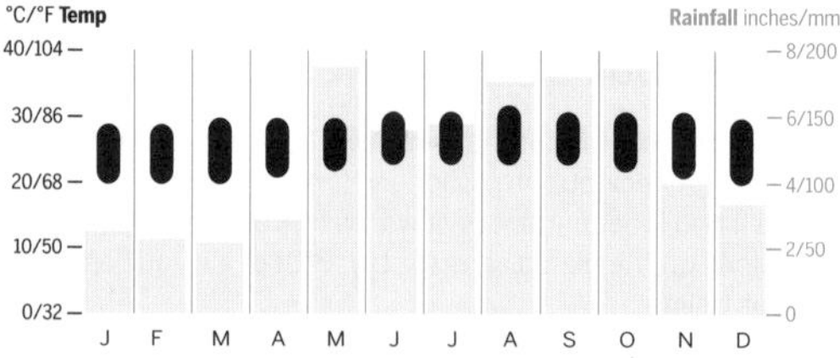

Customs Regulations

Other than the obvious, like weapons, drugs and live animals, there are only a few specific import restrictions for foreigners arriving in the Dominican Republic. Visitors can bring up to 200 cigarettes, 2L of alcohol and gifts not exceeding US$100 duty-free. It's best to carry a prescription for any medication, especially psychotropic drugs.

It is illegal to take anything out of the DR that is over 100 years old – paintings, household items, prehistoric artifacts etc – without special export certificates. Mahogany trees are endangered and products made from mahogany wood may be confiscated upon departure. Black coral is widely available but although Dominican law does not forbid its sale, international environment agreements do – avoid purchasing it. The same goes for products made from turtle shells and butterfly wings – these animals are facing extinction.

It is illegal to export raw unpolished amber from the DR, though amber jewelry is common and highly prized.

Most travelers run into problems with the export of cigars, and it's not with Dominican customs as much as their own. Canada, European countries and the US allow its citizens to bring in up to 50 cigars duty-free.

Electricity

Gay & Lesbian Travelers

As a whole, the Dominican Republic is quite open about heterosexual sex and sexuality, but still fairly closed-minded about gays and lesbians. Gay and lesbian travelers will find the most open community in Santo Domingo, though even its gay clubs are relatively discreet. Santiago, Puerto Plata, Bávaro and Punta Cana also have gay venues, catering as much to foreigners as to locals. Everywhere else, open displays of affection between men are fairly taboo, between women less so. Same sex couples shouldn't have trouble getting a hotel room. Three websites with gay-specific listings and information for the Dominican Republic are **Monaga** (www.monaga.net), **Guia Gay** (www.guiagay.com) and **Planetout.com** (www.planetout.com).

Health

From a medical standpoint, the DR is generally safe as long as you're reasonably careful about what you eat and drink. The most common travel-related diseases, such as dysentery and hepatitis, are acquired by consumption of contaminated food and water (typhoid and hepatitis A and B vaccinations should be considered). Only purified water should be used for drinking, brushing your teeth as well as hand washing.

It's worth noting there's a small risk of malaria (in the western provinces and in La Altagracia, including Punta Cana) and dengue fever (in Santiago, inland and north coast). In these areas, long pants and long sleeves, mosquito repellant and bed nets are recommended (dengue bites are during the daytime). It's worth considering a prescription for a malaria prophylaxis like Atovaquone-proguanil, chloroquine, doxycycline, or mefloquine.

Medical care is variable in Santo Domingo and limited elsewhere, although good privately-run clinics and hospitals can be found in and around the more heavily touristy areas. Many doctors and hospitals expect payment in cash, regardless of whether you have travel-health insurance. Modern pharmacies are easy to find in cities and mid-sized towns.

Some internet resources:

- **Centers for Disease Control** (CDC; www.cdc.gov/travel) Detailed health overview curated with tips and updated notices.
- **MD Travel Health** (www.mdtravelhealth.com) Complete travel health recommendations for every country, updated daily, at no cost.
- **Sitata** (www.sitata.com) Customized medical reports, pre-trip vaccination recommendations, alerts on disease outbreaks and other breaking health news.
- **World Health Organization** (www.who.int/ith) Available online at no cost as well as in book form – *International Travel and Health* – which is revised annually.

Internet Access

The Dominican Republic has a surprisingly limited number of internet cafes; most charge RD$35 to RD$70 per hour. Many of these cafes also operate as call centers.

Wi-fi access is widespread in cafes and restaurants, as well as at midrange and top-end hotels and resorts throughout the country. Travelers with laptops won't have far to go before finding some place with a signal. However, the majority of the all-inclusives, as opposed to most midrange and even budget hotels, charge daily fees (around US$15 and up) for access. Many hotels that advertise the service free for guests only have a signal in public spaces like the lobby and limited or poor access in guest rooms.

Most internet cafes have Spanish language keyboards – the '@' key is usually accessed by pressing 'alt', '6' and '4'.

Legal Matters

The Dominican Republic has two police forces – the Policía Nacional (national police) and the Policía Turística (tourist police, commonly referred to by its abbreviation 'Politur').

Politur officers are generally friendly men and women whose job is specifically to help tourists. Many speak a little bit of a language other than Spanish. They wear white shirts with blue insignia and can usually be found near major tourist sights and centers. You should contact Politur first in the event of theft, assault or if you are the victim of a scam, but you can equally ask them for directions to sights, which bus to take etc.

EMBASSIES & CONSULATES

All of the following are located in Santo Domingo.

EMBASSY	TELEPHONE	ADDRESS
Canadian Embassy	809-685-1136	Av Eugenio de Marchena 39
Cuban Embassy	809-537-2113	Calle Francisco Prats Ramírez 808
French Consulate	809-687-5270	Calle Las Damas 42
German Embassy	809-565-8811	Calle Rafael Augusto Sánchez 23
Haitian Embassy	809-686-5778	Calle Juan Sánchez Ramírez 33
Israeli Embassy	809-920-1500	Calle Pedro Henriquez Ureña 80
Italian Consulate	809-682-0830	Calle Rodríguez Objío 4
Japanese Embassy	809-567-3365	Torre Citigroup Bldg, 21st fl, Av Winston Churchill 1099
Netherlands	809-540-1256	Calle Max Henriquez Ureña 50
Russian Consulate	809-620-1471	Diamond Plaza, 2nd fl, Av Los Proceres
Spanish Embassy	809-535-6500	Av Independencia 1205
UK Consulate	809-472-7574	Av 27 de Febrero 233
US Embassy	809-221-2171	cnr Av César Nicolás Penson & Av Máximo Gómez

It's best to have as little interaction with the Policía Nacional as possible. If a police officer stops you, be polite and cooperate; heavily armed roadway checkpoints aren't uncommon, particularly in regions bordering Haiti – they're looking for drugs and weapons. They may ask to see your passport – you're not required to have it on you, but it's a good idea to carry a photocopy. You might also be asked for a 'tip' in cash or merchandise; feign misunderstanding or simply politely decline. More often than not, you'll simply be waved through.

Money

The Dominican monetary unit is the peso, indicated by the symbol RD$ (or sometimes just R$). Though the peso is technically divided into 100 centavos (cents), prices are usually rounded to the nearest peso. There are one- and five-peso coins, while paper money comes in denominations of 10, 20, 50, 100, 500, 1000 and 2000 pesos. Many tourist-related businesses, including most midrange and top-end hotels, list prices in US dollars, but accept pesos at the going exchange rate.

ATMs

ATMs *(cajeros automáticos)* are common in the Dominican Republic and are, without question, the best way to obtain Dominican pesos and manage your money. Banks with reliable ATMs include Banco Popular, Banco Progreso, BanReservas, Banco León and Scotiabank. Most charge ATM fees (around RD$115 on average); it's worth checking with your domestic bank before you travel whether there are additional fees on their end. And there's a range of frustratingly low maximum withdrawal limits – BanReservas is RD$2000 and Banco Progreso RD$4000 – and limits to the number of withdrawls per day.

As in any country, be smart about where and when you withdraw cash. Most ATMs are not in the bank itself, but in a small booth accessible from the street (and thus available 24 hours).

Credit Cards

Credit and debit cards are more and more common among Dominicans (and more widely accepted for use by foreigners). Visa and MasterCard are more common than Amex but most cards are accepted in areas frequented by tourists. Some but not all businesses add a surcharge for credit-card purchases (typically 16%) – the federal policy of withdrawing sales tax directly from credit-card transactions means merchants will simply add the cost directly to the bill. We've had reports of travelers being excessively overcharged when paying by credit card so always check the bill before signing.

Moneychangers

Moneychangers will approach you in a number of tourist centers. They are unlikely to be aggressive. You will get equally favorable rates, however, and a securer transaction, at an ATM, a bank or an exchange office *(cambio)*.

Post

Mail service in the DR can't be relied upon, no doubt in part because mailing addresses are nonexistent in much of the country. It can take as long as a month for a letter to arrive from the US. Your best bet is FedEx or UPS; within the country, use either Caribe Pack or Metro PAC, each bus company's own package delivery entity is located in their respective terminals.

Safe Travel

The Dominican Republic is not a particularly dangerous place to visit. Street crime is rare in most tourist areas, especially during the day, but you should always be alert for pickpockets and camera snatchers. Avoid walking on beaches at night, and consider taking a cab if you're returning home late from clubs and bars. Car theft is not unheard of, so it's best to not leave any valuables inside your car.

Perhaps the number one annoyance is not being given the proper change after a purchase. In many cases it is a legitimate error in math. But it's not entirely uncommon for waiters, taxi drivers and shop owners to 'accidentally' give you less than warranted. If something's missing, say so right away.

Buying drugs in the DR should be avoided. The seller is often in cahoots with the police who 'catch' the exchange in order to extract a bribe from unwary foreigners. Any transactions involving large amounts can result in significant prison time. Also worth noting is the reputedly 'impure' quality of the cocaine distributed in the DR – public service announcements warn that the majority is more dangerous chemical filler than anything else.

Prostitution is legal (brothel ownership and 'pimping' are illegal) and a big business in the DR (Boca Chica and Sosúa have the highest visible presence). It is definitely illegal to have sex with anyone under the age of 18, even if the offender doesn't know the prostitute's real age. Female prostitutes, when propositioning foreigners, are known to grab and touch aggressively, often a sly attempt at pick-pocketing.

Telephone

Remember that you must dial 1 + 809, 829 or 849 for all calls within the DR, even local ones. Toll-free numbers have 200 or 809 for their prefix (not the area code).

The easiest way to make a phone call in the DR is to pay per minute (average rates per minute: to the US US$0.20; to Europe US$0.50; to Haiti US$0.50) at a Codetel Centro de Comunicaciones (Codetel) call center or an internet cafe that operates as a dual call center.

Calling from a hotel is always the most expensive option.

Cell Phones

Cell (mobile) phones are ubiquitous (bucking trends elsewhere, Blackberry is the most popular smart phone brand) and travelers with global-roaming-enabled phones can receive and make cell phone calls. It's worth checking with your cell-phone carrier for details on rates and accessibility – be aware that per-minute fees can be exorbitant. If you have a GSM phone, and you can unlock it, you can use a SIM card bought from Orange or Claro (prepaid startup kit US$10). Or you can buy a new cell phone (the cheapest is around RD$800; DR cell phones work at 1900 MHZ, the North American standard) and pay as you go (around RD$4 per minute for a call and a recharge costs RD$200). In terms of customer service Orange has a better reputation than Claro.

Phonecards

These can be used at public phones and are available in denominations of RD$50, RD$100, RD$150, RD$200 and RD$250.

Time

The DR is four hours behind Greenwich Mean Time. In autumn and winter it is one hour ahead of New York, Miami and Toronto as well as Haiti –

PRACTICALITIES

- **Newspapers** *El Listin Diario* (www.listin.com.do), *Hoy* (www.hoy.com.do), *Diario Libre* (www.diariolibre.com), *El Caribe* (www.elcaribe.com.do), *El Día* (www.eldia.com.do) and *El Nacional* (www.elnacional.com.do), plus *International Herald Tribune*, the *New York Times* and the *Miami Herald* can be found in many tourist areas. Local papers cost RD$25.
- **Radio & TV** There are about 150 radio stations, most playing merengue and *bachata* (popular guitar music based on bolero rhythms); and seven local TV networks, though cable and satellite programming is very popular for baseball, movies and American soap operas.
- **Weights & Measurement** The DR uses the metric system for everything except gasoline, which is measured in gallons, and at laundromats, where laundry is measured in pounds.

extremely important to keep in mind if heading to or from the border. However, because the country does not adjust for daylight saving time as do the USA and Canada, it's in the same time zone as New York, Miami and Toronto from the first Sunday in April to the last Sunday in October.

Tourist Information

Almost every city in the DR that's frequented by tourists has a tourist office, and a number of less-visited towns do as well. In general, treat the information you get at tourist offices skeptically and double-check with other sources. Some tourist offices offer maps, bus schedules or a calendar of upcoming events, which can be handy.

Travelers with Disabilities

Few Latin American countries are well suited for travelers with disabilities, and the Dominican Republic is no different. On the other hand, all-inclusive resorts can be ideal for travelers with mobility impairments, as rooms, meals and day- and night-time activities are all within close proximity, and there are plenty of staff members to help you navigate around the property. Some resorts have a few wheelchair-friendly rooms, with larger doors and handles in the bathroom. And, it should be said, Dominicans tend to be extremely helpful and accommodating people. Travelers with disabilities should expect some curious stares, but also quick and friendly help from perfect strangers and passersby.

Visas

The majority of would-be foreign travelers in the Dominican Republic do not need to obtain visas prior to arrival. Tourist cards (you don't need to retain this for your return flight) are issued for US$10 upon arrival to visitors from Argentina, Australia, Austria, Belgium, Brazil, Canada, Chile, Denmark, France, Germany, Greece, Ireland, Israel, Italy, Japan, Mexico, the Netherlands, Portugal, Russia, South Africa, Spain, Sweden, Switzerland, the UK and the US, among many others. Whatever your country of origin, a valid passport is necessary.

Tourist Card Extensions

A tourist card is good for up to 30 days from the date of issue. If you wish to stay longer, it's unnecessary to formally extend – instead you'll be charged RD$800 when you depart the country for any stay up to 90 days. Another way to extend your time is to leave the DR briefly – most likely to Haiti – and then return, at which point you'll be issued a brand-new tourist card. (You may have to pay entrance and departure fees in both countries, of course.)

To extend your tourist card longer than three months, you must apply in Santo Domingo at the **Dirección General de Migración** (Map p54; ☎809-508-2555; www.migracion.gov.do; cnr Av 30 de Mayo & Héroes de Luperón; ⏰8am-2:30pm Mon-Fri) at least two weeks before your original card expires (up to nine months will cost RD$1000).

Volunteering

Many NGOs operating in the DR are primarily community networks attempting to develop sustainable ecotourism. Formal volunteering programs may be nonexistent, but if you speak good Spanish and don't mind some elbow grease (or office work), you may be of some use to them. A few more established organizations that accept volunteers include:

CEDAF (Centro para el Desarrollo Agropecuario y Forestal; ☎809-565-5603; www.cedaf.org.do; José Amado Soler 50, Ensanche Paraíso, Santo Domingo) This nationwide NGO helps local farmers develop sustainable ways to use the land.

DREAM Project (Dominican Republic Education & Mentoring; ☎809-571-0497; www.dominicandream.org; Plaza de Patio, Cabarete) Nonconformists will want to avoid this rigidly managed NGO, which otherwise does excellent work in the Cabarete schools.

Fundación Taigüey (☎809-537-8977; www.taiguey.org) This is a network of small NGOs, several of which focus on ecotourism.

Grupo Jaragua (☎809-472-1036; www.grupojaragua.org.do) The largest and oldest NGO in the southwest. Based in Santo Domingo, it concentrates on biodiversity and conservation through microfinancing to assist locals with bee farming etc.

Mariposa Foundation (☎809-571-0610; www.mariposadrfoundation.org; Calle Principal, La Cienega, Cabarete) Dedicated to empowering and educating girls living in and around Cabarete through a 'holistic' program that involves English-language classes, health and wellness seminars, athletics and family involvement. Minimum three month commitment, generally teaching in varying capacities. Located near Kite Beach.

Punta Cana Ecological Foundation (☎809-959-9221; www.puntacana.org) One of the pioneers of sustainable development in the DR; projects targeted at coral reef restoration and preserving the natural environment in the Punta Cana area.

REDOTOR (Red Dominicana de Turismo Rural; ☎809-487-1057; www.redotur.org) Promotes alternative and sustainable tourism projects.

SOEPA (☎809-899-4702) Sociedad Ecologica de Paraiso, founded in 1995, is dedicated to the preservation and protection of the environment and natural resources in the area around Paraiso; it's biggest project is maintenance and development at Cachóte.

Women Travelers

Women traveling without men in the Dominican Republic should expect to receive some attention, usually in the form of hissing (to get your attention), stares and comments like '*Hola, preciosa*' (Hello, beautiful). Although it may be unwanted, it's more of a nuisance than anything else. If you don't like it, dressing conservatively and ignoring the comments are probably your best lines of defense.

But that is not at all to say that women travelers shouldn't take the same precautions they would in other countries, or ignore their instincts about certain men or situations they encounter. Robbery and assaults, though rare against tourists, do occur and women are often seen as easier targets than men. Young, athletic Dominican men who 'target' foreign women, especially in beach resort areas like Punta Cana, are referred to as 'sanky-pankys'. Their M.O. is subtly transactional, usually involving 'promises' of affection in exchange for meals, drinks, gifts and cash from generally older, North American and European women.

Transportation

GETTING THERE & AWAY

Entering the Country

The vast majority of tourists entering the Dominican Republic arrive by air. Independent travelers typically arrive at the main international airport outside of Santo Domingo, Aeropuerto Internacional Las Américas. Passing through immigration is a relatively simple process. Once disembarked, you are guided to the immigration area where you must buy a tourist card (US$10). You're expected to pay in US dollars (Euros and GBP are accepted, but you lose out substantially on the rate); then join the queue in front of one of the immigration officers. You're allowed up to 30 days on a tourist card. The procedure is the same if you arrive at one of the other airports such as Puerto Plata or Punta Cana; the latter is easily the busiest airport in the country in terms of tourist arrivals.

Flights, tours and rail tickets can be booked online at lonelyplanet.com/bookings.

Air

Airports

There are nine so-called international airports, though at least three are used only for domestic flights. For information on most, check out www.aerodom.com. Perhaps the cheapest route between North America and the DR is Spirit Airlines' Fort Lauderdale to Santiago (around US$195 round trip).

Dominican Shuttles, primarily a domestic airline, has regularly scheduled flights from La Isabela in Santo Domingo to Port-au-Price, Haiti (one-way/round trip US$210/340) and Reina Beatrix, Aruba (one-way/round trip US$310/490).

The departure tax of US$20 is almost always automatically included in the price of the ticket.

Aeropuerto Internacional Arroyo Barril (DAB; ☎809-248-2718) West of Samaná, a small airstrip used mostly during whale-watching season (January to March).

Aeropuerto Internacional del Cibao (STI; ☎809-581-8072; www.aeropuertocibao.com.do) Serves Santiago and the interior, but an option worth considering for north coast destinations as well.

Aeropuerto Internacional Samaná El Catey (Presidente Juan Bosch) (AZS; ☎809-338-0094) Located around 40km west of Samaná.

Aeropuerto Internacional de Puerto Plata (Gregorio Luperón) (POP; ☎809-586-1992) Most convenient airport for north coast destinations like the beach resorts around Puerto Plata, Sosúa and Cabarete.

Aeropuerto Internacional La Isabela Dr Joaquín Balaguer (JBQ, Higüero; ☎809-826-4003) This airport is just north of Santo Domingo proper. It handles mostly domestic flights.

Aeropuerto Internacional La Romana (LRM; ☎809-689-1548; Casa de Campo) Near La Romana and Casa de Campo; handles primarily charter flights from the US, Canada, Italy and Germany; some flights from Miami, NYC and San Juan, Puerto Rico.

Aeropuerto Internacional Las Américas (José Francisco Peña Gómez) (SDQ; ☎809- 947-2220) The country's main international airport is located 20km east of Santo Domingo.

Aeropuerto Internacional María Montez (BRX; ☎809-524-4144) Located 5km from Barahona in the southwest; charters only.

Aeropuerto Internacional Punta Cana (PUJ; ☎809-959-2473; www.puntacanainternationalairport.com) Serves Bávaro and Punta Cana, and is the busiest airport in the country.

Airlines

Aerolineas MAS (☎809-682-9399; www.aerolineasmas.com) Daily flights from La Isabela to Port-au-Prince, Haiti and Aruba; soon from Santiago to Haiti as well.

Air Berlin (www.airberlin.com) Charter flights from Germany.

Air Canada (www.aircanada.ca)

Air Europa (www.aireuropa.com)

Air France (www.airfrance.com)

Air Tran (www.airtran.com) Direct flights to Punta Cana.

American Airlines (www.aa.com) Flies to Samaná via San Juan (Puerto Rico); also flies to Santo Domingo, Santiago and Puerto Plata.

Blue Panorama (www.blue-panorama.com) Charter flights from Italy to La Romana.

Condor (www.condor.com)

Continental Airlines (www.continental.com)

Copa Airlines (www.copaair.com) Several flights a week from Santo Domingo to Havana and Port of Spain (Trinidad).

Cubana Air (www.cubana.cu) Twice-weekly direct flights between Santo Domingo and Havana.

Delta (www.delta.com) Direct flights from Atlanta and JFK to Santo Domingo; JFK to Santiago; and Atlanta, Cincinatti, Detroit, JFK, Minneapolis/St Paul and Pittsburgh to Punta Cana.

Iberia (www.iberia.com)

InterCaribbean (Air Turks & Caicos; www.flyairtc.com) Direct flights from Gregorio Luperón to San Juan, Puerto Rico and Providenciales, Turks & Caicos; also from El Catey to San Juan.

JetBlue (www.jetblue.com) Nonstop service between JFK and Puerto Plata, Santiago and Santo Domingo. Also nonstop service from Orlando to Santo Domingo.

Lan Chile (www.lan.com)

LTU (www.ltu.com) Flights from Germany and Austria to Samaná.

Lufthansa (www.lufthansa.com)

Martinair Holland (www.martinair.com) Flights from Amsterdam and Frankfurt to Puerto Plata and Punta Cana.

Seaborne Airlines (www.seaborneairlines.com) Direct flights to San Juan, PR.

Spirit Airlines (www.spiritair.com; Fort Lauderdale) Nonstop flights from Fort Lauderdale to Santo Domingo and Punta Cana.

Thomson Airways (www.flights.thomson.co.uk) Charter flights from the UK.

US Airways (www.usair.com)

Sea

International cruise ships on Caribbean tours commonly stop in Santo Domingo, Cayo Levantado in the Península de Samaná and elsewhere (a new port was being built west of Puerto Plata at Bahia de Maimon).

Caribbean Fantasy, run by **America Cruise Ferries** (www.acferries.com), offers a passenger and car ferry service between Santo Domingo and Puerto Rico (San Juan and Mayagüez). The trip takes about 12 hours and departs three times weekly.

GETTING AROUND

The DR is a fairly small country, so in theory at least it's easy to drive or take public transportation from one side of the country to the other. In practice, however, the inadequate road network will behoove some with limited time and a sufficient budget to consider flying.

Air

If making flight connections in Santo Domingo, keep in mind that it's an hour drive between Aeropuerto Internacional Las Américas and La Isabela. Aerolineas MAS also has flights from Punta Cana to La Isabela and Sanitago. The main domestic carriers and air-taxi companies include the following:

AeroDomca (☎809-826-4141; www.aerodomca.com) Scheduled daily flights between Punta Cana and Arroyo Barril (one-way US$300); charter flights can also be booked elsewhere.

Air Century (☎809-826-4222; www.aircentury.com) Flights from La Isabela to Punta Cana, Puerto Plata, La Romana, Santiago and Samaná.

Dominican Shuttles (formerly Take Off; ☎809-931-4073; www.dominicanshuttles.com) Regularly scheduled flights from SDQ to Punta Cana (one-way/round trip US$120/230); Punta Cana to Arroyo Barril

CLIMATE CHANGE & TRAVEL

Every form of transport that relies on carbon-based fuel generates CO_2, the main cause of human-induced climate change. Modern travel is dependent on airplanes, which might use less fuel per kilometer per person than most cars but travel much greater distances. The altitude at which aircraft emit gases (including CO_2) and particles also contributes to their climate change impact. Many websites offer 'carbon calculators' that allow people to estimate the carbon emissions generated by their journey and, for those who wish to do so, to offset the impact of the greenhouse gases emitted with contributions to portfolios of climate-friendly initiatives throughout the world. Lonely Planet offsets the carbon footprint of all staff and author travel.

DOMINICAN REPUBLIC–HAITI BORDER CROSSINGS

These are the four points where you can cross between Haiti and the DR.

Jimaní–Malpasse This, the busiest and most organized crossing, is in the south on the road that links Santo Domingo and Port-au-Prince.

Dajabón–Ouanaminthe Busy northern crossing on the road between Santiago and Cap-Haïtien (a six-hour drive); try to avoid crossing on market days (Monday and Friday) because of the enormous crush of people and the risk of theft.

Pedernales–Ainse-a-Pietre In the far south; there's a small bridge for foot and motorcycle traffic, cars have to drive over a paved road through a generally shallow river. Relatively easy and calm crossing.

Comendador (aka Elías Piña)–Belladère Least busy and certainly the dodgiest. On the Haiti side, the immigration building is several hundred meters from the actual border. Transportation further into Haiti is difficult to access.

Practicalities

Immigration offices on the Dominican side are usually open 8am to 6pm, and 9am to 6pm on the Haitian side. Arrive as early as possible, so you are sure to get through both countries' border offices and onto a bus well before dark. When deciding between either crossing in the late afternoon or staying an extra night and crossing in the morning, choose the latter – safety concerns aside, onward transportation is less frequent or nonexistent after dark.

Leaving the DR You need your passport and are likely to be asked more questions than if leaving via an airport, usually only out of curiosity that a tourist would travel this way. Officially, you are supposed to pay US$25 to leave the DR, which gives you the right to re-enter at the same point for no extra charge. However, border officials have been known to ask for an extra US$5 to US$10 to leave and the full US$25 to re-enter for no other reason than they can. It's worth politely pointing out that you have already paid the full fee. If you're only interested in leaving without returning the fee should be US$10.

Entering Haiti Pay a US$10 fee (US dollars only).

Public Transportation Caribe Tours and Capital Coach Lines service the Santo Domingo–Port-au-Prince route daily; Caribe Tours also has daily departures at noon from Santiago for Cap-Haïtien. From the north coast it's easy enough to reach Dajabón, but then you have to transfer to a Haitian vehicle on the other side.

Private Transportation Rental vehicles are not allowed to cross from one country into the other, and you need special authorization to cross the border with a private vehicle.

(one-way/round trip US$160/300) charters and Arroyo Barril near Las Terrenas; also between Punta Cana and Arroyo Barril.

Bicycle

The DR's highways are not well suited for cycling, and Dominican drivers are not exactly accommodating to people on bikes; the situation is hectic to say the least. However, mountain biking on the DR's back roads and lesser-used highways can be rewarding, and a number of recommended tour companies operate in Jarabacoa and Cabarete. If you're planning a multiday ride, definitely consider bringing your own bike. If you're joining a bike tour, most tour operators will provide you with one.

Boat

The only regularly scheduled domestic passenger boat route in the DR is the ferry service between Samaná and Sabana de la Mar, on opposite sides of the Bahía de Samaná in the northeastern part of the country. The journey is subject to weather and departures are frequently canceled. There is no car ferry service here, so unfortunately, if you arrive in Sabana de la Mar with a rental vehicle, you'll have to leave it behind and return by the same route you arrived.

Bus

The DR has a great bus system, utilizing buses similar to Greyhound in the US, with frequent service throughout the country. Virtually all first-class buses have toilets in the back and TVs in the aisles showing movies (loudly) en route. Air-conditioning is sometimes turned up to uncomfortable levels. Fares are low – the most expensive first-class ticket is less than US$10 – you must buy your ticket before boarding. Unfortunately, there are no central bus terminals in the majority of cities and each company has its own station location. They almost never stop along the road to pick up passengers but drivers are often willing to drop passengers off at various points along the way; they will not, however, open the luggage compartment at any point other than the actual terminal.

Reservations aren't usually necessary and rarely even taken. The exceptions are the international buses to Port-au-Prince, Haiti, operated by Caribe Tours and Capital Coach Lines. During Dominican holidays you can sometimes buy your ticket a day or two in advance, which assures you a spot and saves you the time and hassle of waiting in line at a busy terminal with all your bags.

First-class carriers include the following:

Capital Coach Line (☎809-531-0383; www.capitalcoachline.com; Plaza Lama, cnr Avs 27 de Febrero & Winston Churchill, Santo Domingo) Air-con service from Santo Domingo to Port-au-Prince, Haiti.

Caribe Tours (Map p60; ☎809-221-4422; www.caribetours.com.do; cnr Avs 27 de Febrero & Leopoldo Navarro, Santo Domingo) One of the country's two main bus companies; has most departures and covers more destinations.

Metro (☎809-566-7126; www.metrotours.com.do; Calle Francisco Prats Ramírez, Santo Domingo) Metro serves nine cities, mostly along the Santo Domingo–Puerto Plata corridor. Fares tend to be slightly more expensive than Caribe Tours.

Guaguas

Wherever long-distance buses don't go, you can be sure a *guagua* (pronounced '*gwa*-gwas') does. *Guaguas* are typically midsize buses holding around 25 to 30 passengers. They rarely have signs, but the driver's assistant (known as the *cobrador*, or 'charger', since one of his jobs is to collect fares from passengers) will yell out the destination to potential fares on the side of the road. Don't hesitate to ask a local if you're unsure which one to take.

Guaguas pick up and drop off passengers anywhere along the route – to flag one down simply hold out your hand – the common gesture is to point at the curb in front of you but just about any gesture will do. Most *guaguas* pass every 15 to 30 minutes and cost RD$35 to RD$70, but unless you have the exact amount some *cobradors* may pocket the change of unwary foreigners. It's a good idea to carry change or small bills and to find out the exact cost in advance. When you want to get off, tap the roof or bang on the side of the van.

Guaguas are divided into two types – the majority are *caliente* (literally 'hot'), which don't have air-conditioning, naturally. For every four or five *caliente* buses there is usually an *expreso*, which typically has air-conditioning, makes fewer stops and costs slightly more. Within these two categories there's a virtual rainbow of diversity in terms of vehicle quality and reliability.

Car & Motorcycle

Though the DR's bus and *guagua* system is excellent, having your own car is invariably faster and more convenient. Even if renting a car isn't in your budget for the entire trip, consider renting one for a select couple of days, to reach sights that are isolated or not well served by public transportation; pretty much a necessity for the southwest.

Driver's License

For travelers from most countries, your home country driver's license allows you to drive in the DR. Be sure it's valid.

Fuel & Spare Parts

Most towns have at least one gas station, typically right along the highway on the outskirts of town. There are a couple of different companies, but prices are essentially the same for all. At the time of research, gas prices were around RD$248 per gallon. Many gas stations accept credit cards and many also have ATMs – all are full service.

With the cost of gas so high, a growing percentage of vehicles have been jerry-rigged to run on much cheaper propane gas (RD$100 per gallon) – you'll usually see a station (Unigas, Propagas or Tropigas) at the exit and entrance of any good-sized town.

Play it safe and always keep your gas tank at least half full. Many *bombas* (gas stations) in the DR close by 7pm, and even when they are open they don't always have gas. If you're traveling on back roads or in a remote part of the country, your best bet is to buy gas from people selling it from their front porch. Look for the large pink jugs sitting on tables on the side of the road.

The most common car trouble is to end up with a punctured or damaged tire caused by potholes, speed bumps and rocks or other debris in the road. The word for tire is *goma* (literally 'rubber') and a tire shop is called a *gomero*. If you can make it to one on your busted tire, the guys there can patch a flat, replace a damaged tire, or just put the spare on.

Insurance

The multinational car-rental agencies typically offer comprehensive, nondeductible collision and liability insurance for fairly small daily fees. Smaller agencies usually offer partial coverage, with a deductible ranging from US$100 to US$2000. Several credit-card companies, including Amex, offer comprehensive coverage for rentals, but you should check your own insurance policy before declining the rental company's.

Maps

If you rent a car, it's worth buying a good map to the area you'll be driving in. In Santo Domingo, **Mapas GAAR** (Map p50; ☎809-688-8004; www.mapasgaar.com.do; 3rd fl, cnr Calle El Conde & Espaillat; ⏰8am-5:30pm Mon-Fri, to 2:30pm Sat) publishes and sells the most comprehensive maps of cities and towns in the DR. Both the *National Geographic Adventure Map* and Boch maps of the Dominican Republic can be recommended.

Rental

Familiar multinational agencies like Hertz, Avis, Europcar, Alamo and Dollar have offices at the major international airports (or pickup service like at Punta Cana), as well as in Santo Domingo and other cities. Not only are their online rates sometimes much less than those of local or national agencies, but their vehicles are of better quality and they provide reliable and comprehensive service and insurance (it should be noted that an additional 'airport terminal charge', around 8%, is tacked on to the bill). If you plan to do any driving on secondary roads along the coast or in the mountains, a 4WD is recommended. Rates typically cost US$30 (for a standard car) to US$120 (for a 4WD) per day. Motorcycles can also be rented, but only experienced riders should do so because of poor road conditions.

Road Conditions

Roads in the DR range from excellent to awful, sometimes along the same highway over a very short distance. The *autopista* (freeway) between Santo Domingo and Santiago has as many as eight lanes, is fast moving and is generally in good condition. However, even here, always be alert for potholes, speed bumps and people walking along the roadside, especially near populated areas. On all roads, large or small, watch for slow-moving cars and especially motorcycles. Be particularly careful when driving at night. Better yet, *never drive at night*. Even the most skilled person with the reflexes of a superhero will probably end up in a ditch by the side of the road.

Some of the highways, including Hwy 3 heading out of Santo Domingo to the east and Hwy 2 leaving the city to the west, have toll fees of fairly nominal amounts (RD$35), while the Santo Domingo–Samaná highway (DR-7) is a relatively whopping RD$412. For the former it's best to have exact change that you can simply toss into the basket and quickly move on.

Road Rules

The first rule is there are none. In theory, road rules in the DR are the same as for most countries in the Americas, and the lights and signs are the same shape and color you find in the US or Canada (speed limit signs are in kilometers per hour). Driving is on the right and seatbelts are required. That said, driving is pretty much a free-for-all. In fact, in 2013, the World Health Organization (WHO) ranked the DR as one of the 'world's most dangerous country for drivers', just ahead of Thailand. Pedestrians, equally indifferent to common sense safety precautions, are also frequently victims. The combination of powerful public transport unions and the general public's opposition to education and licensing regulations are continuing obstacles to improving safety standards.

In small towns, nay in all towns, traffic lights – when working – are frequently ignored, though you should plan to stop at them. Watch what other drivers are doing – if everyone is going through, you probably should, too, as it can be even more dangerous to stop if the cars behind you aren't expecting it. Many city streets are one way and often poorly marked, creating yet another hazard. Often, in lieu of stop signs, culverts (basically, the opposite of speed bumps), deep enough to damage the undersides of low clearance vehicles unless taken at the slowest of speeds, signal stops. Prohibitions against drinking and driving are widely flouted and it's not uncommon to spot a speeding motorcyclist sipping rum.

Hitchhiking

Though hitchhiking is never entirely safe anywhere in the world, Dominicans, both men and women, hitch all the time, especially in rural areas where fewer people have cars and *guagua* service is sparse. It's also common in resort areas like Bávaro, where a large number of workers commute to Higüey or other towns nearby every morning and evening. That said, it is rare to see foreigners hitchhiking, and doing so (especially if you have bags) carries a greater risk than for locals.

Local Transportation

Bus

Large cities like Santo Domingo and Santiago have public bus systems that operate as they do in most places around the world. Many of the larger city buses are imported from Brazil, and are the kind which you board in the back and pay the person sitting beside the turnstile. Other city buses are more or less like *guaguas,* where you board quickly and pay the *cobrador* when he comes around. In general, you will probably take relatively few city buses, simply because *públicos* follow pretty much the same routes and pass more frequently.

Metro

Santo Domingo has a metro system that is continuing to expand.

Motoconcho

Cheaper and easier to find than taxis, *motoconchos* (motorcycle taxis) are the best, and sometimes only, way to get around in many towns. An average ride should set you back no more than RD$30. That being said, you might have to negotiate to get a fair price and we've heard of travelers unknowingly dropped off far short of their intended location. Accidents resulting in injuries and even deaths are not uncommon; ask the driver to slow down *(¡Más despacio por favor!)* if you think he's driving dangerously. Avoid two passengers on a bike since not only is the price the same as taking separate bikes but the extra weight makes scooters harder to control. For longer trips, or if you have any sort of bag or luggage, *motoconchos* are usually impractical and certainly less comfortable than alternatives. By law, drivers are required to wear helmets though it's generally ignored, as are any tickets issued.

Públicos

These are banged-up cars, minivans or small pickup trucks that pick up passengers along set routes, usually main boulevards. *Públicos* (also called *conchos* or *carros*) don't have signs but the drivers hold their hands out the window to solicit potential fares. They are also identifiable by the crush of people inside them – up to seven in a midsize car! To flag one down simply hold out your hand – the fare is around RD$12. If there is no one else in the car, be sure to tell the driver you want *servicio público* (public service) to avoid paying private taxi rates.

Taxi

Dominican taxis rarely cruise for passengers – instead they wait at designated *sitios* (stops), which are located at hotels, bus terminals, tourist areas and main public parks. You can also phone a taxi service (or ask your hotel receptionist to call for you). Taxis do not have meters – agree on a price beforehand.

Language

The official language of the Dominican Republic is Spanish. Some English and German is also spoken by individuals in the tourist business. Dominican Spanish is very much like Central America's other varieties of Spanish. Note though that Dominicans tend to swallow the ends of words, especially those ending in 's' – *tres* will sound like 'tre' and *buenos días* like 'bueno día.'

Spanish pronunciation is relatively straightforward as the relationship between what's written and how you pronounce it is clear and consistent – each written letter is always pronounced the same way. Also, most Spanish sounds are similar to their English counterparts. Note that the kh in our pronunciation guides is a throaty sound (like the 'ch' in the Scottish *loch*), v and b are similar to the English 'b' (but softer, between a 'v' and a 'b'), and r is strongly rolled. If you read our pronunciation guides as if they were English, you will be understood. In our guides, we've also indicated the stressed syllables in italics.

The Dominican Academy of Language published its first Dominican-language-based dictionary in 2013.

BASICS

Hello.	*Hola.*	*o*·la
Goodbye.	*Adiós.*	a·*dyos*
How are you?	*¿Qué tal?*	ke tal
Fine, thanks.	*Bien, gracias.*	byen *gra*·syas
Excuse me.	*Perdón.*	per·*don*
Sorry.	*Lo siento.*	lo *syen*·to
Please.	*Por favor.*	por fa·*vor*
Thank you.	*Gracias.*	*gra*·syas
You're welcome.	*De nada.*	de *na*·da
Yes./No.	*Sí./No.*	see/no

WANT MORE?

For in-depth language information and handy phrases, check out Lonely Planet's *Latin American Spanish Phrasebook*. You'll find it at **shop.lonelyplanet.com**, or you can buy Lonely Planet's iPhone phrasebooks at the Apple App Store.

What's your name?
¿Cómo se llama Usted? ko·mo se *ya*·ma *oo*·ste (pol)
¿Cómo te llamas? ko·mo te *ya*·mas (inf)

My name is ...
Me llamo ... me *ya*·mo ...

Do you speak English?
¿Habla inglés? *a*·bla een·*gles* (pol)
¿Hablas inglés? *a*·blas een·*gles* (inf)

I don't understand.
Yo no entiendo. yo no en·*tyen*·do

ACCOMMODATIONS

I'd like a ... room.	*Quisiera una habitación ...*	kee·*sye*·ra *oo*·na a·bee·ta·*syon* ...
single	*individual*	een·dee·vee·*dwal*
double	*doble*	*do*·ble

How much is it per night/person?
¿Cuánto cuesta por noche/persona? *kwan*·to *kwes*·ta por *no*·che/per·*so*·na

Does it include breakfast?
¿Incluye el desayuno? een·*kloo*·ye el de·sa·*yoo*·no

air-con	*aire acondicionado*	*ai*·re a·kon·dee·syo·*na*·do
bathroom	*baño*	*ba*·nyo
bed	*cama*	*ka*·ma
campsite	*terreno de cámping*	te·*re*·no de *kam*·peeng
guesthouse	*pensión*	pen·*syon*
hotel	*hotel*	o·*tel*
youth hostel	*albergue juvenil*	al·*ber*·ge khoo·ve·*neel*

DIRECTIONS

Where's ...?
¿Dónde está ...? don·de es·ta ...

What's the address?
¿Cuál es la dirección? kwal es la dee·rek·syon

Could you please write it down?
¿Puede escribirlo, por favor? pwe·de es·kree·beer·lo por fa·vor

Can you show me (on the map)?
¿Me lo puede indicar (en el mapa)? me lo pwe·de een·dee·kar (en el ma·pa)

at the corner	*en la esquina*	en la es·kee·na
at the traffic lights	*en el semáforo*	en el se·ma·fo·ro
behind ...	*detrás de ...*	de·tras de ...
in front of ...	*enfrente de ...*	en·fren·te de ...
left	*izquierda*	ees·kyer·da
next to ...	*al lado de ...*	al la·do de ...
opposite ...	*frente a ...*	fren·te a ...
right	*derecha*	de·re·cha
straight ahead	*todo recto*	to·do rek·to

EATING & DRINKING

What would you recommend?
¿Qué recomienda? ke re·ko·myen·da

What's in that dish?
¿Que lleva ese plato? ke ye·va e·se pla·to

I don't eat ...
No como ... no ko·mo ...

That was delicious!
¡Estaba buenísimo! es·ta·ba bwe·nee·see·mo

Please bring the check/bill.
Por favor nos trae la cuenta. por fa·vor nos tra·e la kwen·ta

Cheers!
¡Salud! sa·loo

I'd like to book a table for ...	*Quisiera reservar una mesa para ...*	kee·sye·ra re·ser·var oo·na me·sa pa·ra ...
(eight) o'clock	*las (ocho)*	las (o·cho)
(two) people	*(dos) personas*	(dos) per·so·nas

Key Words

appetizers	*aperitivos*	a·pe·ree·tee·vos
bar	*bar*	bar
bottle	*botella*	bo·te·ya
bowl	*bol*	bol
breakfast	*desayuno*	de·sa·yoo·no
cafe	*café*	ka·fe
children's menu	*menú infantil*	me·noo een·fan·teel
(too) cold	*(muy) frío*	(mooy) free·o
dinner	*cena*	se·na
food	*comida*	ko·mee·da
fork	*tenedor*	te·ne·dor
glass	*vaso*	va·so
highchair	*trona*	tro·na
hot (warm)	*caliente*	kal·yen·te
knife	*cuchillo*	koo·chee·yo
lunch	*comida*	ko·mee·da
main course	*segundo plato*	se·goon·do pla·to
market	*mercado*	mer·ka·do
menu (in English)	*menú (en inglés)*	oon me·noo (en een·gles)
plate	*plato*	pla·to
restaurant	*restaurante*	res·tow·ran·te
spoon	*cuchara*	koo·cha·ra
supermarket	*supermercado*	soo·per·mer·ka·do
vegetarian food	*comida vegetariana*	ko·mee·da ve·khe·ta·rya·na
with	*con*	kon
without	*sin*	seen

KEY PATTERNS

To get by in Spanish, mix and match these simple patterns with words of your choice:

When's (the next flight)?
¿Cuándo sale (el próximo vuelo)? kwan·do sa·le (el prok·see·mo vwe·lo)

Where's (the station)?
¿Dónde está (la estación)? don·de es·ta (la es·ta·syon)

Where can I (buy a ticket)?
¿Dónde puedo (comprar un billete)? don·de pwe·do (kom·prar oon bee·ye·te)

Do you have (a map)?
¿Tiene (un mapa)? tye·ne (oon ma·pa)

Is there (a toilet)?
¿Hay (servicios)? ai (ser·vee·syos)

I'd like (a coffee).
Quisiera (un café). kee·sye·ra (oon ka·fe)

I'd like (to hire a car).
Quisiera (alquilar un coche). kee·sye·ra (al·kee·lar oon ko·che)

Can I (enter)?
¿Se puede (entrar)? se pwe·de (en·trar)

Could you please (help me)?
¿Puede (ayudarme), por favor? pwe·de (a·yoo·dar·me) por fa·vor

Meat & Fish

beef	*carne de vaca*	*kar*·ne de *va*·ka
chicken	*pollo*	*po*·yo
duck	*pato*	*pa*·to
fish	*pescado*	pes·*ka*·do
lamb	*cordero*	kor·*de*·ro
pork	*cerdo*	*ser*·do
turkey	*pavo*	*pa*·vo
veal	*ternera*	ter·*ne*·ra

Fruit & Vegetables

apple	*manzana*	man·*sa*·na
apricot	*albaricoque*	al·ba·ree·*ko*·ke
artichoke	*alcachofa*	al·ka·*cho*·fa
asparagus	*espárragos*	es·*pa*·ra·gos
banana	*plátano*	*pla*·ta·no
beans	*judías*	khoo·*dee*·as
beetroot	*remolacha*	re·mo·*la*·cha
cabbage	*col*	kol
carrot	*zanahoria*	sa·na·*o*·rya
celery	*apio*	*a*·pyo
cherry	*cereza*	se·*re*·sa
corn	*maíz*	ma·*ees*
cucumber	*pepino*	pe·*pee*·no
fruit	*fruta*	*froo*·ta
grape	*uvas*	*oo*·vas
lemon	*limón*	lee·*mon*
lentils	*lentejas*	len·*te*·khas
lettuce	*lechuga*	le·*choo*·ga
mushroom	*champiñón*	cham·pee·*nyon*
nuts	*nueces*	*nwe*·ses
onion	*cebolla*	se·*bo*·ya
orange	*naranja*	na·*ran*·kha
peach	*melocotón*	me·lo·ko·*ton*
peas	*guisantes*	gee·*san*·tes
(red/green) pepper	*pimiento (rojo/verde)*	pee·*myen*·to (*ro*·kho/*ver*·de)
pineapple	*piña*	*pee*·nya
plum	*ciruela*	seer·*we*·la
potato	*patata*	pa·*ta*·ta
pumpkin	*calabaza*	ka·la·*ba*·sa
spinach	*espinacas*	es·pee·*na*·kas
strawberry	*fresa*	*fre*·sa
tomato	*tomate*	to·*ma*·te
vegetable	*verdura*	ver·*doo*·ra
watermelon	*sandía*	san·*dee*·a

Other

bread	*pan*	pan
butter	*mantequilla*	man·te·*kee*·ya
cheese	*queso*	*ke*·so
egg	*huevo*	*we*·vo
honey	*miel*	myel
jam	*mermelada*	mer·me·*la*·da
oil	*aceite*	a·*sey*·te
pepper	*pimienta*	pee·*myen*·ta
rice	*arroz*	a·*ros*
salt	*sal*	sal
sugar	*azúcar*	a·*soo*·kar
vinegar	*vinagre*	vee·*na*·gre

Drinks

beer	*cerveza*	ser·*ve*·sa
coffee	*café*	ka·*fe*
(orange) juice	*zumo (de naranja)*	*soo*·mo (de na·*ran*·kha)

TALKING LIKE A LOCAL

Here are a few typical regionalisms you might come across in the Dominican Republic:

apagón	power failure
apodo	nickname
bandera dominicana	rice and beans (lit: Dominican flag)
bohío	thatch hut
bulto	luggage
carros de concho	routed, shared taxi
chichi	baby
colmado	small grocery store
fucú	a thing bringing bad luck
guapo	bad-tempered
guarapo	sugarcane juice
gumo	(a) drunk
hablador	person who talks a lot
papaúpa	important person
pariguayo	foolish
pín-pún	exactly equal
una rumba	a lot
Siempre a su orden.	You're welcome.
tiguere	rascal
timacle	brave

milk	*leche*	*le*·che
tea	*té*	te
(mineral) water	*agua (mineral)*	*a*·gwa (mee·ne·*ral*)
(red/white) wine	*vino (tinto/ blanco)*	*vee*·no (*teen*·to/ *blan*·ko)

EMERGENCIES

Help!	*¡Socorro!*	so·*ko*·ro
Go away!	*¡Vete!*	*ve*·te

Call a doctor!
¡Llame a un médico! *ya*·me a oon *me*·dee·ko

Call the police!
¡Llame a la policía! *ya*·me a la po·lee·*see*·a

I'm lost.
Estoy perdido/a. es·*toy* per·*dee*·do/a (m/f)

I'm ill.
Estoy enfermo/a. es·*toy* en·*fer*·mo/a (m/f)

It hurts here.
Me duele aquí. me *dwe*·le a·*kee*

I'm allergic to (antibiotics).
Soy alérgico/a a (los antibióticos). soy a·*ler*·khee·ko/a a (los an·tee·*byo*·tee·kos) (m/f)

SHOPPING & SERVICES

I'd like to buy ...
Quisiera comprar ... kee·*sye*·ra kom·*prar* ...

I'm just looking.
Sólo estoy mirando. *so*·lo es·*toy* mee·*ran*·do

May I look at it?
¿Puedo verlo? *pwe*·do *ver*·lo

I don't like it.
No me gusta. no me *goos*·ta

How much is it?
¿Cuánto cuesta? *kwan*·to *kwes*·ta

That's too expensive.
Es muy caro. es mooy *ka*·ro

Can you lower the price?
¿Podría bajar un poco el precio? po·*dree*·a ba·*khar* oon *po*·ko el *pre*·syo

There's a mistake in the check/bill.
Hay un error en la cuenta. ai oon e·*ror* en la *kwen*·ta

Question Words

How?	*¿Cómo?*	*ko*·mo
What?	*¿Qué?*	ke
When?	*¿Cuándo?*	*kwan*·do
Where?	*¿Dónde?*	*don*·de
Who?	*¿Quién?*	kyen
Why?	*¿Por qué?*	por ke

Signs

Abierto	Open
Cerrado	Closed
Entrada	Entrance
Hombres/Varones	Men
Mujeres/Damas	Women
Prohibido	Prohibited
Salida	Exit
Servicios/Baños	Toilets

ATM	*cajero automático*	ka·*khe*·ro ow·to·*ma*·tee·ko
internet cafe	*cibercafé*	see·ber·ka·*fe*
post office	*correos*	ko·*re*·os
tourist office	*oficina de turismo*	o·fee·*see*·na de too·*rees*·mo

TIME & DATES

What time is it?	*¿Qué hora es?*	ke *o*·ra es
It's (10) o'clock.	*Son (las diez).*	son (las dyes)
It's half past (one).	*Es (la una) y media.*	es (la *oo*·na) ee *me*·dya

morning	*mañana*	ma·*nya*·na
afternoon	*tarde*	*tar*·de
evening	*noche*	*no*·che
yesterday	*ayer*	a·*yer*
today	*hoy*	oy
tomorrow	*mañana*	ma·*nya*·na

Monday	*lunes*	*loo*·nes
Tuesday	*martes*	*mar*·tes
Wednesday	*miércoles*	*myer*·ko·les
Thursday	*jueves*	*khwe*·ves
Friday	*viernes*	*vyer*·nes
Saturday	*sábado*	*sa*·ba·do
Sunday	*domingo*	do·*meen*·go

January	*enero*	e·*ne*·ro
February	*febrero*	fe·*bre*·ro
March	*marzo*	*mar*·so
April	*abril*	a·*breel*
May	*mayo*	*ma*·yo
June	*junio*	*khoon*·yo
July	*julio*	*khool*·yo
August	*agosto*	a·*gos*·to
September	*septiembre*	sep·*tyem*·bre
October	*octubre*	ok·*too*·bre
November	*noviembre*	no·*vyem*·bre
December	*diciembre*	dee·*syem*·bre

TRANSPORTATION

Public Transportation

boat	*barco*	bar·ko
bus	*autobús*	ow·to·*boos*
plane	*avión*	a·*vyon*
train	*tren*	tren
first	*primero*	pree·*me*·ro
last	*último*	*ool*·tee·mo
next	*próximo*	*prok*·see·mo

I want to go to ...
Quisiera ir a ... kee·*sye*·ra eer a ...

What time does it arrive/leave?
¿A qué hora llega/sale? a ke *o*·ra *ye*·ga/*sa*·le

Please tell me when we get to ...
¿Puede avisarme cuando lleguemos a ...? *pwe*·de a·vee·*sar*·me *kwan*·do ye·*ge*·mos a ...

I want to get off here.
Quiero bajarme aquí. *kye*·ro ba·*khar*·me a·*kee*

a ... ticket	*un billete de ...*	oon bee·*ye*·te de ...
1st-class	*primera clase*	pree·*me*·ra *kla*·se
2nd-class	*segunda clase*	se·*goon*·da *kla*·se
one-way	*ida*	*ee*·da
return	*ida y vuelta*	*ee*·da ee *vwel*·ta

airport	*aeropuerto*	a·e·ro·*pwer*·to
bus stop	*parada de autobuses*	pa·*ra*·da de ow·to·*boo*·ses
platform	*plataforma*	pla·ta·*for*·ma
ticket office	*taquilla*	ta·*kee*·ya
timetable	*horario*	o·*ra*·ryo
train station	*estación de trenes*	es·ta·*syon* de *tre*·nes

Driving & Cycling

I'd like to rent a ...	*Quisiera alquilar ...*	kee·*sye*·ra al·kee·*lar* ...
4WD	*un todo-terreno*	oon to·do·te·re·no
bicycle	*una bicicleta*	*oo*·na bee·see·*kle*·ta
car	*un coche*	oon *ko*·che
motorcycle	*una moto*	*oo*·na *mo*·to

Numbers

1	*uno*	*oo*·no
2	*dos*	dos
3	*tres*	tres
4	*cuatro*	*kwa*·tro
5	*cinco*	*seen*·ko
6	*seis*	seys
7	*siete*	*sye*·te
8	*ocho*	*o*·cho
9	*nueve*	*nwe*·ve
10	*diez*	dyes
20	*veinte*	*veyn*·te
30	*treinta*	*treyn*·ta
40	*cuarenta*	kwa·*ren*·ta
50	*cincuenta*	seen·*kwen*·ta
60	*sesenta*	se·*sen*·ta
70	*setenta*	se·*ten*·ta
80	*ochenta*	o·*chen*·ta
90	*noventa*	no·*ven*·ta
100	*cien*	syen
1000	*mil*	meel

child seat	*asiento de seguridad para niños*	a·*syen*·to de se·goo·ree·*da* *pa*·ra *nee*·nyos
diesel	*petróleo*	pet·*ro*·le·o
helmet	*casco*	*kas*·ko
hitchhike	*hacer botella*	a·*ser* bo·*te*·ya
mechanic	*mecánico*	me·*ka*·nee·ko
gas/petrol	*gasolina*	ga·so·*lee*·na
service station	*gasolinera*	ga·so·lee·*ne*·ra
truck	*camion*	ka·*myon*

Is this the road to ...?
¿Se va a ... por esta carretera? se va a ... por es·ta ka·re·*te*·ra

(How long) Can I park here?
¿(Por cuánto tiempo) Puedo aparcar aquí? (por *kwan*·to *tyem*·po) *pwe*·do a·par·*kar* a·*kee*

The car has broken down (at ...).
El coche se ha averiado (en ...). el *ko*·che se a a·ve·*rya*·do (en ...)

I have a flat tyre.
Tengo un pinchazo. *ten*·go oon peen·*cha*·so

I've run out of gas/petrol.
Me he quedado sin gasolina. me e ke·*da*·do seen ga·so·*lee*·na

I need a mechanic.
Necesito un/una mecánico/a. ne·se·*see*·to oon/*oo*·na me·*ka*·nee·ko/a (m/f)

Behind the Scenes

SEND US YOUR FEEDBACK

We love to hear from travelers – your comments keep us on our toes and help make our books better. Our well-traveled team reads every word on what you loved or loathed about this book. Although we cannot reply individually to your submissions, we always guarantee that your feedback goes straight to the appropriate authors, in time for the next edition. Each person who sends us information is thanked in the next edition – the most useful submissions are rewarded with a selection of digital PDF chapters.

Visit **lonelyplanet.com/contact** to submit your updates and suggestions or to ask for help. Our award-winning website also features inspirational travel stories, news and discussions.

Note: We may edit, reproduce and incorporate your comments in Lonely Planet products such as guidebooks, websites and digital products, so let us know if you don't want your comments reproduced or your name acknowledged. For a copy of our privacy policy visit lonelyplanet.com/privacy.

AUTHOR THANKS

Michael Grosberg

Thanks to Carly Neidorf for putting up with my long absences and of course to my coauthor Kevin Raub. And on the road to the following for their time, guidance, insight and warmth: Patricia Suriel, Omar Rodriguez, Michael Scates, Mark Rodriguez, Tim Hall, Clare and Jeroen Mutsarrs and Lorenzo Sanssani.

Kevin Raub

Thanks to my wife, Adriana Schmidt Raub, who sure does put up with a lot of travel. Thanks also to my former editor at Lonely Planet, Catherine Craddock-Carrillo; my partner in crime, Michael Grosberg, who had to put up with my early start; and all of the staff we lost in 2013. On the road, Kim Beddall, Nicolas Warembourg, David Cruz, Gordana Stojanovic, Kris and Jill Thomas, Alan Nuñez, Melany Torres, Carla Mathe, Johan Guyot, Kate Wallace, Nathalie Agramonte, Damian Irizarry and Mara Sandri.

ACKNOWLEDGMENTS

Climate map data adapted from Peel MC, Finlayson BL & McMahon TA (2007) 'Updated World Map of the Köppen-Geiger Climate Classification', *Hydrology and Earth System Sciences*, 11, 1633¬44.

Cover photograph: Cascada El Limón, Península de Samaná; Bertrand Gardel/Alamy.

THIS BOOK

This 6th edition of Lonely Planet's *Dominican Republic* guidebook was researched and written by Michael Grosberg and Kevin Raub. The previous edition was written by Paul Clammer, Michael Grosberg and Kevin Raub, and the 4th edition by Paul Clammer, Michael Grosberg and Jens Porup. This guidebook was commissioned in Lonely Planet's Oakland office, and produced by the following:

Destination Editor Helen Elfer

Commissioning Editors Catherine Craddock-Carrillo, Kathleen Munnelly

Product Editor Carolyn Boicos

Senior Cartographer Mark Griffiths

Book Designer Wibowo Rusli

Assisting Editors Justin Flynn, Carly Hall, Kate Kiely, Clifton Wilkinson, Simon Williamson

Assisting Cartographer James Leversha

Cover Researcher Naomi Parker

Thanks to Anita Banh, Sasha Baskett, Fredrik Divall, Ryan Evans, Larissa Frost, Genesys India, Jouve India, Elizabeth Jones, Nadine Lopez, Kate Mathews, Claire Naylor, Martine Power, James Smart, Richard Weil

Index

Map Pages **000**
Photo Pages 000

V

W

Z

Map Legend

Sights

- Beach
- Bird Sanctuary
- Buddhist
- Castle/Palace
- Christian
- Confucian
- Hindu
- Islamic
- Jain
- Jewish
- Monument
- Museum/Gallery/Historic Building
- Ruin
- Sento Hot Baths/Onsen
- Shinto
- Sikh
- Taoist
- Winery/Vineyard
- Zoo/Wildlife Sanctuary
- Other Sight

Activities, Courses & Tours

- Bodysurfing
- Diving
- Canoeing/Kayaking
- Course/Tour
- Skiing
- Snorkeling
- Surfing
- Swimming/Pool
- Walking
- Windsurfing
- Other Activity

Sleeping

- Sleeping
- Camping

Eating

- Eating

Drinking & Nightlife

- Drinking & Nightlife
- Cafe

Entertainment

- Entertainment

Shopping

- Shopping

Information

- Bank
- Embassy/Consulate
- Hospital/Medical
- Internet
- Police
- Post Office
- Telephone
- Toilet
- Tourist Information
- Other Information

Geographic

- Beach
- Hut/Shelter
- Lighthouse
- Lookout
- Mountain/Volcano
- Oasis
- Park
- Pass
- Picnic Area
- Waterfall

Population

- Capital (National)
- Capital (State/Province)
- City/Large Town
- Town/Village

Transport

- Airport
- Border crossing
- Bus
- Cable car/Funicular
- Cycling
- Ferry
- Metro station
- Monorail
- Parking
- Petrol station
- Subway/Subte station
- Taxi
- Train station/Railway
- Tram
- Underground station
- Other Transport

Note: Not all symbols displayed above appear on the maps in this book

Routes

- Tollway
- Freeway
- Primary
- Secondary
- Tertiary
- Lane
- Unsealed road
- Road under construction
- Plaza/Mall
- Steps
- Tunnel
- Pedestrian overpass
- Walking Tour
- Walking Tour detour
- Path/Walking Trail

Boundaries

- International
- State/Province
- Disputed
- Regional/Suburb
- Marine Park
- Cliff
- Wall

Hydrography

- River, Creek
- Intermittent River
- Canal
- Water
- Dry/Salt/Intermittent Lake
- Reef

Areas

- Airport/Runway
- Beach/Desert
- Cemetery (Christian)
- Cemetery (Other)
- Glacier
- Mudflat
- Park/Forest
- Sight (Building)
- Sportsground
- Swamp/Mangrove

OUR STORY

A beat-up old car, a few dollars in the pocket and a sense of adventure. In 1972 that's all Tony and Maureen Wheeler needed for the trip of a lifetime – across Europe and Asia overland to Australia. It took several months, and at the end – broke but inspired – they sat at their kitchen table writing and stapling together their first travel guide, *Across Asia on the Cheap*. Within a week they'd sold 1500 copies. Lonely Planet was born.

Today, Lonely Planet has offices in Franklin, London, Melbourne, Oakland, Beijing and Delhi, with more than 600 staff and writers. We share Tony's belief that 'a great guidebook should do three things: inform, educate and amuse'.

OUR WRITERS

Michael Grosberg

Coordinating Author; Plan Your Trip, Santo Domingo, North Coast, Central Highlands, Understand Dominican Republic, Survival Guide This is the 3rd edition of the Lonely Planet *Dominican Republic* guidebook that Michael has worked on. In addition to his Lonely Planet assignments, he's visited the Dominican Republic on other occasions, going back to his graduate-school days when he was focusing on the literature and culture of Latin America. Michael is based in Brooklyn, New York City, and usually writes just down the street from several Dominican restaurants where he gets his lunch. A reformed academic/journalist by trade, Michael has worked on more than 30 Lonely Planet books.

Read more about Michael at:
lonelyplanet.com/members/michaelgrosberg

Kevin Raub

Punta Cana & the Southeast, Península de Samaná, The Southwest & Península de Pedernales Kevin Raub grew up in Atlanta and started his career as a music journalist in New York, working for *Men's Journal* and *Rolling Stone* magazines. He ditched the rock 'n' roll lifestyle for travel writing and moved to Brazil. On his second run through the Dominican Republic, he found Eden (again!) at the end of the road in Bahía de Las Águilas. This is Kevin's 28th Lonely Planet guide. Follow him on Twitter (@RaubOnTheRoad).

Read more about Kevin at:
lonelyplanet.com/members/kraub

Published by Lonely Planet Publications Pty Ltd
ABN 36 005 607 983
6th edition – Oct 2014
ISBN 978 1 74220 442 0

10 9 8 7 6 5 4 3 2
Printed in China